Empire of Religion

Empire of Religion

Imperialism and Comparative Religion

DAVID CHIDESTER

The University of Chicago Press

CHICAGO AND LONDON

DAVID CHIDESTER is professor of religious studies and director
of the Institute for Comparative Religion in Southern Africa at the
University of Cape Town. He is the author or editor of over
twenty books, most recently, *Wild Religion:
Tracking the Sacred in South Africa.*

The University of Chicago Press, Chicago 60637
The University of Chicago Press, Ltd., London
© 2014 by The University of Chicago
All rights reserved. Published 2014.
Printed in the United States of America

23 22 21 20 19 18 17 16 15 14   1 2 3 4 5

ISBN-13: 978-0-226-11726-3 (cloth)
ISBN-13: 978-0-226-11743-0 (paper)
ISBN-13: 13: 978-0-226-11757-7 (e-book)
DOI: 10.7208/chicago/9780226117577.001.0001

Library of Congress Cataloging-in-Publication Data

Chidester, David, author.
Empire of religion : imperialism and comparative religion /
David Chidester.
pages cm
Includes bibliographical references and index.
ISBN 978-0-226-11726-3 (cloth : alk. paper)—
ISBN 978-0-226-11743-0 (pbk. : alk. paper)—
ISBN 978-0-226-11757-7 (e-book)
1. South Africa—Religion. 2. Imperialism—Religious aspects.
3. Great Britain—Colonies—Africa.   I. Title.
BL2463.C44 2014
200.9171'241—dc23
2013035083

For Jonathan Z. Smith

Contents

Preface

In his magisterial survey of comparative religion published in 1905, Louis Henry Jordan appended a chart that collated information on university programs in the field from all over the world. The continent of Africa was represented in this chart by one university: "Africa, Cape Colony, Cape Town—The University of the Cape of Good Hope." Regarding that university, Jordan's chart inquired, "Which department makes present provision for this subject?" The answer: "None." Looking to the future, the chart asked, "Is such a foundation probable?" In the relevant column appeared the blunt entry "No." According to Jordan, then, the University of Cape Town, the region of southern Africa, and the entire continent of Africa did not support the academic study of comparative religion; moreover, its introduction was unlikely in the foreseeable future.[1] Two years later, though, a report submitted to the colonial secretary of the Cape of Good Hope insisted that the management of the natives of South Africa could be facilitated by the scientific knowledge gained from both comparative philology and the "dangerous principles of Comparative Religion."[2] This government report suggested that comparative religion could be deployed as a science of knowledge and power, as an aid to the containment and control of indigenous populations. Although the academic discipline had not been established in a university department, comparative religion was nevertheless being practiced in South Africa.

In 1969, a Department of Religious Studies was established at the University of the Cape of Good Hope, the University of Cape Town. Since 1984, I have been working there. Dedicated to an open, diverse, intercultural, and interdisciplinary study of religion and religions, the department has been a good place in which to develop critical engagements with the power relations in colonialism, apartheid, and postapartheid nation-building in South Africa. I have also found it to be a good place for thinking about the history of the study of religion. In my graduate training at the University of California, Santa Barbara, I was introduced to a genealogy of the study of religion that began with British imperial theorists. I remember being thrilled to learn that we had a founder, Friedrich Max Müller, but being disappointed when I was almost immediately told that everything he said was wrong. All of the ancestors in this lineage, such as E. B. Tylor, Andrew Lang, and James Frazer, were wrong. After a few years in South Africa, finding myself gradually, sometimes unconsciously, using the word "us" to refer to South Africans or Africans, I again read the work of these imperial ancestors and found that they were not just talking about religion. They were talking about us. As an alternative genealogy of the study of religion, this book tracks back and forth between an imperial center and a colonized periphery. In the end, we might still find that the ancestors of the study of religion were wrong, but we will see how they were wrong in interesting and important ways.

In a previous book—*Savage Systems: Colonialism and Comparative Religion in Southern Africa*—I argued that comparative religion was not only present but that it actually permeated intercultural relations on contested southern African frontiers.[3] From as early as 1600, a "frontier comparative religion" was practiced by European travelers, missionaries, settlers, and colonial agents, as well as by indigenous African comparativists, in their struggles to make sense out of human difference in open frontier zones and closed systems of colonial domination. Among the findings of that book, I mention only two: First, I tried to show that the discovery of the existence of any local, indigenous religion in southern Africa depended upon colonial conquest and containment. Once an African community was placed under the colonial administration of a magisterial system, a location system, or a reserve system, it was discovered to have an indigenous religious system. As a result, frontier comparative religion acted as a science of local control, replicating and reinforcing the colonial containment of Africans. Second, I analyzed the comparative procedures of morphology and genealogy that were employed by travelers and missionaries, settlers and colonial officials, as well as by African comparativists, to trace southern Africans back to the ancient Near East. As unlikely as it might sound, frontier comparative religion in southern Africa during the nineteenth century arrived at the conclusion that the Xhosa were Arabs, the Zulu were Jews, and the Sotho-Tswana were ancient Egyptians. In the practices of comparison and containment, the very categories of "religion" and "religions" were produced and reproduced as instruments of both knowledge and power in specific colonial situations during the nineteenth century in southern Africa.

While *Savage Systems* explored comparative religion on one colonized periphery, this book focuses on the metropolitan center. However, it rediscovers the center of theory production in the study of religion from the perspective of the periphery. *Empire of Religion* documents and analyzes the complex relations between the emergence of a science of comparative religion in Great Britain during the second half of the nineteenth century and the colonial situation in southern Africa. In the process, it provides a counterhistory of the academic study of religion, an alternative to standard accounts, such as Eric Sharpe's *Comparative Religion,* J. Samuel Preus's *Explaining Religion,* and Walter Capps's *Religious Studies: The Making of a Discipline,* that have tracked the internal intellectual development of a European academic discipline but have not been interested in linking the nineteenth-century and early-twentieth-century science of comparative religion with either the power relations or the historical contingencies of the imperial project.[4] Anchoring the study of religion in history, *Empire of Religion* advances an interpretive analysis of imperial comparative religion.

In providing a new history of the study of religion, *Empire of Religion* locates knowledge about religion and religions within the power relations of imperial ambitions, colonial situations, and indigenous innovations. The book uncovers the material mediations—imperial, colonial, and indigenous—in which knowledge about religion was produced during the rise of an academic study of religion between the 1870s and the 1920s in Europe and North America. Focusing on one colonial contact zone, South Africa, as a crucial site of interaction, the book shows how imperial theorists such as Friedrich Max Müller, E. B. Tylor, Andrew Lang, and James Frazer depended upon the raw materials provided by colonial middlemen who in turn depended upon indigenous informants and collaborators who were undergoing colonization. Reversing the flow of knowledge production, African theorists such as W. E. B. Du Bois, S. M. Molema, and H. I. E. Dhlomo turned European imperial theorists of religion into informants in pursuing their own intellectual projects. By developing a material history of the study of religion, *Empire of Religion* documents the importance of African religion, the persistence of the great divide between savagery and civilization, and the salience of complex mediations in which knowledge about religion and religions was produced, authenticated, and circulated within imperial comparative religion.

My history of the study of religion is guided by these three questions:

How is knowledge about religion and religions produced? How is that knowledge authenticated? and How is that knowledge circulated? In imperial, colonial, and indigenous circulations, as we will see, knowledge about religion and religions was not merely replicated but also recast as alternative knowledge, so circulation could also be a means for producing knowledge. While attending to power relations, my story is also an interpretive analysis of enduring methods in the study of religion, such as cognitive studies and cultural studies, which arose from this history. Throughout this book, it must be clear that I do not place myself outside of the genealogy I trace. It is my genealogy. However, by situating this story in South Africa, I hope to make a localized contribution to ongoing efforts in understanding the history of the study of religion.

In recent years, an impressive array of research has been devoted to examining links between knowledge and power in the history of the study of religion. When I started worrying about these matters in the 1980s, my reference points were the works of Michel Foucault, Edward Said, and Talal Asad. Now a considerable body of literature can be consulted. Without listing the many contributors to this literature, I hope I have acknowledged by citations throughout this book my appreciation of their work and my solidarity with the general enterprise of developing a critical, cultural, and historical history of the study of religion. Although I prefer to think that all of us who are developing a critical history of the study of religion are collaborating in a shared project, even when we employ different theories, methods, arguments, and exemplars, I would distinguish my approach in this book as an effort to overcome lingering dualisms—imperial versus indigenous, colonizer versus colonized—by attending to the complex, multiple, and multiplying mediations in which knowledge was produced in and through the material conditions of empire. Binary oppositions, even if dialectical, cannot capture the dynamic interactions of imperial, colonial, and indigenous actors in the production of knowledge about religion and religions. As I hope to establish by showing rather than by saying, imperial comparative religion generated knowledge that was a prelude to empire and a consequence of empire but also an accompaniment to the contingencies of imperial, colonial, and indigenous mediations.

Focusing on representations of indigenous religion in Africa, we will encounter highly problematic terms—*savage, primitive,* and even *indigenous*—that have featured prominently in the formation and development of the study of religion. Generally, although not always consistently, *savage* was a structural term of opposition referring to wild people lacking civilization, while *primitive* was a temporal term designating the earliest or simplest stage of human development. In practice, these terms referred to indigenous people undergoing colonial contacts, relations, and exchanges that often entailed their displacement or containment under an alien political regime. Although *indigenous* seems to be a more neutral or even positive term, it is also a relational term arising out of encounters, struggles, and accommodations with aliens from different imperial centers in a variety of colonial situations. Since they bear traces of a racist triumphalism, the terms "savage" and "primitive" should be placed in "scare quotes," but that would not make them any less scary. Likewise, the nomenclature used to designate Africans often employed terms that are now regarded as racist epithets. We will confront all of these terms directly in analyzing the imperial, colonial, and indigenous mediations that generated the terms and conditions for producing knowledge about religion.

Employing theory as an instrument of surprise, my narrative places familiar figures in unexpected situations, while also introducing new actors into the history of the study of religion. Although the chapters proceed chronologically, my story highlights the reappearance of characters, the recurrence of themes, the revision of texts, and the resonance of this imperial history with basic categories—classification, cognition, myth, and ritual—that continue to be deployed in the academic study of religion. The book is structured by two introductions, setting the scene globally and locally in South Africa; four chapters on the classic theorists Max Müller, Tylor, Lang, and Frazer; one transitional chapter on Du Bois as a theorist of religion, who engaged imperial theory, reversed the flow in knowledge production, and anticipated African theorists; and three conclusions dealing, respectively, with the production, authentication, and circulation of knowledge about religion.

Chapter I, "Expanding Empire," sets out the basic terms of engagement. Recently, some critics have proposed abandoning the term *religion*. As we will see, the same proposal was made in the 1870s. If *religion* was a problematic term, the notion of *religions* was also a problem. In histories of the study of religions, we have seen a transition in scholarship from an earlier emphasis on European discoveries, through critical attention to European inventions, to recent explorations of European and indigenous cocreations of Hinduism, Buddhism, and other religions. In line with the relational focus of recent research, I identify the mediations—imperial, colonial, and indigenous—in which knowledge about religion and religions was produced in relation to South Africa. These mediations, which make up what I will call a triple mediation, provide the material contexts in which I examine knowledge about religion and religions.

In Chapter 2, "Imperial, Colonial, and Indigenous," the triple mediation is displayed in the 1905 meeting of the British Association for the Advancement of Science that was held in South Africa. As a centerpiece of the South African tour, the scientists witnessed a Zulu war dance, which the leading anthropologists of religion, Alfred C. Haddon and E. Sidney Hartland, found to be genuine, although they were relieved that the traditional spears had been replaced by sticks. Presenting indigenous savagery, the war dance was followed by a speech by the Zulu Christian educator John Dube, who emphasized the contrast between savagery and civilization. Also present was Mohandas K. Gandhi, who emphasized the kinship between the British and the Indians as Aryans in the advance of imperial civilization. Reporting on indigenous savagery for the benefit of imperial civilization, local colonial experts, most notably at the 1905 meeting the ethnographer Henri-Alexandre Junod, mediated between the colonized periphery and the metropolitan center in providing raw materials for theory production. Introducing characters who will reappear later, this chapter focuses on the interaction of imperial theory, local experts, and indigenous realities in South Africa.

Chapter 3, "Classify and Conquer," returns to the founder, Friedrich Max Müller, in beginning an examination of key figures in the standard genealogy of the study of religion. Basing his science of religion on a definition of religion as a sense of the infinite and a classification of religions into linguistic families, Max Müller drew evidence from South Africa. From his inaugural lectures in the science of religion in 1870, he referred to the local experts Wilhelm Bleek and Henry Callaway, who were living and working in South Africa, to obtain data for his general theories of language, myth, and religion. As we will see, his exchanges with colonial experts were enabling in providing raw materials, but also disabling in undermining his theoretical projects. As an imperialist, celebrating Queen Victoria as empress of India and defending British sovereignty in South Africa, Max Müller was clearly an imperial theorist. His relations with local experts in South Africa, however, demonstrate both the expansive power and the underlying instability of the empire of religion.

Chapter 4, "Animals and Animism," focuses on E. B. Tylor, the father of anthropology, who defined religion as belief in spiritual beings and tracked religious evolution from primitive animism to superstitious survivals in civilization. Like other imperial theorists, Tylor used data from the work of Henry Callaway, where he found a Zulu diviner who had become a "house of dreams" to provide primary evidence for his dream theory of the origin of religion. The great scientist of evolution, Charles Darwin, shared this interest in identifying the primitive psychology of religion, but he traced the origin of religion further back, to animal psychology. Accordingly, instead of relying on colonial reports about savages, Darwin could observe his own dogs, analyzing their cognitive and emotional dispositions, which turned out to be shared by savages. This chapter, reviewing imperial theories of religious cognition, which were refracted through categories of race, gender, and social class, uncovers the mediations that integrated a Zulu dreamer into the production of Tylor's imperial theory of religion as animism.

Turning from cognitive studies to cultural studies, chapter 5, "Myths and Fictions," focuses on Andrew Lang, the remarkable *litterateur*, who was active in every debate in the study of religion. Focusing on Lang's relations with two adventure novelists, H. Rider Haggard and John Buchan, both of whom lived for a time in South Africa and wrote fictional accounts of African religion, this chapter explores how myth, fiction, and scholarship merged in imagining religion as a global unity, originating in imagination, which was not merely spiritualism but also politics. In these myths and fictions of the religious empire of imagination, the Zulu featured prominently. While maintaining the great divide between savagery and civilization in imperial theory, Lang and the adventure novelists explored the oxymoron of civilized savagery and the irony of savagery as the enduring substratum of civilization.

Chapter 6, "Ritual and Magic," focuses on James Frazer, whose massive compendium of primitive religion and magic, *The Golden Bough*, exemplified (and exhausted) the armchair anthropology of religion. Although Frazer developed his distinction between ritual propitiation and magical coercion in conversation with local researchers in Australia, his primary reservoir of empirical evidence was derived from Africa. One of his conversation partners in Africa, the missionary-ethnographer Henri-Alexandre Junod, was initially guided by Frazer's questions in collecting data for his monograph *The Life of a South African Tribe*, which analyzed the religion of the Thonga. Although Junod adopted and modified Frazer's distinction between religion and magic, his primary theoretical framework was provided by his friend Arnold van Gennep's *Les rites de passage*. Moving between British and French scholarship on religion, Junod's research on ritual and magic was also situated in the expansion of the mining industry in South Africa, where new rites of passage were attending migrant labor.

Beginning with chapter 7, "Humanity and Divinity," we shift from centralized imperial productions of knowledge to alternative productions by focusing on the work of the African American sociologist, historian, and (perhaps surprisingly) scholar of religion W. E. B. Du Bois. In a series of books on the history of Africa and the African diaspora, Du Bois wrestled with representing African indigenous religion. He initially reproduced the evolutionary schema of imperial comparative religion by adopting the terms *fetishism* and *animism* to characterize African religion but gradually revised these representations so that fetishism, for example, no longer referred to the African worship of objects but to a European invention that provided ideological cover for the slave trade. By tracing Du Bois's long history of re-thinking fetishism, indigenous African divinity, and the religious continuity between Africa and African America, we find a theorist of religion reversing the flow between imperial centers and colonized peripheries in the produc-tion of knowledge about religion and religions.

Highlighting reversals in knowledge production, chapter 8, "Thinking Black," examines South African authors who engaged imperial theorists in producing alternative knowledge about religion and religions. The Zulu philologist uNemo unsettled Max Müller; the Manyika diviner John Chava-fambira, in collaboration with the Freudian psychoanalyst Wulf Sachs, im-plicitly challenged Tylorian assumptions about primitive psychology; the historian S. M. Molema cited Max Müller, James Frazer, and William James in proposing his own definition of religion, while also developing a dis-tinctive perspective on the history of religions; and the dramatist H. I. E. Dhlomo drew James Frazer and Jane Ellen Harrison into his revitalization of African arts. Especially in the cases of Molema and Dhlomo, we find African theorists refusing to be data and turning imperial theorists into in-formants for the Africans' own theoretical projects. Although the British imperial theorist E. Sidney Hartland asserted that the key to the study of religion was learning how to "think black," these South African thinkers suggested alternative possibilities for thinking black and thinking back to empire in producing knowledge about religion and religions.

Raising the question of authenticity, chapter 9, "Spirit of Empire," con-trasts three types of comparative religion. Interfaith comparative religion, which privileges the religious insider as the bearer of authenticity, is exam-ined at the Religions of the Empire conference of 1924, organized by the nature mystic Francis Younghusband, which featured a presentation by an African South African, Albert Thoka, who explained the nature mysticism of indigenous African religion. Theosophical comparative religion, which locates authenticity in esoteric wisdom, is illustrated by Patrick Bowen's discovery in South Africa of a secret African brotherhood, the *Bonabakulu*

Abasekhemu, with a Master in every tribe, which taught the secrets of the *Itongo,* the Spirit, as the Zulu equivalent of the Sanskrit *Atma* in Theosophy. Finally, by reviewing how the imperial theorists Max Müller, Tylor, Lang, and Frazer handled the Zulu term *Itongo,* we find a critical comparative religion, adjudicating theory and data, which was underwritten by the footnote, an apparatus for creating effects of authenticity while also opening knowledge claims to disputation. Although these three types of comparative religion—interfaith, theosophical, and critical—were based on dramatically different ways of authenticating knowledge, they all nevertheless emerged within the same empire of religion.

Tracking the circulation of knowledge, chapter 10, "Enduring Empire," provides a brief profile of the transmission of imperial theory in the rise of the study of religion as an academic discipline in the United States. By highlighting the work of Morris Jastrow Jr., whose *Study of Religion* (1901) provided an overview of the entire field, we see the persistence of the great divide between the study of primitive religions and the study of the religions of civilizations. At the same time, we see localized shifts in this circulation of knowledge, as Jastrow argued that researchers in the United States were fortunate in having primitives—Native Americans and African Americans—in close proximity, so they did not have to travel to Africa to study primitive religion. While racialized research on these proximate primitives was central to the development of the sociology and psychology of religion in the United States, research on the religions of civilizations shifted from the British interest in India to an American interest in the ancient civilizations of the Near East. Here, also, Morris Jastrow was active in the circulation of knowledge about the religions of civilizations as an expert on the languages, cultures, and religions of ancient Assyria, Babylonia, and Israel. During the last years of his life, between 1914 and 1920, Jastrow sought to employ his knowledge in the study of religion to establish a just peace in the Middle East.

Empire of Religion thus shows how knowledge about religion and religions was entangled with imperialism, from European empires to the neo-imperial United States. Why do we need to know anything about that? For personal reasons, I must admit, I needed to know where I came from, so my own history circulates through the translocal transactions charted in this book. After all, I was initiated into the genealogy of British imperial comparative religion not in Great Britain but in Santa Barbara, California, before relocating to South Africa, where I learned to think otherwise about the force of imperialism, colonialism, and apartheid in the study of religion. As a result of that trajectory, I needed to know about the material conditions, possibilities, and constraints in which my knowledge was being produced and I was producing knowledge. Without prescribing how anyone else should deal with these matters, I think that going back through the history of the study of religion that I trace in this book provides an opportunity for critical and creative reflection on how we produce, authenticate, and circulate knowledge today. It is against this background that I study religion. In pursuing a critical comparative religion, I see religion as both a problematic term and a human problem. Although I address a broader audience in the humanities and social sciences, on behalf of scholars of religion I ask: Can we be in the empire of religion but not of it? *Empire of Religion* uncovers an imperial history of the study of religion while exploring this possibility.

During twenty years of working on this book, I have valued the participation of many friends, colleagues, students, and research assistants. To them, too many to list, I say: I thank you all. You know who you are. As always, I pay special tribute to the Board of Directors and my wife, Careen.

I also thank various presses that have allowed me to rehearse the ideas contained in this book in earlier form in the pages of their journals and books: portions of "'Classify and Conquer': Friedrich Max Müller, Indigenous Religious Traditions, and Imperial Comparative Religion," in *Beyond Primitivism: Indigenous Religious Traditions and Modernity*, ed. Jacob K. Olupona (London: Routledge, 2004), 71–88; parts of "Real and Imagined: Imperial Inventions of Religion in Colonial Southern Africa," in *Religion and the Secular: Historical and Colonial Formations*, ed. Timothy Fitzgerald (London: Equinox, 2007), 153–76; material from "Religious Animals, Refuge of the Gods, and the Spirit of Revolt: W. E. B. Du Bois's Representations of Indigenous African Religion," in *Re-Cognizing W. E. B. Du Bois in the Twenty-First Century*, ed. Chester Fontenot and Mary Keller (Augusta, GA: Mercer University Press, 2007), 34–60; parts of "Dreaming in the Contact Zone: Zulu Dreams, Visions, and Religion in Nineteenth-Century South Africa," *Journal of the American Academy of Religion* 76, no. 1 (2008): 27–53, published by Oxford University Press; portions of "Darwin's Dogs: Animals, Animism, and the Problem of Religion," in *Soundings: An Interdisciplinary Journal* 92, nos. 1–2 (2009): 51–75, published by the Pennsylvania State University Press, and in *Secular Faith*, ed. Vincent W. Lloyd and Elliot Ratzman (Eugene, OR: Cascade Books, 2011), 76–101, used by permission of Wipf and Stock Publishers (www.wipfandstock.com); material from "Imperial Reflections, Colonial Situations: James Frazer, Henri-

Alexandre Junod, and Indigenous Ritual in Southern Africa," in *Ritual Dynamics and the Science of Ritual*, vol. 4, *Reflexivity, Media, and Visuality*, ed. Axel Michaels (Wiesbaden: Harrassowitz, 2011), 237–64; and I have used material from "Thinking Black: Circulations of Africana Religion in Imperial Comparative Religion," *Journal of Africana Religions* 1, no. 1 (2013): 1–28, published by the Pennsylvania State University Press.

Without imputing any responsibility for anything I have written in this book, I gratefully acknowledge financial support provided over the years by the National Research Foundation of South Africa and the University Research Committee of the University of Cape Town.

In dedicating this book to Jonathan Z. Smith, I acknowledge nearly forty years of inspiration, going back to Santa Barbara, in thinking about religion and the study of religion. As his doctoral dissertation reveals, Smith started out as an Africanist, at least to the extent that he devoted most of his research to subjecting every African datum cited in Frazer's *Golden Bough* to rigorous critical scrutiny. Frazer, as well, could be regarded as an Africanist, as the anthropologist Keith Irvine observed in 1962, because "the development of anthropological literature about Africa would seem to have begun, in a systematic fashion, with the publication of Sir James Frazer's *The Golden Bough* in 1890." In South Africa, Irvine noted, the first ethnographic monograph, written by Henri-Alexandre Junod, was guided by Frazer, making the colonial missionary "one of the first-generation settlers on Frazer's newly-discovered continent."[5] In *Empire of Religion*, such political tropes—imperial discovery, colonial settlement—are taken as points of departure for investigating how Africa became central to an emerging academic study of religion. In a different key, perhaps, this book pursues work on Africa and comparative religion undertaken in the 1960s by Jonathan Z. Smith. Since 2004 I have been using the manuscript of *Empire of Religion*, in various stages of development, as a textbook in a graduate seminar on theory, juxtaposing its chapters on the history of the study of religion with classic essays by Smith on comparison, classification, ancestors, divination, myth, and ritual.[6] In this juxtaposition, students struggle with the challenge of simultaneously engaging in critical reflection on knowledge production, on the one hand, and imagining creative possibilities for producing knowledge about religion, on the other. Exemplifying this challenge, Jonathan Z. Smith has been working in South Africa.

Working in South Africa, I trust this book will also work elsewhere. The key to my history of the study of religion, its analytical engine, is the triple mediation that involved imperial, colonial, and indigenous actors in producing knowledge about religion and religions. Although knowledge arose in a global field of production, authentication, and circulation, specific locations were crucial for all of these actors: imperial theorists, surrounded by texts, in the quiet of their studies; colonial agents on the noisy frontlines of intercultural contacts, encounters, and exchanges; and indigenous people struggling under colonial dispossession, displacement, containment, and exploitation—but also exploring new terms of engagement that included the term *religion*. By bringing these differently situated actors together in the same story, we gain a new appreciation of what has gone into the formation of the study of religion.

CHAPTER ONE

Expanding Empire

The history of the study of religion since the Enlightenment can never be told in full. There is simply too much of it.

ERIC J. SHARPE

In his first lecture introducing the science of religion at the Royal Institution in London on February 19, 1870, Friedrich Max Müller, who has often been identified as the founder of comparative religion, proposed that the real founder was the Mughal emperor Akbar, "the first who ventured on a comparative study of the religions of the world."[1] With a passion for the study of religions, Emperor Jalāl-ud-Dīn Muhammad Akbar (1542–1605) convened regular interreligious discussions at his court, bringing together Muslims, Hindus, Christians, Jews, and Zoroastrians for debates about religion. Establishing a policy of religious toleration in his empire, Akbar also sought to discover the underlying truth in all religions, which he regarded as purely spiritual. His spiritual religion required no prescribed rituals, public ceremonies, or material symbols, except perhaps for the sun, which he saluted in his personal cycle of devotion.[2] Emperor Akbar acquired a library of sacred texts, which he had scholars translate for his own research, and initiated a program of comparative religion.

What kind of comparative religion was this? Based on dialogue between adherents of different religions, it was an interfaith comparative religion. Because it distilled a spiritual essence supposedly shared by all religions, it was a theosophical comparative religion. However, Max Müller focused on Akbar's collection, translation, and analysis of sacred texts. In this academic enterprise, nineteenth-century scholars in Great Britain had a greater abundance than the emperor of India. The original text of the Vedas, for example, "which neither the bribes nor the threats of Akbar could extort from the Brahmans," was now available.[3] Wealthier in texts than the emperor, contemporary scholars were also armed with critical methods of analysis that could distinguish historical layers in the production of sacred texts. Accordingly, Max Müller emphasized a critical comparative religion.

By invoking an emperor as the founding patron of his science, Friedrich Max Müller hinted at the imperial foundation and scope of comparative religion. In collecting the raw material of sacred texts, imperial bribes and threats might not prevail, but the scholars of the nineteenth century nevertheless relied upon imperial expansion, commerce, and force. They depended upon an expanding empire driven by British economic influence and military power, by trade and territorial annexation, by migration and missions, by the steamship and the telegraph, by the law code and the Maxim gun. Where Emperor Akbar had failed, the East India Company succeeded in securing the text of the Vedas. With the company's financial support, Max Müller was able to translate that sacred text for the study of religion. If Emperor Akbar was the founder, he represented a model for the merger of knowledge and power in British imperial comparative religion.

"But this is not all," Max Müller observed. "We owe to missionaries particularly, careful accounts of the religious belief and worship among tribes far lower in the scale of civilization than the poets of the Vedic hymns."[4] Christian missionaries, all over the world, were a crucial source for new texts of savage religion. Turning from India to South Africa, Max Müller devoted considerable time in his first lecture to the religion of the Zulu. Although earlier travelers, missionaries, and colonial agents had reported that the Zulu had no religion, more recent reports from the Anglican missionary Henry Callaway, author of *The Religious System of the Amazulu* (1868–70), provided new texts for Zulu religion. These texts were not obtained by bribes or threats, but their collection also depended upon an expanding empire. As Callaway transcribed Zulu voices, Max Müller included the Zulu in an imperial study of religion.

Following the lead of Max Müller, if not Emperor Akbar, we will explore the importance of empire in the formation of comparative religion. As an imperial enterprise, a new comparative religion emerged in the 1870s at a specific historical juncture. Realities of empire, which had previously seemed remote from domestic interests, were increasingly supported in Great Britain by an ideology of imperialism, a vision of a global Greater Britain.[5] In the context of European rivalry, British imperialism assumed a new meaning. While attending to that history, we will also have to use *imperialism* as a generic term, since it will apply to other empires, such as the German empire or the Japanese empire, which were also expanding their scope over territory, people, and knowledge. If we adopt Edward Said's definition of imperialism as "the practice, the theory, and the attitudes of a dominating center ruling a distant territory," we will have to look for multidimensional relations between a dominant imperial center and subordinate colonial peripheries, a network of relations of domination—*imperium*—but also of cultural circulation, theoretical formulation, and knowledge production.[6] In these terms, we will ask, How did the realities of empire and the ideology of imperialism inform an imperial comparative religion?

At the same time, we need to ask, Why is comparative religion a significant index to empire? If this science were merely a supplement to empire, then any other science could do. As many historians have recognized, nineteenth-century science was frequently entangled with the requirements of empire. For example, in his study of the geologist Roderick Murchison, the historian Robert A. Stafford has argued that the "mediation provided by natural science gave Europeans intellectual as well as actual authority over colonial environments by classifying and ultimately containing their awesome dimensions. This new level of control, linked with the technology representing its practical application, also conferred prestige on the metropolitan power as a civilizing force, helping legitimate imperial rule *vis-à-vis* subject races, domestic masses, and rival great powers." In its practical effects, imperial science was an important element in Europe's "grid of cultural, political, economic, and military domination."[7] Like the natural sciences, the human sciences could also reinforce imperial authority, particularly through the power of representation. During the nineteenth century, the construction of an "English" or "British" national identity depended heavily upon the colonization of others through the process of representing them. As Philip Dodd has noted, "a great deal of the power of the dominant version of Englishness during the last years of the nineteenth century and the early years of the twentieth century lay in its ability to represent both itself to others and those others to themselves."[8] These imperial sciences were inherently ambiguous, because they contained not only an implicit sense of global power but also the pervasive anxiety of powerlessness in the face of perceived degeneration at home and resistance to imperial authority abroad.[9] Nevertheless, natural and human sciences in this era were engaged in the imperial project of maintaining, extending, and reinforcing empire.

During the second half of the nineteenth century, comparative religion emerged in Great Britain as an important imperial enterprise, at the nexus of science and representation, which promised to extend the global scope of knowledge and power within the British Empire. This science of comparative religion addressed not only internal debates within a European intellectual tradition but also the intellectual and practical dilemmas posed by increased exposure to exotic or savage forms of religious life from all over the world, particularly those beliefs and practices encountered in the colonized regions of exotic India and savage South Africa. More than any other imperial science, comparative religion dealt with the essential identities and differences entailed in the imperial encounter with the exotic East and savage Africa. Comparative religion, therefore, was a crucial index for imperial thinking about empire.

As the great historian of comparative religion Eric J. Sharpe observed, "The history of the study of religion since the Enlightenment can never be told in full. There is simply too much of it."[10] Likewise for the history of imperialism, there is too much to tell. In a classic review of imperial studies, David Fieldhouse proposed focusing on a single colonial site, but with attention to that site as a "zone of interaction" with the metropolitan center.[11] Accordingly, we will focus the history of the study of religion on one site, South Africa, with special attention to the zone of interaction that produced knowledge about African religion, especially Zulu religion, in imperial comparative religion. Although this specific focus might seem restrictive, we will find that this attention to one zone of interaction has the potential to tell the whole story of the study of religion.

Throughout this book, we will ask, How was knowledge about religion and religions produced, authenticated, and circulated? Not a history of religious beliefs, practices, experiences, and social formations, this book is a history of representations of religion. In tracking representations of religion, we will attend to what I will call a triple mediation—indigenous, colonial, and imperial. In the indigenous mediation, indigenous people negotiated between ancestral traditions and Christian missions. In the colonial mediation, which moved between conditions on the colonial periphery and the demands of the metropolitan center, local experts generated reports about indigenous religious systems. In the imperial mediation, which situated the present between hypothetical reconstructions of the archaic primitive and contested civilizing projects, the indigenous and the colonial were absorbed into imperial theory. Although this triple mediation might raise ethical concerns, my focus throughout this book is epistemological: How do we know anything about religion and religions? Since knowledge is entangled with power, as well as with the contingencies of history, a genealogy of the production of knowledge in imperial comparative religion will reveal important dynamics of the formation of a scientific study of religion and religions.

TRIPLE MEDIATION

In the development of the imperial science of comparative religion, the production of theory—the process of turning raw religious materials into intellectual manufactured goods—involved a complex process of intercultural mediation, a triple mediation between indigenous, colonial, and imperial actors that was crucial to the formation of theory in imperial comparative religion. This process can be clearly identified in relations between British imperial comparative religion and a colonized periphery such as South Africa.

First, metropolitan theorists applied a comparative method, or what came to be known as *the* comparative method, that allowed them to use the raw religious materials from colonized peripheries to mediate between contemporary savages and the primitive ancestors of humanity.[12] "Though the belief of African and Melanesian savages is more recent in point of time," Max Müller observed in his foundational 1870 lectures on the science of religion, "it represents an earlier and far more primitive phase in point of growth, and is therefore as instructive to the student of religion as the study of uncultivated dialects has proved to the student of language."[13] E. B. Tylor put it this way in 1871: "[The] hypothetical primitive condition corresponds in a considerable degree to modern savage tribes, who, in spite of their difference and distance . . . seem remains of an early state of the human race at large."[14] Despite occasional disclaimers that contemporary savages could not be exactly equated with primitive humanity, reports about savages remained primary evidence for any theory of the primitive.[15] Whatever their differences, metropolitan theorists, such as Max Müller, Tylor, John Lubbock, Herbert Spencer, Andrew Lang, William Robertson Smith, and James Frazer, deployed a comparative method that inferred characteristics of the primitive ancestors of humanity from reports about contemporary savages living on the colonized peripheries of empire.

For these theorists, the empire was both opportunity and obstacle, simultaneously a context for theorizing and a problem to be theorized. On the one hand, the expanding scope of empire dramatically increased the available data for thinking about religion. As Max Müller observed, the British Empire provided unprecedented access to the sacred texts of the world and accounts of the religious beliefs and practices of colonized people. By weaving this data together, imperial theorists had the opportunity to produce a universal theory of religion. As we will see, the theories that resulted from this opportunity differed dramatically. But they shared the same means of production. Without leaving home, they could accumulate and process colonial texts. But they could also visit imperial exhibitions, from the Colonial and Indian Exhibition of 1886 to the British Empire Exhibition of 1924–25, to theorize about religion and religions. As we trace the development of theorizing about religion in the context of such exchanges and events, we will gain insight into the centralized engine of theory production.

On the other hand, as obstacle, the empire was a problem because it raised the contradiction between liberal ideals of liberty and the realities of colonial coercion. As the central contradiction of the British Empire, this gap between liberty and coercion was an enduring problem for politicians and scholars. While politicians generally tried to deal with this problem by proclaiming political freedom at the center and enlightened despotism at the periphery, imperial theorists of the human sciences generated accounts of the primitive, whether African, Indian, or Irish, that could be used to justify coercion while awaiting the long evolutionary delay in their trajectory to civilized liberty.[16] Generally racialized, these accounts of the primitive were useful to empire. As a science of primitive religion, imperial comparative religion might also have been useful, but the linkage between knowledge and power is more complex. In the matrix of knowledge production, imperial comparative religion was simultaneously preparation, accompaniment, and result of empire, an academic enterprise that might provide justification for domination while being shaped by relations of domination, but it was contemporary with the conflicts and confusions of imperial expansion.

Focusing on classic theorists of religion, we will examine their relations with empire. As we have already seen, Friedrich Max Müller, who invoked an emperor as the founder of his academic discipline, developed a British imperial perspective for the study of religion. Although he was a German immigrant, he advanced the British imperial cause with passion. Editor of *The Sacred Books of the East*, Max Müller also built general theories of language, myth, and religion that were heavily dependent upon the colonial extraction of raw materials from the peripheries of empire. Similarly dependent upon these extractions, E. B. Tylor, the father of anthropology, was a classic theorist of religion who pioneered the psychological or cognitive study of religion. Drawing evidence from savages, such as the Zulu of South Africa, Tylor developed a theory of religion as primitive mentality. Arguing against both Max Müller and Tylor, the literary entrepreneur and scholar of religion Andrew Lang built his theories of religion on the same raw materials but also in conversation with adventure novelists H. Rider Haggard and John Buchan, who had lived in South Africa. As a result, Lang's work raises questions about the relations among religion, fiction, and scholarship. The greatest, or at least the most prolific, synthesizer of imperial comparative religion, James Frazer, produced his monumental survey of primitive religion out of the same materials. *The Golden Bough*, spinning out of control to twelve volumes, was a compendium of the foolishness of primitive humanity. Ostensibly intended to solve a problem in Greek classics, asking why the priest of Diana at Nemi was killed, Frazer sought data in Africa. As Jonathan Z. Smith observed, "Frazer's use of African evidence constitutes the sole 'empirical' demonstration of his thesis."[17] For example, Frazer used a traveler's report about the Zulu as evidence of Africans who killed their divine kings. Relying on the unreliable account of the British trader Nathaniel Isaacs, who recounted that the Zulu king Shaka valued Rowland's Macassar Oil, which was advertised as preserving, strengthening, and beautifying the hair, Frazer found in 1890, "It seems to have been a Zulu custom to put a king to death as soon as he began to have wrinkles or gray hairs."[18] In his revised and expanded edition of 1911, Frazer added to this report his own conjecture that the Zulu killed their king "by the simple and perfectly sufficient process of being knocked in the head."[19] Imperial theorists in the study of religion, in a variety of ways, were bringing colonized people into the center of theorizing about the nature of religion. Colonial situations at the same time enabled and destabilized their theories of religion.

Second, on the periphery, European observers, primarily travelers, missionaries, and colonial agents, mediated between the metropolitan theorists and indigenous people. As Max Müller often observed, he relied upon the authority of European scholars on the colonized periphery, colonial experts like Henry Callaway, Wilhelm Bleek, and Theophilus Hahn in South Africa, who had mastered the local languages, collected the myths, and documented the customs of savages. By his own account, Max Müller corresponded with these local experts on the periphery and submitted his tentative work to them for correction. He deferred to them as the "highest authorities."[20] Other local experts in South Africa, such as the historian George McCall Theal, the author Dudley Kidd, and the missionary-ethnographer Henri-Alexandre Junod, developed similar relationships with metropolitan theorists. As mediators between colonial situations and the metropolitan center, these local experts enabled the collection of data in imperial comparative religion. However, as we will see, their local research, embedded in specific colonial relations, could also occasionally undermine imperial theory.

South Africa was important to the new British imperialism emerging in the 1870s. The discovery of mineral wealth—diamonds in 1867 and gold in 1886—attracted immigrants, entrepreneurs, and capital investment with imperial consequences, most spectacularly in the financing of the empire-building of Cecil Rhodes. In counterpoint to British imperial expansion, indigenous resistance resulted in major imperial wars, the Anglo-Zulu War of 1879 and the Anglo-Boer War of 1899-1902. In her analysis of the rise of imperialism, Hannah Arendt placed South Africa, "the culture-bed of Imperialism," at the center of its capitalist ventures, military coercion, and territorial annexation.[21] Even if we grant Bernard Porter's argument that the British generally ignored their empire before the 1870s, subsequent events in South Africa certainly drew attention. They coincided with a time in Great Britain, as Porter observed, when "the empire and society began to need each other."[22] A review of British newspapers during the 1890s has found that "South Africa more than any other colonial region captured the news in all sectors of the British press."[23] As we will see, the imperial theorists of comparative religion were well aware of South Africa. Local experts in the study of religion, however, were on the frontlines of imperial expansion and colonial conflict. Dedicated to the enterprise of colonial collecting, which has often been identified as crucial to the expansion of imperial knowledge and power, local experts mediated between colony and empire by providing the raw materials of savage religion that were necessary for manufacturing general theories of religion.

Two local experts were most prominent in this exchange between South Africa and imperial comparative religion. Both were missionaries, the medical doctor turned ethnographer Henry Callaway, author of *The Religious System of the Amazulu* (1868-70), and the entomologist turned ethnographer Henri-Alexandre Junod, author of *The Life of a South African Tribe* (1912-13; second edition 1927). Their exchanges with imperial theorists corresponded with two phases in the development of the study of religion. Between 1870 and 1900, while Max Müller, E. B. Tylor, and Andrew Lang dominated debates about religion in Great Britain, Henry Callaway provided the most authentic data for savage religion. After 1900, with leading anthropologists of religion Alfred C. Haddon and E. Sidney Hartland visiting South Africa in 1905, Henri-Alexandre Junod was guided by questions about savage religion provided by James Frazer. In the process, while Junod is often regarded as the author of the first ethnographic monograph, Callaway's work has been relegated to antiquarian interest in the prehistory of the anthropology of religion. Nevertheless, both were engaged in mediating between imperial theory and changing colonial situations, which ranged from the dispossession and displacement of Callaway's Zulu to the incorporation and exploitation of Junod's Thonga, in defining the experience of indigenous people in South Africa.

Finally, the African informants employed by the local experts were themselves engaged in a third mediation between indigenous tradition and the force of European colonization. Comparative religionists in their own right, many of these informants can be identified—the Bushman informants //Kabbo, Dia!kwain, and Qing; the Zulu informants Ngidi, Mabaso, and Kumalo; the Thonga informants Libombo, Mboza, Tobane, and Mankhelu—but many others remain nameless translators, or converts at remote mission stations, or even prisoners at Cape Town's Breakwater Prison. Nevertheless, indigenous Africans acted as important intercultural mediators in the formation of theory in comparative religion. As a result of their own ambivalent position, often as recent Christian converts, these African informants mediated the contradictions of the colonial context in ways that in turn colonized the production of theory in the science of comparative religion.

In 1870, the most important indigenous expert on African religion in South Africa was Mpengula Mbande. Born in Griqualand East, south of the British colony of Natal, Mbande grew up in the Gwala clan, amaPepete tribe, which British administrators of Natal included in their colonial construction of the Zulu nation. After losing his parents in colonial conflict, he grew up under the care of an uncle who was a diviner; his brother Undayeni was also a ritual expert in traditional medicines, dreams, and relations with ancestral spirits. Leaving his family during a time of domestic crisis, Mbande moved to the colonial town of Pietermaritzburg, where he joined the American Board mission of Jacob Ludwig Döhne. There he met his wife, Mary, who had fled to the mission to avoid an arranged marriage, and the Anglican missionary Henry Callaway, who had recently arrived with Bishop John William Colenso. Accompanying Callaway in 1857 to his new mission station at Springvale, Mbande prospered as a maize farmer, but he also rose in the Anglican Church. As Callaway recalled, on first impression, he thought that Mbande was "as soft and unprepossessing a specimen of a native in a transition state between heathen and Christian as I ever saw."[24] However, recognizing Mbande's ability, Callaway ordained him as the first indigenous Anglican priest in South Africa, with responsibilities for preaching Sunday sermons, teaching Sunday school, and confirming converts; eventually Callaway installed him as a deacon of the church. Callaway also involved Mpengula Mbande in the collection of native folklore, customs, and traditions. As we will see, Mbande was more than an informant; he was the primary author of *The Religious System of the Amazulu*. In one striking incident in the collection, Mbande relates the ordeal of a Christian convert, James, who underwent the calling of a diviner. He was called by ancestral spirits, through dreams, and became a "house of dreams." While the Zulu diviner James came to feature prominently in imperial theories of religion, especially in providing evidence for E. B. Tylor's theory of animism, he also returned to Springvale when Mbande suddenly died in January 1874, diagnosing the cause as witchcraft.[25] Mediating between ancestral traditions and colonial situations, Mpengula Mbande lived on in imperial comparative religion.

For Henri-Alexandre Junod, the most important indigenous experts on African religion were the Christian convert Elias "Spoon" Libombo and the traditional diviner and political leader Mankhelu. A former diviner, or "bone-thrower," Libombo had converted to Christianity and by 1907 had become a church elder, as Mbande had become a deacon, in Junod's mission. Like Mbande, Libombo provided accounts of African ancestral religion that could be distilled into a colonial synthesis of the religious system of an African tribe. By contrast, the diviner, politician, and military strategist Mankhelu resisted Christian conversion and military containment but nevertheless also provided data for Junod's colonial research. Compared to Mbande, however, these African collaborators in Junod's project had less scope for interjecting their own voices. They answered his questions, which were formulated by James Frazer, and they fit into his theory of religion, which was largely derived from the work of Arnold van Gennep, who had recently highlighted the importance of rites of passage in the human life cycle and social formation. Nevertheless, reading between the lines of Junod's work, we can hear the voices of Africans reflecting on the problem of religion. Most dramatically, we will hear emerging leaders in African politics—such as John Dube, the founding president of what became the African National Congress, whom Junod met on a ship to London—refusing to answer Junod's questions about Zulu religious beliefs and practices. Instead of answering, Dube turned the tables by questioning Junod about European beliefs in mesmerism. As the colonial expert became informant, reversing the flow in knowledge production, Junod bemoaned the fact that these politicized Africans were less compliant than his Thonga informants.

The potential for reversing the flow of power relations in the production of knowledge about African religion was advanced by W. E. B. Du Bois, who was, among other vocations, a theorist of religion. Over a long career as a sociologist, historian, and political activist, Du Bois struggled to think through the web of relations in which knowledge about African religion and religions was being produced. After initially defending African fetishism, he eventually developed a critique of the very notion of the fetish as an ideological cover for relegating Africans to a subhuman status and justifying slavery. Identifying with the indigenous, hoping to hear indigenous voices speaking for themselves at the Universal Races Conference in 1911, Du Bois developed a critical engagement with the problem of indigenous African religion that stands in counterpoint to the constructions of primitive religion by classic theorists of imperial comparative religion. Reading Du Bois in South Africa, African intellectuals such as S. M. Molema and H. I. E. Dhlomo also reversed the flow of knowledge production between the metropolitan center and the colonized periphery in the study of religion. Treating imperial theorists as if they were informants, they sought to fashion their own local understandings of religion. Although they might not have been entirely successful, these African theorists must be regarded as active participants in the mediations of the study of religion.

Imperial, colonial, and indigenous—this triple mediation mixed and merged in complex ways in the formation of the study of religion. While indigenous informants recorded religious arguments and tensions, changes and innovations, confusions and contradictions, or sometimes their own Christian critiques of indigenous religion, the local colonial experts on the periphery distilled a system, a distinct, coherent, and functional religious system. When their reports about that local system got to the metropolitan center, however, imperial theorists treated their data as unmediated raw materials for reconstructing the origin and development of religion in a linear progression from the primitive to the civilized or a structural opposition between the lower and the higher races. In most cases, this complex, contradictory mediation became thoroughly and perhaps intentionally obscured in the process of theoretical production. Although clearly dependent upon colonization, the theorists of imperial comparative religion consistently erased any traces of that dependence by developing theories about the prehistoric rather than the historical situation of empire in which they were operating. By attending to the multiple mediations of knowledge, we can recover what they erased.

RELIGION AND RELIGIONS

In *God's Empire*, a survey of religion and British colonialism during the nineteenth century, the historian Hilary M. Carey stated that the term *religion* was not a useful category for historical analysis. "We must talk instead," he asserted, "about churches and their ethnic and political character."[26] In different ways, Christian churches represented the "spiritual realm" of British imperial expansion and colonial settlement. Ethnic origins and political positions were more useful in analyzing that spiritual realm. Nevertheless, for convenience, Carey retained the term *religion*, including it in the subtitle of his book, *Religion and Colonialism in the British World, c. 1801–1908*, even if his focus on Christian churches and colonial missions dramatically narrowed the potential scope of the term. In *Empire of Religion*, we will explore the ways in which *religion* is a useful term for analysis in tracing the mediations of knowledge production in the British Empire.

For reasons different from the historian's, during the rise of comparative religion in the 1870s, some anthropological theorists argued that the term *religion* should be abandoned entirely in the science of anthropology because it was inherently incoherent, burdened with historical associations, and theologically loaded. In a presentation to the Anthropological Institute in 1877, the naturalist W. L. Distant, who played an active role in debates on religion, proposed that it would be "better to discard the use of the term Religion in anthropological discussions altogether as being an undefined term, and as such not admissible in science." According to Distant, *religion* was a problem not only because it lacked a coherent, general definition but also because it was so thoroughly imbued with theological convictions and controversies that it should be left to theology. He placed religion on the side of theology and outside of the sphere of science, observing, "It can be no offence to theology to leave its subject matter solely to itself, science reserving the like claims on its own behalf." Anticipating recent arguments for abandoning the term *religion* in the human and social science and replacing it with "culture" or "communions" or "cosmographic formations," Distant concluded that a true science of humanity had "to give the word 'religion' some universal definition, cease to use it altogether, or in its place to substitute a term alike capable of being conceived and incapable of being misunderstood."[27]

Imperial theorists of religion tried to provide a universal definition of their key term. For Friedrich Max Müller, religion was an affective sense of the infinite, while for E. B. Tylor it was a cognitive belief in spiritual beings. Combining the affective and the cognitive, the Dutch scholar of religion C. P. Tiele, who has been advanced as the founder of modern comparative religion, in competition with Max Müller, defined religion as both the "original, unconscious, innate sense of infinity" and "belief in the superhuman."[28] Studying this religious essence required different methods: philology and history for Max Müller; psychology and anthropology for E. B. Tylor; chronology, morphology, and what came to be known as phenomenology for C. P. Tiele. In principle, these theorists distinguished their methods of inquiry from theology while retaining the term *religion* for science. As we will see, there were different ways of adjudicating the relations between religion and science in imperial comparative religion.

For some theorists who wanted to retain the term for science, religion could be explained empirically by scientific measurements of human capacities and constraints. For the phrenologist Cornelius Donovan, who shared the platform with E. B. Tylor at a meeting of the Ethnological Society in 1870, phrenology was a naturalistic method for discerning mental, emotional, and even religious capacity in human beings by measuring skulls.[29] Although far removed from twenty-first-century methods of cognitive science or evolutionary psychology, phrenology shared the commitment to empiricism that runs through these scientific approaches to the explanation of religion. Leading modern-day theorists in the cognitive study of religion would probably not recognize the leading British phrenologist of the 1870s as their ancestor. Cornelius Donovan's measurement of the cephalic index for "veneration" is more in line with the search for the "religious gene" than with their rigorous theoretical programs and empirical research. Nevertheless, like the phrenologist, they have retained the term *religion* for science instead of abandoning it entirely to the theologians.[30]

Although they might have been sympathetic to W. L. Distant's critique of the term's incoherence and theological associations, there were theorists who retained the term *religion* not only for scientific explanation but also for scientific intervention. E. B. Tylor, for one, agreed that the term lacked scientific precision—despite his attempt to provide a minimal definition, "belief in spiritual beings"—and carried too much weight as a "survival" of primitive psychology that dragged against human progress. Tylor might have abandoned the term, leaving it to theology, but he wanted to use it to mark out harmful superstitions lingering in the modern world that had to be destroyed. Accordingly, Tylor identified his science of religion as a "reformer's science," proclaiming: "It is a harsher, and at times even painful office of ethnography to expose the remains of crude old culture which have passed into harmful superstition, and to mark these out for destruction. Yet this work, if less genial, is not less urgently needful for the good of mankind. Thus, active at once in aiding progress and in removing hindrance, the science of culture is essentially a reformer's science."[31] Twenty-first-century campaigners for scientific atheism share this interest in retaining the term *religion* in order to mark it out for destruction. For example, the

philosopher Daniel Dennett proposed that the best antidote for the harmful superstition of religion would be education about religion in schools. If
children learned the facts about religious beliefs, practices, and organizations, they might develop immunity to religion's superstitious appeal.[32] In
this respect, Dennett continued Tylor's reformer's science of religion.

Strategically and perhaps ironically intervening in the terms—science,
theology, and religion—some theorists made a religion out of science.
Clearly, Thomas Huxley, who declared himself the bishop of the "church
scientific"—preaching "lay sermons," singing "hymns to creation," developing a "molecular teleology"—engaged in such a strategic inversion of terms.[33]
Flourishing with the "entire absence of theology," Huxley's religion was
located in the depths of human nature and the progress of science. He developed a "religion" of science similar to what Richard Dawkins has called
"Einsteinian religion," investing science with a kind of religious significance and perhaps spiritual awe. Complaining about the confusion caused
by Einstein's occasional recourse to religious language, Dawkins observed,
"Much unfortunate confusion is caused by failure to distinguish what can be
called Einsteinian religion from supernatural religion. Einstein sometimes
invoked the name of God (and he is not the only atheistic scientist to do
so), inviting misunderstanding by supernaturalists eager to misunderstand
and claim so illustrious a thinker as their own."[34] Dawkins was interested
in saving Einstein's "natural" religion from his general condemnation of
"supernatural" religion as delusional. According to Dawkins, Einstein was
only using religious metaphors for scientific insights. However, the investment of science with religious significance ran deep in the debates about
religion in the emerging science of religion during the 1870s in Britain. Max
Müller, for example, found religion within science. In a presentation to the
International Congress of Orientalists in 1874, Max Müller addressed the
difficulty in deciding whether or not a savage tribe had a religion. Observing
that he personally had found the introduction to Herbert Spencer's *First
Principles* to be "deeply religious," he doubted whether any traveler who
came upon a remote tribe of devoted Spencerians would report that those
savages had a religion.[35] Even for Max Müller, therefore, a science of religion contained the possibility of a "deeply religious" science.

Although Eric Sharpe's claim "Darwinism makes it possible" is over-
stated, Charles Darwin played a crucial role in these deliberations about
the essence of religion.[36] In his personal life oscillating between respect for
religious faith and commitment to secular faith, Darwin pursued scientific
methods of inquiry into religion. Leaving theology to the best minds, or at

least some of the best minds, to resolve, he investigated the animal psychology of religion, finding in dogs the key to explaining religion as a universal capacity shared by animals and humans. Subsequently, Darwinism has provided a basis for cognitive and evolutionary explanations of religion as well as for campaigns against religion in the name of a reformer's science. Darwinism has also been enlisted into a division of labor, or negotiated truce, in what Stephen Jay Gould called the "respectful noninterference" between the "Non-Overlapping Magisteria" of religion and science.[37] But Darwinism has also been identified as a "secular religion," breaking the truce, with an extension of the term *religion* to scientific inquiry that might very well reinforce W. L. Distant's concerns in the 1870s about the inherent incoherence and problematic application of the term in the science of human culture.[38]

Affective and cognitive definitions of religion, both of which essentially called for psychological methods of inquiry, were eventually supplemented by social definitions and sociological methods. Pioneered by John Ferguson McLennan and William Robertson Smith, the social definition of religion crystallized during the 1890s in the academic controversy over totemism, a totalizing term that merged spiritual attention to objects, sexual relations, and social formations in an all-encompassing approach to defining and studying religion. According to cultural analyst W. J. T. Mitchell, this expansive definition of religion as totemism corresponded to the interests of an expanding empire that was encompassing subjectivities, sexualities, and social formations all over the world.[39] As an important theorist in debates about totemism, Andrew Lang extended this expansion of the term *religion* by directing attention to the politics of religion. Expansion, however, also entailed reduction. James Frazer, who emerged from his classical studies to become an expert on totemism, ultimately reduced religion to the basic biological functions of eating and sex, of procuring food and producing children. While these needs could be addressed by religious propitiation of superhuman beings, they could also be dealt with by their magical coercion. Familiar with these developments in British imperial comparative religion, the French sociologist Emile Durkheim formulated his classic social definition of religion as "beliefs and practices relative to sacred things . . . which unite into one single moral community . . . all those who adhere to them."[40] By the early twentieth century, therefore, religion was firmly established in comparative religion as something that was not merely psychological or emotional but also practical and ultimately social.

In his review of definitions of religion published in 1912, James H. Leuba classified them as affective, intellectualist, and social (or voluntaristic), and he organized forty-eight definitions into these categories. While Winston King cited this catalog, in a textbook for the study of religion originally published in the 1950s, to suggest that religion cannot be defined, Jonathan Z. Smith countered that Leuba's collection actually proved that religion can be defined in many ways.[41] In the mediations of imperial comparative religion, we will encounter many definitions of religion, all of which can be analyzed not only for their meaning but also for their use in the imperial, colonial, and indigenous mediations in which knowledge about religion and religions was being produced.

This book is a contribution to the history of the study of religion. Against the background of classic overviews, such as those provided by Jacques Waardenburg, Eric Sharpe, J. Samuel Preus, and Walter Capps, it contributes to the ongoing work of providing new narratives for the history of the study of religion by situating the subject-field within cultural, social, and political dynamics both inside and outside of the modern West.[42] Certainly, narratives of the study of religion can find origins within the West, whether in the European Renaissance, the Reformation, or the Enlightenment, for an intellectual engagement with religion and religions.[43] Moving into the late nineteenth century, however, entails engaging a different political terrain in which the study of religion correlated with the expansion of European empires.

Tracing the development of the study of religion in Europe during this period, Hans Kippenberg reviewed major theorists and schools of thought. But he also sought to identify those academic interests as engagements with the rise of modernity.[44] His history of the field, therefore, was more flexible in its inclusion of social factors and forces that might be regarded as extraneous in a purely internal account of the development of the study of religion. Nevertheless, his account was an exclusively European narrative.

Counternarratives for the study of religion have been produced, calling attention to aspects of the engagement with religion and religions previously ignored or suppressed. Turning anthropological methods back on the West, Talal Asad investigated the disciplinary practices and historical conflicts that gave rise to the religious and the secular in Europe.[45] As Asad's interventions have addressed how we think about religion, they have also had implications for how we understand the history of the study of religion. In addition to its entanglement with imperialism and colonialism, the study of religion has been on the frontlines of the production of modern ideologies of secularism. Other counternarratives have been noteworthy. John P. Burris focused on international expositions, which were material display rather than "pure" academic research, as occasions for both public exhibition and public education about the diversity of religions that represented a significant counterpoint to the development of the academic study of religion.[46] Uncovering the history of theorizing magic, the supposed contrary of religion, Randall Styers developed an insightful historical analysis of the emergence and significance of the basic categories of religion, magic, and science in the study of religion and in the modern world.[47] Retracing the genealogy of the academic study of religion in Europe and North America, Tomoko Masuzawa's close reading of the history of the idea of "world religions" advanced an alternative narrative of the history of religious studies by exploring how Christian universalism and European hegemony were both displaced and retained by discourses of religious pluralism.[48]

Multiple narratives of the study of religion outside of Europe have also proliferated. They have resituated attention to "religion" as both an intellectual problem and a political project all over the world. From a variety of vantage points, the history of the study of religion has been rendered in colonial and postcolonial perspectives. Asian religions, according to earlier scholarship, were discovered in Europe, with the "British discovery of Hinduism" or the "British discovery of Buddhism" providing the premise for stories about internal intellectual developments within European philological and historical research.[49] Even if discovery seemed more like invention, the story was situated in Europe, because Buddhism, according to Philip Almond, "was created, and discourse about it determined, by the Victorian culture in which it emerged as an object of discourse."[50]

By contrast, attention to colonial situations has demonstrated the ways in which European discoveries were embedded in the power relations established by the conquest and control of colonized populations. For example, the invention of Hinduism as a religion has been attributed to British colonial interventions.[51] A collection of essays edited by Donald S. Lopez Jr. in 1995, *Curators of the Buddha,* has suggested that a variety of Buddhisms were not simply discovered but actually invented under different colonial conditions from Sri Lanka to Tibet.[52] Multiple narratives of the study of religion, situated in colonial contexts, demystifying earlier accounts of heroic European discoveries, have included colonial agents, from administrators to missionaries, in the invention of knowledge about the religious traditions of Asia.[53]

However, these histories of invented traditions might very well give too much weight to European imperial ambitions. As Lopez observed, varieties of Buddhism were invented not solely by European Orientalists, but in "the networks of exchange that existed between the Orientalizer and the

Orientalized."[54] Under colonial conditions, religious categories were not simply discovered or purely invented by outside observers. They emerged through complex interrelations, negotiations, and mediations between alien and indigenous intellectuals. In recent research on the invention of "Hinduism," for example, analysts have argued that Europeans discovered religious category formations that were already shaped in India out of distinctively Indian cultural, social, and political interests.[55] But this new emphasis on indigenous agency retains the earlier insights into the invention of traditions by arguing that the category of "Hinduism" actually emerged out of both indigenous and alien inventions in an ongoing process of intellectual production. Similarly, the emergence of the academic study of Chinese religions in Europe depended upon Asian and European intellectuals discovering each other in relations of reciprocal reinvention. The category of religion throughout East Asia was a product of Western and indigenous actors operating within contingent intercultural relations.[56] In these changing narratives of our intellectual past, moving from discoveries through inventions to intercultural mediations, we are gaining greater insight into the complex formations of basic categories in the academic study of religion. As a contribution to the history of the study of religion, this book focuses on African indigenous religion, especially Zulu religion, as a nexus for reflecting on the mediations in which knowledge was produced about religion and religions.

AFRICAN RELIGION

African religion has undergone a similar history in which scholarship has focused on discovery, invention, and cocreation. After a long history of denial, Europeans discovered African religions, and the discovery often coincided with the colonial containment of particular African populations, as African religious systems were recognized within colonial administrative systems. Analyzing these discoveries, critical scholarship has shown how the invention of African traditional religion was part of a larger imperial project of inventing Africa.[57] Uncovering the cocreation of African religion, the historian Paul S. Landau has highlighted the ways in which both African indigenous religion and African Christianity emerged simultaneously in southern Africa out of colonial encounters in which the Christian God was Africanized and African ancestors were "spiritualized and sacralized" in contingent intercultural mediations.[58] By the end of the twentieth century, these discoveries, inventions, and mediations had been formalized in the academic study of religion by the inclusion of African traditional religion as a variety of the broader category of indigenous religion.[59]

However, as I will argue, Africa was central to the emergence of the academic study of religion from its founding, or refounding, which was signaled by Max Müller's lectures in 1870. During the European Enlightenment, as Guy G. Stroumsa has observed, Africa was "a continent practically ignored in most studies of the religions of humankind at the time."[60] This neglect of Africa during the Enlightenment was strange, given the fact that Charles de Brosses's publication in 1760 of *Du culte des dieux fétiches* provided both a comparison of ancient Egyptian and contemporary West African religion and a term, *fetish*, which became central to European thinking about religion and eventually about economy and sexuality.[61] Certainly philosophical denigration of Africa, most notoriously in Hegel's assertion that Africa "is no historical part of the World," contributed to this neglect.[62] But Africa did not impinge directly upon European politics, economic interests, or self-understanding until the second half of the nineteenth century. In counterpoint to the discovery of mineral wealth in South Africa, beginning in the 1860s and expanding through the rest of the century, British theorists of religion began mining South Africa for religious data. As noted, Max Müller highlighted the Zulu in his inaugural lectures in the science of religion; we will see that he also featured the Zulu in his introductory essay to the multivolume series *The Sacred Books of the East*. In the first general survey, *The Religion of Africans*, published in 1877, Henry Rowley profiled Zulu religion, giving special attention to Mpengula Mbande, whose accounts of Zulu myth were "valuable only as showing the workings of the native mind when brought into contact with the superiority of Europeans."[63] Racial superiority, as one feature of the ideological cluster of imperialism, was conjoined with territorial expansion.

At the Berlin Conference between November 15, 1884, and February 26, 1885, the entire continent of Africa (with the exception of Liberia and Ethiopia) was divided up among European imperial nations. While this annexation of Africa was brokered among rival European powers to extend their political spheres of influence and economic interests, it was also underwritten by a liberal mission of religious toleration that was important to the late-imperial project. At the Berlin Conference, European powers agreed that in their dealings with Africa, "freedom of conscience and religious toleration [would be] expressly guaranteed to the natives, no less than to subjects and foreigners."[64] Although earlier forms of European imperialism had linked conquest with religious conversion, this new imperialism in

Africa proclaimed religious liberty, toleration, and peace among adherents of different religions. Under this liberal imperial mandate, knowing about the religions of African natives and other subjects of empire could serve the interests of imperial peace. In Great Britain, initiatives to foster religious toleration and understanding, such as the Universal Races Conference in 1911 and the Religions of the Empire conference in 1924, which we will visit, consciously sought to advance this imperial objective. However, the same spirit of religious toleration was embedded in the Berlin Conference that divided up Africa for European domination, exploitation, and immiseration. In South Africa, the Zulu and all other Africans were on the frontlines of this peculiar imperial mix of liberal mission and territorial expansion.

The long history of British engagements with the Zulu, which in Great Britain eventually made *Zulu* "almost a household word,"[65] went through many permutations—the traveler's reports of Nathaniel Isaacs, who claimed in the 1820s that the Zulu "tyrant" Shaka had ceded land to Britain; the colonial reports following the British annexation of Natal in 1843, from Theophilus Shepstone, who developed a system of indirect rule over the Zulu; and the missionary reports from John William Colenso, who furthered his gospel by immersing himself in Zulu language and culture but also developed critical biblical scholarship that scandalized the church. The Anglo-Zulu War, especially the Zulu defeat of British troops at the Battle of Isandhlwana in 1879, galvanized British interest in the Zulu. Learning of this defeat, which included the death of the son of Louis Napoleon, British prime minister Benjamin Disraeli reportedly responded, "A very remarkable people, the Zulu. They defeat our generals; they convert our bishops; they have settled the fate of a great European dynasty."[66] After his eventual defeat, Zulu king Cetshwayo went to London to meet Queen Victoria. Years later, the Zulu Christian educator John Dube, who later became the first president of the African National Congress, led a political delegation to London in 1909 to appeal for African rights in the Union of South Africa.

Although these mediations of the Zulu in Great Britain were primarily conducted in texts—travelers' reports, missionary accounts, colonial archives, parliamentary debates, newspaper stories, periodical articles, and adventure novels—they were also transacted in other media.

International exhibitions, for example, were significant media for generating representations of religion. In London, staged shows featuring Zulu "savages" were popular attractions, from the 1853 exhibition at St. George's Gallery, Hyde Park Corner, London, which featured dramatic displays of Zulu divination, marriage rites, and war dances, inspiring Charles Dickens's diatribe against the "noble savage"; through the popular Zulu shows staged by the impresario Guillermo Antonio Farini; to the museum exhibition "Briton, Boer, and Black in Savage South Africa" mounted in 1899 at the beginning of the South African War.[67] The London *Daily Telegraph* reported in 1879 that the Zulu shows put on by Signor Farini were entertaining and educational, "throwing some light on the manners and customs of barbarous nations."[68] These shows were media for meditating on the opposition between savagery and civility, a mediation explicitly structuring the performances of South Africa's African Choir, which toured England in the early 1890s, performing a program divided into two parts, "Africa Uncivilized" and "Africa Civilized."[69] But these exhibitions also mediated representations of Zulu religion, with special emphasis on the martial religion of the "war dance."

Visual illustrations also mediated perceptions of "savage" religion. Wood-engraved drawings, a prominent feature of popular periodicals, were a medium for representing Zulu religion. The massive anthropological compendium assembled by Rev. J. G. Wood, published between 1868 and 1870 as *The Uncivilized Races; or, Natural History of Man*, was richly illustrated by "over 700 fine illustrations . . . engraved by the brothers Dalziel," the most famous wood engravers of the Victorian era.[70] Eight of those illustrations depicted various aspects of Zulu religion—*Unfavourable Prophecies*; *Sacrificing the Bull*; *Approach of the Prophetess*; *Prophet and Inquirers*; *Old Prophets*; *Prophet and His Wife*; *The Prophetess at Work*; and *Smelling for a Wizard*. They were eventually included in 1913 in the second South African edition of Henry Callaway's *Religious System of the Amazulu*.[71] Circulating back to South Africa, these images reinforced a certain kind of knowledge about Zulu religion.

In South Africa, Zulu identity was emergent, fluid, and contested. It was not anchored in a primordial ethnicity or a stable polity. Beginning with the military conquests by Shaka in the 1820s, the Zulu were a royal house, while tributary groupings of people, known collectively as *amantungwa*, were outsiders, often referred to by the Zulu with derogatory epithets, indicating their subordinate status from a Zulu perspective. Between the 1820s and the 1860s, this restricted notion of the Zulu persisted, although it came under pressure from the Boer Republic of Natalia established in 1838, which was usurped by the British as the Colony of Natal in 1843. For these colonizers, every African in the region could be designated as Zulu by virtue of language, culture, and religion. Accordingly, considerable effort went into studying these features of Zulu life. As we will see, the philologist Wilhelm

Bleek and the ethnographer Henry Callaway embarked on their research in this colonial context of defining the Zulu. At the same time, for Africans in the region, greater unity among separate chiefdoms was motivated by pulling together under Zulu leadership in opposition to the Boers and the British. Under the reign of the Zulu king Cetshwayo between 1872 and 1879, these pressures culminated in mobilizing for war against the British Empire. After the Zulu defeat, the British colonial administration partitioned Africans into thirteen chiefdoms, with chiefs all appointed by the colonial government, in a system of indirect rule. Although one of the chiefs, John Dunn, was Scottish, all of the Africans contained in this system were defined as Zulu. The ethnogenesis of the Zulu, therefore, was intimately related to colonial conflicts and imperial expansion in South Africa.[72]

Although the historian Hilary M. Carey proposed abandoning the unhelpful term *religion* while focusing on allegedly more stable terms, such as churches, ethnicity, and politics, all of these terms were unstable in the colonial context. Operating in what the historian Norman Etherington has identified as "one of the most heavily evangelized regions of the globe,"[73] Christian churches were crucial in the emergence of Africans in the region who identified with Zulu ethnicity. African Christian converts were active in promoting Zulu identity, often in alignment with the politics of the British colonial administration. However, this same Zulu ethnicity could be mobilized against colonial political interests, as occurred in the uprising of 1906, the Bhambatha Rebellion, which drew both Christians and traditionalists into military action against the British. By 1912, the Christian educator John Dube was a Zulu entering progressive politics at the birth of the African National Congress, in counterpoint to the coalition of Christians, landowners, and remnants of the Zulu royal house that in 1924 formed the Zulu political organization, Inkatha, to advance traditional interests. While John Dube was deposed from his presidency of the African National Congress in 1917 for being too traditional, Inkatha was eventually credited as the bastion of authentic Zulu tradition in the self-proclaimed Christian Republic of South Africa.[74]

The term *religion* might very well prove to be useful in tracking indigenous, colonial, and imperial mediations. In the frontier zone of the 1820s and 1830s, the British traveler Nathaniel Isaacs reported that the Zulu had no religion.[75] This discovery of an absence, which was endlessly repeated by Europeans in other frontier contact zones, signaled a strategic intervention in contests over land, livestock, and labor. By the 1850s and 1860s, when Henry Callaway was conducting his research, this alleged absence of religion became a religious system, the religious system of the Zulu, which mirrored their containment, in principle, under a colonial administrative system. As reports of this Zulu religious system were transmitted to Great Britain, however, imperial theorists disaggregated that system, taking it apart, breaking it into bits and pieces that could be appropriated as evidence for a variety of theories of primitive religion. Data, of course, is crucial to any theory, but the ways in which religious raw material was extracted by imperial comparative religion reveals both the power and the instability of that comparative religion, demonstrating its expansive capacity for absorbing the Zulu while exposing its theoretical project to being undermined by the Zulu under changing colonial conditions. By retaining *religion* as a key term, while paying attention to the imperial, colonial, and indigenous mediations in the production of knowledge about religion and religions, we will gain insight into the expanding but unstable empire of religion.

CHAPTER TWO

Imperial, Colonial, and Indigenous

South Africa affords a most favorable field for the study of the ethnology of the
lower races and the sociology of the higher.

ALFRED C. HADDON

In 1905 the British Association for the Advancement of Science held its annual
meeting in South Africa. Traveling by Union-Castle steamships, 380 overseas delegates attended this academic congress in a region still recovering from the recent war—the Anglo-Boer War/South African War (1899-
1902)—that had challenged British control over South Africa. In his travel
diary, the astronomer James Stark Browne (1853-1931) observed that the
association's South African hosts had made arrangements for this academic
visit that were "worthy of the love for the mother country which the colonies entertained; and of the importance of the scientific body about to visit
their shores."[1] The British Association certainly was well received and entertained, not only by formal ceremonies and academic presentations but
also by excursions to hotels and seashores, observatories and dynamite fac-
tories, gold mines and diamond mines, and ethnographic displays of native
rituals. But the relations among imperial Britain, colonial South Africa, and
the indigenous Africans working in the mines and dancing in the displays
were complex and conflicted, certainly too complex to be captured by a
visiting delegation of scientists. Nevertheless, this visit raised crucial questions about the production of knowledge within an imperial science that
stretched from the stars to the soul.

While the president of the association, the astronomer George H. Darwin,
son of Charles Darwin, was preparing en route to give his keynote address
on the heavenly bodies when they arrived in Cape Town, the passengers
on the ship were entertaining themselves with academic debates and diver-
sions. Professor of botany J. Reynolds Green, for example, entertained the

gathering with an "intensely serious" exposition of the science of phrenology, a science for discerning mental capacity, if not the soul, by measuring the size and shape of the skull, which he illustrated with pictures of the skulls of Julius Caesar, Simple Simon, and the eighteenth-century English highwayman Dick Turpin, accomplishing "an admirable bit of fooling with the air of a dry professor at a college class."[2] In a debate on the question "Yellow Peril: Is It a Reality to Be Feared?" many argued that it was not, most notably "our Japanese friend Iwasaki." Iwasaki Koyata was the twenty-six-year-old heir to the Mitsubishi Corporation, studying at Cambridge, who observed that the tropical heat must have affected the travelers' brains to make them even ask such a question; he hoped they would be all right again when they returned to England. Also arguing against this proposition was the German anthropologist Felix von Luschan, who refocused the question on religion. The rise of Japan, Luschan argued, was an "immense gain to the thought of the world," because the religious ethos of Japan, embodied in the *bushido* code of warriors, was superior to the Christianity that was taught in European Protestant churches. Based on "common sense," *bushido* was also vastly superior to the "miserable superstition" and "ikon-worship" of Roman Catholic and Greek Orthodox Christianity.[3] Drawing out general scientific findings from this comparison of religions, Luschan concluded that encounters with the rest of the world were leading to "an awakening of Europeans to the truth that they had not a monopoly of all the virtues of religion"; that it was possible, given the diversity of religious faiths in the world, to trace "the effects of their faiths upon the characters of different nations"; and that Europeans, in their ongoing engagements with Japan, could only "greatly benefit by intercourse with the ideas of a young and vigorous nation."[4]

Professor Luschan's speech, Browne recalled, "was much applauded." He explained, "I need scarcely say that with such a party as ours the broadest views prevailed on religious questions, and it was like a breath of fresh air to talk to some of our companions on these subjects."[5] We might pause, however, to consider the implications of Luschan's assertions about religious diversity, the relation between religions and nations, and the invigorating influence of interchange among young imperial nations.

First, religious diversity, which might always have been a fact of life, had only recently been invested with a positive evaluation, most notably by the work of the philologist Friedrich Max Müller, who has often been regarded as the founder of the modern study of religion. In European encounters with religious difference, the classical Greco-Roman opposition between *religio* and *superstitio*, and the Christian opposition between religious faith and heresy, were gradually modified to account for a multiplicity of religions. Beginning with the polemical opposition between two religions, Protestant and Catholic, when the English theologian Richard Hooker in 1593 first used the plural term *religions*, European encounters with religious variety resulted in the eighteenth-century formula of four religions—Christianity, Judaism, Islam, and Paganism—and the nineteenth-century formulation of world religions, which Max Müller identified as eight religions with sacred texts: Christianity, Judaism, and Islam; Hinduism, Buddhism, and Zoroastrianism; Confucianism and Taoism.[6] In his inaugural lectures for a science of religion in 1870, Max Müller suggested that all of these religions contained glimmers of truth. Reading these lectures in South Africa as they were serialized in *Fraser's Magazine*, the Anglican missionary, medical doctor, and ethnographer Henry Callaway, who had been conducting research on the language, folklore, and religion of the Zulu, felt that Max Müller's lectures on the science of religion confirmed what he had deduced from Christian scripture as the inspiration for his ongoing research into Zulu religion: that "the opinion which restricts the knowledge of God . . . to Christian countries, is a godless heresy."[7] Callaway was inspired by Max Müller's assertion that "there is no religion that does not contain a spark of truth."[8] Based on his understanding of Christian revelation and supported by his reading of Max Müller, Callaway was convinced that European Christians did not hold a monopoly on religious virtue. His missionary project, however, could not admit the possibility, as Luschan asserted about Japanese *bushido*, that indigenous Zulu religion might have virtues that were superior to the religious promise of Christianity.

Second, Luschan's assertion about the link between religious faiths and nations also had a recent history. Certainly the treaty of Westphalia in 1648, ending the European wars of religion, had produced a formula for linking religions and nations—*cuius regio, eius religio*, whoever rules determines the religion that will be observed within a territory. In an early exploration of religious diversity in the eighteenth century, an observer in South Africa, Peter Kolb, assumed this linkage between religions and nations, noting that "different nations have different notions" when he described the "pissing ceremony" practiced by the "Hottentots" (Khoikhoi) living in the Cape of Good Hope. Although being pissed upon might be a sign of dishonor in European nations, according to Kolb it was the greatest honor in the religion of this savage nation.[9] But the notion of nation invoked by Luschan was informed by more recent theoretical developments, such as Ernest

Renan's assertion in 1882 that a nation was "a soul, a spiritual principle," which suggested that nations embodied a quasi-religious spirit.[10] Of course, a nation, however romanticized, could never be purely spiritual. In Max Weber's classic formulation, a national state is the organized exercise of legitimate violence over a territory, so the relations between religious faiths and nations must necessarily be embedded in the material realities of violent force and territorial control.[11] Nevertheless, following Luschan, a study of religions could ignore these material factors and forces in attributing the spirit of nations to their religious faiths.

Finally, Luschan's praise of Japan as a "young and vigorous nation" could only refer to Japan's recent emergence as an imperial nation with its military victory over Russia.[12] During the shipboard debate about the "yellow peril," the Japanese defeat of Russia must have been on everyone's mind, because the only scholar to argue that the peril was real gave a lecture on the virtues of the Russian empire. Japan was a young empire, having established its first colony in Taiwan in 1895. But Japan certified its imperial status by entering Korea in 1905 and formally annexing Korea in 1910 as part of the Japanese empire. According to Luschan, Europe could learn from the spirit of this young and vigorous empire. But his German empire, established in 1871, was also relatively young and was vigorously establishing colonies in eastern and southern Africa. By sharing assumptions about race and culture, empires, young and old, were learning from each other not only in practical politics but also in the academic study of physiology, psychology, sociology, and religion.

Iwasaki Koyata (1879-1945), who had entertained his fellow passengers by dressing up as Kaiser Wilhelm and joking about the yellow peril, returned to Japan from this South African academic excursion in 1906 to assume the responsibility of vice president of the Mitsubishi Corporation. He became president of Mitsubishi in 1916. Having studied in England, "learning from the world's most advanced country," Iwasaki returned to Japan as "an idealistic entrepreneur."[13] He also returned as an imperialist. As Iwasaki would have discerned from the British model, imperialism was not only a matter of conquering; it was also an enterprise of collecting artifacts and converting natives. While he assembled an impressive collection of Chinese bronze antiques by 1911, his brother purchased the personal library of Max Müller for Tokyo Imperial University.[14] Turning to the work of conversion, Iwasaki Koyata sponsored the missions of the Japanese Congregational Church into occupied Korea.[15] As the largest corporate sponsor of this Japanese imperial initiative, Iwasaki put his financial resources behind an enterprise that recalled the British imperial slogan "Christianity,

Commerce, and Civilization" but was being recast in a Japanese idiom that registered conquest as a kind of conversion or "assimilation" (*doka*) into Japanese culture and Japanese civilization (*bunmei*) as a standard for measuring "primitive" Koreans. As the study of religion was established in Japan, with Masaharu Anesaki assuming the first professorship in the subject at Tokyo Imperial University in 1905, it developed in this context of expanding colonization and imperial ambition.[16]

Felix von Luschan (1854–1924), despite his broad and refreshing views on religion, also became engaged in an imperial enterprise, not by converting souls but by collecting skulls from German colonies in Africa. Inventor of the widely used chromatic scale for identifying thirty-six shades or "types" of skin pigmentation, Luschan used scientific measurement to identify racial origins and distinguish racial forms. Conversing with him on the ship, Browne found that Luschan was intensely interested in southern Africa. He had read a recent book on the Bushmen and speculated that the ancient ruins of Zimbabwe could not be of African origin, unaware that their African origin was being proved by the excavations of David Randall-MacIver, sponsored by the British Association for the Advancement of Science.[17] During the meetings of the British Association, Luschan presented a paper, "The Racial Affinities of the Hottentots," which argued primarily on the basis of language that the Khoikhoi were relatively recent arrivals from North Africa who had interbred with indigenous Bushmen.[18] But his visit to South Africa gave Luschan opportunity to supplement his research on language with the measurement of bodies. Visiting the Breakwater Prison in Cape Town, Luschan was delighted to find "a greater number of Bushmen, Hottentots and Griqua . . . than had ever before been placed at the comfortable disposal of a scientific traveler."[19] This South African prison solved a research problem that had troubled Luschan during the Colonial Exhibition of 1896 in Berlin when he found it difficult to take scientific measurements of the Africans and Pacific Islanders, not only because they were averse to being naked and scrutinized, but also because of "the complete impossibility of exercising any coercion over them."[20] The Breakwater Prison provided a controlled environment for scientific investigation. The long sea voyage provided another controlled environment for Luschan to collect anthropometric measurements, in this case measuring members of the British Association. He confided to Browne that he found the average size of their heads was larger than normal.[21]

Not as a phrenologist, but as a physical anthropologist, Felix von Luschan was interested in collecting skulls. Returning to Berlin, he saw the genocidal warfare against the Herero in the German colony of South West Africa as an opportunity to enhance his collection. Between 1904 and 1907, the German policy of extermination reduced the Herero population from eighty thousand to twenty thousand and confined many survivors to concentration camps.[22] Luschan wrote to Lieutenant Ralf Zürn to ask if there was "any possible way in which we might acquire a larger number of Herero skulls." Lieutenant Zürn responded that skulls could be best collected in the camps, "since in the concentration camps taking and preserving the skulls of Herero prisoners of war will be more readily possible than in the country, where there is always a danger of offending the ritual feelings of the natives."[23] Arguably, Zürn showed some sensitivity to the religious questions involved in Luschan's scientific inquiry by calling attention to African religious rituals for the dead. Nevertheless, Lieutenant Zürn and other colonial administrators sent skulls, skeletons, dried skin, and hair from South West Africa to anthropological collections in Germany. As the historian Andrew Zimmermann has assessed this exchange, the cooperation in collecting skulls for scientific investigation "transformed administrators and soldiers into anthropological collectors and colonial raids and massacres into scientific expeditions."[24] A similar exchange was taking place between British scientists and the British military in South Africa.[25]

The production of knowledge in physical anthropology depended upon such exchanges between imperial centers and colonial peripheries. Indigenous raw materials, in this case skulls, were accumulated and transported by colonial agents, who acted as middlemen, to the imperial center to be transformed by theory into intellectual goods. However, the relations between center and periphery were not entirely efficient. While Luschan was collecting Herero skulls for the Berlin Ethnological Museum, German politicians were vigorously debating the brutality and the cost of the imperial campaign in South West Africa. As a result of those debates, the Reichstag was dissolved in December 1906 and elections were called for January 1907. These were commonly referred to as the "Hottentot elections," and historian Erik Grimmer-Solem has characterized them as "a national referendum on the entire German colonial endeavor."[26] At the imperial center, therefore, we find political actors adopting different positions—promoting imperial ambitions, opposing colonial campaigns, and arguably developing principles and practices from Africa into a program of racial extermination—that shows diversity at the center.[27] But all of these positions at the center were worked out in the same imperial field that encompassed indigenous resources, colonial agents, and metropolitan interests.

In the global relations between powerful imperial centers and the subjugated peripheries, where indigenous people were dominated, dispossessed, and displaced, the center seems at first glance to hold a monopoly on all of the power and knowledge, apparently presiding over a one-way flow of resources from colonized periphery to imperial center. However, as the historian Bernard Cohn observed with respect to the British colony of India, center and periphery must be seen as a single field of contacts, relations, and exchanges; the "metropole and colony have to be seen in a unitary field of analysis."[28] Following this insight, Catherine Hall has observed that "colony and metropole are terms which can be understood only in relation to each other," but she added that for the British Empire "the identity of colonizer is a constitutive part of Englishness."[29] Although this assertion has been resisted by historians who want to diminish the importance, intentionality, or impact of empire at the British center,[30] recent research has explored the British imperial field not as relations between a fixed center and changing peripheries, but as networks and exchanges,[31] as "webs of empire" and "bundles of relationships,"[32] as "imperial formations" in which power and knowledge were circulating.[33] In the case of the British Association, the visit to South Africa was an important event in this circulation, illustrating Hall's assertion that the British world was "defined by its outsides: without Empire there was no England, without barbarism there was no civilization."[34] Visiting South Africa in 1905, the British Association for the Advancement of Science entered a field of circulations—indigenous, colonial, and imperial—that were crucial to the production of knowledge in all of the sciences as well as within the empire of religion.

SAVAGE SOUTH AFRICA

In his presidential address in Cape Town, George H. Darwin (1845–1912) began by reflecting on the distance between Europe and Africa, which was shrinking: whereas Bartholomeu Diaz, the discoverer of the "Cape of Storms," had taken sixteen months and Vasco da Gama four months to reach the Cape, the British Association had arrived by steamships in two weeks.[35] As he revealed on another occasion, George Darwin had a personal interest in South Africa, because his father, visiting during his voyage on the *Beagle* in 1836, wanted to get off the ship and walk across the interior but was prevented by a storm, a South African storm, George Darwin quipped, which made his own birth possible by saving his father from certain death.[36]

Although Cape Town was a colonial periphery of the imperial metropole, the city had long been a center of global networks and cultural circulations. During the 1830s, Lady Margaret Herschel, wife of the astronomer John Herschel, reflected on this central role of Cape Town. "If London is the centre of civilized Europe, this seems to be the centre of the rest of the world—for we live in the midst of accounts and arrivals from India, China, Australia and America—all teem with interest."[37] As a nexus for such global exchanges, South Africa, in general, was a transcultural space, a contact zone in which indigenous Africans, European settlers, and Asian immigrants had a long, often violent, sometimes collaborative, history of intercultural relations.

Indigenous Africans had generally suffered from these relations, undergoing conquest, dispossession, and displacement. The confinement of Africans, as Felix von Luschan discovered, could be an advantage for research, a situation that delegates found throughout South Africa, as the president of the anthropological section of the association, Alfred C. Haddon, noted: "Prison authorities also gave us facilities and by these means Bushmen, Hottentots and representatives of various Bantu-speaking peoples were studied."[38] Mining compounds provided another controlled environment for research. But the visiting scientists, especially those with anthropological interests, were most impressed when they moved from the Cape to Natal and witnessed genuine Zulu rituals performed in savage regalia in their natural habitat.

On August 23, 1905, George H. Darwin and other delegates of the association were received by Marshall Campbell, owner of the Mount Edgecombe Sugar Estate near Durban. As they approached this extensive plantation, James Stark Browne recalled, they saw bands of Zulu men "in all their savagery of war array" approaching, singing, and shouting, all "with very weird effect." After a guided tour of the sugar refinery, the delegates proceeded to an open field where they witnessed a dramatic display of Zulu savagery. According to Browne, the authenticity of this performance, something that "needed to be seen to be properly appreciated," was certified by the savage costumes, rhythms, and ferocity of the Zulu dancers. In their "barbaric array of skins, ornaments, feathers, and most wonderful variety of headdresses," some nearly naked, others in "fantastic costumes as quite to baffle description," the dancers appeared "grotesque in the extreme." For over an hour, these dancers enacted wild dances that Browne found "almost equally impossible to describe, for their full meaning, even to sightseers, was difficult to grasp." Describing the indescribable, Browne reported: "First the whole line, three or four deep, began to stamp and move about, rhythmically keeping time to a monotonous chant which they all intoned together. While this was going on, the chiefs and braves, one after the other, dashed out of the ranks and went through the pretence of sanguinary conflicts with imaginary foes, shouting and capering wildly and stabbing with their sticks with devilish ferocity all the time." Browne speculated that this wild dance, with its "pretended conflicts," was a war dance, reenacting past conflicts, preparing for future conflicts, and transforming dancers into frenzied warriors as it served "to work on the spirit of the men, exciting them to prodigious deeds of valour and emulation." At certain points in the ritual, the dancers rushed toward the delegates of the British Association, "as if about to annihilate our entire party," but then retreated "as though regretting that they dared not touch us." The strange costumes and wild rhythms; the shrieking, yelling, and groaning; the threatening prospect of savage attack—the "effect of this upon our inexperienced nerves," Browne recalled, "was very thrilling." The dancers, as well, seemed to be thrilled, excited by the war dance, so Browne felt that "it was well that the Government had taken away their assegais and curtailed the size of their shields, for after dances of this sort they might be tempted to do some mischief."[39]

This war dance was certainly a highlight of the South African tour for delegates of the British Association. In a review of the meetings published in the journal *Man*, the correspondent recalled this Zulu war ritual, noting that the "dances were genuine . . . except that the performers carried staves instead of assegais."[40] Leaders of the anthropological section of the British Association were particularly impressed. Reporting on their visit to Edgecombe, the anthropologist E. Sidney Hartland described the dancing, with "magical intent," which they had witnessed. "A war-dance was first performed," he recalled. "It was of a most exciting description, for the men were gradually wrought up into what looked a perfect fury, dancing, leaping, and yelling." Hartland, as well, was relieved that the Zulu dancers had been prevented from carrying assegais. "Had they had spears, as they would in their natural condition, instead of thin long sticks or wands which they actually carried," he reported, "it would have required some amount of nerve to witness it unmoved."[41] President of the anthropological section Alfred C. Haddon reported that the "natives danced war and other dances for our delectation," suggesting that the delegates could regard the dancing as entertainment because of the absence of real weapons. Zulu war dances, which the association witnessed at the sugar estate, and again two days later near Pietermaritzburg under the auspices of the governor of Natal, supreme chief of all the Zulu, were such monumental events, in Haddon's estimation, that it was "improbable that they will ever be repeated on a similar scale."[42]

In their encounter with this savage Zulu war dance, the imperial visitors were confronted with several colonial constructions. As the designation of the colonial governor as supreme chief should have indicated, any independent Zulu political sovereignty had been broken. In a report in 1905 on the natives of Natal, the linguist Alice Werner (1859–1935) explained that the Zulu people, divided into 312 tribes, were organized under different types of jurisdiction in locations, Crown lands, private lands, or mission reserves. "The distribution is somewhat irregular," Werner acknowledged, "having been arranged, to some extent at least, on the principle of *Divide et impera*."[43] Dividing and ruling, in this case, also meant containing and taxing. During August 1905, while the British Association was visiting, the colonial government proposed a new poll tax, incumbent on all adult Zulu males, which was incurring resentment and resistance. A few weeks later, in October 1905, people opposed to the new tax gathered for a strengthening and purifying ceremony. As the historian Jeff Guy has argued, the term *war dance* was a colonial construction that was applied to any collective ceremony that Europeans found threatening, so this ritual ceremony was inevitably interpreted by colonial observers as a "war dance" or "war doctoring."[44] When an armed uprising against colonial taxation broke out in 1906, colonial observers insisted that the Zulu rebellion, the so-called Bhambatha Rebellion, began with a war dance. "There is no act, passive in its nature, which a Native can commit that betrays hostile intent more plainly than being doctored for war," the colonial administrator James Stuart observed in his report on the uprising. "Once such ceremonies are held, all that remains is to await the signal for a simultaneous rising."[45] This colonial focus on Zulu religious ritual, recast as a war dance, deflected attention from the material conditions of oppressive taxation and labor extraction as if this ritual were the cause of the uprising.[46]

While witnessing a savage "war dance" in a region that would soon be at war, the delegates of the British Association were subjected to a staged display of barbarity and civilization. As the Zulu warriors, who were employees of the sugar plantation, retreated, they were replaced by a group of "native Christians," dressed in European clothing and performing "God Save the King," "Home Sweet Home," and other popular songs. "Of course," as Browne recognized, "this was all done to show us the contrast between the heathen and the Christianized Zulus."[47] Other delegates also noted the "object lesson" in this staged contrast between heathen and Christian Zulus. As J. D. F. Gilchrist reported to the scientific readership of *Nature*, "The contrast afforded by a Zulu war dance and a demonstration by Christian native girls was an object lesson which many were glad to have seen."[48]

British delegates could have stayed home to see such public displays of the contrast between heathen and Christianized Africans. For example, the African Choir, touring England in 1891 and 1892, performed the first half of their concerts in savage attire, the second half in civilized Christian dress.[49] For their host at Edgecombe, Marshall Campbell, "an ardent believer in and supporter of missions," staging such a drama of heathen savagery and Christian civilization was the whole point of the visit.[50]

The leading anthropologists of the British Association, Alfred C. Haddon (1855–1946) and E. Sidney Hartland (1848–1927), omitted the Christian half of this equation in their accounts of the Zulu rituals they attended. These heathen ceremonies were "genuine," they reported, even though the dances were performed by employees of their host as a prelude to songs by Zulu Christians and a speech by a Zulu pastor, a "native missionary," as Browne recalled, who "addressed us and in a forcible and humorous speech appealed to us for funds to help on his work in that locality." Advocating industrial education along the lines developed by Booker T. Washington in the United States, this Zulu pastor argued that learning the "dignity of labour" was the key for the regeneration of Africans. But he also identified the "object lesson" that the delegates were supposed to learn from their visit as he "drew a comparison between the simple civilized performance to which [they] had just listened and the brutal savage display enacted outside, and claimed that these results came from training the children early in life." The delegates were so moved by this Zulu preacher that according to Browne they immediately donated £75 to his Christian missionary project of industrial education.[51]

This native missionary was John Langalibalele Dube (1871–1946), educated in the United States at Oberlin College in Ohio, who had returned to Natal to found a school and a newspaper; in 1912 he became the first president of the African National Congress.[52] Although the delegates of the British Association at Edgecombe were impressed by his speech, even donating money to his cause, they could not have appreciated Dube's political role in South Africa. Another guest at the proceedings, however, who knew John Dube very well, described him as someone "one should know." Mohandas K. Gandhi reported that Dube had given a "very impressive" speech to the members of the British Association, in which he argued that for Africans "there was no country other than South Africa; and to deprive them of their rights over lands, etc., was like banishing them from their home."[53]

Gandhi, who had been in South Africa since 1893, with a home in his settlement at Phoenix in Natal since 1904, for a while shared his printing press with John Dube, producing both Gandhi's *Indian Opinion* and Dube's *Ilanga lase Natal*. Although Dube raised some funds from the delegation, Gandhi wanted more from the British Association. As he wrote in an article published in *Indian Opinion*, Gandhi wanted the association to convene in India. Celebrating the South African visit of this "body of illustrious scientists," Gandhi maintained that their time in the colony would not only advance science but also achieve "a more important result in drawing together South Africa and Britain, and the Colonies with one another." Looking forward to the day when the British Association, "one of the greatest assets of the Empire," would come to India, Gandhi proposed that the association should change its name to "THE BRITISH EMPIRE ASSOCIATION FOR THE ADVANCEMENT OF SCIENCE."[54]

Although they had wide interests in anthropology and folklore, Haddon and Hartland were both experts in "savage" religion. The following year Haddon published his introduction to primitive religion, *Magic and Fetishism*; three years later Hartland convened the section on the "religions of the lower cultures" of the International Congress for the History of Religions held at Oxford in 1908.[55] Both had developed an interest in South Africa before the visit of the British Association. In 1900 Haddon and Hartland were instrumental in drafting a memorandum on behalf of the Anthropological Institute and the Folklore Society to the British secretary of state for the colonies, Joseph Chamberlain, advocating imperial support for the "scientific study of the native laws and customs of South Africa." Although their appeal was signed by the most prominent British scholars, including the founder of modern British social anthropology, E. B. Tylor, the office of Secretary Chamberlain casually dismissed their proposal by observing in 1900, "The time has, of course, not yet arrived when such a Commission could be appointed with any advantage"; he repeated in 1902, "[The secretary] regrets that he cannot regard the present time as a suitable one for such an appointment." Their imperial interest in the natives of South Africa, therefore, received no official imperial support. Nevertheless, Haddon and Hartland tried to provide compelling imperial arguments for conducting research on native religion, laws, and customs in South Africa—the natives were not going away; conflicts between Europeans and natives arose from "ignorance by the former of the customs and superstitions of the latter"; and "accurate knowledge of the customs, institutions, and superstitions of the natives" had practical value in the colonial administration of the natives in South Africa.[56]

What did Haddon and Hartland learn about the natives during their visit to South Africa in 1905? Certainly their visit confirmed what they wrote to Secretary Chamberlain: "This native population . . . does not tend to die out in consequence of contact with Europeans." Accordingly, the natives "are likely to remain a permanent element of the population." However, this insight was commonplace in British reflections on South Africa. For example, it was formulated in 1904 succinctly in an article in the popular periodical the *Nineteenth Century* on "The Black Peril in South Africa" by citing Lord Arthur Balfour's observation about Africans in South Africa: "They are there, they are going to remain there."[57] Although the visit enabled the British anthropologists to see for themselves the living "customs, institutions, and superstitions" of the natives of South Africa, they were entangled in a contradiction between the scientific demand for "accurate knowledge" and the pragmatic requirements of colonial management.

Seeking accurate knowledge, they witnessed "genuine" African rituals that were carefully staged by the owner of a sugar plantation in Natal as an "object lesson" in the contrast between savagery and civilization. They would witness other genuine African rituals organized by the governor of Natal, the mine owners of Johannesburg, and the colonial administrators of Rhodesia. As they sought accurate knowledge, the authenticity of their visit was certified by colonial agents. During the British Association's visit to Natal, Sidney Hartland acquired an authentic necklace from a Zulu witch doctor, a ritual necklace like those he had seen in the Zulu war dances. But the authenticity of this ritual artifact was certified for Hartland in a document provided by the dealer he bought it from in Durban: "The witch-doctor's necklace, made of horns, etc., belonged to a Zulu well known to myself. He belongs to a tribe near Tugela. This doctor was on a visit to Durban for the purpose of trading, and was wearing this necklace when I purchased it. He was very unwilling to part with it."[58] Dated August 22, 1905, and signed by the dealer, F. W. Flanders, this certificate served to authenticate the necklace for Hartland and eventually for the collection of the Pitt Rivers Museum at Oxford. Authenticity was underwritten by coercion, because the witch doctor did not want to part with it.

Although the anthropologists sought "accurate knowledge of the customs, institutions, and superstitions of the native," their encounters with Africans were managed by colonial administrators, facilitated by prison officials, staged by wealthy hosts, and certified by entrepreneurs. If they were not gullible in these exchanges, perhaps they were complicit. Did they collude with the colonial distinction between ethnic African subjects and racialized white citizens of South Africa? Perhaps they did, personally. But personal feelings were not the issue. In an unpublished essay on imperialism written around 1891, Haddon had expressed his personal opposition to "the red paint of British aggression" and had identified with the victims of that violence who "would be less than men if they did not rebel."[59] But the issue was not personal but professional. They definitely reinscribed the imperial divide between the savage and the civilized as a matter of academic method and discipline, since Haddon concluded from his visit: "South Africa affords a most favorable field for the study of the ethnology of the lower races and the sociology of the higher."[60] In the empire of religion, this disciplinary distinction between sociology and ethnology marked the great divide between citizens of the world's religions and subjects of native superstitions. South Africa was on the frontlines of that divide.

LOCAL EXPERTS

In their plea for an imperial commission, the Anthropological Institute and the Folklore Society proposed that this body should consist of "persons familiar with native life in South Africa," drawing upon the knowledge of local experts but also including "at least one person, unconnected with South Africa, of recognized eminence in the study of savage customs and superstitions in general." The commission, therefore, would bring together local and imperial expertise in the study of savage life. The only example of a local expert "familiar with native life in South Africa" who was cited in this appeal was Henry Callaway, author of *The Religious System of the Amazulu*, "whose name is never to be mentioned without respect."[61] Although his primary research on Zulu religion deserved respect, Callaway was also praised for applying his knowledge in the expert testimony he had presented before colonial government commissions of inquiry into African customs.

As Alice Werner confirmed in her review of native affairs in 1905, conflict in Natal and Zululand could be resolved only by such expert knowledge. She agreed with the imperial scholars that the "real and only remedy is, *to know the native.*" But this knowledge should be produced not through collaboration between imperial scholarship and local experts but by building trust between colonial officials and indigenous Africans. She invoked the advice of James Stuart, who was both colonial official and local expert, that the colonial government should "create an independent Department which, by devoting its whole time to inquiring into the affairs of these people, would become so authoritative as to be a guide as well to the Government as to the entire European community." This government department, Stuart urged, should be "organized with the co-operation of hereditary Chiefs and responsible heads of other sections of Natives, all directly under European officials, as fairly to voice Native feeling." Knowledge of the native, from this perspective, had to be based on cultivating trust, demonstrating the kind of sympathy that James Stuart found best exemplified by the secretary for native affairs, Theophilus Shepstone, and the Anglican bishop John William Colenso. By taking an interest in Africans and seeking to understand them, Shepstone and Colenso, according to Stuart, had gained the people's trust. Stuart said, "It is in no small degree due to the action of these prominent men that Europeans are respected as much as they are."[62]

During the visit of 1905, the British Association entered this colonial field of knowledge production, an arena animated by what I have called a triple mediation—imperial, colonial, and indigenous. For the imperial anthropologists interested in knowing something about the natives in the interest of mediating between savages and primitive humanity, the most useful interaction was with local experts, since the visit facilitated a face-to-face exchange between eminent theorists of savage religion and "men on the spot" who knew the languages, cultural repertoires, and religious beliefs and practices of the natives in South Africa. Ultimately, however, the imperial theorists were interested in how this local knowledge might contribute to expanding "the study of savage customs and superstitions in general." Accordingly, they sought to frame the theory and pose the questions in ways that might contribute to that general knowledge.

Local experts were also interested in such questions, participating in the conceptual mediation between "savage" Africans and the primitive ancestors of humanity. South African scholars presenting papers in the anthropological section of the association seemed to welcome the opportunity to collaborate with metropolitan scholars. But they also had to mediate between colonial situations, which included the demands of governance introduced by Shepstone and the demands of missions represented by Colenso, and the indigenous Africans who acted as their informants or collaborators in generating accounts of the religious beliefs, practices, and institutions of the natives. Africans, of course, were engaged in complex mediations, as we have seen, which ranged from staged displays of war dances to armed rebellion against colonial taxation. Mediating between indigenous traditions and colonial situations, Africans who converted to Christianity adopted a new "gospel of work," or the industrial education advocated by John Dube, but African Christians also participated in both the displays and the rebellions.[63]

The anthropological section of the British Association, Section H, featured twenty-seven academic presentations during the 1905 meetings in Cape Town and Johannesburg. The keynote address, delivered by the president of the section, Alfred C. Haddon, provided a general overview of ethnology in South Africa that drew upon his wide reading of the work of travelers, missionaries, colonial agents, and local experts. Advocating the collection of more anthropometric data for comparative physiology, Haddon also called upon the local experts to engage in more work to salvage knowledge about Africans whose lives or lifestyles were "doomed" by the advance of civilization. Their research, Haddon urged, could rescue the "memory of these primitive folk from oblivion."[64]

If physical data could be organized according to a racial theory, how could cultural data, the "memory of these primitive folk," be organized? In his presentation at the South African meetings, E. Sidney Hartland demonstrated how this cultural data might be organized by drawing South African evidence into the theoretical controversy that had been occupying social anthropologists in Britain, the controversy over totemism.

Although the theoretical definition and viability of the term were hotly debated, totemism had become commonplace in the academic study of religion. Everyone had to deal with it. Adapted from an Ojibway word for kinship and introduced into the study of religion by John McLennan in his essay titled "The Worship of Animals and Plants," published in 1869–70, which defined totems as "animal or vegetable gods," the totem gradually replaced the fetish as a focus of attention in the anthropology of religion. In McLennan's account, the totem was like the fetish, an object that was worshipped, but it also organized social relations, since members of the same totem clan were prohibited from marrying each other and kinship was traced through the mother's line. Part of the term's appeal, therefore, was the way it connected religion with society, a connection developed by William Robertson Smith in his analysis of the totemic basis of Semitic religion.[65]

But leading theorists of religion, such as Max Müller or E. B. Tylor, who were more interested in primitive psychology than sociology, were slow to engage totemism as a significant theoretical problem in the study of religion. In 1897 Max Müller formulated his understanding of totemism as a developmental progression: "A totem is a clan mark, then a clan name, then the name of the ancestor of the clan, and lastly the name of something worshipped by the clan."[66] Two years later Tylor published his observations on totemism, noting that he had been reluctant to write about a topic of such "bewildering complexity," a subject surrounded with "various and vague ideas." He only hoped that "further research among the races of the lower culture would clear its outlines."[67] Tylor's own proposal that the totem originated in ancestor worship and formed a link between animals and humans, connecting an animal species with a human clan so they were "united in kinship and mutual alliance," did not reduce the confusion or complexity of totemism in the study of religion.[68] Other theorists eagerly embraced the topic. Andrew Lang and James Frazer published extensively on totemism, although they adopted very different approaches, with Lang emphasizing the totem's role in social differentiation and organization and Frazer variously explaining the totem in terms of primitive magic, economy, and sexuality.

Why did the term *totemism* come to assume such prominence in imperial theories of religion during this period? After all, as Edmund Leach observed, the key terms of nineteenth-century theory—fetishism, animism, and totemism—basically referred to the same thing, a primitive ignorance, allegedly displayed by savages all over the world, of the meaning and value of material objects.[69] In a sweeping proposal, the cultural theorist W. J. T. Mitchell has argued that the transition from interest in the fetish to the obsession with the totem can be correlated with the historical development of the British Empire. The term *fetish*, which originally emerged out of the intercultural trading zone of West Africa, served to represent a savage ignorance of the value of objects. Accordingly, as a theory of the origin of religion, fetishism suited the interests of mercantilist, seafaring empires in representing trading relations with indigenous people. Totemism, however, combined the fetishistic regard for objects with a wider range of savage beliefs and practices relating to sex, marriage, kinship, and social organization. As a more encompassing term, totemism was a theory of the origin of religion that suited the interests of "the mature, that is to say, British form of empire, combining mercantilism and territorial expansion, the spread of trading monopolies and religious missions."[70] Interest in totemism, therefore, can be situated in this expanding empire because the term enabled theorists to include a wider range of human activity, from sexuality to society, within the study of religion.

In expanding the empire of totemism, the Anthropological Institute and the Folklore Society published detailed schedules of questions, "Notes and Queries," to be used by travelers, missionaries, government officials, and other "investigators on the spot" in the colonial peripheries of the British Empire.[71] Defining totemism as a "religious and social system" revolving around a "sacred object," the queries about totemism addressed not only social divisions and religious reverence but also intimate questions about sexual intercourse, marriage, and kinship relations among indigenous people. Representing the most primitive structure of human relations, simultaneously sexual, social, and religious, totemism also provided a baseline for speculating on the historical development of religious systems. In a set of questions asking about "traces of the transitions of totemism into a more advanced worship," the Zulu featured as a model for such transitions. "Are the dead, or the spirits of the dead, worshipped? If so, what is their name (Zulu *Amatongo*)? And have these any relation to animals, and especially to snakes (Zulu *Ihlozi*), or to those animals whose name the clan bears? Are such animals considered to bring luck or to represent ancestral or guardian spirits? Is there a supernatural being, a kind of great father, who first gave being to men? And if so, what is his name (Zulu, *Unkulunkulu*)?"[72] In these questions, the Zulu, the only indigenous people mentioned by name in the twenty-nine sets of questions about totemism, were used to illustrate an evolutionary scheme in which religious development proceeded from primitive totemism, through ancestor worship, to the emergence of beliefs in gods. Although this evolutionary scheme was being contested, most persistently by Andrew Lang, who used Zulu evidence to support his theory of the original "high gods of lower races," these notes and queries served to circulate the term *totemism* as an organizing principle for research in the colonies.

As E. B. Tylor observed, the theory of totemism had to be animated by "further research among the races of the lower culture."[73] Much of that research was coming from Australia, where local experts W. Baldwin Spencer and Francis J. Gillen were collaborating with metropolitan theorists.[74] But South Africa was also a site for research on totemism. Imperial theorists read recent publications for evidence supporting their positions; one report might be read to reinforce the arguments of E. B. Tylor and another might lend support to arguments advanced by Andrew Lang.

The seventh volume of *Records of South-Eastern Africa*, edited by George McCall Theal, official historian for the Cape government, provided evidence for Tylor's proposal that totemism originated in ancestor worship. According to this South African historian, "The Bantu believed that the spirits of the dead visited their friends and descendants in the form of animals. Each tribe regarded some particular animal as the one selected by the ghosts of its kindred, and therefore looked upon it as sacred."[75] Calling attention to Theal's account, James Frazer found that Bantu religion confirmed Tylor's general theory of totemism. He concluded, "If Dr. Theal's

account is correct (and I know no reason to doubt it), the totemism of the Bantu tribes of South Africa resolves into a particular species of the worship of the dead; the totem animals are revered incarnations of the souls of dead ancestors."[76] However, the South African research of G. W. Stow seemed to confirm Lang's theory that the origin of totemism could be found in the names given to groups of people by outsiders. Such nicknames, or sobriquets, originally marking social difference, were embraced as objects of worship as totemism developed from its social origin to religious elaboration. Stow proposed that the South African evidence suggested that the totems "among these tribes arose from some sobriquet that had been given to them; and that in course of time, as their superstitions and devotional feelings became more developed, these tribal symbols became objects of veneration and superstitious awe."[77]

Clearly, these exchanges between local experts and imperial theorists did not resolve the theoretical debates about totemism. As they mediated between the colonial periphery and the metropolitan center, local experts often incorporated the theories of leading scholars of religion such as Max Müller, Tylor, Lang, or Frazer into their reports. Recognizing that this exchange distorted the evidence, the folklorist N. W. Thomas proposed that "in dealing with South African problems we clear our minds of totemism as a necessary part of the solution."[78]

In his presentation at the South African meetings, "The Totemism of the Bantu," E. Sidney Hartland sought to test local African data against a general theory of totemism. Beginning with a local reference, he invoked the authority of the French missionary to the Basotho Eugène Casalis, who had observed fifty years earlier that Africans and Native Americans had similar beliefs and practices, in order to place Africans in a broader comparative framework. Hartland's analysis depended upon comparing underlying religious structures with conjectural histories of the evolution or degeneration of African religion. As a result of this method, he could conclude that Bantu religion had originated in the basic structure of totemism but had undergone a "process of decay" that obscured the original structure with an overlay of ancestor worship. This religious change, he speculated, resulted from contact with "the pure Negro along the west coast" and a shift from tracing kinship from the mother to the father that provided the social basis for ancestor worship. However, by going back through this historical process of decay to a pure totemic origin, Hartland could conclude, "There is no essential difference between the Bantu practices and belief and what is generally recognised as totemism elsewhere."[79]

One of the local experts, the missionary W. C. Willoughby (1857–1938), also presented a paper on totemism, "Notes on the Totemism of the Becwana," which speculated on the underlying totemic structure of the indigenous religion of the Tswana-speaking people of South Africa. Although people were currently organized around "tribal totems," which were designated by animals, these particular animal emblems did not feature prominently in the most important religious rituals of birth, adulthood, marriage, and death. Like Hartland, Willoughby speculated that these various tribal totems had to be a more recent development or decay overlaying an original totemic structure. This original structure, he speculated, must be the ox-totem, not only because the ox featured prominently as the most important animal in Tswana sacrificial ritual but also because this sacrificial significance of the ox was shared widely by indigenous Africans. Accordingly, Willoughby argued, Africans in South Africa shared the same totemic origin in a generic "Bantu religion" underlying the diversity of beliefs, practices, and associations that might be observed within the indigenous religion of the region.[80]

Hartland and Willoughby, the imperial theorist and the local expert, addressed the same topic, South African totemism, by following a similar trajectory: identifying an original structure and charting a history of decay. But the differences in their analyses are revealing. Hartland's history of Bantu religion began with a generic totemism, which was the same as "what is generally recognized as totemism elsewhere." Willoughby's history, by contrast, began with a specific totem, the ox-totem, as the original structure of indigenous religion in South Africa. Although they both began by positing an original, originating religious structure, the imperial theorist posited a universal totemism while the local expert distilled a specific totem. Both sketched a history of degeneration from that origin. However, by contrast to Hartland's history of a loss of the original totemism in the shift to ancestor worship, Willoughby presented a history of the proliferation of totemism, an expansion of "tribal totems," which divided Africans and separated them from their original unity.

Although they adopted the same theoretical framework and participated in a shared intellectual project, the imperial theorist and the local expert were very differently situated. While Hartland was looking for data from Willoughby and other local experts that he could marshal in imperial debates about the primitive origin of religion, Willoughby was introducing the imperial theory of totemism into ongoing colonial arguments about the tribal divisions and the underlying unity of indigenous people in South

Africa. Putting the matter bluntly: Under colonial governance, Africans were all the same, excluded from citizenship but all divided into tribal units, as Alice Werner suggested, by the principle *divide et impera*, in the interest of managing and controlling the natives. Willoughby's account of African religion, with its dual emphasis on underlying unity and tribal divisions, was clearly located within this colonial mandate.

The meetings of the British Association featured other presentations by local experts on African religion. Some were purely descriptive, such as C. A. Wheelwright's account of circumcision rituals in the Transvaal or the reports by William Grant, A. E. Mabille, and J. W. Shepstone about African tribal life.[81] But imperial theory lingered in the proceedings, even though any evolutionary theorist would have been frustrated when Rev. E. Gottschling outlined Venda religion by observing that all three stages of religious development—totemism, ancestor worship, and belief in gods—existed simultaneously.[82] The missionary and ethnographer Henri-Alexandre Junod, who would emerge as one of the leading local experts on indigenous religion in southern Africa, gave his presentation, "The Ba-Thonga of the Transvaal," which also adapted imperial theory.[83] In conversation with imperial theorists and the latest theoretical developments, Junod was a colleague on the periphery. His presentation was particularly appreciated by the imperial theorists, as Haddon reported, not only because Junod had already published valuable works on the natives, but also because he "enlivened his bright paper by singing native songs; he also provided a native to sing and play upon a xylophone."[84] Even local experts could be valued by imperial theorists for providing entertainment.

The meetings of the anthropological section, however, were serious business, entertaining religion, as a subject of interest, between the serious demands of psychology and physiology. Canon William Crisp, presenting a paper titled "The Mental Capacity of the Bantu," could provide anecdotes about the "native shrewdness" of Africans in their dealings with Europeans, but Professor Felix von Luschan was there to insist on the scientific validity of linking psychology with physiology and the scientific necessity of collecting anthropometric data from the natives. Louis Péringuey, director of the South African Museum in Cape Town, who presented a paper, "The Stone Age in South Africa," returned to Cape Town to make plaster casts of Bushmen.[85] These transactions displayed the undercurrents of imperial scientific theory—psychology could be measured by physiology, and culture could be derived from race—in which any academic study of religion would have to find its way.

IMPERIAL THEORY

In the empire of religion, as we have noted, imperial theory operated with a distinction, sometimes explicit, often implicit, between text-based "world religions" and savage religions, a distinction duplicating the bifurcated system of colonial governance that established different laws for racialized citizens and ethnic, tribal, or savage subjects. Imperial theory established different methods of inquiry into the citizens of world religions and the subjects of savage religions. While world religions were explored through textual translation, historical reconstruction, and philosophical reflection, savage religions were subjects for administrative intervention, ethnographic reporting, and psychological explanation, resulting in Haddon's dual mandate in South Africa for studying the sociology of the higher races and the ethnology of the lower races.

At the center of empire, as Haddon and Hartland insisted, the British had an interest in the study of savage religion. On the one hand, scientific knowledge about the beliefs and practices of the natives could serve the political requirements for their colonial management. On the other, stable colonial governance could enable the gathering of scientific data. The interests of imperial science and governance coincided because they both depended upon creating and exercising colonial control over submissive natives, whether the natives were submitting to excessive taxation or anthropometric measurement. Although "political and scientific interests do not always concur," Hartland observed, "in dealing with savage races they are very often identical."[86]

Ultimately, the British Empire had to recognize that it was engaged in an imperial competition. While the Dutch had long provided financial support for research in their colonies, Germany was now devoting substantial expenditures to supporting anthropological inquiries in its new colonies in Africa and the Eastern Archipelago. Great Britain could not afford to fall behind in this imperial competition, Hartland warned, "or all the much-vaunted practical British genius for government and colonization will not save us."[87]

Since the British government, through its secretary for the colonies, Joseph Chamberlain, refused the appeals for financing a commission to study the savages of South Africa, we have to assume that imperialists at the center were unconvinced by these arguments. But imperialism depended not only on military force, political control, and economic exploitation; it also required accumulating and archiving information.[88] Germans engaged

in colonial archiving before they had an empire;[89] the Japanese underwrote their imperial claims on Korea by archiving folklore.[90] By the beginning of the twentieth century, the British had assembled an extensive archive of savage beliefs, practices, laws, and customs all over the world. Even without formal imperial support, that archiving of savage information continued as an important component of empire.

At the center of empire, the British were also showing an interest in gaining knowledge about world religions. Between 1877 and 1905, the book series "Non-Christian Religious Systems" produced eleven volumes on Hinduism, Buddhism, Islam, Confucianism, and Taoism, with many of the volumes going through numerous printings and selling many copies.[91] Sponsored by the Society for the Promotion of Christian Knowledge, this series promoted knowledge about the religious texts and traditions of the world. Another book series, Archibald Constable's "Religions, Ancient and Modern," which began with Haddon's *Magic and Fetishism* in 1906, advertised its twenty-two volumes as "presenting the Salient Features of the great Religions of the Human Race."[92]

If the empire of religion had a jewel in its crown, it must have been the monumental publication of *The Sacred Books of the East*, under the general editorship of Max Müller, which resulted in fifty volumes published between 1879 and 1910.[93] In his "Preface to the Sacred Books of the East," which appeared with the first volume in 1879, Max Müller celebrated both the hard work of translation, which included collecting and collating manuscripts, reviewing commentaries, and laboring over the meaning of ancient texts, and the opportunity provided by these translations of sacred texts for readers' hearts to "quiver with the first quivering rays of human thought and human faith, as revealed in those ancient documents."[94] Although this publication project was extensive, it omitted Jewish and Christian scripture, over Max Müller's objection, and ignored any texts from or about indigenous religions. Perhaps Max Müller was acknowledging this second exclusion in his preface to the series when he reflected on why the sacred books were sacred. By being preserved and transmitted from generation to generation, often in oral performance, these texts "became sacred heirlooms, sacred, because they came from an unknown source, from a distant age." Drawing on recent research on savage religion, Max Müller explained, "There was a stage in the development of human thought, when the distance that separated the living generation from their grandfathers or great-grandfathers was as yet the nearest approach to a conception of eternity, and when the name of grandfather and great-grandfather seemed the nearest expression of God." These texts were sacred, therefore, not because they were written by sacred authors, but because they bore traces of the earliest human sense of eternity, the continuity of generations, which could be most clearly seen, Max Müller indicated in the first footnote to appear in his "Preface to the Sacred Books of the East," in the Zulu religious beliefs and practices collected in "Bishop Callaway, Unkulunkulu, or the Tradition of Creation, as Existing among the Amazulu and Other Tribes of South Africa."[95] In this gesture of recognition, Max Müller indicated that the imperial line between world religions and savage religions could be blurred, especially if the Zulu provided a model for understanding how the sacred texts of the world became sacred in the first place.

If the line between savage and civilized could be blurred, the distinction between a fixed imperial center and subservient colonized peripheries could also be contested. As we recall, Mohandas K. Gandhi (1869–1948), who lived and worked in South Africa between 1893 and 1914, was present at the excursion of the British Association in Natal. Having studied law in London, where he arguably became a Hindu through his participation in the Vegetarian Society and the Theosophical Society and his reading of the sacred books of the East, Gandhi subscribed to British ideals of citizenship and justice during his time in South Africa, an adherence to imperial ideals that motivated his call for renaming the British Association as the British Empire Association, but he rejected this idealized empire around 1914 for God and India.[96] In Gandhi, therefore, relations between imperial center and colonial periphery, West and East, and Europe and Africa were being constantly renegotiated.

During March 1905, Gandhi was invited to present a series of lectures on religion at the Masonic Temple in Johannesburg, sponsored by the Johannesburg Lodge of the Theosophical Society. Since its founding by Helena Petrovna Blavatsky and Henry Steel Olcott in 1875, Theosophy had developed what the anthropologist Peter van der Veer has called an "anti-Christian comparative religion," a study of religions with special attention to the wisdom of the East, which was outside the scope of Christian missions or colonial control.[97] Gandhi's lectures on religion were published in the local Johannesburg newspaper, the *Star*, and in his own periodical, *Indian Opinion*. As Gandhi showed in his lectures on religion in 1905, it was possible to recast an imperial theory of religion with India as its center. Providing an overview of the history of religions, he started with the North Pole, because the Indian scholar and political prisoner B. G. Tilak, on the basis of astronomical calculations, had determined that the Vedas bore traces of people who had lived in the Arctic Circle around 10,000 BC.[98] After those northerners entered and colonized India, the subsequent history of religions unfolded as a series of challenges posed to this imperial Hindu establishment in India. From this perspective, the history of religions had to follow a specific chronology that was very different from the conventional chronology assumed in Europe. In chronological order, following the original Hinduism (or Aryanism), the history of religions unfolded with the advent of Buddhism, then Islam, and then finally Christianity.[99]

These lectures in Johannesburg illustrated what Gandhi had learned from the academic study of religion, especially from Max Müller, but they also showed what he could do with that knowledge. Gandhi observed in his first lecture on March 4, 1905, "The study of different religious systems [was] most praiseworthy, tending, as [it] did, to widen people's sympathies, and enlarge their comprehension of the motives and beliefs underlying the actions of those who were strangers in creed and colour."[100] Gandhi had found this spirit of informed and sympathetic toleration advanced by Max Müller. In a letter of April 27, 1902, to Sir John Robinson, premier of Natal, Gandhi wrote: "I am very glad that you liked Professor Max Müller's book. Nothing to my mind can conduce better to an understanding between the Western and the Eastern branches of the Imperial family than a fair knowledge, on the part of either, of the best of the other."[101] In his Johannesburg lectures on religion, however, Gandhi identified his intention as cultivating understanding and respect for religions not merely to facilitate imperial family recognition between West and East but "to remove the prejudice and ignorance that existed concerning his own people" in the struggle for the rights of citizenship in South Africa.[102]

In his lecture of March 4, 1905, Gandhi began his outline of the Hindu faith by observing that "Aryanism would have been a better descriptive word than Hinduism."[103] During his time in South Africa, Gandhi frequently urged British colonial officials to recognize that both the British and "the Indians in South Africa belong to the Indo-Germanic stock or, more properly speaking, the Aryan stock," noting that the books of "Max Müller, easily obtainable in Pretoria, also support this view."[104] In a letter to Sir John Robinson of June 29, 1894, Gandhi insisted that "both the Anglo-Saxon and the Indian races belong to the same stock." Referring to imperial authorities on the topic of Aryanism, he noted that "Max Müller . . . and a host of other writers with one voice seem to show very clearly that both the races have sprung from the same Aryan stock, or rather the Indo-European as many call it."[105] Although Max Müller proposed "Aryan" as a genus of language, culture, and religion, refusing the identification of language with race, Gandhi had a local interest in using Max Müller's authority to assert a racial solidarity between the British and the Indians in South Africa.

Continuing his lecture, Gandhi emphasized the Hindu religious commitment to self-denial and duty, which had been vividly demonstrated in South Africa during the Anglo-Boer War, he recalled, by an indentured Indian laborer who had served, at great personal risk, to warn the British army of impending Boer attacks. This Hindu sense of duty, which Gandhi could have derived from the central concept of *dharma*, was also distilled from the writings of Max Müller and deployed in relation to the British Empire. Celebrating the 1905 centenary of Horatio Nelson, whose motto was "England expects that every man will do his duty," Gandhi wrote a tribute to Admiral Nelson as an imperial founder who was "worshipped in the Empire . . . because he was a living embodiment of duty." According to Gandhi, Indians could easily identify with this commitment to duty. He suggested that Hindu *dharma* and British imperial duty were essentially the same, because "Max Müller has acknowledged in his writings that in Indian philosophy the meaning of life is summed up in four letters spelt—DUTY."[106]

Based on their shared racial origin and common commitment to imperial duty, Gandhi argued, the British and the Indians in South Africa should be able to recognize each other as citizens of the same empire. His theosophical audience at the Masonic Lodge in Johannesburg in March 1905, however, probably would have been happier if Gandhi had offered some glimmer or "quiver" of the secret wisdom of the East. During his time in South Africa, Gandhi's proof text for the wisdom of India was provided by Max Müller, who wrote: "If I were asked under what sky the human mind has most fully developed some of its choicest gifts, has most deeply pondered on the greatest problems of life, and has found solutions of some of them which well deserve the attention even of those who have studied Plato and Kant, I should point to India."[107] But Gandhi did not cite that text in his lectures on religion. Instead, he used it in formal legal proceedings, such as his submission on the Dealers' Licenses Act of 1894 that restricted Indian trading and in formal petitions to the colonial government, such as a submission of July 1, 1894, to the legislature of Natal.[108] In that petition, calling for the extension of the franchise to Indians, Gandhi extended the quotation from Max Müller: "And if I were to ask myself from what literature we have here in Europe, we who have been nurtured almost exclusively on the thoughts of the Greeks and Romans, and of one Semitic race, the Jewish, may draw that corrective which is most wanted in order to make our inner life more perfect, more comprehensive, more universal, in fact, more truly human—a life not for this life only, but a transfigured and eternal life—again I should point to India."[109] Here again, Gandhi's use of imperial theory was situational, deploying Max Müller's research on religion within local colonial struggles over Indian citizenship and trading rights in South Africa. Imperial theory, therefore, was not always controlled by the metropolitan center.

IMPERIAL CONFERENCES

Knowledge about religion and religions, as we have seen, was being produced in and through the ongoing mediations of imperial theory, colonial expertise, and indigenous realities. The visit of the British Association for the Advancement of Science to South Africa in 1905 has offered a focusing lens for highlighting the constructions and contradictions in the production of knowledge in the scientific study of religion. We will continue to attend to this triple mediation in the formation of comparative religion.

Returning to the United Kingdom, scholars of religion could participate in these mediations at home. A series of international conferences brought the entire empire of religion to Britain—the International Congress for the History of Religions at Oxford in 1908; the World Missionary Conference at Edinburgh in 1910; and the Universal Races Conference held in London in 1911. For our purposes in exploring the dynamics of knowledge production in comparative religion, we can briefly examine each conference as representing a different facet of the triple mediation that generated knowledge about religion.

First, the International Congress for the History of Religions that convened during September 1908 was the third meeting of an association of scholars that began at the international exposition in Paris in 1900. The Oxford congress was committed to adhering to the terms of engagement that had been formulated in Paris as a Fundamental Rule: All discussions about religion would be of an essentially historical nature and all confessional or dogmatic polemics would be strictly forbidden. While pursuing their serious work in the historical study of religions, delegates in Oxford were also entertained by a welcoming event in the Town Hall, garden parties, and evening receptions. By purchasing a ticket for £1, a price set "for Ladies as well as Gentlemen," delegates were entitled to participate in all meetings and receptions and to receive a copy of the conference proceedings. However, "Ladies tickets," at a price of 10 shillings, covered everything except a copy of the transactions. As it turned out, about 600 delegates participated, almost 250 of them women.[110] The congress was divided into nine sections, with one devoted to method in the history of religions and the rest focusing on different regions within the empire of religion, dealing with religions of the lower culture; the Chinese and the Japanese; the Egyptians; the Semites; the Indians and the Iranians; the Greeks and the Romans; the Germans, Celts, and Slavs; and the Christian religion.

As president of the section on the religions of the lower culture, E. Sidney Hartland convened a panel of leading theorists on savage religion. The most important and most influential paper, "The Conception of Mana," was presented by R. R. Marett (1866–1943), who had succeeded E. B. Tylor as the leading anthropologist of religion at Oxford. Attempting to identify an evolutionary stage in the development of primitive religion that preceded Tylor's animism, with its "belief in spiritual beings," Marett used the indigenous Melanesian term *mana* to represent a quality of religious awe in relation to supernatural power that was prior to any beliefs about spirits. In constructing his argument for this "pre-animistic" stage in the evolution of religion, Marett revealed the basic dynamics of knowledge production in imperial theory. Although the term *mana* was indigenous among Melanesian Islanders and had been translated for a European audience by the missionary R. H. Codrington, the imperial theorist had to erase these local, contingent factors in appropriating the term for a general theory of religion. As Marett explained, "When the science of Comparative Religion employs a native expression such as mana, or tabu, as a general category, it is obligated to disregard to some extent its original or local meaning." By disregarding, even if only to some extent, the indigenous meanings or local conditions under which this term arose, Marett showed how a native word such as *mana* could be extended as a basic principle in a general theory of religion. Evoking a recurring theme in imperial rhetoric and colonial interventions, Marett argued that this appropriation of an indigenous term would actually benefit the natives "by the advantage of thus enabling savage mentality to express itself as far as possible in its own language."[111] Encouraged by the response to this paper at the Oxford congress in 1908, Marett included his presentation on *mana* in his influential book *The Threshold of Religion*. As an advance in imperial theory, this book countered earlier intellectualist understandings of religion, such as Tylor's animism, by focusing on religious awe and emotion, ritual and performance, in relation to supernatural power, arguing that religion was danced out rather than thought out. Nevertheless, by intentionally disregarding the indigenous realities and colonial conditions of his subject, R. R. Marett exemplified imperial theory.

Second, the World Missionary Conference that met in Edinburgh in 1910 was a landmark in Christian missions. Although the delegates might not have been conversant with the most recent debates among imperial theorists of religion, they also had a global view of the religions of the world. Adhering to E. B. Tylor's theory of animism, they specifically addressed the problem of "animistic religions" in the published report, *The Missionary Message in Relation to Non-Christian Religions*. As W. H. T. Gairdner recalled, the missionary conference devoted considerable time and attention to trying to understand non-Christian religions. Outlining a global perspective, the conference undertook a "review of the great world-religions and their interaction with the Gospel of Christ."[112] Setting Christianity outside the scope of the world religions to be engaged by the gospel, the conference examined five "great religious systems": animism, Chinese religion, Japanese religion, Hinduism, and Islam. Gairdner observed that animism was "the generic name for the religious beliefs of more or less backward or degraded peoples all over the world." Although he clarified this generic definition by explaining that animists believed in the occult power of individual souls and the power of other spirits, ranging from plants and animals to powerful deities, Gairdner's reference to "backward or degraded peoples" suggested that animism was the religion of savages. Whether they had remained behind in the progress of evolution or had degenerated from some higher state, the "savages" of Africa, the Americas, India and Asia, and the Pacific Islands were all animists. But animism turned out to be the religion of most of the world, especially if Chinese religion was "animism, in the form of ancestor worship," and Japanese religion was "fundamental animism," in contrast to the spiritual "pantheism" of Hinduism, the "Eastern theism" of Islam, and the Christian gospel.[113]

In the published report "Animistic Religions," the missionary conference began with E. B. Tylor's definition but quickly moved from imperial theory to colonial missions. Research into animism had to be based not on theory but on reports from the field. "The missionaries in their ministry have come in contact with all classes of tribal society," the report observed. "Their knowledge of animism, therefore, is comprehensive and their opinions are based on wide experience."[114] Two Christian missionaries, in particular, were given prominence in the report on animistic religions by the World Missionary Conference: Henry Callaway, who had worked among the Zulu, and Henri-Alexandre Junod, who had worked among the Thonga, both operating as missionary-ethnographers in South Africa.[115] Their knowledge of animistic religions, according to the World Missionary Conference, was more reliable than the speculations of any imperial theorist. Having lived with the natives in direct contact, they were able to convey knowledge about animistic religions that was not distorted by imperial theory. However, both

of these missionaries were engaged in ongoing communication with imperial theorists; they formulated their research questions, analyzed their data,
and reported their findings in conversation with imperial theorists such as
Friedrich Max Müller, E. B. Tylor, and James Frazer. Although the missionary conference assumed that they provided direct access to knowledge
about indigenous religions, these missionary-ethnographers were engaged
in the ongoing exchanges between metropolitan centers and colonial peripheries in the production of knowledge about religion.

Nevertheless, the World Missionary Conference called attention to the importance of local researchers, such as Henry Callaway and Henri-Alexandre
Junod, as producers of knowledge about religion. Despite their exchanges
with metropolitan theorists, they did not intentionally disregard what R. R.
Marett called the "original or local meaning" of religious beliefs and practices. They immersed themselves in local beliefs; they attended to local customs; and they struggled with the problem of translating the meaning of
beliefs and practices. However, these missionary-ethnographers inevitably
became entangled in local colonial situations, mediating between colonial
interventions and indigenous people who were caught up in webs of colonial displacement, containment, and exploitation. Accordingly, their research findings could never provide direct, unmediated access to the beliefs
and practices of indigenous religion, let alone a comprehensive knowledge
of the "animistic religions" of the world.

Third, during the following year, the Universal Races Conference, con-
vening in London in 1911, promised to give scope for indigenous voices
from all over the world to be heard at the imperial center. At least one of
the delegates, the American sociologist W. E. B. Du Bois (1868–1963), anticipated such an exchange. Looking forward to the event, Du Bois wrote,
"The chief outcome of the Congress will be human contact—the meeting of
men; not simply the physical meeting, eye to eye and hand to hand of those
actually present, but the resultant spiritual contact which will run round
the world." Du Bois imagined that this conference would bring together
people of all races to speak for themselves. He especially looked forward to
the opportunity for those who had been oppressed by imperialism, colonialism, and slavery to speak in their own voices. "Only the man himself can
speak for himself," he asserted. "The voice of the oppressed alone can tell
the real meaning of oppression and, though the voice be tremulous, excited
and even incoherent, it must be listened to if the world would learn and
know."[116] In this conference, Du Bois hoped, the words of oppressed people
would not be appropriated by imperial theorists or translated by Christian

missionaries. Indigenous voices of people of color, whether from colonized South Africa or the segregated United States, would speak together and finally be heard throughout the world.

In its organization, however, the Universal Races Conference was a large-scale imperial enterprise. With the support of the British government, from the top, and a host of honorary sponsors, patrons, and allied organizations, including the international courts of the Hague, the organizing committee convened the entire world, beginning with delegates from "Great and Greater Britain," who were subdivided into two categories—(a) British Empire, excluding India; and (b) India. In the first category, delegates from South Africa included John Tengo Jabavu, who spoke on "The Native Races of South Africa," the Muslim leader Abdullah Abdurahman, the novelist Olive Schreiner, and, from Zululand, Alfred Mangena, who was a lawyer in Pretoria. In the second category of "Great and Greater Britain," delegates from India included the art historian Ananda K. Coomaraswamy, the president of the Theosophical Society Annie Besant, and Mohandas K. Gandhi, who was identified as a lawyer from Johannesburg, South Africa. But the entire world was present. Outside of Greater Britain, delegates came from everywhere. When they were not listening to presentations or engaging in discussions, the delegates were informed and entertained by ethnographic displays that were staged by the director of exhibitions, Alfred C. Haddon.

As a vice president of the Universal Races Conference, Felix von Luschan gave a keynote presentation on the anthropological understanding of race. In a rambling presentation, full of anecdotes and aphorisms, Luschan asserted that anthropology should study "how races developed and changed through migration and interbreeding." He declared that determining the number of races was a matter of pointless speculation, so he settled for a conventional classification of Indo-European, East-Asiatic, and African races. Luschan's science of race, however, was overwhelmed by anecdotes and aphorisms. Considering the scientific validity of arranging races in a hierarchy from inferior to superior races, he observed that "certain white men may be on a lower intellectual and moral level than certain coloured Africans." Instead of extending this observation to conclude that race could not be regarded as a determining factor in intellectual or moral capacity, Luschan found that this discrepancy was a "theoretical statement and of little practical value, except for the Colonial Service." Any colonial agency, he continued, should remove such deficient white men from service, since they posed a danger to the natives and their home nation. The only "savages" in Africa, he quipped, were white men who had gone native. In his anthropology of race, Luschan was less concerned with migration than with interbreeding, asserting that racial barriers had to be preserved. Invoking what he called a "well known proverb," he recited a religious aphorism for maintaining racial purity: "God created the white man and God created the black man, but the Devil created the mulatto."[117] Although he was a vice president of the Universal Races Conference in London, Luschan was president of the Race Hygiene Society in Berlin. His anthropological science, therefore, held practical interest.

While W. E. B. Du Bois must have been disappointed by hearing this anthropology of race, Felix von Luschan was disappointed by the entire conference, complaining when he returned to Berlin that it was full of a "large number of coloured scholars from all over the world, theosophians, Esperanto-people, idealists, peace-dreamers struggling to form an ill-assorted unified whole."[118] In his presentation, Luschan had explicitly attacked the "peace-dreamers," asserting that "the brotherhood of man is a good thing, but the struggle for life is a far better one." In the ongoing evolutionary struggle for survival, nations and races must contend against each other, Luschan concluded, invoking another proverbial aphorism, *si vis pacem, para bellum*, if you want peace, prepare for war.[119] The organizers of the Universal Races Conference, who had published an agenda for facilitating friendship among all races and nations, must have been startled by this declaration of war. But Felix von Luschan was only making explicit the unspoken terms of engagement—imperial, colonial, and indigenous—in the formation of the conference.

Religion was a battlefield. In his address to the conference, T. W. Rhys Davids (1843-1922), a professor of comparative religion at the University of Manchester, spoke on "Religion as a Consolidating and Separating Influence." Invited to consider the role of religion in interracial contact, Rhys Davids observed, "This is precisely one of the problems to which the young science of Comparative Religion hopes eventually to be able to give attention." In this hopeful observation, he implicitly acknowledged that the scientific study of religion had not previously paid attention to this problem, even though the entire enterprise arose out of interracial, intercultural, and interreligious contacts and exchanges. Having never given the question much attention, Rhys Davids could only suggest that religion could be both separating and consolidating. If religion is identified with a race, it can be divisive and lead to conflict; if religion transcends the barriers of race, it can provide a basis for peaceful consolidation.[120] This formula, however, was contradicted by indigenous voices from Japan and South Africa. In their presentation on Japan, the sociologists Tongo Takebe and Teruaki Kobayashi argued that the racially pure religion of ancient Japan was a consolidating influence. "In ancient Japan," they explained, "morality was religion; and religion was at the same time politics, so that Japanese society was perfectly harmonized."[121] According to these Japanese sociologists, a religion based on racial purity could build harmony instead of conflict. In his presentation on the "Native Races of South Africa," John Tengo Jabavu, despite his own Christian commitments, indicated that a universal Christianity, transcending the barriers of race, could be divisive, even intensifying divisions between races and resulting in racial separation and conflict.[122]

Indigenous voices, therefore, were not necessarily confirming the assumptions of imperial theorists. But they were also not speaking independently of imperial theory or colonial missions. After all, the Japanese sociologists had embraced the imperial notion of religion, and the South African minister had identified with the aims and objectives of the Christian mission. Accordingly, the voices of the oppressed, speaking for themselves, which W. E. B. Du Bois wanted to hear resounding from the Universal Races Conference, were subtly but thoroughly infused by the orchestrations of empire and the hymns of colonial missions. Under the influence of the imperial center, they were nevertheless finding new ways to recenter religion within regions peripheral to Europe. Knowledge about religion, therefore, depended upon the ongoing mediations of these indigenous initiatives, local colonial expertise, and imperial theory.

CHAPTER THREE

Classify and Conquer

Let us take the old saying, *Divide et impera*, and translate it somewhat freely
by "Classify and conquer."

FRIEDRICH MAX MÜLLER

During the last year of his life, Friedrich Max Müller (1823-1900), the eminent Indologist, philologist, mythologist, and founder of the modern science of comparative religion, was preoccupied with the South African War
(1899-1902). As England sent imperial troops against the Boer republics
of the Transvaal and Orange Free State, Max Müller, weakened by illness,
wrote essays on the religions of China, dictated his autobiography, and worried about the imperial situation in South Africa. "To the end he enjoyed
being read to," his wife recalled, "and took keen interest in the newspapers,
and all that concerned the war in South Africa."[1] Max Müller's interest in
this imperial conflict resulted in the last of his publications to appear before his death, *The Question of Right between England and the Transvaal,* a
pamphlet that was printed and widely distributed by the Imperial South
African Association. Drawing together in translation a series of essays that
had originally appeared between February and April 1900 in the *Deutsche
Revue,* this pamphlet was a lively defense of England's imperial sovereignty
over South Africa. England's claim, Max Müller argued, was based not on
greed for land and gold but on treaties signed at the time of the Congress
of Vienna in 1814 that ensured English suzerainty over all of South Africa.
He recalled that England's right over the entire region had been demonstrated by the emancipation of slaves in 1834, the annexation of the Orange
River State in 1848, the Sand River Convention of 1852, and the granting of
conditional independence to the Transvaal Republic in 1881. That history,
Max Müller contended, demonstrated England's legal right. By contrast,
Boer claims, which could be based, for example, on the prior Dutch settle-
ment of the Cape, were "pre-historic things which can have no legal value."

Based on international law and historical precedent, therefore, Max Müller concluded that England held "supreme authority in South Africa."[2] As a result, Boer resistance was nothing more than unjustified rebellion against legitimate imperial authority.

How do we account for this interest in South Africa? First, Max Müller indicated that he had a personal, family connection with South Africa by recalling that his cousin, Captain John Elliot, had been killed during the first Anglo-Boer War (1880–81). The Boers, Max Müller observed, had remembered their martyrs, but "their own misdeeds, as the cold-blooded murder of Captain John Elliot . . . [had] been forgotten, and never revenged."[3] Second, in Germany, public sentiment about the South African War had been mobilized against England. As a German immigrant in England for more than a half century, Max Müller was concerned not merely to defend his adopted country but also to maintain close relations between England and Germany. Beginning his defense of England's right to South Africa with an appeal for Anglo-Saxon unity, he argued that England and Germany shared common interests because "blood is thicker than ink."[4] However, German response to Max Müller's intervention in the public debate about the South African War was overwhelmingly negative. One German correspondent proposed that Max Müller should be hung on the gallows between British secretary of state for the colonies Joseph Chamberlain and South African mining magnate Cecil Rhodes, "the thieves on the right-hand and the left!"[5] According to a biographer, this polemic cast a shadow over Max Müller's entire career, providing "one of the reasons why his name was forgotten in Germany."[6] Third, the immediate pretext of the war, England's defense of the rights of English foreigners, or *uitlanders*, in the Transvaal Republic, might have resonated with Max Müller's own position in England as an *uitlander*, a foreigner who had adopted a British imperial perspective on the world. From that perspective, England presided over a beneficent global order. If, as Max Müller asserted, Canada, Australia, New Zealand, the West Indies, West Africa, Malta, Gibraltar, Cyprus, and Ceylon were all satisfied with "this desperate yoke of English sovereignty, why not the Boers, who even enjoy greater privileges than they do?"[7] Significantly, Max Müller omitted India, the land of his greatest professional interest and expertise, from this inventory of contented submission to the political yoke of the British Empire. However, he did draw a pointed analogy by asserting that England "can retire from South Africa as little as from India."[8] These two imperial possessions, he suggested, were essential for maintaining the global power and authority of the British Empire.

Because he was an academic expert on the language, myth, and religion of India, Max Müller's scholarly work often depended upon the resources and intersected with the interests of the British Empire. While his edition of the *Rig Veda* was made possible by the support of the East India Company, his academic authority was occasionally drawn upon to provide symbolic reinforcement for British rule over India. For example, he translated "God Save the Queen" into Sanskrit in 1882; in 1884 he advocated the Ilbert Bill, which expanded the scope of Indian judges, because it demonstrated that "the Imperial word has been kept sacred"; and he provided a Sanskrit translation in 1890 for the erection of a statue of the prince consort in Windsor Park as part of the Women's Jubilee offering to the queen.[9] In response to the opening of the Colonial and Indian Exhibition in 1886, Max Müller remarked, "It is well that England should sometimes be reminded of her real greatness and her enormous responsibilities."[10] Like the Colonial and Indian Exhibition, the South African War was an occasion for reminding England of its imperial power, rights, and responsibilities. Therefore, at the end of his life, Max Müller assumed a dual mission to defend the English abroad and remind the English at home of their global empire, an imperial order that was fixed on the twin poles of India and South Africa.

As his pamphlet on the South African War revealed, Max Müller had undertaken a fairly thorough reading of journalism, history, travel literature, and novels about South Africa. Anyone who had followed his academic career closely, however, would not be surprised by this interest in the region. Max Müller had a long history of professional involvement with the study of South African language, myth, and religion. Although he could claim specialized expertise on the subject of India, his broader academic reputation was built on lectures, essays, and books that dealt with general comparative themes in the fields of philology, mythology, and the science of religion. In those fields, Max Müller often invoked South African evidence to draw comparative conclusions. His use of those materials revealed significant facets of what I am calling imperial comparative religion—its global scope, its mode of intellectual production, and the complex process of intercultural mediation that made it possible.

CLASSIFYING

The series of four lectures Max Müller delivered at the Royal Institution during February and March 1870 has often been regarded as the founding gesture of the comparative study of religion.[11] Defining religion broadly as "the faculty of apprehending the Infinite," Max Müller attempted to place the study of religion on a scientific foundation.[12] However, his science of religion bore traces of a poetic sensibility, influenced by early-nineteenth-century romanticism, which found the heart of religion in profound emotion and expansive feeling. While establishing his academic reputation in philology during the 1850s, Max Müller published a romance novel, *German Love*, in which his central definition of religion, a sense of the infinite, was at the center of a love story between the narrator and his beloved, Maria. In their wide-ranging conversations on love, nature, mysticism, and religion, the German lovers identified the essence of religion, which was held in common by all religions, "Persians or Hindoos, Heathens or Christians, Romans or Teutons," as the "element of infinity that seems to lie behind them—a far-reaching glance into the eternal—a power of rendering divine that which is meanest and most transitory."[13] Religion, as a universal human faculty, was distinguished from theology, the intellectual discourse of an elite class of specialists, which inevitably distorted the simple essence of the human sense of infinity. "It is a wonder," the narrator exclaims, "that the theologians have not robbed us ere now of all religion," and he goes on to observe that theologians, priests, and other specialists have not only distorted religion but also alienated the masses of people. He explains, "There has never yet been a religion in the world which its priests, whether they be Brahmans or Schamans, Bonzes or Lamas, Pharisees or Scribes, have not corrupted or undermined. There they are, quarrelling and disputing in a language which is unintelligible to nine-tenths of their flock."[14] Throughout his academic career, Max Müller operated with this distinction between the underlying unity of religion, grounded in the universal human faculty for apprehending the infinite, and the observable diversity of religions that could be organized by scientific classification.

Max Müller insisted that a science of religion had to be based on comparison, since "all higher knowledge is acquired by comparison, and rests on comparison."[15] In adopting a global scope for the science of religion, Max Müller argued that comparison had to be guided by classification. "Let us take the old saying, *Divide et impera*," he declared, "and translate it somewhat freely by 'Classify and conquer.'"[16] More than merely a rhetorical flourish, this motto signaled Max Müller's imperial project, the promotion of a science of religion that generated global knowledge and power. In developing his imperial science, he dismissed several possible classifications, such as the distinctions between true and false; revealed and natural; national and individual; and polytheistic, dualistic, and monotheistic religions, on the ground that they were not sufficiently scientific. Only a classification based on language, he argued, could provide a firm foundation for a science of religion. For Max Müller, language was the defining human faculty, distinguishing humans from animals, a universal human capacity that could be classified into families. Accordingly, he classified the world of religion by reinstating his taxonomy of language—Aryan, Semitic, and Turanian—as the organizing principle of the global empire of religion. In Max Müller's taxonomy, each language family had developed distinctive religions, the Aryan (Hinduism, Buddhism, and Zoroastrianism), the Semitic (Judaism, Christianity, and Islam), and the Turanian (Confucianism and Taoism). "With these eight religions," Max Müller observed, "the library of the Sacred Books of the whole human race is complete."[17]

However, with this global inventory of world religions, the science of religion had only just begun. "But after we have collected this library of the sacred books of the world, with their indispensable commentaries, are we in possession of the requisite materials for studying the growth and decay of the religious convictions of mankind at large? Far from it. The largest portion of mankind,—ay, and some of the most valiant champions in the religious and intellectual struggles of the world, would be unrepresented in our theological library."[18] Max Müller retained the basic distinction between the study of book-religions and the study of religions without books throughout his career.[19] He observed in 1892 that he had long been convinced that "a study of the religions of uncivilised races would help us to reach a lower, that is, a more ancient and more primitive stratum of religious thought than we could reach in the sacred books of the most highly civilised races of the world."[20] Accordingly, by revealing the most primitive basis of religion, savage religions without books might even provide keys for interpreting the library of the sacred books of the world.

Max Müller's concern for including religions without books in the science of religion mirrored his attention to spoken dialects in the science of comparative philology. He observed in his 1861 lectures on the science of language, "Dialects which have never produced any literature at all, the jargons of savage tribes, the clicks of the Hottentots . . . are as important, nay for the solution of some of our problems, more important, than the poetry of Homer, or the prose of Cicero." He complained frequently that literacy shackled language, because its creativity and regeneration, its "continual combustion," was blocked by "literary interference."[21] If religions without books were to be included in a science of global comparison, however, they could only be incorporated, ironically, if they were transformed into texts.

Their spoken character had to be recorded and transcribed. A truly global science of religion, therefore, had to be engaged in the production of new sacred texts for the nontextual religions of the world.

The mode of intellectual production that generated new sacred texts for nonliterate religions emerged as an international enterprise. Raw religious materials, which were contained in the reports of travelers, missionaries, and colonial administrators, were extracted, exported, and transformed into intellectual manufactured goods at metropolitan centers of theory production. As Max Müller acknowledged, missionaries, in particular, had provided useful accounts of religious beliefs and practices among savages. Like many other metropolitan theorists, however, Max Müller frequently advocated a more thorough and extensive collection of these raw materials from the colonized peripheries of the British Empire. In 1870 he appealed to the Colonial Office to initiate a centralized plan of ethnographic collection. He repeated that request in 1872, noting, "Accurate knowledge of really wild-grown and autochthonic forms of religion would be of the greatest advantage for a comparative study of religions, a branch of inquiry which will become more important with every year."[22] The Colonial Office refused to dedicate resources for this project, but Max Müller repeated his appeal yet again in 1874 and in 1880. "If I have been less successful in stimulating ethnological research in the Colonies," he wryly observed in his first Gifford Lectures of 1888, "it has not been altogether my fault."[23]

Even without official imperial support, Max Müller could conclude that in the empire of religion there was "no lack of materials for the student of the Science of Religion."[24] But to obtain those materials, Max Müller had to rely on reports from the periphery by local scholars, including the South African experts Wilhelm Bleek, Theophilus Hahn, and, most importantly, Henry Callaway. They were the essential middlemen in transforming the resources of savage religions into texts. In the process, however, because the colonial situation in which these experts worked influenced their research findings, many of the frontier conflicts and contradictions of South Africa were introduced into Max Müller's global science of imperial comparative religion.

While presenting his introductory lectures on the science of religion in 1870, Max Müller was well aware that one religious book, the Bible, had been at the center of theological controversy, heresy trials, and legal actions in England during the preceding decade. The 1860 publication of seven chapters of critical Christian scholarship in the book *Essays and Reviews* began what historians have identified as "the greatest religious crisis of the Victorian age," "the greatest crisis of Victorian faith."[25] By publishing and popularizing the findings of German biblical research, the authors in *Essays and Reviews* set out to "interpret the Scripture like any other book."[26] The authors, all liberal Christians, abandoned a literal adherence to biblical authority by using alternative textual and archaeological sources for religious history and by proposing a developmental process of religious progress. Directly challenging the scientific credibility of the Bible, they rejected miracles for the laws of science and questioned the scientific credibility of the creation account in the book of Genesis.

Widely read, with thirteen editions published in England between 1860 and 1869, *Essays and Reviews* generated intense attacks by conservative defenders of biblical authority. In the first salvo published in a popular journal, the *Westminster Review*, Frederic Harrison (1831-1923) accused the book of undermining "the broad principles on which the Protestantism of Englishmen rests." He objected to three recurring themes in the chapters— the notion that human thought and morality evolved; the use of German critical methods, which might be appropriate for studying ancient Greek and Roman texts, for the analysis of scripture; and the rejection of the divine inspiration and literal inerrancy of the Bible. As a result, Harrison complained, the Bible appeared as "a medley of legend, poetry, and oral tradition, compiled, remodeled, and interpolated by a priestly order centuries after the times of its supposed authors."[27] Although this rendering of the Bible eventually came to be taken for granted in biblical scholarship, during the 1860s it brought authors of *Essays and Reviews* before ecclesiastical tribunals and secular courts on charges of heresy. Rowland Williams, the first to be charged, had written a chapter on the critical biblical research of Baron Christian von Bunsen, a Prussian linguist, diplomat, and ambassador to England, who had questioned biblical chronology on the basis of a thorough analysis of textual and archaeological evidence from ancient Egypt. Baron Bunsen also happened to be a patron of Max Müller. Max Müller had other connections with *Essays and Reviews*. As an expert on comparative mythology, he had been invited to contribute but did not; he was scheduled to write on "The Eastern Religions" for a proposed second volume that never appeared. Nevertheless, he was caught up in the theological backlash, as Dean Arthur Stanley observed in his defense, by "the partisan party alignments against Max Müller for his liberal theology and German nationality in the election of the Chair of Sanskrit at Oxford."[28]

In the midst of this controversy over the credibility and authority of the Bible, in 1862 the bishop of Natal John William Colenso (1814-1883) published the first volume of his commentary on the first six books of the Old Testament, *The Pentateuch and the Book of Joshua Critically Examined*. Using science, logic, and mathematical analysis, Colenso sought to demonstrate that these biblical texts were essentially "fictions" rather than reliable historical accounts. Colenso's *Pentateuch* was even more popular than *Essays and Reviews*, selling ten thousand copies in the first few weeks of its appearance in England. According to Colenso, his critical investigations of the Bible were inspired by his experience as a missionary among the Zulu, especially by the probing questions posed by his Zulu assistant William Ngidi during their collaboration in translating the Bible. As Colenso explained in the preface to his commentary,

> While translating the story of the Flood, I have had a simple-minded, but intelligent native—one with the docility of a child, but the reasoning powers of mature age—look up and ask, "Is all that true? Do you really believe that all this happened thus—that all the beasts, and birds, and creeping things, upon the earth, large and small, from hot countries and cold, came thus by pairs, and entered into the ark with Noah? And did Noah gather food for them *all*, for the beasts and birds of prey, as well as the rest? My heart answered in the words of the Prophet, "Shall a man speak lies in the Name of the Lord?" Zech. Xiii.3. I dared not do so.[29]

In this extraordinary passage, Bishop Colenso retained his Christian faith, with the integrity of the biblical prophet Zechariah, by refusing to preach the fictions of the Bible. He was convinced that his critique of biblical inerrancy would serve the interests of Christian missions. On the one hand, "being no longer obliged to maintain every part of the Bible as an infallible record of past history," the missionary could present the truth of divine love rather than the unbelievable fictions of the Bible to "the Mahomedan and Brahmin and Buddhist, as well as the untutored savage of South Africa."[30] On the other hand, as a corollary, the Christian missionary could advance religious truth by finding it in other religions, including a Sikh prayer, a Hindu invocation, or the questions of an intelligent Zulu.

Like *Essays and Reviews*, Colenso's biblical criticism produced an intense theological backlash that also found him eventually charged with heresy before an ecclesiastical court. The role of the intelligent Zulu, however, drew as much attention as his biblical scholarship, resulting in popular jokes about how the Zulu had converted the Bishop of Natal. This mockery, however, must be regarded as nervous laughter, as the historian Jeff Guy has argued, because it arose from a "disturbing reversal of the idea of colonizer and colonized which switched dominated for dominant, unlearned for learned, heathen for Christian, savage for civilized, the self and the other."[31] Although turning the Bible into fiction might have shaken the foundations of English Protestantism, this exchange between the Christian bishop and the "Zulu philosopher" violated basic classifications underpinning knowledge and power in the British Empire.

Rushing to attack Colenso in a popular journal, the poet, essayist, and literary critic Matthew Arnold (1822–1888) set out "to try the book of the Bishop of Natal, which all England is now reading," on the bases of another classification, the distinction between the few who belong to a "much-instructed" elite and the masses comprising the "little-instructed" many. Summoning him before the court of literary criticism, Arnold found Colenso guilty of crimes against aesthetic taste and philosophical sophistication, but he ultimately condemned him for allegedly failing to edify the many or inform the few. While arguing that Colenso had nothing new to teach the educated elite, Arnold charged that he did great damage to the masses of "little-instructed" Christians by stripping them of the Bible and only comforting them with "a fragment of Cicero, a revelation to the Sikh Gooroos, and an invocation of Ram." Arguably, Arnold himself showed little regard for the masses in this essay, since he observed that "knowledge and truth, in the full sense of the words, are not attainable by the great mass of the human race at all."[32] In the end, as if he were presiding over an ecclesiastical book-burning, Arnold concluded that literary criticism "must deny the Bishop's book the right of existing, when it can justify its existence neither by edifying the many nor informing the few."[33] Although Arnold's rigid distinction between the educated elite and the uneducated masses—a distinction that Arnold sought to soften in his subsequent work—was most prominent in this essay, his vehement rejection of the African bishop, with his intelligent Zulu and his Asian wisdom, implicitly reinforced the basic distinction between civilization and savagery in the empire of religion.

As we have seen, the production of knowledge about religion, as well as the ongoing contestation of that knowledge, can be situated in multiple mediations—imperial, colonial, and indigenous. In his indigenous mediations between ancestral traditions and Christian conversion, William Ngidi collaborated with Bishop Colenso, not only by translating between English and Zulu, but also by negotiating on behalf of the Anglican mission with local Zulu authorities. Both activities required Ngidi to mediate between conflicting orientations. For example, when negotiating with the Zulu prince Cetshwayo in 1859, Ngidi realized that they gave very different meanings to the Zulu phrase for "over there": the prince assumed that it meant "over there" in the colony of Natal across the Tugela River, while Ngidi used the phrase to mean "over there" across the ocean in England.[34] Struggling with such contrasting orientations, Ngidi eventually left Colenso's Christian mission, reportedly starting his own mission that drew on both Christianity and Zulu ancestral religion. After being deposed by the British in 1879, King Cetshwayo underwent his own reorientation by going "over there" to England to plead with the queen and the Foreign Office, with the support of Colenso and his family, for the restoration of his kingdom.[35]

John William Colenso, mediating between the colonial periphery and the imperial center, pursued critical biblical scholarship that he thought would be good for both. Widely read, but also roundly criticized, ridiculed, and rejected by the intellectual and ecclesiastical establishment, Colenso's efforts were not generally appreciated at the center of empire. Benjamin Disraeli, for example, drew out the political implications of the "great scandal" of Colenso's "conversion" by an intelligent Zulu when he declared that it was like royalty giving way to democracy, "almost as bad as Kings becoming Republicans."[36] Colenso found support, however, from Max Müller, who in 1865 described clerical attempts to censure or silence Colenso as "a disgrace to the nineteenth century." In the midst of preparing his lectures on the science of religion in 1870, Max Müller defended Colenso in a letter to Dean Stanley, proposing that Colenso had merely demonstrated that "the Old Testament was not originally written in the language of the nineteenth century, but in old, heavy, poetical phraseology." In 1874, while Colenso was visiting Oxford as his guest, Max Müller again defended the bishop. "The time will come," he observed, "when they will thank Colenso for having shown that the Old Testament is a genuine old book, full of all the contradictions and impossibilities which we have a right to expect in old books."[37] At the end of his life, as he reflected in his autobiography about the practical religion that he had learned from his mother, Max Müller noted that he "never was frightened or shaken by the critical writings of [David Friedrich] Strauss or [Heinrich] Ewald, of [Ernest] Renan or [John William] Colenso."[38] All had produced critical and controversial scholarship—Strauss's *Life of Jesus, Critically Examined*, Ewald's *History of Israel*, Renan's *Life of Jesus*, and Colenso's *Pentateuch*—that challenged orthodox or conventional assumptions about the literal truth of the Bible. Clearly, Max Müller's defense of Colenso indicated where he stood in one of the major religious controversies of the nineteenth century. Although he disapproved of Colenso's mathematical method, Max Müller argued that the bishop had performed a service to the science of religion by demonstrating that the Bible was a poetic rather than a historical or scientific text.

In their shared appreciation of the poetry of the Bible, Max Müller and Colenso also shared a conviction about the unity of religion, whether that unity was configured as a human sense of the infinite or as divine love, which could be distinguished from the diversity of religions that all contained the light of truth no matter how much that light might be distorted by theologians. While confirming Max Müller's understanding of the poetry of book religions, Colenso also represented a link in his expanding collection of data on religions without books. When Colenso arrived in Natal to assume his responsibilities as Anglican bishop in 1855, he was accompanied by the philologist Wilhelm Bleek and the priest Henry Callaway. Over the next decades, while Colenso was scandalizing British theology with his critical biblical scholarship, Bleek and Callaway became leading authorities on the indigenous religions of South Africa. As Max Müller established ongoing relations and correspondence with these local experts on African religion, they directly influenced his theoretical work in the science of religion by providing access to indigenous religions without books.

RELIGION OF THE SKY

Sharing the same patron, the Prussian diplomat and scholar Baron Christian von Bunsen, Max Müller and Wilhelm Bleek (1827–1875) had much in common. Both had been encouraged by Bunsen to study language as the key to ancient history, myth, and religion. Max Müller responded not only by developing principles of classification based on language but also by proposing a linguistic theory of the origin of religious myth. Under the notorious phrase the "disease of language," Max Müller argued that myth resulted from a primitive proclivity for transposing words for natural phenomena into supernatural persons. He proposed in his first series of lectures on the science of language in 1861, "Mythology, which was the bane of the ancient world, is in truth a disease of language. A mythe [sic] means a word, but a word which, from being a name or an attribute, has been allowed to assume a more substantial existence. Most of the Greek, the Roman, the Indian, and other heathen gods are nothing but poetical names, which were gradually allowed to assume a divine personality never contemplated by their original inventors."[39] In his second series of lectures on language, Max Müller reiterated this generative theory of myth. "The mischief begins when language forgets itself," he declared, "and makes us mistake the Word for the Thing, the Quality for the Substance, the *Nomen* for the *Numen*."[40]

In between these two series of lectures, Max Müller had received corroboration from South Africa that lent new substance and precision to his theoretical speculations about the linguistic origin of myth. "I received lately," Max Müller noted, "a Comparative Grammar of the South-African Languages, printed at the Cape, written by a most learned and ingenious scholar, Dr. Bleek."[41] In that comparative grammar, Wilhelm Bleek had classified the indigenous languages of South Africa into two major families, the "Hottentot" and the "Bantu." The "Hottentot" language was spoken by Khoisan people in the Cape, while the "Bantu" language family took in Africans who would emerge from the nineteenth century under the designations Xhosa, Zulu, and Sotho-Tswana. Although he argued that the study of these languages promised to answer many questions in the science of language, replacing, he hoped, Oriental with African studies as the leading field in comparative philology, Bleek also stressed the importance of South African languages for the study of religion.

Bleek spent more than a year with Colenso in Natal, engaged in studying the Zulu language and compiling a book on Zulu religion, which, significantly, in the light of the demand to produce new sacred texts for indigenous religions without books, arranged oral testimony into chapters and verses as if it represented a Zulu Bible.[42] He then moved to Cape Town to enter the employment of Sir George Grey (1812–1898). Having served as a governor in Australia and New Zealand, Grey was not only an imperial administrator; he was also a collector of texts about the languages, cultures, and religions of indigenous people in the colonies. Bleek was immediately put to work in cataloging the Grey collection, producing an inventory that was eventually published in Cape Town, London, and Leipzig. As an example of the mediation between imperial centers and colonial peripheries, the Grey library also exemplified the colonial networks of circulating knowledge that linked such disparate places as the Pacific Islands, Australia, New Zealand, and South Africa.[43] Pursuing his own research in Cape Town, Bleek published his *Comparative Grammar of South African Languages* (1862), but he also documented "Hottentot" folklore in his popular compendium *Reynard the Fox in South Africa* (1864), which played a significant role in European theoretical debates over the historical diffusion or independent parallel development of folklore, myth, and religion.[44] While he served as librarian for the collection of George Grey, Bleek devoted himself to learning Bushman languages, struggling not only with vocabulary, grammar, and syntax, but also with the unfamiliar clicks that were an integral part of Khoisan languages. Initially, he interviewed Bushman informants within the controlled environment of the Breakwater Prison. But he gradually brought a few of the freed prisoners into his household, where his interests in Bushman language, culture, and religion were shared by his sister-in-law, Lucy Lloyd. Through a remarkable collaboration, Bleek, Lloyd, and their houseguests produced a rich archive of Bushman tradition.[45]

Conducting local research in his home in Cape Town, Wilhelm Bleek was always aware of the global significance of his work. In 1869, when the president of the Anthropological Society, Thomas Huxley, called for a global collection of photographs of indigenous people from all British colonies, Bleek was eager to provide photographs from the Cape Colony that conformed to the standardized specifications set in London. Finding his subjects back at the Breakwater Prison, he assembled a portfolio of pictures of African prisoners, including photographs of a "Kafir," a "Damara," a "colonial Hottentot," and several "Bushmen" in the collection that he sent to the Anthropological Society. Bleek explained in the notes that accompanied his submission, "In this set of photographs there are, therefore, represented the three distinct races of men (and families of languages) extant in South Africa; viz. the Bantu (in the Kafir and the Damara), the Hottentot, and the Bushmen." He distinguished among these three African races by noting differences in their ways of life, politics, language, and numeracy. But he also emphasized differences in religion: "The Bantu" were "addicted to ancestor worship" and "eminently prosaic in their ideas and literature"; the "Hottentot or Khoikhoi," who were noted for "worshipping in former days the moon," were "poetical in their ideas with a traditionary literature full of myths and fables"; and the "Bushmen," who were known for "worshipping moon, sun and stars," were also "poetical in their ideas with an extensive mythological traditionary literature."[46]

In his *Comparative Grammar of South African Languages*, Bleek had fused Khoikhoi and Bushman under the single designation "Hottentot," placing their languages in contrast to the languages of Bantu-speaking Africans in South Africa. Bleek's submission to the Anthropological Society in 1869 continued that basic opposition. Although he identified three races in his photographs, Bleek persisted in reinforcing the contrast between two indigenous families of language, one based on prose, the other on poetry, with the prosaic Bantu "addicted to ancestor worship" and the poetic Khoisan "worshiping moon, sun and stars." As Bleek had argued in his *Comparative Grammar*, these two indigenous families of language could be distinguished on the grounds that the Hottentot language organized nouns by grammatical gender while the Bantu languages did not. Accordingly, because they spoke a sex-denoting language that attributed gender to nouns, the Hottentots had developed a rich mythology that personified the moon and sun, the night and dawn, as supernatural beings. Therefore, this mythological personification of heavenly phenomena, or what Bleek called the sidereal religion of the Hottentots, was generated by the grammatical structure of their language. By contrast, Bantu languages, without grammatical gender, had not supported the personification of nouns upon which the development of myth depended. Instead of sidereal religion, the grammatical structure of Bantu languages supported the emergence of an alternative type of religion, the worship of the dead. According to Bleek's theory, therefore, two original forms of religion—sidereal worship and ancestor worship—were derived from the two different grammatical structures that had been preserved in their most primitive forms among the indigenous people of South Africa.

When he gave his lectures on the science of religion in 1870, Max Müller invoked Bleek's findings as crucial evidence in support of a theory of religion that was based upon language. Indeed, as Max Müller quoted Bleek quoting Max Müller, he indicated the symbiotic relationship between their theoretical projects. Max Müller explained,

> In order to guess with some hope of success at the original meaning of ancient traditions, it is absolutely necessary that we should be familiar with the genius of the language in which such traditions took their origin. Languages, for instance, which do not denote grammatical gender, will be free from many mythological stories which in Sanskrit, Greek, and Latin are inevitable. Dr. Bleek, the indefatigable student of African languages, has frequently dwelt on this fact. In the Preface to his Comparative Grammar of the South-African Languages, published in 1862, he says: "The forms of a language may be said to constitute in some degree the skeleton frame of the human mind whose thoughts they express. . . . How dependent, for example, the highest products of the human mind, the religious ideas and conceptions of even highly civilized nations, may be upon this manner of speaking has been shown by Max Müller, in his essay on Comparative Mythology (Oxford Essays, 1856). This will become more evident from our African researches."[47]

Not only confirming the premise that language held the key to religion, Bleek actually advanced the theoretical work of Max Müller by broadening the base of relevant evidence. In South Africa, Bleek's African researches suggested a global classification of both language and religion into two general families, the sex-denoting languages, which included the Hottentots, but also the Semitic and the Aryan, and the prefix-pronominal languages that included the Bantu, the Negro, and the Polynesian. Max Müller invoked Bleek's findings as confirmation of his own theory. He even deployed Bleek's researches in a polemical aside against E. B. Tylor, who might have had interesting things to say about savage religion but did not admit "the identity of language and thought." "He thinks," said Max Müller, "that the simple anthropomorphic view is the fundamental principle of mythology, and that 'the disease of language' comes in at a later period only."[48] According to Max Müller, therefore, Bleek had convincingly demonstrated the linguistic origin of religion. Following Bleek, Max Müller concluded that "the religions of savages, too, will have to submit hereafter to the same treatment which we apply to the sacred traditions of the Semitic and Aryan nations." And, as Bleek had shown, "there [was] no solid foundation for the study of the religion of savages except the study of their languages."[49]

In 1890 Max Müller continued to invoke Bleek's distinction between two indigenous language families that had generated different religions in South Africa. Max Müller noted that indigenous South Africans could be divided between the "Hottentots and Bushmen in the South," on the one hand, since the "best judges now consider these two races, in spite of striking differences in language and religion, as originally one," and, on the other, the "Bantu races," who have "spread from East to West across the whole continent." Max Müller recalled, "Dr. Bleek, who was the first to establish the relationship of the best-known Bântu languages on a truly scientific basis, was also the first to show the influence which such languages would naturally exercise on the religious ideas of those who spoke them. Being without grammatical gender, in our sense of the word, these languages do not lend themselves easily to the personification of the powers of nature. Worship of ancestral spirits is very general among these Bântu tribes."[50] Throughout his life Max Müller cited Wilhelm Bleek as a colleague in establishing the crucial connection between language and religion. Imperial center and colonial periphery, in this exchange, were coordinated in discovering language as the key to religion.

However, in one important respect, Bleek's researches in African languages and religion actually undermined Max Müller's theoretical project. On the colonial periphery, Bleek found that Max Müller's global classification, his method of dividing and conquering the empire of religion, was inadequate. Instead of identifying three global language families, the Aryan, Semitic, and Turanian, which Max Müller had used to organize the empire of religion, Bleek found that the two local language families that had emerged on the colonial frontier in South Africa, the "Hottentot" and the "Bantu," more clearly demonstrated the origin and development of religion. Reinscribing this colonial distinction in his theory of the origin of religion, Bleek identified two basic forms of religion, represented by Hottentot sidereal worship and Bantu ancestor worship. In pushing this distinction further, however, Bleek argued that ancestor worship, practiced by the Xhosa, Zulu, and Sotho-Tswana people of South Africa, had preserved the original form of religion performed by primitive human beings before sex-denoting languages had "filled the sky with gods."[51] Although language was certainly foundational, the "disease of language" that had generated mythic personifications occurred, according to Bleek, at a later period in human evolution. Therefore, while Max Müller's linguistic theory had framed Bleek's research, Bleek's research findings undermined Max Müller's theory.

Max Müller's colleagues in the academic study of religion in Britain also took up this challenge, arguing against the originating force of the "disease of language" as the metaphoric origin of religious myth. "For myself," E. B. Tylor argued, "I am disposed to think (differing here in some measure from Professor Max Müller's view of the subject) that the mythology of the lower races rests especially on a basis of real and sensible analogy, and that the great expansion of verbal metaphors into myth belongs to more advanced periods of civilization."[52] Here Tylor echoed Bleek's argument that mythic personifications arose in a later, more advanced state of religious evolution. But Bleek's argument also reflected his colonial situation, in which he found the Zulu ancestor-worshippers to be more primitive, more opposed to Europeans, while he found the sky-worshipping Khoisan people of the Cape, under European control, to be closer linguistically to the more advanced and civilized European languages, culture, and religion. By contrast to the Khoisan, Bleek found the Bantu to be alien to the European, observing "a much greater congeniality between the Hottentot and European mind than we find between the latter and any of the black races of Africa."[53] Accordingly, in charting an evolutionary progression from the primitive Bantu, addicted to ancestor-worship, through the Hottentot, whose language had filled the sky with gods in ways that were congenial to the European mind, Bleek implicitly inscribed the South African colonial opposition between Europeans and Bantu-speaking Africans into his theory of religion.

When Max Müller presented his foundational lectures on the science of religion in 1870, the Bushmen appeared as the leading contenders for the title of "Urmenschen," the original, primitive human beings, in imperial comparative religion, but they seemed to be disappearing not in the mists of primordial time but under the weight of European colonization. The "Bushmen," as Bleek lamented, were a "dying out race."[54] As he struggled to preserve their language, myth, and religion, Bleek was also dying, adding urgency to his salvage ethnography. Max Müller indicated that he appreciated Bleek's dilemma:

> Dr. Bleek, the excellent librarian of Sir George Grey's Library at the Cape, who has devoted the whole of his life to the study of savage dialects and whose

Comparative Grammar of the South African languages will hold its place by the side of Bopp's, Diez's, and Caldwell's Comparative Grammars, is most anxious that there should be a permanent linguistic and ethnological station established at the Cape. . . . Dr. Bleek has lately been enabled to write down several volumes of traditional literature from the mouths of some Bushman prisoners, and he says, "my powers and my life are drawing to an end, and unless I have some young men to assist me, and carry on my work, much of what I have done will be lost." There is no time to be lost, and I trust, therefore, that my appeal will not be considered importunate by the present Colonial Minister.[55]

Republishing this essay in 1881, Max Müller noted that Bleek had died in 1875 but that there was hope that a successor as librarian of the Grey collection would be appointed. That successor was the missionary, linguist, and ethnographer Theophilus Hahn (1842-1905), who maintained the close link between Max Müller and the study of Khoisan religion in South Africa. Hahn's major work on the religion of the "Hottentots," which Max Müller arranged to be published, showed the influence of the linguistic approach to the analysis of sidereal religion. Opening his book on Khoikhoi religion with an epigraph from Max Müller—"The facts of language, however small, are historical facts"—Hahn stated his intention to provide a solid foundation for the study of "the Science of Religion as regards the Khoikhoi branch." Hahn, however, seemed too eager to fit his evidence into imperial theory, insisting, for example, on dubious etymological grounds, that the Khoikhoi deity was actually the rising sun, with a name that was "intended for nothing else than to illustrate metaphorically the change of day and night."[56] Nevertheless, through Theophilus Hahn, Max Müller was able to remain conversant with one side of Bleek's classification of religion, the poetic Hottentots and Bushmen who worshipped the moon, sun, and stars.

The other side of Bleek's classification, represented by the Bantu, or often simply by the Zulu, who prosaically worshipped their ancestors, was developed by the researches of the priest, missionary, medical doctor, and ethnographer Henry Callaway, who emerged as the leading nineteenth-century authority on Zulu religion and, by extension, on all savage religion. Although he was situated on the colonial periphery, Henry Callaway, like Wilhelm Bleek, acted as a mediator in the formation of theory within the science of imperial comparative religion.

RELIGION OF THE ANCESTORS

The Anglican priest Henry Callaway (1817-1890) provided the most important link between the imperial theorists of comparative religion and South

Africa. In addition to his work as priest, missionary, and medical doctor, Callaway took an active interest in comparative religion and anthropology.[57] From his mission station at Springvale, near Pietermaritzburg, Callaway engaged in researches on Zulu religion that enabled him to know the Zulu religious system better than the Zulu did, because, he claimed in 1862, he had "entered far deeper, than the natives themselves could penetrate."[58] As a local expert, Callaway mediated between Zulu indigenous religious tradition in South Africa and theorists in England. He served as the local secretary in Natal of the Anthropological Society in London and corresponded with Max Müller and E. B. Tylor.[59] However, it was Callaway's major text *The Religious System of the Amazulu* (1868–70) that marked his most enduring contribution, because the collection of oral testimony, arranged in two columns, where the original Zulu was juxtaposed with an English translation, seemed to provide direct access to a savage religion from the mouths of the savages themselves.

In his 1870 lectures, Max Müller used Callaway's findings to consider "the old controversy whether there are any tribes of human beings entirely devoid of religious sentiment." Although the Zulu had been accused of lacking any trace of religion, Callaway, by learning their language and gaining their confidence, had extracted a coherent account of the Zulu religious system. In Max Müller's summary: "They all believe, first of all, in an ancestor of each particular family and clan, and also in a common ancestor of the whole race of man. That ancestor is generally called the Unkulunkulu, which means the great-great-grandfather. When pressed as to the father of this great-great-grandfather the general answer of the Zulus seems to be that he 'branched off from a reed,' or that he 'came from a bed of reeds.'" In Sanskrit, Max Müller observed, the term *parvan*, a knot or joint in a cane, could signify a family, while the term *vamsa*, a reed or bamboo cane, could refer to the human race or a lineage. Involving a similar metaphorical extension, the Zulu term for reed, *uhlanga*, could indicate the original source of all life. However, through the "disease of language," the term "was personified, and thus became the mythical ancestor of the human race."[60]

· Drawing on Callaway's evidence, Max Müller could support his linguistic theory of the origin of myth. However, Henry Callaway's account of a Zulu religious system was entangled in the local conditions of a specific colonial frontier on at least three counts. First, Callaway framed his research agenda in terms of what he saw as the needs of the Christian mission. In this regard, he conducted his research on Zulu religion in the context of a theological polemic against Bishop Colenso. On theological grounds,

Callaway argued that Colenso's adoption of the God-name uNkulunkulu was inappropriate for a frontier mission that had to distinguish itself from a surrounding heathendom. Accordingly, Callaway discovered, against the findings of both Colenso and Bleek, that uNkulunkulu was understood by the Zulu not as God but as their original ancestor.

Second, Callaway collected evidence for this conclusion primarily from informants who had sought refuge at his mission station in Springvale. Like the residents of other Christian missions, these informants were social outcasts or refugees from African communities.[61] Furthermore, since they came from different regions that ranged from the remote northern Zulu territory to the Eastern Cape, Callaway's informants had undergone different experiences of the expanding colonial frontier. As a result, instead of holding a single, coherent Zulu religious system, Callaway's informants asserted a spectrum of religious positions that can be correlated with varying degrees of colonial contact. At least seven different religious positions can be distilled from the oral testimony Callaway collected. Located in the colonial situation, Zulu religious statements can be correlated with the advance of the mission and administration, so that, for example, relatively intact political groupings to the north regarded uNkulunkulu as the ancestor of their particular tribes, political groupings broken or displaced by colonial warfare redefined uNkulunkulu as the original ancestor of all human beings, and Zulu in conversation with the mission had learned a new theological discourse in which uNkulunkulu could be understood as a supreme being.

Third, positioned at the center of this colonial argument, Callaway's principal informant and assistant, the convert, catechist, and eventually deacon Mpengula Mbande (d. 1874), actually authored *The Religious System of the Amazulu*. Although Callaway transcribed and edited the volume, providing footnotes and occasional commentary, the majority of the text appeared in the words of Mbande, reflecting, at many points, Mbande's own ambiguous position on the colonial frontier as a recent Christian convert. Mediating between the colonial mission and traditional African society, Mpengula Mbande's ambivalent personal position defined the dominant perspective on Zulu religion that emerged in Henry Callaway's *Religious System of the Amazulu*. As a Christian, however, Mbande mediated intercultural relations in that colonial situation by advancing his own scathing Christian critique of indigenous Zulu religion, insisting, at one point, that whatever African traditionalists said about religion "has no point; it is altogether blunt."[62] Nevertheless, Mbande's account became the standard version of an indigenous Zulu religious system.

In one of his most important contributions to *The Religious System*, Mpengula Mbande related the "account which black men give white men of their origin." According to this creation myth, black men emerged first from the *uhlanga*, the place of the origin of all nations, coming out, however, with only a few things. They emerged with some cattle, corn, spears, and picks for digging the earth. Arrogantly, with their few possessions, the black men thought that they possessed all things. When the white men emerged, however, they came out with ox-drawn wagons, bearing abundant goods, and able to traverse great distances. By displaying this new, unexpected use for cattle, the whites demonstrated a superior wisdom that had been drawn from the *uhlanga*. In relation to the power and possessions of white men, black men recognized that they were defenseless. As Mbande explained:

> We saw that, in fact, we black men came out without a single thing; we came out naked; we left everything behind, because we came out first. But as for the white men, we saw that they scraped out the last bit of wisdom; for there is every thing, which is too much for us, they know; they know all things which we do not know; we saw that we came out in a hurry; but they waited for all things, that they might not leave any behind. So in truth they came out with them. Therefore, we honour them, saying, "It is they who came out possessed of all things from the great Spirit; it is they who came out possessed of all goodness; we came out possessed with the folly of utter ignorance." Now it is as if they were becoming our fathers, for they come to us possessed of all things. Now they tell us all things, which we too might have known had we waited; it is because we did not wait that we are now children in comparison with them.

Therefore, Mpengula Mbande concluded, Europeans had not achieved victory over Africans by their superior force of arms. Rather, their wisdom had conquered. According to Mbande, European colonizers had been "victorious by sitting still." They had not required military force. The wisdom, wealth, and virtue that whites had drawn from the *uhlanga* were sufficient to overpower the black people, who reflected among themselves, as Mbande reported, that "these men who can do such things, it is not proper that we should think of contending with them, as if because their works conquer us, they would conquer us by weapons."[63]

In this mythic account, Mpengula Mbande recorded an indigenous religious rationale for submission to the colonial government and its Christian mission. Obviously, this myth was not some primordial Zulu cosmogony. It was a critical reflection on the contemporary Zulu colonial situation. In Mbande's account, this story was the relevant creation myth in the living religious system of the Zulu. In Max Müller's handling of this myth, as we recall, *uhlanga*, the original source of all life, illustrated the "disease of language" through which the term, "reed," or "bed of reeds," was "personified, and thus became the mythical ancestor of the human race." However, for Mbande, the primordium was clearly located in the colonial situation. Accordingly, Zulu religion revealed its most dynamic, creative character not in trying to recover a forgotten past, but in the struggle to make sense out of the violent oppositions of the colonial present.

Rather than a single, coherent Zulu religious system, therefore, *The Religious System of the Amazulu* contained an intercultural argument, orchestrated around Mpengula Mbande's Christian critique, which displayed the religious tensions and contradictions of the colonial situation in Natal. Accordingly, this text provided an unstable foundation for theory-building in the science of imperial comparative religion.

During the 1890s, Max Müller began to recognize that the imperialcolonial exchange in the study of religion was both an enabling and a disabling nexus for producing knowledge. On the one hand, he observed in 1888, African language, culture, and religion, which were so far away from Oxford, "were brought near to me many years ago through my personal intercourse with the late Dr. Bleek" and subsequently by personal correspondence with Dr. Theophilus Hahn and Dr. Henry Callaway in South Africa. "I should have hesitated to avail myself of the rich materials which the folk-lore of African races supplies to the student of mythology," he continued, "had I not been able to confer personally with such scholars as Dr. Callaway and Dr. Hahn on every point on which I wished to speak as elucidating dark corners in the mythology of India and Greece." Remarkably, this interchange with scholars in South Africa enabled Max Müller to write not only about such African topics as the metaphorical meaning of the Zulu *uhlanga*, the mythology of the Hottentots, and the relations between language and religion in Africa generally, but also to use the African research of local experts in South Africa to illuminate aspects of the religious literature of ancient Greece and India.[64] This exchange with local experts, therefore, was vital to Max Müller's entire enterprise in the scientific study of religion.

On the other hand, the imperial-colonial exchange could be disabling, as Max Müller observed in 1892, because of the untrustworthiness of the material it often generated for the study of religion. Unreliable witnesses, whether sailors, traders, or missionaries, had produced reports that imperial scholars "copied out, classified and tabulated, without any attempt at testing the credibility of these witnesses." As these reports multiplied, any centralized synthesis increasingly became impossible because "the contradictions became so glaring, the confusion so complete, that serious students declined altogether to listen to this kind of evidence." But imperial scholars, according to Max Müller, were also starting to lose confidence in any easy correlation between savages and primitive humanity. Observing that careful research had shown that "the customs of savage races were often far more artificial and complicated than they appeared at first," reflecting "historical development as in that of more civilized races," he argued against the prevailing assumption of imperial comparative religion by asserting that "savage and primitive are very far indeed from meaning the same thing." In the light of shifting theory and unreliable evidence, Max Müller announced a "new epoch in the study of uncivilized races," which would be guided by two principles: authorities on savages must be eyewitnesses, free of racial or religious prejudice, and they must be sufficiently conversant in the language of the natives to enter into sensitive topics. As exemplars of these two principles, he cited "a real Hottentot scholar, like Dr. Hahn," and "the books of Dr. Callaway on the Zulus," regarding both Callaway and Hahn as colleagues in producing reliable knowledge for a science of religion that encompassed every region and every stage of religion, whether primitive, savage, or civilized.[65]

A few years later, however, Max Müller had to confront the instability of this exchange more directly when he read a report from Natal that called into question the reliability of Henry Callaway, his authority on Zulu religion and collaborator in the science of religion. "Nothing could be more interesting and valuable than the works of the late Bishop Callaway on the customs and superstitions of the Zulus," he observed in 1897. "They belong to the very best of this class of works." As an eyewitness who was free of prejudice and conversant in the native language, Callaway embodied Max Müller's principles for pursuing research that would gain reliable knowledge about savage religion. In praising Callaway's research, Max Müller also celebrated the interest they shared in comparing the religions of South Africa with the religions of India. He posed the rhetorical question: "Who has not admired his account of Unkulunkulu, the great-grandfather who, as he represented him, was clearly an ancestral spirit and had nothing whatever to do with the class of physical gods, such as Dyaus and the Devas of the Veda." Recently, however, the authority of Henry Callaway had been challenged by an alternative report about uNkulunkulu emanating from the Zulu of South Africa. Max Müller noted, "We now receive from Zululand itself an account of

Unkulunkulu from the hand, as it would seem, of a native, very different from that given by Bishop Callaway." This native account, published in the periodical *Inkanyiso yase Natal,* contradicted Callaway's version not only by identifying uNkulunkulu as a sky god, but also by claiming that biblical stories—Adam and Eve, the Flood, the story of Joseph—were all part of indigenous Zulu tradition.[66]

This publication that Max Müller received from South Africa, *Inkanyiso yase Natal,* was an Anglican periodical established in Pietermaritzburg, in the colony of Natal, in 1889. Claiming a large Zulu readership, in 1895 the periodical was transferred to Zulu editors and became the first newspaper in South Africa to be edited by Africans.[67] The articles in question appeared in six issues during 1895 and argued on the basis of etymology, as if applying the philological method of Max Müller, that "the real origin of the name of Unkulunkulu, in all its local varieties, must be found in a word expressing originally the material sky." In this conclusion, the Zulu author of the articles for *Inkanyiso yase Natal* contradicted the findings of Callaway by asserting that uNkulunkulu was the heavenly deity rather than the original ancestor of the Zulu. Although Max Müller confessed that he could not adjudicate the accuracy of the etymological arguments in this report from Zululand, he was clearly disturbed by its challenge to the authority of Henry Callaway, which showed "how uncertain is even the very best evidence which we receive concerning the language, the customs and myths of savage tribes." Zulus, writing for themselves, called into question the entire enterprise of a comparative religion that had been structured on the mediations between local colonial experts and imperial theorists. As Max Müller recognized, the challenge from Natal affected both ends of this imperial-colonial exchange. "If our Zulu informant can say that Bishop Callaway 'got bogged in a philological mess,' " Max Müller lamented, "what would he say of us if attempting to build on such boggy foundations tall structures of mythological philosophy?"[68]

Max Müller's distress pointed to a larger crisis in imperial comparative religion. "If we can no longer quote Callaway on Zulus, or Hahn on Hottentots," he complained, "whom shall we quote?"[69] This dilemma was inherent in the triple mediation that had created the conditions of possibility for an imperial comparative religion. Max Müller's theoretical mediation between colonized savages and the original primitives of humanity depended upon quoting Henry Callaway, while Callaway's mediation between the colonized periphery of South Africa and the metropolitan centers of theory production in Europe depended upon quoting Zulu informants.

In the colonial context of Natal, however, Mpengula Mbande was faced with his own problem of mediation, a problem he addressed, among other ways, in the idiom of religious myth. Although he certainly quoted elements of a traditional religious heritage, Mbande reconfigured those traditional resources in response to the colonial present, producing, perhaps not without some measure of irony, the original myth "which black men give white men of their origin." Mbande was celebrated in missionary literature as "an educated, intelligent, Christian native."[70] He was proclaimed as a "Zulu philosopher."[71] However, in the missionary agenda, Mbande's account was valued because it exposed the degradation of indigenous African religion. As the missionary Thomas B. Jenkinson observed, "The account given by the late Native Deacon Umpengula of the state of the native mind on the subject of their ancestor worship and degraded state is very good."[72] In Great Britain, as interreligious conflicts on the frontier were absorbed into the emerging science of comparative religion, Mpengula Mbande's mythic account became authoritative. However, in the earliest book-length overview of African traditional religion, when Mbande's myth was quoted, it was found to be "valuable only as showing the workings of the native mind when brought into contact with the superiority of Europeans."[73] In these blatantly racist terms, therefore, Mbande was incorporated at the center of empire into an imperial comparative religion.

As middlemen in this exchange, Wilhelm Bleek and Henry Callaway simultaneously enabled and undermined Max Müller's science of religion. By providing access to religions without books, they made it possible for Max Müller to fashion a global science of religion that included indigenous religious traditions. At the same time, however, because they incorporated local colonial conflicts and contradictions into their research findings, Bleek and Callaway provided extremely unstable foundations for global theory building. By the end of his career, Max Müller was forced to recognize this inherent instability in the construction of theory within imperial comparative religion. Perhaps his vigorous defense of England's imperial power in his last publication to appear before his death should be read as a compensatory gesture in response to a growing uneasiness about the foundations of imperial knowledge in the global science of comparative religion. With the failure of knowledge, Max Müller had to settle for an assertion of power.

CONQUERING

The preceding discussion calls for a reassessment of the role of Friedrich Max Müller as the founder of the modern study of religion. Of course, the study of religion cannot be bound to its founder, especially since that founder is most often treated as a myth of origin that is best forgotten. Nineteenth-century comparative religion was fed by many intellectual streams. The philology of Max Müller, the evolutionary anthropology of E. B. Tylor, the folklore studies of Andrew Lang, and the nascent support provided by James Frazer for the practice of local ethnography all contributed to the formation of a comparative study of religion. However, despite their internal disagreements, these scholars all collaborated in the production of an imperial comparative religion, contributing, in different ways, to its global scope, its centralized intellectual production, and the complex relations of intercultural mediation that linked the imperial center with the colonized peripheries of empire.

Central to any reassessment of the history of comparative religion is the question of the relation between knowledge and power. Although they could be regarded, for the most part, as liberal imperialists, the theorists of imperial comparative religion were not obviously in positions of political power in Britain. Max Müller, for example, might have corresponded regularly with Prime Minister William Gladstone, but he had no direct influence on imperial policy; he even failed to interest the Colonial Office in supporting the collection of ethnographic data. Nevertheless, Max Müller operated at the symbolic nexus of knowledge and power that made the empire a reality. Basic features of that imperial-colonial nexus can be suggested by Max Müller's participation in imperial pageantry.

Present at the opening by Queen Victoria of the Colonial and Indian Exhibition on May 4, 1886, Max Müller witnessed the royal procession led by Victoria and the Prince of Wales that moved through South Kensington to the Royal Albert Hall. There the queen sat on a golden throne from India, a throne that had been taken during the British conquest of Lahore, and presided over the opening ceremonies, which featured an imperial poem by Tennyson and a rendition by the royal choir of "God Save the Queen," two verses of which were performed in Sanskrit, as translated by Max Müller. Later, reflecting on the vast global power represented by that imperial ceremony, he declared: "I feel grateful that I went and witnessed what was not a mere festivity, but an historical event. Behind the gorgeous throne and the simple dignified presence of the Queen, one saw a whole Empire stretching out, such as the world has never known, and an accumulation of thought, labour, power, and wealth that could be matched nowhere else. It is well that England should sometimes be reminded of her real greatness and her enormous responsibilities."[74] In this imperial epiphany, this vision of imperial history, expansion, centralized accumulation, and global mandate, Max

Müller's testimony hinted at the location of power in imperial comparative religion.

First, comparative religion was a science of symbols that could distinguish between mere ceremonies and real historical events. As we recall, in Max Müller's pamphlet on the South African War, England's sovereignty was based on real historical events; Boer claims were allegedly based on "prehistoric things which can have no legal value."[75] Imperial ritual, Max Müller suggested, was entirely different from such "prehistoric things." Since the empire relied heavily upon new imperial symbols, myths, and rituals, those invented traditions that signified British power at both the center and the periphery of empire, imperial comparative religion could certify their reality in and through the process of disempowering the alternative symbolic forms of the exotic or savage colonized. While the colonized acted out "mere festivity," the "disease of language," "primordial stupidity," "superstitious survivals," or a "magical mentality," British imperial ceremony enacted a real historical event.

Imperial pageantry, as many analysts have argued, made the empire a living reality at home in Britain. The *Pall Mall Gazette* described the Colonial and Indian Exhibition of 1886 as a "revelation of Empire."[76] Looking back at the Victorian era of imperial ceremony, in 1924 Lord George Askwith observed that "it was not until the Indian and Colonial Exhibition and the Jubilee Pageants of 1887 and 1897 that the nation began to awake to a better knowledge of the import of the British Empire." The public then came to realize "that the British Empire [was] a living and growing entity, bound together in a manner different from any other known to history."[77] Similarly, Max Müller found these events making history, not only as historical events in themselves, but also as creating and reinforcing a public sense of the historical significance of a British Empire that was unique in human history.

The Colonial and Indian Exhibition was a prelude to the festivities of the Queen's Jubilee in 1887. As a participant in these imperial rituals, Max Müller was involved in both receiving and giving ceremonial gifts to mark this auspicious occasion. From India, he was contacted by a prominent Hindu who was conducting a ceremony in his family temple, which included presenting green and white checked shawls as gifts to all the learned priests. He sent one of these shawls to Max Müller. "Unless you are willing to accept it," he said, "the service at our family temple will be incomplete." By accepting this gift from the British colony of India, Max Müller was able to complete the local Hindu ceremony for the Queen's Jubilee. A few weeks later, however, he was commanded to Buckingham Palace to present the

Queen's Jubilee offering from the "German colony in England," a picture of the German royal family.[78] Again, for Max Müller, these ritual exchanges were not "mere festivities" because they enacted real historical relations of empire.

Second, as the queen's throne displayed the entire empire, imperial comparative religion also focused and condensed its vast global scope. In nineteenth-century comparative religion, "one saw a whole Empire stretching out, such as the world has never known." For Max Müller, and other imperial theorists, the empire of religion stretched not only from the center to the periphery but also from the present to the past, even extending to the origin of humanity. These two global extensions, in space and time, were necessarily related, as imperial theorists mediated between the colonized savages and the original primitives of the human race. However, the time and space of imperial comparative religion also configured global power. "To be able to exercise intellectual power over the problematic mythology of the past," the cultural analyst Steven Conner has observed, "was a promise of being able to exercise the same power over the subject races who were the producers of such mythologies."[79] Like imperial exhibitions, imperial comparative religion collected, condensed, and displayed the empire as a sign and signal of its global scope and domination.

Empire provided a frame of reference, a metaphoric horizon, for organizing knowledge about religion. Perhaps, in his inaugural lectures on the science of religion in 1870, Max Müller's use of the phrase *divide et impera*—divide and rule, classify and conquer—was in fact merely a rhetorical flourish, a figure of speech bearing no relation to imperial policy or the kind of colonial practice of *divide et impera* identified by Alice Werner in the British control and management of Africans in South Africa.[80] After all, he changed his gloss of *divide et impera* from "classify and conquer" to "classify and understand" in the revised version of his lectures published in 1882.[81] Nevertheless, it was the horizon of empire that enabled his expansive global collection, collation, and classification of data about religion from the furthest reaches of the colonial periphery to the deepest recesses of human prehistory.

Empire also provided Max Müller with a metaphoric horizon for situating the theoretical controversy between two contending approaches to the study of religion, the historical school, which studied religion through language and sacred texts, and the theoretical or anthropological school, which based its research on conjectures about human nature and reports about savages, on "psychophysiological experiments" and "the creeds of living savages."[82] Advocating the study of language, philological methods, and the translation of texts, Max Müller placed himself in the historical school, perhaps as its leader, but this approach was being overtaken by followers of the theoretical school initiated by E. B. Tylor in the anthropology of religion. Addressing this controversy in 1890, Max Müller adopted an expansive perspective, suggesting that both schools were doing good work in mining for the same gold, which ultimately would be of benefit to the study of religion, even though the vehemence of academic debates and disputes had produced "the same disparaging remarks made by one party of the other, which you may be accustomed to hear from the promoters of rival gold mines in India or in the South of Africa."[83] Here, also, gold mining is certainly just a metaphor, a rhetorical flourish, but it arose from the same imperial horizon in which Max Müller saw the queen's throne representing a global empire that "can retire from South Africa as little as from India."[84]

Third, as Max Müller testified, imperial power was the power of centralized accumulation, not only the gathering of wealth and the exploitation of labor for the benefit of the metropolitan center, but also the accumulation of thought "that could be matched nowhere else." This notion of the British Empire absorbing the best of the world was a commonplace in imperial thinking. Frederick Temple had maintained in his chapter "Education of the World" in *Essays and Reviews* that England had absorbed conscience from the Hebrews, will from the Romans, reason and taste from the Greeks, and spiritual imagination from Asia, and he added, "Other races . . . may yet have something to contribute."[85] Mathew Arnold, with his vision of England drawing together Hebraic and Hellenic streams of culture, also assumed that Britain absorbed the best of the world.[86]

Imperial exhibitions, as many analysts have observed, put the British absorption of its colonies on display.[87] Exhibits featured gold from India and diamonds from South Africa. At the same time, they brought Indians, Africans, and other natives from the colonies as both workers on the exhibits and objects for ethnographic display. Impressed by the opportunity for research, the Anthropological Institute held four meetings during the Colonial and Indian Exhibition of 1886, advertised as "Anthropological Conferences on the Natives of the British Possessions." They included academic papers and guided visits to the various regional "courts" of the exhibition. The current president of the institute, Francis Galton, observed, "The opportunity is unprecedented of meeting men from all parts of the Empire who are familiarly acquainted with its native races, and of inspecting collections of high ethnological interest that have been arranged with cost and pains in the various courts."[88] During the meeting devoted to the races of Africa on June 1, 1886, for example, participants listened to presentations on the natives of the Cape of Good Hope, Natal, and the Gold Coast and then adjourned for a tour of the African exhibits guided by the speakers. Clearly, the Anthropological Institute's "unprecedented opportunity" for accumulating knowledge was made possible by what Max Müller saw as the imperial "accumulation of thought, labour, power, and wealth that could be matched nowhere else."

Max Müller celebrated the centrality of the British Empire for the study of religion. During his first Gifford Lectures, delivered in Edinburgh in 1888, he specifically outlined the advantages of conducting his research at the center of empire. "Living in England," he observed, "I naturally tried to avail myself of the splendid opportunities which this country offers for linguistic and ethnological studies." The opportunities for research, however, were not local but global, not focused on local British language, culture, and religion, but on the vast scope provided by the British Empire. As Max Müller recounted, he had availed himself of the colonial and missionary networks that spanned the British Empire. On the one hand, South Asia, his primary focus, was brought closer to England through imperial relations to such an extent that "at Oxford, for instance, it is almost as easy to study the language, manners, and customs of the Veddahs [of Ceylon] as the Gaels." Other colonies, as well, were brought within the imperial orbit, so that there should be "no difficulty in obtaining through the Colonial Office any information that could be of use for the study of civilised or uncivilised tribes from Canada to New Guinea." On the other hand, Christian missionary networks, the "wonderful net which Missionary enterprise has spread from England over the whole world," provided opportunities for "gathering valuable information for the proper study of mankind."[89] Expressing his gratitude to the East India Company, the India Office, the Colonial Office, and the various missionary societies, Max Müller acknowledged their enabling role in advancing his global research in the science of religion.

In the practice of imperial comparative religion, this centralized accumulation of thought, this concentration of ways of thinking about others, was, by unspoken definition, as a matter of implicit principle, incomparable, a kind of knowledge "that could be matched nowhere else." It could compare without being compared. As we have seen, relations between center and periphery in imperial comparative religion, the complex triple mediation that made it possible, were asymmetrical relations of power. In the *Notes and Queries* sent out to the colonies for accumulating information about savages, one of the questions asked, "Do they eat everything?"[90] As formulated in a letter to his colleague Bishop Colenso in 1883, William Ngidi implicitly turned the question back on the English: "I hope that now you know that the Zulus are set at loggerheads by the coming of the white men, who want to eat up their land."[91] Comparing without being compared, eating without being eaten, imperial comparative religion was based on the centralized accumulation of knowledge from colonized people.

Finally, Max Müller celebrated the imperial pageantry because it was "well that England should sometimes be reminded of her real greatness and her enormous responsibilities." At the end of his life, defending England's sovereignty in South Africa, Max Müller took the opportunity to again remind England of that greatness and responsibility by insisting that England had to maintain its imperial control over South Africa just as it was exercising sovereign power over India. As Max Müller suggested, these two imperial possessions, the twin poles of his academic work, were essential for maintaining the global power and authority of the British Empire. With power, however, also came responsibility. Max Müller, along with other imperial theorists, hoped that imperial rule might actually be beneficial for the people under its domain.

Obviously, for colonized people, any benefit of empire was an ideal that was not necessarily realized in practice. Liberal imperialists generally found this distinction between the imperial ideal and contingent colonial practice important, since any harm done to the natives could be attributed to local departures from enlightened imperial policy. Accordingly, liberal imperialists might question colonial practice. In welcoming the abundant opportunities for research provided by the Colonial and Indian Exhibition of 1886, the president of the Anthropological Institute, Francis Galton (1822–1911), observed, "It will be one of our principal objects to learn the condition of the native races at the present moment and to gather opinions concerning the influence of the white man upon them; whether it has been directed as judiciously as might be desired, seeing that it has tended more frequently to degrade than to elevate—to destroy rather than build up."[92] Coming from Francis Galton, the pioneer of eugenics, whose early book on his travels in South Africa included instructions on how to tie up natives with rope, this concern for the destruction of native races might be surprising.[93] But it was based on an imperial confidence that the Anthropological Institute could analyze data, render judgment, and guide imperial policy toward building up rather than destroying the natives in the empire.

At the same time, liberal imperialists might challenge imperial policy by seeking to extend its scope in the colonies, as the Anthropological Institute and Folklore Society tried to do in relation to South Africa by petitioning the Colonial Office to establish a commission to study "native customs, institutions, and beliefs." Such a commission, E. Sidney Hartland argued, was "an urgent necessity both for missionaries and for purposes of government." Not only good for colonial governance and missionary networks, as Alfred C. Haddon insisted, such a commission, with imperial support, was essential "both for the sake of science and of the natives themselves."[94] Imperial science, colonial governance, and Christian missions might all be served; but how would such a commission for anthropological inquiry ever benefit the natives of South Africa?

During the last year of his life, Friedrich Max Müller, who had championed the "historical school" in the study of religion, defended the justice of England's cause in the South African War, while Hartland and Haddon, the current leaders of the "anthropological school," petitioned the Colonial Office to establish an imperial research commission for the benefit of science, government, missions, and the natives of South Africa. Opposing schools of thought, therefore, came together in the empire. Despite their theoretical differences, they worked within the same imperial horizon, which Max Müller beheld in his vision of Queen Victoria's throne, of "a whole Empire stretching out" from center to periphery, from history to prehistory, absorbing the entire world.

CHAPTER FOUR

Animals and Animism

As for the man who is passing into the morbid condition of the professional
seer, phantoms are continually coming to talk to him in his sleep, till he becomes as the expressive native phrase is, "a house of dreams."

E. B. TYLOR

At a meeting of the Ethnological Society in London on April 26, 1870,
chaired by Professor Thomas Huxley, an eminent scholar and a promoter
of evolutionary theory, two academic papers were presented, one by
Dr. Cornelius Donovan, the other by Mr. Edward B. Tylor, Esq. In the first
presentation, Dr. Donovan, who was a fellow of the Ethnological Society, a
doctor of philosophy and a professional phrenologist, read his paper, "On
the Brain in the Study of Ethnology." Proposing that researchers should be
working "to ascertain the mental condition of the various races of men," he
argued for the usefulness of phrenology, the science of measuring the size,
shape, and weight of skulls, in determining mental capacity. Such a scientific method, he argued, was crucial for anthropological research, because
it demonstrated that the "comparatively low state of intellectual and moral
development exhibited by most uncivilized races" could be attributed to "a
corresponding inferiority in 'the quality, quantity, and form of the brain.'"
In conclusion, Cornelius Donovan urged European travelers among such
"uncivilized races" to advance this science—presumably by measuring
skulls—that was dedicated to "analyzing the mental constitution of each
race, and of determining the relation which it bears to that of the normal
European."[1]
　　Cornelius Donovan (c. 1820–1872) was an eminent phrenologist with
an active practice in London. Among his many clients was the scientist
Francis Galton, who had received a personality profile from Dr. Donovan.
Cornelius Donovan was also an active participant in the major academic
associations—the Anthropological Society and the Ethnological Society—
that were undertaking research on savages. During one meeting of the

Anthropological Society, which was run by the adamantly racist president, James Hunt, Donovan objected not to the racism but to the implicit atheism in the leadership of the society. Exclaiming that he "stigmatized the whole lot of them," Donovan submitted a motion "that the Society viewed with regret and disapprobation the fact that a great majority of the Council [were] professed atheists." Donovan's motion was not seconded, and the leadership of the society, under James Hunt, was reelected.[2] For Cornelius Donovan, therefore, a science of race had to be pursued in harmony with religion.

In his popular text *A Handbook of Phrenology*, published in 1870, Donovan argued that his science had demonstrated that humans are inherently religious, showing how every human being "is innately a moral and religious, as well as an animal and intellectual, being." According to phrenology, the size, shape, and weight of the skull could reveal a faculty of faith, a capacity for worship, and an instinct for religious veneration. Donovan explained, "[Veneration] is the instinct whose highest object is the Deity. The worshipping emotion is innate, inalienable, natural." Long heads, in particular, revealed this capacity for veneration, although sometimes they might be "deficient in length at the top, leaving no room for 'Veneration' to develop itself fully."[3] As the frontispiece to his book, Donovan reproduced images of Pope Alexander VI, Martin Luther, and Philipp Melanchthon, which he had copied from an earlier phrenological textbook by Johann Gaspar Spurzheim, *Phrenology, in Connexion with the Study of Physiognomy*, published in 1826. Although Donovan did not comment on the illustrations that introduced his book, they captured the importance of the correlation between skulls and religion in the science of phrenology. If we were familiar with the phrenological diagnosis of Spurzheim, we would know that Luther's skull showed a "great deal of brain at the basis of the head" and that Melanchthon's skull showed the "brain of an extraordinary man" but that the skull of Alexander VI showed a "cerebral organization" that was "despicable in the eyes of a phrenologist." Spurzheim declared, "Such a head is unfit for any employment of a superior kind, and never gives birth to sentiments of humanity."[4] Accordingly, these skulls were indicators of Luther's humanity, Melanchthon's extraordinary humanity, and Pope Alexander VI's inhumanity, with all of the attendant religious implications for Protestant polemics against Catholics.

Measuring religion, therefore, was part of the science of phrenology. Alongside the distinction between Protestant and Catholic skulls, phrenologists developed an interest in research on civilized and savage skulls, although Cornelius Donovan cautioned, "The savage races will have to be studied after the civilized are well known."[5] Certainly such scientific research was undertaken in British colonies, collecting and measuring skulls to infer mental and moral qualities of "savages" and other "uncivilized races."[6] These research findings could be arranged in an evolutionary sequence from the most primitive origins to the most civilized developments, an arrangement conventionally proceeding from the "savage" African to the "normal European."

Cornelius Donovan does not appear in any history of the anthropology of religion. His expertise as a professional phrenologist has been forgotten along with the rejection of his science of measuring skulls to determine mental capacity. But the author of the second paper, E. B. Tylor (1832–1917), has endured. His minimal definition of religion as animism or "belief in spiritual beings"; his theory of the origin of religion as an attempt to deal with the anomalies posed by dreams and death; and his focus on basic intellectual or cognitive processes in dealing with these dilemmas—all of these features of Tylor's theoretical work have persisted in the academic study of religion.[7] Looking back on the meeting of the Ethnological Society in April 1870, we might be grateful to be able to trace the genealogy of the anthropology of religion back to the "intellectualist" theory of Edward B. Tylor, rather than to the blatant racism of Dr. Cornelius Donovan. In contrast to Donovan's reduction of mental and moral capacity to physiology, Tylor focused on philosophy, identifying a primitive "philosophy of religion" in which religious ways of thinking were revealed in the origins and survivals of human culture. His title, however, resonated with the previous presentation: "The Philosophy of Religion among the Lower Races of Mankind."

E. B. Tylor's theoretical work on religion drew together the multiple genealogies of travel narratives, poetic correspondences, and philosophical distinctions that might be regarded as the European prehistory of the anthropology of religion. Although he traveled to Mexico and wrote about his visit, E. B. Tylor based his theory of religion on reports from all over the world by European travelers, missionaries, and colonial administrators.[8] While Cornelius Donovan urged travelers to adopt a single method of reporting by measuring skulls, Tylor sifted through this chaos of information to look for recurring, underlying patterns of thinking in human culture. Tylor found the most fundamental pattern, the underlying basis of all correspondences in the history of religion, in the animism that set "the groundwork of the philosophy of religion at large, from the religion of savagery to that of civilized life."[9] However, in keeping with Enlightenment rationalism, Tylor ultimately had to base his anthropology of religion on distinctions. He tried to establish those distinctions at home and abroad.

At home, in adopting the designation *animism*, Tylor admitted that he might have preferred identifying the underlying essence of religion as "spiritualism" if that term had not already been appropriated by a "peculiar modern sect," the spiritualist movement that had developed in North America and Europe to commune with spirits of the dead. Eventually, he investigated this modern sect, attending séances and recording his observations.[10] But Tylor chose the term *animism* not only to distinguish his anthropological science from this modern spirituality but because he was convinced that modern spiritualists, with their "extreme spiritualistic doctrines," could not be regarded as "typical of the theory of spiritualism among mankind at large."[11] Tylor's anthropology of religion was located in a larger world.

Looking abroad, relying on travelers' reports for his evidence about the spirituality of "mankind at large," Tylor came up against the limits of those accounts. They lacked a familiarity, an intimacy, with the languages, cultures, and religions of the people they portrayed. "What is wanted," he urged, "is a declaration by observers intimately acquainted with the language of the tribe, and also intimate enough to gain confidence on a subject on which savages are less apt to be confidential than any other."[12] Nevertheless, drawing his evidence from admittedly unreliable reports about savages, Tylor built a general theory of religion, as animism, beginning with the "natural theology of the lower races," based on emergent spiritual concepts such as the notion of a soul, "which served to explain many of the great phenomena of [human] existence—life, death, sleep, dreams, visions, ecstasy, disease," and proceeding through "the Polytheism of low races," which anticipated the "supremacy of one great deity, and thus faintly foreshadows the coming of Monotheism."[13] In all of these distinctions, arranged in an evolutionary progression, Tylor nevertheless insisted on an underlying psychology of animism at every stage.

Tylor's fundamental distinction was between internal and external life, between subjectivity and objectivity. Animism, whether demonstrated in "savage psychology" or modern "survivals" such as spiritualism, was a failure to make such a crucial distinction. "This is unknown to the savage, who (these Africans may serve as a type) is a man who scarcely distinguishes his subjectivity from objectivity, hardly knows his inside from his outside."[14] The anthropology of religion, therefore, had to distinguish between religious subjectivity, which is animated by delusions, and scientific objectivity.

Cornelius Donovan, who deduced human mentality, morality, and spirituality from the shape and size of skulls, could also have been accused of confusing inside with outside. Although Tylor did not refer to Donovan's paper, he included physiology in his theory of animism by observing that "a whole theory of savage biology is here, which explains life and death, sleep and waking, swoons and illness, dreams and visions." But Tylor was not really interested in physiology. He was interested in psychology. He based his theory of religion on "savage psychology," but he also reflected on how animism was "retained in modern psychology," even if he deflected that persistence by insisting that "we should find among modern peasants that a much more nearly savage state is retained."[15] Tylor advanced a science of distance, drawing data from distant savage races, but also a science of difference that could explain social distinctions in England.

At the April 1870 meeting, E. B. Tylor's anthropology of religion, which he based on arguments concerning the "savage psychology" of animism, received two kinds of criticism: He was not sufficiently historical and he was not sufficiently psychological. These arguments have also persisted in the study of religion.

On the one hand, the historian Osbert H. Howarth responded that a history of religions, even if it tried to push back through history to the origin of religion, had to be based on sound historical records rather than hypothetical conjectures. Tylor's psychology, he found, was not grounded in "the earliest records we possess," which were not recent travelers' reports about savages but the historical and archaeological records of ancient civilizations. The anthropology of religion should begin with textual records, as solid historical evidence, which might show, Howarth suggested, that the animism of savages was derived from the monotheism of ancient civilizations.

On the other hand, the civil engineer, banker, and comparative linguist Hyde Clarke responded that Tylor's "comparative psychology" had not gone far enough because he had not considered "the animistic tendencies of animals." He urged Tylor to include dogs in his anthropology of religion, because, the "mind of a dog being constituted like that of a man, he has, there can be no reasonable doubt, the same phenomena of dreaming, and in the disordered condition of the senses at the moment of waking would see distorted images, which are treated as actual experiences." Anthropological inquiry into religion should begin with the psychology of dogs, Hyde Clarke argued, and develop as a science that "accounted for the growth of superstition in animals."[16] The study of religion should be a kind of animal psychology.

In his brief response at the end of this meeting, Tylor countered the historical objection by insisting on the explanatory power of his "savage psychology" to account for the religions of all civilizations, both ancient and modern. He insisted that "the religions of savage races afford explanations of otherwise obscure beliefs and rites of the civilized world." Accordingly, he concluded, "it is rather in the doctrines of low tribes than among high nations that original theological conditions are to be sought."[17] Unfortunately, Tylor did not say anything about dogs. Although he was a social evolutionist committed to the notion of human progress from primitive to civilized, which was underwritten by its distinction between the "low tribes" of colonized people all over the world and the "high nations" in Europe with imperial ambitions, Tylor was trying to work out a psychology that bridged these divisions. His "savage psychology," as Hyde Clarke proposed, might even blur the distinction between humans and animals in the study of religion. It could explain the superstitions of dogs, savages, rural peasants, and even urban spiritualists as "survivals" from a primitive psychology.

DOGS AND SAVAGES

John Lubbock (1834–1913), in his popular survey of human evolution, *The Origin of Civilization and the Primitive Condition of Man*, originally published in 1870, explained that religion originated as the result of the primitive tendency to attribute animation to inanimate objects. To illustrate this primitive "frame of mind" and "tendency to deification," Lubbock cited evidence from South Africa, relying on the early-nineteenth-century report from the traveler Henry Lichtenstein that the Xhosa in the Eastern Cape assumed that an anchor cast ashore from a shipwreck was actually alive. In a footnote, Lubbock observed, "Dogs appear to do the same."[18] This analytical link between the behavior of dogs and the primitive origin of religion was not uncommon in imperial comparative religion. In *Descent of Man*, Lubbock's friend and mentor Charles Darwin made this link explicit. According to Darwin, religion could be explained in terms of two features of canine behavior in which dogs attribute animation to inanimate objects and submit to a higher power. In both of these respects, the dog could provide the basic theoretical model for explaining the origin and evolution of religion.

Charles Darwin (1809–1882) was certainly a crucial figure in the academic study of religion, as he was in other scientific fields. Eric Sharpe, in his survey of the history of comparative religion, titled his chapter on nineteenth-century social evolutionists "Darwinism Makes It Possible."[19] Although Darwin provided inspiration for evolutionary theories of religion, he also addressed religion directly in his own writings. Darwin's first publication, coauthored with the captain of HMS *Beagle*, Robert FitzRoy, appeared in 1836 in the Cape Town periodical *South African Christian Recorder*. In this article, FitzRoy and Darwin recounted their recent travels in Tahiti and New Zealand, but they seemed more interested in dealing with the controversy over the role of Christian missionaries in South Africa. During their stay in the Cape between May 31 and June 18, 1836, they had learned that many European settlers were resentful of missionary interventions among the natives. "A very short stay at the Cape of Good Hope is sufficient to convince even a passing stranger," they wrote, "that a strong feeling against the Missionaries in South Africa is very prevalent." Arguing against European settlers who insisted that Africans could never evolve, FitzRoy and Darwin cited the precedent of European "savages," those "irreclaimable barbarians" the tribes of Danes and Saxons, who evolved in Europe into the "most industrious, intelligent, orderly, and humane of the dwellers upon earth." If those European savages could evolve, why not African savages? "If it is said that the races of men above mentioned always surpassed the Hottentots, the Bushmen, or the Caffers in natural abilities and disposition," FitzRoy and Darwin demanded, "are there any tribes of savages in the world in a state more degraded than those just named?"[20] Even the most degraded savages, whether European or African savages, had the potential for development. Accordingly, FitzRoy and Darwin concluded, Christian missionaries were an important civilizing agency that should be accepted by European settlers and supported by the British government.

This advocacy of Christian missions, even if the young Darwin had just signed on as coauthor in this publication of 1836, might seem surprising coming from a scientist who in his autobiography related that he had in his early years thought of becoming a country parson but then had gradually, effortlessly lost his faith in Christian doctrine and theology. During 1836 and 1837, Darwin recalled, "I had gradually come, by this time, to see that the Old Testament from its manifestly false history of the world . . . and from its attributing to God the feelings of a revengeful tyrant, was no more to be trusted than the sacred books of the Hindoos, or the beliefs of any barbarian."[21] Like so much of his theoretical work, the publication of Darwin's thinking about religion was long delayed. But his writings on the topic suggest two principles that were important for the academic study of religion: the rejection of theology in favor of "religion" as a universal category and the explanation of religion on the basis of the psychology of dogs.

In his discussion of religion in *Descent of Man*, Darwin began with the question of religion's universality. If religion was defined as belief in a supreme being, sufficient reports had been collected, "not from hasty travelers,

but from men who [had] long resided with savages," that many people had
no idea of an omnipotent God.[22] As indicated in a footnote, Darwin valued a discussion of this question, "On the Universality of Belief in God,"
which had been presented in 1864 by Rev. F. W. Farrar (1831–1903) to the
Anthropological Society in London. Collecting reports about savages, including observations by "hasty travelers," Farrar found that belief in God
was not a human constant. In reviewing African beliefs, for example, Farrar
cited the evidence for an absence of any concept of God among indigenous
Africans, noting, for example, "[A] missionary, the Rev. [George] Brown,
tells us of the Kaffirs, 'That they have not in their language *any word to use
as the name, or to denote the being, of a God*—of any God.'"[23] Quickly reviewing similar reports about Australians, the Malagache, Eskimos, Andaman
Islanders, and the Veddahs of Ceylon, Farrar concluded that these testimonies, which could be multiplied, were sufficient to settle the question of the
universality of belief in God. "A vague fear of the Unknown," he conceded,
might be universal, because it is "found even among animals." But such a
feature of animal psychology is "widely different from the belief in God."[24]
Therefore, if defined as belief in a supreme being, religion is not a human
universal.

Darwin subscribed to this conclusion that "numerous races have existed
and still exist, who have no idea of one or more gods." He distinguished this
historical or ethnographic finding from the issue of the existence of God,
"a Creator and Ruler of the universe." This theological question, he noted,
"has been answered in the affirmative by the highest intellects that have
ever lived."[25] Here also Darwin's assertion about intellectuals believing in
God could be read historically, as simply recording that the greatest minds
in history have affirmed the existence of a supreme being, rather than as
stating his own theological conviction. The ambivalence at the heart of this
sentence might account for a slight revision in the second edition, where
Darwin changed "the highest intellects" to "some of the highest intellects
that have ever lived."[26] In any case, Darwin was more interested in animal
psychology, including the "fear of the unknown" that was dismissed by
Farrar as a defining feature of religion, than he was invested in theology.

If he was going to analyze the universal characteristics of religion,
Darwin needed a different definition from "belief in a supreme being." He
found that definition in the "belief in unseen or spiritual agencies." This
redefinition of religion as belief in spirits, which pointed to something that
was most likely universal among "less civilized races," was central to the research of leading contemporary theorists. Darwin cited and recommended
John Lubbock's "three striking chapters on the Development of Religion"

in *The Origin of Civilization*; John McLennan's proposal that primitive humans explained natural phenomena and forces as spiritual agencies; and Herbert Spencer's theory of the primitive emergence of the notion that humans had a "double essence, corporeal and spiritual."[27] He particularly focused on E. B. Tylor's theory of animism, which traced the origin of the belief in spirits to dreams. Darwin noted, "It is probable, as Mr. Tylor has clearly shewn, that dreams may have first given rise to the notion of spirits; for savages do not readily distinguish between subjective and objective impressions. When a savage dreams, the figures which appear before him are believed to have come from a distance and to stand over him; or 'the soul of the dreamer goes out on its travels, and comes home with a remembrance of what it has seen.'"[28] Although he appreciated all of these accounts of the origin of religion as belief in spirits, Darwin was convinced that there was "a still earlier and ruder stage" that preceded such primitive attempts to explain either nature or dreaming. These theories, he worried, presumed that the primitive human being already had well-developed mental faculties of reasoning, without which, Darwin argued, "his dreams would not have led him to believe in spirits, any more than in the case of a dog."[29]

To find the origin of religion, we must turn to dogs. Over the years, Charles Darwin developed close relations with dogs. There were the terriers Nina, Spark, Pincher, and Sheila, the retriever Bob, the Pomeranian Snow, and the Scottish deerhound, a hunting dog, named Bran. The terrier Polly featured prominently in his later years, providing reference points for his research on the expression of emotions in humans and animals.[30] Darwin enjoyed sitting with Polly on his veranda as she barked at passersby whom he called "the naughty people," taking his dog's side against the humans.[31] A great lover of dogs, Darwin was convinced that dogs could dream and dogs could reason. Without language, which some philosophers had regarded as the defining feature of humanity, dogs exhibited such characteristic features of human psychology as dreaming and reasoning. Darwin observed that "a long succession of vivid and connected ideas," independent of language, could pass through "the prolonged dreams of dogs." He found that "retriever-dogs are able to reason to a certain extent; and this they manifestly do without the aid of language"[32] Although dogs could dream and reason, they did not seem to be able to reason about their dreaming in the ways that E. B. Tylor and the other theorists imagined as religion's origin. Revealing an earlier stage, the rude behavior of dogs demonstrated two psychological factors, the tendency to regard objects as alive and the disposition to submit to a higher power, that were instrumental in the origin of religion.

First, with respect to giving life to inanimate objects, Darwin explained the "tendency in savages to imagine that natural objects and agencies are animated by spiritual and living essences" by relating an anecdote about his own dog, "a full-grown and very sensible animal," who one afternoon noticed an open parasol lying on the lawn and moving in the breeze. If someone had been carrying the parasol, Darwin surmised, the dog would have disregarded its movements as normal. But here the parasol seemed to be moving by itself. Every time it moved, the dog growled and barked. "He must," Darwin concluded, "have reasoned to himself in a rapid and unconscious manner, that movement without any apparent cause indicated the presence of some strange living agent." So, here a spiritual agency was attributed to the unknown, which was also mixed with fear, because for Darwin's dog "no stranger had a right to be on his territory."[33] Fear of the unknown generated a dog's belief in the spiritual agency of inanimate objects.

Such a belief in spiritual agency, Darwin argued, could easily develop into beliefs in supreme beings, because "savages would naturally attribute to spirits the same passions, the same love of vengeance or simplest form of justice, and the same affections which they themselves experience."[34] Beginning with the attribution of life to inanimate objects, religion evolved by projecting human emotions onto the spirits, eventually resulting in beliefs in divine beings who displayed such human passions as love and vengeance. This origin and development of religion, however, was revealed not by scriptural authority, archaeological evidence, or historical records but by the behavior of a dog on a sunny afternoon.

Other theorists were developing this analysis of the psychology of dogs in their efforts to explain the origin of religion. Herbert Spencer (1820–1903), whose "ghost-theory" of the emergence of religion was appreciated but also criticized by Darwin for not being sufficiently early or rude, discussed primitive religion and dog psychology in the first volume of his *Principles of Sociology*, published in 1871. Spencer also related an anecdote about a dog, a large and ferocious dog, half mastiff, half bloodhound, which often played with a stick. But one day the stick injured the dog's palate, causing pain but also causing the dog to reclassify the stick from inanimate to animate object, capable of independent agency. "Similarly," Spencer concluded, "in the mind of the primitive man, knowing scarcely more of natural causation than a dog, the anomalous behavior of an object previously classed as inanimate, suggests animation." While the anomalous is regarded as animated, it also is feared because "there arises a tendency to regard the object with alarm, lest it should act in some other unexpected and mischievous way." Fear of the unknown, therefore, also featured in Herbert Spencer's explanation of the origin of religion in terms of dog psychology, although he argued that this "vague notion of animation" would eventually be filtered through the "ghost-theory" to identify more specific spiritual agents, such as the dead, the ancestors, the gods and goddesses, or a supreme being "to which such anomalous behavior can be ascribed."[35]

Pursuing this line of inquiry, George Romanes (1848–1894) shifted from anecdote to experimentation in his research on fetishism in animals. An expert on animal intelligence, Romanes had been entrusted by Darwin with the challenge of clarifying mental evolution. Inspired by reading the account of Darwin's dog and the parasol, Romanes conducted experiments on a Skye terrier—"a remarkably intelligent animal"—by making a bone move with an invisible thread and by blowing soap bubbles across the floor. In both experiments, the intelligent dog thought inanimate objects were alive. But the dog also displayed fear of the unknown. In the case of the moving bone, "his astonishment developed into dread, and he ran to conceal himself under some articles of furniture, there to behold at a distance the 'uncanny' spectacle of a dry bone coming to life." In the case of the soap bubbles, when one bubble burst, the dog was convinced that the object was alive and even capable of causing harm. From these experiments, Romanes adduced that his dog displayed the awe and fear that must have motivated "primitive man" to attribute spiritual agency to inanimate objects. Confronted by mysteriously moving bones and bursting bubbles, his dog "must have felt the same oppressive and alarming sense of the mysterious which uncultured persons feel under similar circumstances."[36]

Second, with respect to submitting to a higher power, Darwin found the source of religious devotion in dogs. Recognizing that feelings of religious devotion are complex, involving love, fear, and dependence on an "exalted and mysterious superior," Darwin argued that we can find traces of this state of mind "in the deep love of a dog for his master, associated with complete submission, some fear, and perhaps other feelings."[37] For understanding this sense of dependence, Darwin recommended in a footnote that the reader should consult another paper presented to the Anthropological Society, this one by Luke Owen Pike, "On the Psychical Elements of Religion." In a wide-ranging survey of the history of religions from a psychological perspective, Pike had observed, "Every widely accepted religion gives play to the emotions, and every religion which gives play to the emotions introduces a power which is propitiated and therefore feared."[38] Although Pike made no reference to dogs, Darwin found this religious disposition inherent in a dog's submission to its master. Citing the authority of Wilhelm Braubach, Darwin proposed that we might even conclude that "a dog looks on his master as a god."[39] In the second edition of *Descent of Man* (1882), he reinforced this notion that dogs regard their masters as gods by invoking the authority of the natural philosopher Francis Bacon and the poet Robert Burns.[40] By demonstrating a "strong sense of dependence" on their masters, dogs exhibited a crucial feature of religion, perhaps exemplifying what Friedrich Schleiermacher identified as religion's defining essence, a profound sense of absolute dependence on a superior being.[41]

Following this line of analysis regarding the canine psychology of religious submission, dependence, and propitiation of superior powers, Herbert Spencer related another anecdote about a dog. He told of an intelligent retriever, skilled at fetching birds that had been shot by the master, who apparently came to regard this activity with a kind of religious devotion: the dog would replicate the hunt by fetching and presenting leaves or other small objects in order to "perform this act of propitiation as nearly as practicable in the absence of a dead bird." In this act of symbolic substitution, motivated by devotion to the master, Spencer found the kernel of a primitive psychology of religion in which a "kindred state of mind" with this dog "prompts the savage to certain fetichistic observances of an anomalous kind."[42] Religious acts of propitiation, therefore, could be explained by the submission of dogs to their masters, as dogs seek to gain the favor and avoid the wrath of their superiors.

Examining this aspect of a dog's sense of absolute dependence on a superior being, George Romanes again wanted to proceed from anecdote to scientific experimentation. Having tested his intelligent terrier with moving bones and bursting bubbles to establish that the dog could attribute life to inanimate objects, Romanes further experimented on the dog's "sense of the mysterious" by testing his devotion to his master. Alone with the dog in a room, Romanes made "a series of horrible grimaces." He ignored the dog's "caresses and whining," while continuing to make faces at the dog. Distressed by this unusual behavior of the master, the dog "became alarmed and slunk away under some furniture, shivering like a frightened child." The dog's distress, he deduced, could only be explained as "the violation of his ideas of uniformity in matters psychological." Romanes confessed that he had repeated this experiment on less intelligent and sensitive terriers "with no other effect than causing them to bark at me." Nevertheless, he concluded from his successful experiment that dogs have a "sense of the mysterious," like their dread of thunder, in relation to a superior power.[43] By implication, religious dependence on superior beings is born out of similar arbitrary fluctuations between love and fear.

In *Descent of Man,* Darwin recognized that an anthropological theory of religion had to be based on evidence provided not by "hasty travelers" but by observers "who have long resided with savages."[44] As we have seen, however, more immediate evidence could also be gained by observing dogs. Having long resided with dogs, Darwin found it convenient to substitute dogs for savages, letting dogs stand in as representatives of indigenous people living on the colonized peripheries of empire. Darwin's dogs served as surrogates for representing savage dreaming, reasoning, and feeling, all of which, supposedly, indicated the primitive origin of religion. Arguably, this identification of indigenous people with dogs can be read as a political subtext in imperial theorizing about religion—colonizers are to colonized as humans are to animals. But Darwin insisted on the continuity between animals and humans. As a result, religion was recast from a marker of difference between savage and civilized to a medium of continuity between animals and human beings.[45]

Max Müller complained about this equation of canine and religious behavior. He blamed it on a misreading of Hegel. Against Schleiermacher's definition of religion as absolute dependence, Hegel had argued that religion should rather be understood as perfect freedom. If the sense of dependence constituted religion, then the dog might be called the most religious animal. "What was considered a rather coarse joke of Hegel's," Max Müller objected, "has now become a serious doctrine."[46] Adhering to this doctrine, many theorists of religion, myth, and ritual followed Darwin in viewing dogs as a model for indigenous African religion. In a discussion of "Animal Concepts of the Supernatural," for example, John H. King asserted, "The dog engages occasionally in rites similar to those of negro fetishism."[47] For Max Müller, this focus on dogs marked a crisis over what it meant to be human, since he held that the human was constituted by language, with speech standing as the Rubicon that no animal could ever cross. As an extension of language, religion also marked an impenetrable boundary between the animal and the human. Indicating the seriousness of this issue, when Max Müller confronted Darwin with this premise, Darwin reportedly declared, "You are a dangerous man."[48]

Others objected, too. "No man will ever develop religion out of a dog," exclaimed a reviewer of Darwin's *Descent of Man.*[49] But Darwin's dogs had established new terms, representing a kind of watershed, for thinking about religion. They embodied a definition of religion not as belief in a supreme being or an omnipotent God but as intellectual, emotional, and physical engagements with spiritual agencies. This definition of religion was crucial for

Darwin, since he began his analysis of religion by observing that belief in God was not universal among human beings but beliefs in spiritual agencies seemed to be universal. Subsequent debates about Darwinism and religion followed the two tracks marked out by these definitions.

Reverting to the definition that Darwin rejected, the entire controversy between religion and science, whether engaged by theists or atheists, focused on the viability of belief in a supreme being. This theological question, Darwin wrote in a letter in 1860, "is too profound for the human intellect. A dog might as well speculate on the mind of Newton."[50] So, while dogs might have invented religion, they could not be expected to solve the question of theology.

But a more profound distinction between theology and religion was taking shape in these reflections. Thomas Huxley (1825–1895), who was known as "Darwin's bulldog," recognized this distinction in 1864. Distinguishing between theology, which required belief, and religion as an "unshakeable" feature of human nature, Huxley proposed that religion was not in conflict with science. "Religion has her unshakeable throne in those deeps of man's nature which lie around and below the intellect, but not in it. But Theology is a simple branch of Science or it is nought."[51] Huxley, the agnostic, even found "religion" in his own life, but only by recognizing "that a deep sense of religion was compatible with the entire absence of theology."[52] By contrast to religion, theology, to the extent that it made knowledge claims, would have to compete in the same arena as contemporary science.

Leaving theological questions for the highest or at least some of the highest intellects to resolve, Darwin wanted to take the study of religion out of the sphere of theology. Accordingly, his definition of religion as belief in spiritual agencies called for different types of theoretical inquiry drawing on evidence that ranged from the beliefs of dogs to the variety of human beliefs in spirits.

MIND AND BODY

The redefinition of religion was directly related to a reevaluation of mind and body. As we have seen, a certain dualism persisted in distinguishing between inside and outside, between subjective and objective phenomena. E. B. Tylor found that the African savage "scarcely distinguishe[d] his subjectivity from objectivity, hardly [knew] his inside from his outside," an assertion echoed by Charles Darwin in noting, "Savages do not readily distinguish between subjective and objective impressions."[53] This dualism, however, was being undermined by contemporary research on both mind and body. While new research was being conducted on the mental life of animals and plants, which would have implications for any "intellectualist" theory of primitive religion, scientists were also debating the relevance for religion of such embodied features of human life as race, gender, and social class.

William Lauder Lindsay (1829-1880), who had been referenced by Darwin in the second edition of *Descent of Man* for providing further confirmation that dogs regard their masters as gods, was at the forefront of research into the mental life of animals, paying special attention to their mental pathology or insanity.[54] But Lindsay also identified features of mental activity, such as sensation, memory, and consciousness, in the mind of plants. Arguing against any clear "Psychical Line of Demarcation" that would separate the mental life of plants, animals, and humans, Lindsay concluded that it was necessary "to regard mind, and all its essential or concomitant phenomena, as common in various senses or degrees to plants, the lower animals, and man."[55] Likewise, John Lubbock found mental life in ants. As president of the Entomological Society of London, Lubbock advised scientists to recognize the rationality of insects. "Look, then, at the ants," he urged. "They build houses, they keep domestic animals [aphids], and they make slaves." Discerning mental life in these activities, he found that ants displayed reason in domesticating their environment and forming social hierarchies. Lubbock concluded from his study of the mental life of ants, linking entomology with anthropology, "If we deny to them the possession of reason we might almost as well question it in the lower races of Man."[56]

Of course, some European commentators had in fact alleged that "lower races" lacked reason. James Hunt, president of the Anthropological Society, was on record for denying the mental capacity of Africans.[57] John Lubbock never did. Likewise, E. B. Tylor was always clear that savages, although supposedly displaying "inveterate ignorance," were nevertheless rational beings. Contemporary research in psychology, however, was exploring the ways in which plants, insects, and animals could also think, demonstrating basic mental capacities shared between these lower life forms and the "lower races" of human beings. Intellectualist theories of religion thus focused on primitive mental life against the background of this scientific research into the mental life of plants, insects, and animals.

This egalitarian psychology, attributing mind to all animated beings, was entangled with countervailing scientific assumptions about the salience of race, gender, and social class in human mental life. Put bluntly, while plants and animals could think, blacks, women, and lower-class Europeans could not think very well at all. This embodied psychology had a number of implications for the study of religion. Was religion determined by race? Was religion perpetuated by women? Was primitive religion better studied among the lower classes of London than among the savages in distant colonies?

Luke Owen Pike (1835-1915), who had been praised by Darwin for his profile of the psychological aspects of religion, was struggling through the embodied features of religion associated with race, gender, and social class. In a presentation to the Anthropological Society, "On the Alleged Influence of Race upon Religion," Pike argued that race was not a defining or determining factor in the distribution of religion. A heated discussion followed, with many members of the society insisting on the correlation between race and religion. Invoking conventional wisdom, they pointed to the divisions within European Christianity, where Protestants were found to have long, narrow heads and Catholics short, round heads, the long, narrow dolichocephalic Protestants distinguished from the short, round brachycephalic Catholics by using the cephalic index of cranial measurement, which served to distinguish among the races of humanity.[58]

Indicating the persistence of this racialized history of religion, decades later Isaac Taylor (1829-1901) restated this conventional wisdom: "The dolichocephalic Teutonic race is Protestant, the brachycephalic Celto-Slavic race is either Roman Catholic or Greek Orthodox." The shape and size of skulls, therefore, persisted as an indicator of religious formation because cranial measurements were assumed to reveal states of mind. The long skulls of the Teutonic race were suited for a Protestant Christianity in which the traits of "individualism, willfulness, self-reliance, independence are strongly developed," while the round skulls of the Celto-Slavic race were only capable of a religious life that was "submissive to authority and conservative in instincts." Analyzing the geographical distribution of these racial, cranial, and mental types, Isaac Taylor concluded, "Roman Catholicism, or the cognate creed of the Greek and Russian Orthodox churches, is dominant in all those lands where the brachycephalic race prevails; Protestantism is confined to the dolichocephalic Teutonic region."[59]

In this racialized theory of Christianity, we can see the prominence of race in the study of religion. Throughout his life, Friedrich Max Müller fought against this tendency to racialize language, culture, and religion. His studies of Aryan language, Max Müller insisted, were not about any

Aryan race, so that any scholar "who speaks of Aryan race, Aryan blood, Aryan eyes and hair, is as great a sinner as a linguist who speaks of a dolichocephalic dictionary or a brachycephalic grammar."[60] Max Müller's joke, however, only suggested that these technical terms for cranial measurement were commonplace in racialized theories of human difference and diversity.

Gender also functioned as a marker of difference in theories of religion. At another meeting of the Anthropological Society, Luke Owen Pike took up the topic of women in politics. Although he wanted to maintain conventional gender distinctions, he recognized that women were claiming new public roles. Here again, Pike encountered resistance from members of the society who insisted that women ought to keep to their place. For the study of religion, however, the significance of this debate was found in the consensus among all the men in drawing a correlation between women and primitive religion. The terms had been outlined by Karl Vogt (1817-1895), who was cited by Darwin as the authority on gender differences. Vogt proclaimed, "Woman is the conservator of old customs and usages, of traditions, legends and religion." With respect to a woman's mind, which could also be analyzed by skull measurements, Vogt found that the "type of the female skull approaches in many respects that of the infant, and still more that of the lower races." As a result, "she preserves primitive forms, which but slowly yield to the influence of civilization."[61] As these gendered observations were echoed by Charles Darwin, they reinforced an analogy between the female and the primitive in opposition to the analogy between the male and the civilized. For the study of religion, female preservation of the primitive, only slowly yielding to male civilization, operated as a gendered subtext.

Imperial comparative religion explained savages in terms that could easily be transposed onto subclassified persons at home. For example, it has often been noted that the analogy between savages and children was central to this enterprise. In an 1867 essay on the "early mental condition of man," Tylor argued that primitive tribes displayed childlike minds. "In the working of the minds of early tribes," he proposed, "we trace a childlike condition of thought in which there is a wonderful absence of definition between past and future, between fact and imagination, between last night's dream and to-day's waking." In their childlike state of mind, savages displayed remarkable absences, including the inability to distinguish between dreaming and waking. This incapacity was crucial for the evolution of religion, Tylor proposed: "Out of this state of mind we find arising all over the world a consistent, intense, and all-pervading spiritualism."[62] Although he had re-named that all-pervading spiritualism "animism" in 1871, Tylor persisted in finding its origin in a childlike mentality. He observed in *Primitive Culture*, "We may, I think, apply the often-repeated comparison of savages to chil-dren as fairly to their moral as to their intellectual condition."[63] While the progress of intellectual, moral, and religious evolution moved on from this original mentality, savages remained behind as permanent children.

In South Africa, the analogy between indigenous people and children clearly served the interests of colonial domination. What interests, however, were served at the center of empire? In the analysis of the imperial theorists of comparative religion, who were the religious, superstitious, or primitive dogs that inhabited the immediate context of urban London? Tylor pro-vided hints in *Primitive Culture*, by pointing to children, peasants, and the urban working class, which suggested that his theory of religion, for all its social Darwinism, evolutionary theory, and commitment to progress, was formulated in the face of a perceived intellectual degeneration and moral decay in contemporary British society. For example, Tylor observed, "The inmates of a Whitechapel casual ward and of a Hottentot kraal agree in their want of the knowledge and virtue of the higher culture," but he noted that drawing this analogy between the poor of London and the savages of South Africa "was like comparing a ruined house to a builder's yard."[64] The savages of London were worse than those of South Africa, because they had allegedly degenerated, like a ruined house, from the achievements of higher culture.

Twenty years later, when Tylor delivered a paper titled "Limits of Savage Religion" to the Anthropological Institute, he was confronted again with this comparison between a Whitechapel slum and an African kraal in a response from the entomologist W. L. Distant (1845–1922), who had spent several years in South Africa. Distant brought the analysis home to London by insisting that more could be learned in Whitechapel than in South Africa about the nature of savage religion. Distant argued:

> It seems likely that we shall never really understand the religious or speculative ideas of so-called savages, until we commence the study of the opinions held on these matters by the masses at home. What is the idea of the "Great Spirit" among the savages (to use a misleading word usually applied to other races) found in our own great cities; and would it not be better to commence the study in Whitechapel rather than proceed at once to Africa or Australia? Among the South African Bantu Kafirs I have lately visited, I found the majority ready to believe anything and everything told them by their elders, whilst the chiefs,

who are always more intellectual, sometimes exhibit a healthy scepticism. Is it not just the same in England, and would not the enquiry proceed much more rapidly if we investigated at first the crude and often simple ideas held on these matters by our own people, and thus be better able to formulate a method of enquiry to be applied to other races.[65]

Imperial comparative religion could bring its analysis home from the colonies to provide terms and conditions for explaining the "religion" of children, social deviants, and the working class in metropolitan London. As a result, not only dogs, but also the insane, criminals, women, peasants, and the urban poor could be explained as unwarranted survivals from human prehistory. They all shared the same primitive mentality. While Tylor and Distant looked to the impoverished residents of Whitechapel, others looked to the criminal element in London; C. G. Leland insisted that "Fetish or Shamanism [was] the real religion of criminals."[66] These outcasts from modern society supposedly perpetuated the religion found among the savages of colonized peripheries. At the center of empire, they were the savages within.

Turning the ethnographic method back on the metropolitan center, seeking out the spiritual ideas among the savages of the great cities of Europe, was part of the critical project of Karl Marx (1818–1883). Publishing the first volume of *Capital* a year after Darwin's *On the Origin of Species*, Marx suggested a connection between biology and political economy. Now that Darwin had explained the organs of plants and animals, which served as instruments of production for biological life, Marx demanded: "Does not the history of the productive organs of man in society . . . deserve equal attention?"[67] A history of these material organs—the means, modes, and forces of economic production and social reproduction—would be easier to formulate than Darwin's natural history, Marx suggested, because it was a history shaped by human beings themselves. Marx envisioned a material history of labor, the working of mind and body, brains and hands, in the production of value. Under capitalism, however, value was being alienated from productive minds and bodies by systems of exchange that he called commodity fetishism. Just like the "misty realm of religion" that anthropologists found in savage fetishism, the economic relations inherent in the commodity invested life in inanimate objects. In the savage religion of fetishism, Marx observed, "the productions of the human brain appear as autonomous figures endowed with a life of their own. . . . So it is in the world of commodities with the products of men's hands."[68] A capitalist economy based on this fetishism of commodities turns relations between human beings into imaginary relations among animated objects.

Others had used the term *fetishism* to reflect critically on the beliefs and practices of civilization. In 1864 an anonymous article published in the periodical edited by Charles Dickens, *All the Year Round*, questioned the fetishism of civilized society. Asking, "What is a fetish?" the author defined the savage fetish as "a bundle of rags, a mass of rubbish, a muttered charm." Out of these worthless materials and meaningless words, "the poor benighted savages . . . make something which thenceforth rules their lives and determines their actions." Noting that the civilized mocked this savage worship of objects, the author found a similar fetishism in civilized society: "We laugh at their fetishes, but are our own much better? Analyze them, and I think we shall come to rags, rubbish [and] a muttered charm of words." In this critical reflection on civilized fetishism, however, the author's main evidence was drawn from the vagaries of women's fashions in London.[69] Marx clearly advanced a more substantial and radical critique of the entire system of commodity relations. The commodity fetish was not merely a desired object; it was an animated object in an entire system of exchange that had been thoroughly mystified. Obscuring the reality of human labor, capitalist relations of exchange enveloped the commodity in a dreamlike fog that was similar to the dreamlike illusions of the "misty realm of religion." In his critical analysis of religion, Marx was clearly influenced by the work of Ludwig Feuerbach, who had argued that religion was a projection of human ideals and desires onto an imaginary God. Feuerbach observed, "Religion is the dream of the human mind."[70] All religion, in this respect, was like a dream, projecting a fantasy world that alienated human beings from reality.

In building his "dream theory" of the origin of religion, E. B. Tylor could draw upon a long history of European thinking about dreams as the threshold between illusion and reality. During the eighteenth-century Enlightenment, the ability to distinguish between dreaming and waking was often regarded as a uniquely human accomplishment. As Buffon observed, "the only difference between us and the brutes is, that we can distinguish dreams from ideas or real sensations."[71] In the rise of anthropology during the nineteenth century, however, this same distinction was used to mark the difference not only between humans and animals but also between civilized and savage humans. During the 1860s, Adolf Bastian (1826–1905), the leading anthropologist in Germany, formulated this assumption that savages, like animals, were incapable of distinguishing between dreaming and waking: "Tribes in the state of nature surrender passively to the all too overwhelming impressions of the external world. For them, hallucinations and illusions maintain a half-conscious oscillation between dreaming and waking as a normal condition. Their entire mental condition enables them to create supernatural agencies or to believe in these unconditionally, with an intensity and to an extent, to the direct understanding of which luckily our logical thinking has long ago destroyed the bridge, or at least should have done so."[72] According to this account, normal life among savages blurred dreaming and waking, as savages lived in a kind of semiconscious fog. What Marx called the "misty realm of religion" emerged out of that fog, creating the illusion of supernatural beings. This analysis of savage consciousness became commonplace in the anthropology of religion. Herbert Spencer insisted that savages could not distinguish "I saw" from "I dreamed that I saw"; James Frazer maintained forty years later, "What a savage sees in a dream is just as real to him as what he sees in his waking hours."[73] E. B. Tylor placed savage dreaming at the center of his theory of religion.

E. B. Tylor built a theory of religion—animism, the belief in spiritual beings—that explicitly linked the animal and the human by focusing on the cognitive constraints and capacities of human psychology. Everyone, he observed, "who has ever dreamt a dream, has seen the phantoms of objects as well as of persons."[74] Like animals or children, however, savages were unable to distinguish between the sense impressions of dreams and waking life. Accordingly, they incorporated dream phantoms into their waking reality and ultimately into their primitive religion.

DREAMING

Zulu dreaming provided important evidence for E. B. Tylor's theory of religion. Like Max Müller, Tylor was impressed by the apparently unmediated access to savage religion afforded by Callaway's *Religious System of the Amazulu*. In September 1871, Tylor tried to raise funds, by making an appeal through the *Colonial Church Chronicle*, to subsidize the completion and publication of Callaway's work. He declared, "No savage race has ever had its mental, moral, and religious condition displayed to the scientific student with anything approaching to the minute accuracy which characterizes" *Religious System*.[75] In his major work, *Primitive Culture*, Tylor observed that Callaway's account represented "the best knowledge of the lower phases of religious belief."[76] Reviewing an ethnography on the natives of South Africa in 1874, Tylor criticized the author for "describing the Zulu religion without mention or apparently knowledge of the remarkable native documents collected by Dr. (now Bishop) Callaway," because Callaway's documents shone "such clear light not only on the religious ideas of these barbarians, but on the origin and development of religion among mankind at large."[77] Unlike Max Müller, however, who used Callaway's book as a resource for studying language, analyzing the play of metaphors in Zulu religion, Tylor harvested evidence for the cognitive origin of religion.

As we have seen, in Tylor's theory of religion, animism was derived from the primitive inability to distinguish between dreams and waking consciousness. When the primitive ancestors of humanity dreamed about deceased friends or relatives, they assumed that the dead were still alive in some spiritual form. Out of dreams, therefore, evolved "the doctrine of souls and other spiritual beings in general," a doctrine that was "rational," even if it was enveloped in "intense and inveterate ignorance."[78] Tylor certainly found evidence of an active dream life among Callaway's Zulus. As many European reporters had observed, the Zulu often saw the shade or shadow of deceased ancestors in dreams.[79] However, Callaway's volume included a detailed account about one Zulu man, an aspiring diviner, who had become so overwhelmed with visions of spirits that he had described his own body as "a house of dreams."[80] According to Tylor, all Zulu people, as savage survivals of the primitive, were subject to dream visions. He said, however, "As for the man who is passing into the morbid condition of the professional seer, phantoms are continually coming to talk to him in his sleep, till he becomes as the expressive native phrase is, 'a house of dreams.'"[81]

Although Tylor appropriated him as an archetype of the primitive, this particular Zulu man, who served Tylor as a savage survival of the original "house of dreams" from which religion originated, can be identified as James, a Christian convert for twelve years, who had recently left the mission with the initiatory sickness associated with becoming a diviner, torn between the promises of the Christian mission and the demands of indigenous tradition. While Henry Callaway's principal informant and collaborator Mpengula Mbande went one way, becoming a catechist for the Christian mission, James struggled in the other direction, striving to keep an ancestral dream alive under increasingly difficult colonial conditions. In this case, therefore, the "house of dreams" was not a primitive but a colonial situation, the product of contemporary conflicts in southern Africa.

In order to distill a primitive religious mentality, E. B. Tylor had to erase all of the social, political, and military conditions under which his data was being collected. As a matter of method, he insisted on erasing the intercultural exchanges in which his data was being produced as "religious" data. In his use of evidence, Tylor was capable of entirely obliterating the meaning and significance of data supplied by experts in colonial situations, such as Henry Callaway, who provided him with his classic case of animism in the account of the Zulu diviner who had become a "house of dreams." In the case of the "professional seer" who becomes a "house of dreams" because "phantoms are continually coming to talk to him in his sleep,"[82] Tylor substantially distorted his data. In Callaway's account, the phantoms were not coming merely to talk to the diviner. They were coming to kill him.

In the Zulu conversations recorded by Mbande, which form the bulk of Callaway's *Religious System*, we learn the basic principles of an indigenous hermeneutics of dreams. In the interpretation of dreams, according to Mbande, the Zulu had developed basic principles of correlation and contrast for discerning the meaning of dream symbolism.

First, Zulu dream interpretation observed the correlation of summer with good dreams and winter with bad dreams. "People say, summer dreams are true," Mbande observed. By contrast, "winter causes bad dreams." Therefore, in this hermeneutics of dreams, Zulu dream interpretation found a correlation—summer dreams are true, winter dreams are false—which Mbande underscored by reporting, "It is said there is not much that is false in the dreams of summer. But when the winter comes the people begin to be afraid that the winter will bring much rubbish, that is, false dreams." However, in this Zulu hermeneutics of dreams, with its winter rubbish and summer revelations, Mbande introduced an element of indeterminacy by cautioning about summer dreams that Zulu people "do not say they are always true."[83] While the correlation was important in establishing basic principles for interpretation, this indeterminacy was even more important because it opened a space for creative and critical reflection on the potential meaning of dreams.

Second, Zulu dream interpretation observed a principle of contrast, holding that dreaming "goes by contraries."[84] According to a number of Zulu informants recorded in *Religious System*, dreaming of a wedding means that someone will die, while dreaming of a funeral means that someone will get married, or get well, or otherwise flourish. As Mbande related his own experience, he recalled, "I have dreamt of a wedding dance, and the man died; again, I have dreamt of the death of a sick man, but he got well."[85]

In Britain, imperial theorists of religion were intrigued by this principle of contrast. Referring to these Zulu reports, E. B. Tylor noted, "This works out, by the same crooked logic that guided our ancestors, the axiom that 'dreams go by contraries.'"[86] Similarly, Andrew Lang took these reports to indicate an unexpected link: "Dr. Callaway illustrates this for the

Zulus . . . [proving that] savages, indeed, oddly enough, have hit on our theory, 'dreams go by contraries.' "[87] However, the conversations collected in *Religious System* about the hermeneutical principle "dreams go by contraries" reveal profound struggles with indeterminacy. Like the correlation of good summer dreams and bad winter dreams, the principle "dreams go by contraries" was true but not always true. Mbande acknowledged, "I have not yet come to a certain conclusion that this is true; for some dream of death, and death occurs; and sometimes of health, and the person lives." His friend Uguaise Mdunga accepted the principle that dreams go by contraries but then recounted that he had just dreamed of a wedding and a funeral. According to the principle of contraries, a "dream of a funeral lamentation is good; the dream of a wedding is bad." But what if you dream of both?[88]

As these Zulu deliberations about the hermeneutics of dreams indicate, dreams could be correlated with the seasons, but not always, and dreams could go by contraries, but not always. And sometimes, as Uguaise observed, "sleep has filled my mind with mere senseless images."[89] This indeterminacy in the interpretation of dreams was related to the uncertainty and instability of daily life under colonial conditions. Dreams were not merely "texts" to be interpreted. They were calls to action. They demanded a practical response, whether through exchanges with ancestral spirits or through asserting ancestral claims on a territory.

In the first instance, as Uguaise Mdunga observed, dreams often required a sacrificial offering for an ancestor, calling the dreamer to action. "You will see also by night, you will dream; the Itongo [ancestor] will tell you what it wishes," he observed. "It will also tell you the bullock it would have killed."[90] This exchange between the living and the "living dead," the ancestors, was a central feature of Zulu religious practice. Dreams were a medium of communication; but they were also a call to action, with detailed attention to the specific ancestral spirit, the sacrificial offering, and, of course, the dreaming human being who must be brought into relationship with the deceased ancestor in this exchange.

In the second instance, dreams often required actions to assert or reassert claims on territory, as when dreaming of the dead (or, according to one report, even not dreaming of the dead) required the living to perform certain ritual actions so that the dead might be "brought back from the open country to his home."[91] In such ancestral dreams, practical steps had to be taken to reestablish the territorial integrity of domestic space shared by the living and the dead.

Under colonial conditions, the meaning of dreams might have become increasingly uncertain. But the energetics of dreams was radically disrupted.[92] As Africans were deprived of the means of exchange and access to territory, dream life was dramatically altered. Increasingly, according to reports collected in *Religious System*, Africans turned to ritual techniques for blocking dreams because they were unable to fulfill the practical obligations to their ancestors that were conveyed by dreaming. Techniques for blocking dreams included using a black medicinal herb, performing symbolic actions to throw the dream behind (without looking back), and enacting rituals to remove the dream from the home and secure it in a remote place.[93] Conversion to Christianity could also be a technique for blocking ancestral dreams.

In the ritual energetics of exchange, Africans deprived of cattle could not fulfill the requirements of sacrifice. Recounting a recent dream, Uguaise Mdunga noted, "I have seen my brother." His deceased elder brother, appearing in a dream, called for a sacrificial offering, which placed a solemn and sacred obligation on Uguaise to respond. But Uguaise had no cattle. Addressing the spirit of his brother, he cried, "I have no bullock; do you see any in the cattle-pen?" Unable to achieve the necessary exchange, Uguaise could only feel the anger of his brother. "I dreamed that he was beating me," he reported, noting that in further dreams this spirit kept "coming for the purpose of killing me."[94] The result of this blocked exchange, he felt, would only be suffering, illness, and death.

A few decades earlier, European Christian missionaries had complained that they could not gain converts among the Zulu because the people were too wealthy in cattle.[95] Now, ironically, when people had less cattle, ancestors were increasingly appearing in dreams to demand sacrifice. As a result, people dreamed but did not talk about their dreams. Mbande observed, "Although they have dreamed and in the morning awoke in pain, [they] do not like to talk about it themselves; for among black men slaughtering cattle has become much more common than formerly, on the ground that the Idhlozi [ancestor] has demanded them."[96] Under colonial conditions of dispossession, dreams of ancestors calling for cattle apparently increased, but the living, unable to fulfill this exchange, no longer were able to talk about what they had seen in their dreams. Increasingly, Africans sought ritual means to block their dreams, as Callaway observed, "lest the frequent sacrifices demanded should impoverish them."[97]

Under colonial conditions, Africans tried to block their dreams, but their dreams were also blocked by colonial conditions. In addition to calling for sacrificial exchange, dreams called upon people to keep their ancestors in the home or bring them back to the home. However, for people displaced from their homes, this aspect of the energetics of dreams became very difficult. As Mbande recounted, his own family, which had been displaced by colonial warfare, struggled with their ancestral dreams of home. Forced to flee to another country, they employed the traditional ritual means of transporting ancestors under the sign of snakes. As a symbolic trace of the ancestor, the snake communicated through dreams, Mbande noted: "Perhaps the snake follows; perhaps it refuses, giving reasons why it does not wish to go to that place, speaking to the eldest son in a dream; or it may be to an old man of the village; or the old queen."[98]

In the case of Mbande's family, however, their ancestral dreams were blocked by the colonial incursions of the Dutch and the British. As they were "flying from the Dutch," the head of the family, Umyeka, dreamed that their paternal ancestor was demanding that they reclaim their home: "It was said to him in a dream, 'Why do you forsake your father?'" But they could not return home, "fearing their feud with the Dutch." Blocked from returning to their ancestral territory, they dreamed of relocating their ancestor. Mbande recalled, "Our father whilst asleep dreamt the chief was talking with him, [saying] it would be well for you to make a bridge for me, that I may cross on it and come home; for I am cold, and the water makes me colder still." With considerable ritual effort, they built a bridge for their ancestor to relocate to a new home. But this dream of a new home was also shattered, because they were soon driven out at the order of the British colonial administrator, secretary for native affairs Theophilus Shepstone. As a result, Mbande reported, "We were scattered and went to other places."[99] The energetics of dreams, therefore, was radically disrupted by such colonial conditions of dispossession and displacement.

In *The Religious System of the Amazulu*, a convert at Callaway's mission station, who is identified only as James, features prominently as a dreamer. After living for over ten years at the Christian mission, James left to pursue his own dreams. He showed all of the symptoms of being called by the ancestors to be a diviner, including suffering an illness (Mbande notes that such matters are "not intelligible among Christians"), and went off to live alone, subject to dreams, his body becoming a "house of dreams."[100] When Mbande and his fellow Christian convert Paul went to see him, James related that his initiatory sickness had caused him to leave the mission, noting, "This disease has separated me from you," but he also observed that his dreams had given him new access to the entire world. "There is not a single place in the whole country which I do not know; I go over it all by night in my sleep; there is not a single place the exact situation of which I do not know."[101] In this new freedom, however, his dreams were still blocked. In his dreams, he was told where to find medicinal plants, but he did not find them; he dreamed of antelope telling him where to find an aloe tree, but it was not there. He dreamed of ancestors, calling for meat, but he could not provide the cattle. The Word of God and the bell of the church, Mbande advised, would drive away all of these dreams. But James seems to have found these ancestral dreams already blocked. Nevertheless, he continued to dream. He told Mbande and Paul, "On the night before you came I saw you coming to me, but you were white men."[102] Going by contraries, perhaps, this dream nevertheless suggested that James now perceived these African Christian converts as aliens.

Every night, in dreams, James saw wild animals, dangerous snakes, and rushing rivers. "All these things come near to me to kill me," he said. On the day of his meeting with his Christian friends, James reported that the previous night he had been attacked by men. James explained, "I dreamt many men were killing me; I escaped I know not how. And on waking one part of my body felt different from other parts; it was no longer alike all over." As a result, James found, "My body is muddled today."[103] The Zulu term for "muddled"—*Dungeka, Ukudunga*—was a metaphor derived from stirring up mud in water. Although it could be applied to a state of mind, signifying a confusion of mind, it could also be applied to the disturbance of a household by a house-muddler (*Idungandhlu*) or the disturbance of a village by a village-muddler (*Idungamuzi*).[104] All of these meanings, certainly, were at play in the dreams of a Zulu man who experienced his body, his home, his family, and his sense of community stirred up and under attack by forces threatening to kill him.

Mbande reminded James of an old dream that James had related to Mbande when they were both Christians, in which James crossed a river, in a boat of faith, and was saved from being killed by wild dogs. In Zulu geography, the river was a powerful liminal zone in between the sacred space of home, which was built up through ritual relations with ancestors, and the wild, dangerous zones of the bush or forest that contained alien spirits. Mediating between home space and wild space, the river represented both ancestral protection and spiritual danger, a place of potential for both life and death.[105] As James learned during his initiatory sickness, the dreams of a diviner were filled with rushing rivers. Mbande, as a Christian, interpreted these dream rivers as a test of faith. The dreamer, according to Mbande, must cross these rivers in the boat of Christian faith. Remembering this old dream, in which he had been saved by the boat of faith, James had now arrived at a new interpretation. Yes, James said, "the boat is my faith, which has now sunk into the water. And the dogs which I saw are now devouring me." If he could not be saved by Christian faith, Mbande demanded, "Who will save you?" Nothing, James replied: "I am now dead altogether."[106]

Under colonial conditions, all of the Zulu dreams we have considered bear traces of a changing world, a colonial world in which indigenous people were undergoing dispossession, displacement, and despair. As a result, in the hermeneutics and energetics of dreams, the principles of dream interpretation became increasingly indeterminate and the ways of practically engaging with the demands of dreams by entering into ancestral exchange or affirming ancestral territory became increasingly impossible. These were realities of the colonial situation revealed through dreams.

ANIMISM AND MATERIALISM

In the history of the study of religion, E. B. Tylor has been celebrated and criticized for pioneering an "intellectualist" theory of religion. According to Tylor, religion was essentially a way of thinking. Although primitives suffered from primordial stupidity, Tylor argued that they nevertheless exercised their limited intellectual powers to develop explanations of the world in which they lived. Unfortunately, in support of this proposition, Tylor cited Callaway's catechist, Mpengula Mbande, who had observed that in ancestral Zulu religion, people "are told all things, and assent without seeing clearly whether they are true or not." However, Mbande's point in this statement was that most Zulu people adhered to their ancestral religion, unthinkingly, because they had not been exposed to Callaway's new Christian gospel.[107] Rather than offering evidence of primordial stupidity or inveterate ignorance among savages, Mbande was announcing his recently acquired Christian commitment by criticizing adherents of ancestral religion. Clearly, Mbande agreed with Tylor that religion was a way of thinking, but his Christian critique of Zulu thinking was situated in interreligious relations.

Although Tylor's "dream theory" was the centerpiece of his account of the origin of religion, dreaming did not provide the only evidence for Tylor's theory of animism. The involuntary physical phenomenon of sneezing also featured in Tylor's argument. Here again Callaway's Zulu evidence was definitive. As Tylor observed in *Primitive Culture*, sneezing was "not originally an arbitrary and meaningless custom, but the working out of a principle. The plain statement by the modern Zulus fits with the hints to be gained from the superstition and folklore of other races, to connect the notions and practices as to sneezing with the ancient and savage doctrine of pervading and invading spirits, considered as good or evil, and treated accordingly."[108] From Callaway's *Religious System of the Amazulu,* Tylor derived the ethnographic facts that the Zulu thought their deceased ancestors caused sneezing; that sneezing reminded Zulu people to name and praise their ancestors; that the ancestors entered the bodies of their descendants when they sneezed; and that Zulu diviners regularly sneezed as a ritual technique for invoking the spiritual power of the ancestors.[109] These Zulu concepts and practices, Tylor concluded, were remnants of a prehistoric era in which sneezing was not merely a "physiological" phenomenon, "but was still in the 'theological stage.'"[110] Nevertheless, despite this brief reflection on the theology of sneezing, Tylor focused primarily on the hallucinations of dreams as the fundamental origin of religion.

In 1871 Henry Callaway presented a paper to the Royal Anthropological Institute in London on the results of his research into the dreaming, divination, and religious life of the Zulu of South Africa. Ordinary dreams and extraordinary visions, Callaway proposed, could be explained as "brain-sensation" that took the form of "brain-sight" and "brain-hearing." Brain-sensation, he clarified, is "a condition of brain which, without external causes in operation, is attended by feeling, hearing, and sight, just as it would if there were external causes in operation, capable of producing such sensations." Drawing upon the Zulu accounts and interpretations of such "subjective apparitions," which he had recently published in his *Religious System of the Amazulu,* Callaway illustrated brain-sensation through examples of "spectral vision or *brain-sight*" and *"brain-hearing*—that is . . . the same condition of brain as there would be if the sounds actually reached it through the ear."[111] This extrasensory seeing and hearing, Callaway speculated, could be cultivated by a kind of self-mesmerism. Referring to the theory of animal magnetism developed by Franz Mesmer and popularized by public performances of hypnosis, telepathy, and clairvoyance, Henry Callaway suggested that Zulu diviners were expert in entering such trance states. Their extrasensory perception, therefore, could be explained by analogy to mesmerism. In the discussion that followed, one member of the institute, Walter Cooper Dendy, vehemently dismissed Callaway's analysis, complaining that it was "the most prolix and monotonous paper read before the Institute during this session; indeed, it was a real infliction." Outraged by this account of Zulu self-mesmerism, Dendy declared, "If we hear nothing from south-eastern Africa more rational, the sooner the district is tabooed the better."[112]

Back in South Africa, Mpengula Mbande was also skeptical about the sights and sounds experienced in dreams, visions, and divination. He had personally experienced what Callaway called brain-sight and brain-hearing in his encounters with dreamlike phantoms—a deadly snake, a fearsome leopard, a terrifying warrior with an assegai—that attacked him while he was praying alone before dawn. Disciplining his senses to simply accept these phantoms, Mbande finally realized that he was being attacked by "fantasy" and "deceived by fantasies." By dismissing these sights and sounds as insubstantial hallucinations, Mbande certainly demonstrated, if any proof were necessary, that he could distinguish between dreaming and waking, fantasy and reality.[113] While converting dreams into Christian heuristic devices, he conquered fantasy through a discipline of the senses and reasoned skepticism.

Henry Callaway's analysis did not do justice to his data, because he reduced the dynamic Zulu hermeneutics and energetics of dreams, which were situated in contested colonial situations and interreligious relations, to a cognitive psychology of "brain-sensation." Dreaming under colonial conditions, as we have seen, could not be adequately explained as a mentality and certainly not as a "primitive mentality" preserving original cognitive processes of an animism that confused dreaming and waking. In order to distill a primitive religious mentality from Callaway's data, E. B. Tylor had to erase all of the social, political, and military conditions under which the data had been collected. In fact, as a matter of method, Tylor insisted on the necessity of erasing the intercultural exchanges in which such "religious" data was emerging in colonial contact zones. According to Tylor, savage religions had to be abstracted from their living contexts in order to be used in an evolutionary history of human culture that began with primitive animism. "In defining the religious systems of the lower races, so as to place them correctly in the history of culture," Tylor observed in 1892, "careful examination is necessary to separate the genuine developments of native theology from the effects of intercourse with civilized foreigners." Any trace of more advanced religious concepts, such as ideas of deity, morality, or retribution in an afterlife, could only have entered savage religion, Tylor argued, through such foreign intercourse with higher races. Factoring out colonial contacts, relations, and exchanges, he argued, "leaves untouched in the religions of the lower races the lower developments of animism."[114] According to this method, therefore, animism appeared as the original religion—the earliest, the lowest—only by erasing the actual colonial situations in which indigenous people lived. As a result, the theory of animism provided an ideological supplement to the imperial project.

Nineteenth-century Zulu dreams were not symptoms of some original "primitive mentality." Instead, they were situated within the violent disruptions of a colonial contact zone. An undercurrent of violence runs through these dreams, as dreamers are threatened by neglected ancestors, enemy warriors, wild animals, or dangerous rivers. This violent dream imagery can be related to the breakdown in the religious practices of ancestral exchange and spatial orientation that were important features of Zulu religion. But some of these dreams, especially the dreams of James, also revealed the interreligious nature of the contact zone, a space in which Africans were negotiating new Christian and indigenous religious understandings of a changing world.

Both of these modes of understanding—indigenous African and African Christian—were erased by E. B. Tylor in abstracting Zulu dreams from the intercultural and interreligious relations of the contact zone. But they were also destined for destruction within his imperial understanding of the mission of a scientific study of religion. Tylor imagined that his anthropological investigations were providing "new evidence and method in theology." But his ethnographic theology, comparing "evidence of religion in all stages of culture," advanced a discipline of demystification that was not unlike Mpengula Mbande's demystification of dreams and visions as merely fantasy. "It is a harsher, and at times even painful office of ethnography," Tylor asserted, "to expose the remains of crude old culture which have passed into harmful superstition, and to mark these out for destruction."[115] As we have seen, colonial interventions in Zulu dream life, which eroded the material means of ancestral exchange and territorial orientation, had already been far more destructive than E. B. Tylor, from his study at Oxford, could ever have hoped to be.

In *Primitive Culture*, E. B. Tylor attempted more than defining and explaining animism; he used his "dream theory" to mark out the great divide between animism and materialism in the modern world. Arising from a common origin in primitive animism, all religions, whether practiced by the "savage fetish-worshipper" or the "civilized Christian," shared the same "mental connexion" that confused dreams with reality. Accordingly, Tylor insisted that any distinctions that might be made within the religious world, such as the divisions among intolerant and often hostile religious sects, were superficial. The only meaningful distinction, the "deepest of all religious schisms," was the opposition between animism and materialism.[116] For E. B. Tylor, scientific materialism was real. Animism, as the defining essence of religion, was not real, since it was derived from mistaking dreams for reality. Whether animism appeared among the Zulu *isanusi*, who became a "house of dreams," or among the spiritualists conducting their popular séances in London, it was a superstitious survival of the primitive that was out of place in the reality of secular modernity.

Objections to Tylor's "dream theory" of religion initially came from colleagues who were interested in scientifically exploring the claims being made by modern spiritualists. Alfred Russel Wallace (1823–1913), codiscoverer of the theory of evolution with Charles Darwin, had developed a personal interest in spiritualism, seeing its promise of spiritual development as consistent with the biological evolution of the human species. On scientific grounds, he argued, the phenomena experienced by people at spiritualist séances had to be regarded as facts, however those facts might be interpreted, rather than being immediately dismissed as delusions. In a review of Tylor's *Primitive Culture* in 1872, Wallace proposed as a "possible solution to the problem of animism, that the uniformity of *belief* is due in great part to the uniformity of the underlying *facts*."[117] Similarly, Andrew Lang, who had been converted to anthropology by reading *Primitive Culture*, came to reject Tylor's "dream theory" of the origin of religion precisely because it did not take the sensory phenomena of dreams, visions, hallucinations, and other spiritualist phenomena seriously as facts. Lang observed in 1898, "Facts do not cease to be facts because wrong interpretations have been put on them by savages."[118] Spiritualist facts, according to Wallace and Lang, had to be investigated through methods of psychic research, or what emerged as a specialized psychology of religion. Turning from psychological facts to social facts, the sociologist Emile Durkheim eventually rejected Tylor's "dream theory" of religion on the grounds that religion could not be reduced to a system of "hallucinatory representations" with no objective foundation in human life. In his *Elementary Forms of the Religious Life*, published in 1912, Durkheim discovered that objective foundation in the order and rhythms of society.[119]

Although it was posed as a scientific explanation of the origin and development of religion, the theory of animism also addressed dilemmas in nineteenth-century European society regarding the meaning of materiality. Despite the expansion of scientific materialism, with its implicit challenge to religious belief, the séances of spiritualism were gaining popularity in Europe, promising material proof of spiritual survival of death. According to E. B. Tylor, contemporary spiritualist practices in Europe were a "survival" of primitive religion because, like the religious beliefs and practices of indigenous people on the colonized peripheries of empire, the spiritualist séance represented an unwarranted persistence in the modern world of attributing life to the dead. As a European intellectual problem, therefore, the theory of animism can be situated in the context of nineteenth-century distress about the religious implications of scientific materialism and the scientific implications of a new religious practice such as spiritualism.[120] At the same time, this theory of the animation of dead matter was developed in the midst of the consolidation of commodity capitalism in Europe and North America. The commodity, as Karl Marx provocatively proposed, was not dead matter, because it was animated by a "fetishism of commodities," similar to savage religion, which attributed life to objects "abounding in metaphysical subtleties and theological niceties."[121] While drawing evidence from remote savages on the colonized peripheries of empire, the theory of animism was entangled in European struggles to understand the materiality of spiritualism and the spirit of capitalism.

CHAPTER FIVE

Myths and Fictions

My empire is of the imagination.

AYESHA, IN *SHE*, BY H. RIDER HAGGARD

The great detective Sherlock Holmes was a scholar of religion. He had expert knowledge about Hindus and Muslims in India, observing that the "Hindu proper [had] long and thin feet," while the "sandal-wearing Mohammedan" had a big toe that was separated from the others.[1] Holmes was also familiar with the origin of primordial religion in tree worship and the development of new religious movements such as the Mormons in the American territory of Utah.[2] In solving the difficult case related by Dr. John Watson in "The Adventure of Wisteria Lodge," which first appeared in *Strand Magazine* in 1908, Holmes was left with evidence that could be explained only by understanding the beliefs and practices of savage religion. A strange object belonging to an African native from South America had been left in the home of the criminals. "The man was a primitive savage," Holmes explained, "and that was his fetish." In the kitchen of that home, investigators had found the gruesome evidence of a pail of blood, a dismembered bird, and the charred bones of an animal. To find an explanation for this evidence, Holmes spent a morning in the British Library reading the classic work on savage religion, Eckermann's *Voodooism and the Negroid Religions*. There he found an authoritative account of savage ritual sacrifice. Holmes quoted Eckermann: "The true voodoo-worshipper attempts nothing of importance without certain sacrifices which are intended to propitiate his unclean gods. In extreme cases these rites take the form of human sacrifices followed by cannibalism. The more usual victims are a white cock, which is plucked in pieces alive, or a black goat, whose throat is cut and body burned." All of these aspects of voodoo-worshipping sacrifice—the blood offering, the plucked cock, and the burned goat—had been performed by the native in the kitchen of Wisteria Lodge. "So you see," Holmes concluded, "our savage friend was very orthodox in his ritual."[3]

In this adventure from the casebook of Sherlock Holmes, we find a fictional detective, who was often mistaken by readers as real, citing a fictional text, by a fictional authority, about a fictional savage religion. This chapter explores this mystery: How do we adjudicate relations among religion, fiction, and scholarship about religion?

To explore the relations among myth, fiction, and scholarship, we will focus on the career of Andrew Lang. A prominent scholar of religion, myth, and ritual, Lang was also a *litterateur*, writing fiction that displayed the subversive strategies of irony, parody, and humor but also celebrating the mythic narratives he found in the imperial romance adventures by Robert Louis Stevenson, H. Rider Haggard, and Rudyard Kipling. In his scholarship in the fields of anthropology, religion, and literature, Lang was a serious scholar, adept at footnotes, committed to factual accuracy. For example, he criticized his friend Arthur Conan Doyle for misrepresenting Andamanese islanders as cannibals in the Sherlock Holmes novella *The Sign of Four*.[4] However, Lang's scholarship also displayed a capacity for myth-making. In his celebration of romance novels, he argued that this genre of fiction was primordial, full of the supernatural, and presently poised to revitalize a disenchanted modern society in Britain. According to Lang, "As this visible world is measured, mapped, tested, weighed, we seem to hope more and more that a world of invisible romance may not be far from us."[5] H. Rider Haggard, the best-selling author of the era, made common cause with Lang in theorizing romance novels by transforming this fictional genre into myth. In his article "About Fiction," Haggard maintained: "The love of romance is probably coeval with the existence of humanity. So far as we can follow the history of the world we find traces of it and its effects among every people, and those who are acquainted with the habits and ways of thought of savage races will know that it flourishes as strongly in the barbarian as in the cultured breast. In short, it is like the passions, an innate quality of mankind."[6] Haggard thought that the anthropologist Andrew Lang was most acquainted with the beliefs and practices of savages. Lang felt the same way about the novelist Rider Haggard. This merger of fiction and scholarship was crucial for Andrew Lang. As Robert Michalski has observed, "The popular romance, more than any other fictional form, offered Lang the same kind of encounter with the alien and the strange that he experienced in his anthropological work."[7] By analyzing the exchanges between Andrew Lang and adventure novelists, with special attention to Zulu religion in South Africa, we can see knowledge about savage religion being produced through scholarship, fiction, and imperial mythmaking.

In 1901 Andrew Lang praised the new "exotic" literature that had been produced by writers who had "at least, seen new worlds for themselves."[8] Among others, Lang was certainly thinking of his close friend H. Rider Haggard, who had both seen new worlds in South Africa and fictionalized them in his adventure novels. For his part, Haggard returned the compliment from a South African perspective by praising scholars like Lang "who collect traditions from the natives and try to make out a little piece of the history of this dark land."[9] The relation between Lang and Haggard highlights significant questions about the roles of myth, folklore, fiction, and history within nineteenth-century imperial comparative religion. In *The Savage in Literature*, Brian Street noted that the line between fiction and scholarship was often blurred in scientific theory building. "The embodiment of these theories in fictitious characters planted them more firmly in the popular mind than abstract debates by scientists could ever do," Street observed, "though the scientists themselves sometimes resorted to similar methods in order to make a point."[10] As an extraordinarily prolific author of novels, poetry, histories, biographies, literary criticism, and anthropological scholarship, Andrew Lang operated at the intersection of myths and fictions. His links to the adventure novelists Rider Haggard and John Buchan, who had both lived and worked in South Africa, further suggested that Lang also operated within the broad arena of imperialism, colonial exchanges, and popular culture. By focusing on Lang's interest in South African adventure novels, we can gain perspective on the role of comparative religion in popular imaginative literature and the place of the imagination in imperial comparative religion.

Andrew Lang (1844–1912) is included in standard histories of comparative religion for his expansive anthropological approach to myth and folklore, his commitment to the premise that high gods stood at the origin of religion, and his vigorous polemics against Max Müller's philological analysis of Aryan myth, E. B. Tylor's theory of animism, Herbert Spencer's hypothesis of original ancestor worship, and James Frazer's scheme of religious evolution.[11] Lang was actively involved in every theoretical debate in the study of religion. He described himself, however, as a "hodman of letters," indicating, with characteristic humor, the humble building trade of popular literature in which he worked. In his obituary in the London *Times* on July 22, 1912, Andrew Lang was described as "one of the most remarkable men of letters of our day."[12] He was a significant scholar, the wide range of his expertise suggested by his nearly twenty entries in the ninth edition of the *Encyclopedia of Britannica* (1875–99), which included articles on apparitions and poltergeists, ballads and mythology, and the family and totemism. His dedication to the anthropology of religion was evident in countless articles and reviews and in numerous books: *Custom and Myth* (1884), *Myth, Ritual, and Religion* (1887; revised 1899), *The Making of Religion* (1898), *Magic and Religion* (1901), *The Origins of Religion* (1908), *Social Origins* (1903), and *The Secret of the Totem* (1905). R. R. Marett recalled that one night when they were walking together at Oxford, Andrew Lang poignantly remarked, "If I could have made a living out of it, I might have been a great anthropologist!"[13] Lang's sense of humor, according to his contemporary Salomon Reinach, a French historian of religions, prevented him from being taken entirely seriously as an anthropologist. Reinach also had a sense of humor, which was evident in his definition of religion as "a sum of scruples which impede the free exercise of our faculties."[14] In a tribute to Lang, Reinach exclaimed:

> Poor Lang! He suffered from one great fault; he was too witty. Had he been a German professor, heaping up ponderous materials wrapped in obscure language, rewarding his readers by the meritorious discovery of involved truths, we should not have been told in many obituary notices, after words of praise of his poetry, novels and Greek scholarship, that he also dealt with folk-lore and mythology. All his books on mythology sold well; several of them have been translated; but there is something about them that deters the reader from taking them quite seriously. That "something" is more and worse than wit: it is a certain misuse of it. Lang was not only witty but jocular; he found it difficult to abstain from fooling, from affecting "naughtiness."[15]

While he engaged in often heated intellectual controversies with other imperial theorists of comparative religion, Lang seemed to hold greater affinity with popular adventure novelists such as H. Rider Haggard and John Buchan who were linked with South Africa. Certainly the novelists acknowledged Lang as a model and mentor. Meeting Lang in 1885, Rider Haggard praised him as "*par excellence* a *litterateur* of the highest sort, perhaps the most literary man in England or America." Rising to hyperbole, Haggard identified Lang as "the tenderest, the purest and the highest-minded of human creatures, one from whom true goodness and nobility of soul radiate in every common word or act, though often half-hidden in jest, the most perfect of gentlemen."[16] Where Haggard found human perfection,

John Buchan discovered a high god in Andrew Lang, noting that after read-ing his work in 1892, a decade before embarking upon his own career in South Africa, Lang became "the chief deity in my pantheon."[17]

For both novelists, South Africa was formative. Henry Rider Haggard (1856–1925) went to South Africa in 1875, at age nineteen, to work for the secretary for native affairs, Theophilus Shepstone. Impressed by Shepstone, Haggard identified with his strategic opposition to the Boers and his in-terest in knowing the natives, and he served in Shepstone's delegation to Pretoria for the British annexation of the Boer Republic of the Transvaal. Haggard developed a fascination with Zulu religion. While serving on the staff of Sir Henry Bulwer, he witnessed a Zulu "war dance" during a visit to the kraal of Chief Phakade, but most of the information Haggard gained about Zulu religion was derived from local experts, such as Shepstone's translator, Fred B. Fynney, who related vivid tales about the mysteries of Zulu spiritualism and the terror of Zulu religious politics.[18] Returning to England in 1881, Haggard incorporated such tales in his writing. After pub-lishing in popular magazines articles titled "The Transvaal" and "A Zulu War Dance," Haggard's first book, *Cetywayo and His White Neighbours*, ap-peared in 1882, to coincide with the British visit of the deposed Zulu king. Haggard's breakthrough as a best-selling novelist came with the publication of *King Solomon's Mines* in 1885. Reviewing the manuscript, Andrew Lang was delighted with this novel of savagery and civilization. He told Haggard that they must find the best—meaning, the most profitable—way of getting the novel published. But Lang was also enthralled by the way Haggard's novel intersected with his own anthropological interests in savage religion. Lang praised Haggard's "native gift of savagery."[19] One literary critic has re-cently observed, "Haggard was also adept in picking out and making cred-ible the mythology of such people as the Zulu, with an emphasis on magic, communication by some fashion superior to the telegraph, and fortune-telling developed to a fine art."[20] Developing a close friendship that ex-tended over many years, Lang and Haggard collaborated not only in their publications but also in imagining the nature of savage religion. They made plans to go together on a book tour of South Africa the year before Lang's death.

John Buchan (1875–1940), like Andrew Lang, was born in Scotland, in the Borders. He developed an interest in classical philosophy and literature. Influenced by his reading of Andrew Lang, Buchan was drawn to the primi-tive power of myth in human history. In his novels and his politics, Buchan advanced the myth of imperialism as a "religious faith," as a "church of empire."[21] In the aftermath of the South African War, Buchan joined the staff of Lord Alfred Milner at age twenty-seven and served in "Milner's Kindergarten" of young men overseeing reconstruction and designing the blueprint for a new Union of South Africa. In his account of that process, *The African Colony: Studies in the Reconstruction*, published in 1903, Buchan paid attention to religion, noting that political unification would require "a wide toleration for local customs and religions." He observed, "We cannot fuse the races by destroying the sacred places of one of them, but only by giving the future generations some common heritage."[22] However, since the entire project of unification was directed at whites in South Africa, this religious toleration and respect applied only to the Boers. Black South Africans, excluded from citizenship, were not included in the spirit of religious toleration that Buchan found essential for building a new South Africa. Although he generally ignored Africans in his blueprint for the imperial reconstruction of South Africa, Buchan focused on African religion in his novel *Prester John* (1910). In this adventure novel, a self-proclaimed African messiah mobilized religion, both savage and Christian, to threaten the sovereignty of whites in South Africa.[23]

In the fiction of imperial adventure, Andrew Lang found true stories of savage life. Reviewing *King Solomon's Mines* in the popular press, Lang praised the realistic accounts of savagery from an author so "intimately acquainted with the wild borders of Zululand," an author with "a most sympathetic knowledge of the Zulu." Revealing that the "Kukuanas of the tale are, in fact Zulus," he said he had found Haggard "so correct in his descriptive touches and pictures of African life."[24] Lang was not alone in using Haggard's fiction for ethnographic data. A South African respondent to *Notes and Queries* observed that, among the Zulu, "a white ox is slaughtered on declaration of war." For further detail, he advised, "*See* Rider Haggard's very accurate *Nada the Lily*."[25] But fiction had always conveyed savage truth for Lang. As he recalled in a tribute to E. B. Tylor in 1907, his early childhood interest in savages had been stimulated by the novel *The Last of the Mohicans*, by James Fenimore Cooper, whose vivid depictions of Native Americans seemed to provide reliable anthropological data.[26] The adventure novelist Rider Haggard, who apparently had an intimate familiarity with the Zulu, continued to expand Lang's data about savages, even providing evidence in novels that Lang found worthy of citing in his academic publications on myth, ritual, and religion. Not only providing data but also theorizing, novelist John Buchan underwrote imperial comparative religion by insisting on the unique position of the British for understanding other people. "We call ourselves insular," Buchan wrote in 1916, "but the truth is that we are the only race on earth that can produce men capable of getting inside the skin of remote people."[27] British scholars of religion, in particular, thought they were adept at getting inside savage skins.

What did the adventure novelists find in the comparative religion of Andrew Lang? The truth of religion, according to Lang, was its global uniformity, imaginative origin, and political character. Lang identified these features of religion among savages. But he also played with the opposition between savagery and civilization, revealing his haunting suspicion that "as man advanced in social progress, he became more deeply stained with religious cruelty."[28] As we will see, these themes in the imperial study of religion were developed at the intersection of scholarship and fiction.

GLOBAL UNITY

Andrew Lang insisted upon a global unity, a vast narrative uniformity, in the entire history of religions. Whether in Great Britain, South Africa, or anywhere else in the world, he found, "All peoples notoriously tell the same myths, fairy tales, fables and improper stories, repeat the same proverbs, are amused by the same riddles or devinettes, and practise the same, or closely analogous, religious rites and mysteries."[29] Despite the apparent diversity of religions, Lang identified the underlying uniformity, as well as recurring repetition, in the myths and rituals of the religions of the world.

What provided evidence for this global uniformity of religious narratives and practices? Like other imperial theorists, Lang relied upon reports from local experts on the colonized peripheries of empire. "Our best evidence," he held, "is from linguists who have been initiated into the secret Mysteries. Still more will missionaries and scholars like Bleek, Hahn, Codrington, Castren, Gill, Callaway, Theal, and the rest, sift and compare the evidence of the most trustworthy native informants." Of these seven local experts cited by Lang, four worked in South Africa, suggesting the importance of evidence from that region for theory building in imperial comparative religion. In Lang's method, reports from Robert Henry Codrington in Melanesia, Matthias Alexander Castrén among the Finns, and William Wyatt Gill among the Mangaia in the South Pacific had to be compared with the reports of other local experts, including Wilhelm Bleek, Theophilus Hahn, Henry Callaway, and George McCall Theal in South Africa. According to Lang, the narrative unity of religion was revealed only when such evidence was tested by cross-checking accounts from other regions of the world. In testing the reliability of data, Lang asked, "Does Bleek's report from the Bushmen and Hottentots confirm Castren's from the Finns? Does Codrington in Melanesia tell the same tale as Gill in Mangaia or Theal among the Kaffirs?" Evidence was validated if it was confirmed, not by additional reports from the same region, but by reports from widely divergent areas of the globe. If local experts in different regions told the same stories, Lang concluded, "then we may presume that the inquirers have managed to extract true accounts from some of their native informants."[30] Lang's method of verification required correlating, comparing, and contrasting local reports within a global framework.

Local experts did not always cooperate with such an imperial plan. Wilhelm Bleek and Henry Callaway in South Africa both enabled and undermined the theoretical work of Friedrich Max Müller: they enabled his work by providing data but undermined it by developing contradicting theory and explanation. R. H. Codrington (1830–1922), one of the experts praised by Lang for being "initiated into the secret Mysteries," was busy undermining the theories of E. B. Tylor and James Frazer. In his local reports from Melanesia, Codrington found among the natives no evidence of animism based on dreams or visions, no evidence of any "belief in a spirit which animates any natural object," and no evidence of a primitive inability to "distinguish between animate and inanimate things."[31] As for totemism, in response to questions posed by Frazer in 1888, Codrington reported that among the Melanesians he had found no evidence of "any real *totem*."[32] Instead, Codrington wrote to Max Müller in 1877, "The religion of the Melanesians consists, as far as belief goes, in the persuasion that there is a supernatural power belonging to the region of the unseen, and, as far as practice goes, in the use of means of getting this power turned to their own benefit."[33] Revolving around the term *mana*, a supernatural power inspiring awe, which was engaged by rituals of prayer and sacrifice, Melanesian religion as reported by Codrington did not conform to the underlying unity of religion represented by either Tylor's animism or Frazer's totemism.

In assessing ambiguous accounts in Callaway's *Religious System of the Amazulu*, Lang reiterated this principle of cross-checking reports from all over the world. Although he found Callaway "honest but confused," Lang nevertheless invoked him as an important source for establishing not only the validity of religious data but also the uniformity of religion.[34] In 1894 Callaway featured prominently in Lang's reflections on twenty years of controversy between philological and anthropological methods in the academic study of religion. Lang recalled,

When Anthropology first challenged the interpretations of myths given by Philologists, we were told that Anthropology relied on mere travellers' tales. It was answered that the coincidence of report, in all ages and countries, and from all manner of independent observers, unaware of each other's existence, was a strong proof of general accuracy, while the statements of learned and scholarly men, like Codrington, Callaway, and many others, confirmed the strange stories of travelers like Herodotus, of missionaries, traders, and adventurers.[35]

As we will see, the inherent ambiguity in Callaway's *Religious System* did not stop Lang from using this Zulu evidence to reinforce his theories of both primitive theism and primitive spiritualism.

In adopting Lang's notion of the global uniformity of all religious narratives, adventure novelists could also relate the same stories. Haggard's hero put it this way in the novel *She*, which was dedicated to Andrew Lang: "All great Faiths are the same, changed a little to suit the needs of passing times and people."[36] However, Haggard's fictional constructions of indigenous religions in Africa were underwritten by his anthropological understanding of the human imagination of nature and fear of death.

In *Allan Quatermain* (1887), Haggard's imaginary Zu-Vendis, roughly based on the Zulu, are ruled by a high priest, Agon, who learns from his encounter with the British intruders into his domain that the British have as many as ninety-five different religions. The Zu-Vendis subscribe to only one natural religion, the worship of the sun. "As regards their religion," the hero Allan Quatermain reports, "it is a natural one for imaginative people who know no better, and might therefore be expected to turn to the sun and worship him as the all-Father." Here Haggard seems to be providing an ethnographic report, which could be cross-checked with other reports, confirming Lang's theory of primitive monotheism, which found the origin of religion in the natural intuition of a supreme being. But this indigenous religion of the Zu-Vendis remained a savage religion, which could not "be justly called elevating or spiritual," even though it provided another example of what Lang called the worship of "savage supreme beings." Although the Zu-Vendi spoke of the sun as "the garment of the spirit," Quatermain suspects that "What they really adore is the fiery orb himself." Accordingly, he concludes, "I cannot say that I consider this sun-worship as a religion indicative of a civilised people, however magnificent and imposing its ritual."[37]

During the same year this novel was published, Haggard gave a lecture in Edinburgh on the Zulu. Here he provided an outline of indigenous Zulu religion that emphasized the importance of supreme beings, the Almighty uNkulunkulu and the Queen of Heaven, Inkosana-y-Zulu:

They believe in a God, the Unkulunkulu—the Almighty, the Greatest Great, he is the Creator, the Source of all life. The Zulu mind does not indeed venture to define the Deity, or to measure his attributes. To them he is a force, vague, immeasurable, pressing round them as air, and as the air impalpable, and as the air all-present. They believe, too, in guardian spirits who watch over the individual, interposing at times to ward off danger from him. In the same way the nation has a guardian angel, Inkosana-y-Zulu, the Queen of Heaven, who, in the form of a young and lovely woman, appears at moments of national importance and makes a communication to some chosen person.[38]

"Strangely," as his daughter, Lilias Rider Haggard noted in her biography of her father, the Zulu imagined the Queen of Heaven as "a white woman, a fact H.R.H. used in many tales," most powerfully in his creation of Ayesha, She-Who-Must-Be-Obeyed.[39] The white goddess worshipped by the Zulu was a powerful trope for imperial fiction and politics in the empire of Queen Victoria.[40]

Haggard's novel *She* (1887) focused on the royal priestess Ayesha, who exercised imperial power from the Caves of Kôr, but it also engaged questions of religion, as the narrator and hero Horace Holly asked, "What was her real religion?" Holly tells Ayesha about his religion, based on the teachings of the "Hebrew Messiah." In this interchange, the colonial encounter is rendered as an opposition between alternative ways of life. "Ah!, she said; I see—two religions." Despite this opposition, Haggard maintained an underlying unity of all religions by tracing the production of religions to the fear of death. Their discussions of religion in the realm of Ayesha followed a trend, according to Holly, which was familiar to him from debates about the origin of religion in nineteenth-century Britain. The human tendency to fear death and cling to life, we learn, "breeds religions."[41] Religion, therefore, is not merely an imaginative engagement with nature; it is also fear and even terror of the unknown.

As unifying factors in savage religion, awe, fear, and even terror were considered by Andrew Lang. In an early essay, "Fetichism and the Infinite," Lang argued that religion could not be confined to beliefs in spiritual beings or feelings of the infinite, because it arose out of "a development of ideas of Force," which human beings engaged through an "interested search" for ways to harness "something practically *strong* for good or evil."[42] Accordingly, the underlying unity of religion might be found in dramatic conflicts between forces of good and evil.

John Buchan's novel *Prester John* was centered on savage terror, while also evoking a civilized terror of savagery, as exemplified by the Zulu

Christian messiah John Laputa, who was organizing an African revolt against European rule in South Africa. In this novel, the problem was not finding religious unity but fighting religious syncretism represented by Laputa's "Ethiopianism," which Buchan identified as "a kind of bastard Christianity" that mixed up "Christian emotion and pagan practice."[43] The problem in *Prester John* was not an opposition between two religions, as in Haggard's *She*, but an illicit merger of two religions. How did this aversion to religious syncretism, this contempt for the illicit mixing of Christian and pagan religions, fit with Lang's notion of the underlying unity of all religions? If all religions were the same, their mixing should not pose any problem. Celebrating James Fenimore Cooper's Mohicans or Rider Haggard's Zulus, Lang had embraced the underlying, unifying savagery of all human civilization. Buchan's idea of religious unity, however, had been thoroughly racialized by his experience in South Africa, so that his "wide toleration for local customs and religions" applied only to white people in the unity of the British Empire.[44] As a racialized purity, religious unity assumed a different character for John Buchan in early-twentieth-century South Africa.

As a unifying undercurrent in human civilization, the very notion of savage religion was ambivalent, sometimes invoked as a shared beginning, sometimes as a stark opposition. For the study of religion, this savage ambiguity was crucial. On the one hand, Andrew Lang and E. B. Tylor, despite their theoretical differences, could always find common cause in looking to savages for evidence of the shared origin of humanity. Conflicting in prose, these imperial theorists could collaborate in poetry; Lang and Tylor together wrote verses for "The Double Ballade of Primitive Man," concluding with the lines: "Theologians all to expose,—/'Tis the MISSION of Primitive Man."[45] Therefore, the academic study of religion, by basing its scientific findings on reports about savages, was unified against Christian theology in its efforts to understand religion. On the other hand, theology persisted as a crucial religious reference point in these scientific efforts. In publishing "The Double Ballade of Primitive Man," Andrew Lang dedicated its satirical poetry to James Anson Farrer (1849–1925), who in 1879 had written in *Primitive Manners and Customs* that all theology went through three developmental stages. Its primitive origins and civilized decadence were harmless, but its middle stage of full flowering was "abominable and cruel." As an illustration of this middle stage of theology, Farrer cited the British Christian missions that had been "forced" upon the Zulu king Cetshwayo, charging that the missionaries were imperial agents and colonial spies working against the Zulu kingdom.[46] While unifying against theology, imperial scientists also had to recognize the importance of the interventions as well as the syncretisms that had resulted from Christian missions.

While presenting fictional accounts of African indigenous religion, the adventure novelists mediated between Africa and the center of empire by rendering colonial relations in highly charged terms that raised problems about religion, religions, and religious difference. For Haggard and Buchan, as well as for Lang, different religions could not be organized into a system of classification, such as the system of eight text-based religions of the world devised by Max Müller, under the slogan "classify and conquer," as a formula for a science of religion.[47] Nor were they interested only in reducing all religious diversity to one primitive principle of origin, such as E. B. Tylor's theory of animism, which remained the core of all "savage" religion and persisted in unwarranted "survivals" of primitive superstition in the religious beliefs and practices of advanced civilizations.[48] Instead, Lang and the novelists created a vast narrative uniformity of religion out of colonial reports, whether factual or fictional, in which all religions were essentially the same. Although different religions might be identified, and reporters might distinguish between two religions or multitudes of religions, Lang, Haggard, and Buchan collaborated in reinforcing what the cultural analyst Jeremy Stolow has called "the fiction of a unitary and integral world of religious others."[49] Essentially, all savage religions were the same when compared to civilization.

IMAGINATIVE ORIGINS

Asserting the global unity of religion, myth, and ritual, Andrew Lang argued that it resulted not from intercultural borrowings or historical diffusion but from the creative power of the human imagination. In his 1873 essay "Mythology and Fairy Tales," Lang began his attack against Max Müller's philological exegesis of Aryan myth by arguing, "There are necessary forms of the imagination, which in widely separated peoples must produce identical results." Similar mental and social conditions, he proposed, generated forms of imagination that produced the same narratives and practices. Clearly, Lang drew upon a long history of nineteenth-century romantic theorizing about the creative power of imagination and fancy. On the basis of this romantic legacy, he argued against Max Müller's own romantic account of the linguistic origin of myth by insisting, "The Aryan and the lower races have had to pass through similar conditions of imagination and of society, and therefore of religion."[50] In 1884 he reasserted this conviction that myths were produced by human beings "in similar mental conditions of ignorance, curiosity, and credulous fancy."[51] However, Lang's model for the credulous and creative imagination also drew extensively upon reports about the myths and rituals of the Zulu of South Africa, who demonstrated the "necessary forms of imagination" that had originally produced religion. According to Lang, Henry Callaway's Zulu informants had successfully refuted the theories of the origin of religion that had been advanced by Friedrich Max Müller and Herbert Spencer, as if these "primitives" had embarked on a mission to expose not only Christian theologians but also imperial theorists of religion.

With respect to Vedic myth, Max Müller's special province and privileged case for analyzing the linguistic origin of religion, Lang asserted in 1873 that Callaway's reports from South Africa proved that it was "plain that these [Vedic] tales [went] back to the time when our Aryan forefathers were in the mental condition of Dr. Callaway's [African] instructor in the Zulu language," the Christian convert and later deacon Mpengula Mbande.[52] Lang implied that the religion of ancient India could be better understood by analyzing the "mental condition" of Mbande than by explicating Sanskrit etymology. Max Müller's philological approach to the study of religion, which traced the origin of mythology to a breakdown in language, a primitive "disease of language" in mistaking metaphors for deities, confusing *nomina* for *numina*, was persistently critiqued by Lang, who has often been credited with demolishing this philological method in the anthropological study of religion, myth, and ritual. Invoking the Zulu in support of this ongoing critique of Max Müller, Lang observed in *Myth, Ritual, and Religion* that when Zulu ritual specialists in rainmaking, who were known as "heaven-herds," looked to the skies, they were not confusing poetic metaphors with numinous beings. They were literally herding clouds. According to Lang, "The Zulus conceive of the thunder-clouds and lightning as actual creatures, capable of being herded like sheep. There is no metaphor or allegory about the matter, and no forgetfulness of the original meaning of words. The cloud-herd is just like the cow-herd."[53]

As for Herbert Spencer's theory that religion originated in ancestor worship, Lang found, "That inquiring race, the Zulus, are as subversive of the fancy of Mr. Spencer as of the early orthodoxy of Bishop Colenso."[54] As noted, Lang realized that the Zulu evidence collected by Callaway was ambiguous. When asked about the meaning of the term *uNkulunkulu*, which had been adopted by Bishop Colenso to signify the Christian God, Zulu informants gave many different answers, rendering uNkulunkulu as the first ancestor of a particular political grouping, as the first ancestor of all humanity, or as a supreme being. Accordingly, Lang admitted, "The truth is that both the anthropological theory (spirits first, Gods last), and our theory (Supreme Being first, spirits next) can find warrant in Dr. Callaway's valuable collections." Lang realized that the dispute over the originating impetus of ideas of supreme beings or spirits could not be "settled by the ambiguous case of the Zulus alone" but "must be solved after a survey of the whole field of savage and barbaric religion."[55] Nevertheless, he continued to deploy the ambiguous case of the Zulu to support his theory of an original intuition of supreme beings and an enduring intuition of spirits.

In his Gifford Lectures of 1888, which were published in substantially revised form as *The Making of Religion* ten years later, Lang focused on these two originating features of religious imagination, belief in supreme beings and interaction with supernatural spirits.

According to Lang, from the beginning, as shown among the "lowest savages," human beings had developed the notion of a supreme being who was eternal, moral, and powerful. Referring to a Bushman interpretation of South African rock art published in 1874 in the *Cape Monthly Magazine*,[56] Lang found that Cagn, who had been thought to be a revered insect invoked in hunting magic, or a glorified medicine-man celebrated in myth, was actually a supreme being. A Bushman by the name of Qing, who "had never before seen a white man except fighting," suggested that Cagn was regarded as a heavenly being, existing before the Sun, the maker of all things, who was addressed through prayers but did not receive offerings in sacrificial ritual. In this account, Cagn appeared as an eternal and powerful being but also as a moral being, with the Bushman Qing's qualification that this supreme being's ethics had been diminished by conflict. "At first Cagn was very good," Qing related, "but he got spoilt through fighting so many things." Ignoring these implicit references to colonial conflict—Qing fighting white men, Cagn fighting many things—Lang concluded that Cagn was originally a savage supreme being, a "deity of a rather lofty moral conception," who did not "need . . . [to] be propitiated by human sacrifices or cold chickens."[57] Lang's analysis of the Bushman Cagn who did not require or receive sacrificial offerings was central to his distinction between elevated supreme beings—remote and lofty, eternal, moral, and powerful—and spirits, who were closer to human beings because they were "bribable" through offerings.

In his reading of the "honest, but confused" evidence about Zulu religion supplied by Henry Callaway, Lang also distinguished between the idea of a lofty supreme being, who was not worshipped through offerings, and ancestral spirits who received such material exchanges in the hope of practical benefit. According to Lang, the fact that uNkulunkulu "was not worshipped" was no proof that he had not originally been an eternal, moral, and powerful supreme being. Despite the conflicting testimony in *Religious System*, Lang argued that we might still discern the notion of a God, even though that "heavenly King" had been overtaken by a more immediate and more recent interest in ancestral spirits. In a remarkable summary of Zulu religion, Lang brought the evidence into line with his theory—supreme being first, spirits next:

> On this examination of the evidence, it certainly seems as logical to conjecture that the Zulus had once such an idea of a Supreme Being as lower races entertain, and then nearly lost it; as to say that Zulus, though a monarchical race, have not yet developed a King-God out of the throng of spirits (Amatongo). The Zulus, the Norsemen of the South, so to speak, are a highly practical military race. A Deity at all abstract was not to their liking. Serviceable family spirits, who continually provided an excuse for a dinner of roast beef, were to their liking. The less developed races do not kill their flocks commonly for food. A sacrifice is needed as a pretext. To the gods of Andamanese, Bushmen, Australians, no sacrifice is offered. To the Supreme Being of most African peoples no sacrifice is offered. There is no festivity in the worship of these Supreme Beings, no feasting, at all events. They are not to be "got at" by gifts or sacrifices. The Amatongo are to be "got at," are bribable, supply an excuse for a good dinner, and thus the practical Amatongo are honoured, while, in the present generation of Zulus, Unkulunkulu is a joke, and the Lord in Heaven is the shadow of a name. Clearly this does not point to the recent but to the remote development of the higher ideas, now superseded by spirit-worship.[58]

According to this rendering of Zulu religious history, uNkulunkulu was originally a supreme being. Certainly Lang could find testimony to this effect in Callaway's *Religious System*. For example, an old woman interviewed by Mpengula Mbande recounted that uNkulunkulu was "the Creator, who is in heaven, of whom the ancients spoke," but then damaged her testimony, as Lang noted, when she "began to babble humourously of how the white men made all things."[59] Undeterred by such colonial confusion, Lang outlined a conjectural history of Zulu religion in which uNkulunkulu, as a remote or abstract supreme being, had been turned into a joke because the martial Zulu needed more immediate gratification of their needs in war and peace. Accordingly, they had turned to ancestral spirits, who could be bribed with gifts, sacrifices, and a good dinner, in developing religious beliefs and practices to serve these more practical interests.

Rider Haggard knew he was intervening in the problematic production of knowledge about indigenous Zulu religion. In his preface to *Nada the Lily* (1892), which was dedicated to Theophilus Shepstone (1817-1893), Haggard observed that the Zulu accounts of uNkulunkulu collected in Henry Callaway's *Religious System of the Amazulu* were ambivalent, since his "character seems to vary from the idea of an ancestral spirit, or the spirit of an ancestor, to that of a god."[60] In this recognition that Callaway's evidence was "honest, but confused," Haggard might have been more perceptive than the imperial theorists Max Müller, E. B. Tylor, or even Andrew Lang about the fluid and contested negotiations over the meaning and force of this religious term *uNkulunkulu* on a violent colonial frontier in South Africa. However, as a novelist, Haggard could make his choice among these different options for dramatic effect. In *Nada the Lily*, he decided that his character the Zulu Mopo would understand uNkulunkulu as God. In this decision, which was perhaps no more arbitrary than the decisions made on this particular question by the metropolitan theorists Max Müller, Tylor, or Lang, the novelist also made a theoretical intervention in the study of religion. "In the case of an able and highly intelligent person like the Mopo of this story," he argued, "the ideal would probably not be a low one, therefore he is made to speak of Umkulunkulu [*sic*] as the Great Spirit, or God."[61] Opting for this lofty understanding of uNkulunkulu, Haggard related how Mopo prayed to the spirits of his ancestors but also "dared to pray to the Umkulunkulu, the great soul of the world, who moves through the heavens and the earth unseen."[62] This supreme being drew out the "great pattern" of fate with his own hand, Mopo explained. "[Human lives] are but a little bit of the pattern, which is so big that only the eyes of Him who is above, the Umkulunkulu, can see it all."[63] In making this fictional choice to render uNkulunkulu as God, Haggard implicitly sided with Lang's theory of an original supreme being—supreme being first, spirits next—against any competing evolutionary scheme that saw religious development proceeding from beliefs in spirits, through polytheism, to a supreme being.

By contrast, in *Prester John* the novelist John Buchan made the opposite choice by rendering uNkulunkulu as the original Zulu ancestor, asserting that the Zulu "worshipped a great Power who had been their ancestor, and the favourite Zulu word for him was Umkulunkulu." Although Zulu religious belief had changed over time, being "perverted into fifty different forms," this adherence to an original ancestor remained their central creed—that "Umkulunkulu had been the father of the tribe, and was alive as a spirit to watch over them."[64] The spirit of the original ancestor was embodied in a great snake, which Buchan described as the fetish, totem, and most sacred possession of the Zulu. Although he was an educated Christian and charismatic preacher, the Zulu messiah John Laputa ultimately drew his power from possessing this most sacred object, the necklace of the great snake, which allowed him to "assume the collar of Umkulunkulu in the name of our God and the spirits of the great dead."[65] Adventure novelists, therefore, could adopt different positions in the theoretical controversy over the origin of religion: Haggard subscribed to the formulation "Supreme Being first, spirits next," while Buchan found spirits first, God last.

Although savage supreme beings were important in Lang's theoretical work on the origin of religion, spirits also featured prominently. As a founding member of the Society for Psychical Research, Lang was interested in examining contemporary evidence of clairvoyance, telepathy, and other psychic phenomena. Describing himself at one point as a "psycho-folklorist," Lang was fascinated with the modern spiritualist séance as an ethnographic site and noted that his interest in a famous medium such as Leonora E. Piper, who had been verified as legitimate in a report of the society, was purely anthropological.[66] Challenged at the Savile Club by an academic colleague, Edward Clodd, with the verse "The devils also believe and tremble" from the Bible (James 2:19), Lang playfully confessed, "I don't believe, but I tremble."[67] Certainly Lang was not alone in this anthropological interest in spiritualism, although he does not seem to have become an adherent, as did Alfred Russel Wallace, Darwin's competitor in the development of evolutionary theory.[68] While commending E. B. Tylor for his fieldwork in actually attending séances, Lang pursued his own research on spiritualism by textual analysis.[69]

In *The Making of Religion*, he embarked upon a textual investigation of spiritualist phenomena by drawing upon the Zulu expression "opening the gates of distance," which he found in Callaway's *Religious System of the Amazulu* and used for the title of his chapter on spiritualism. Lang explained, "'To open the Gates of Distance' is the poetical Zulu phrase for what is called clairvoyance, or *vue à distance*. This, if it exists, is the result of a faculty of undetermined nature, whereby knowledge of remote events may be acquired, not through normal channels of sense. As the Zulus say: 'Isiyezi is a state in which a man becomes slightly insensible. He is awake, but still sees things which he would not see if he were not in a state of ecstasy (nasiyesi).'"[70] In addition to this account from Callaway, Lang also found the phrase "opening the gates of distance" in a chapter titled "Zulu Spiritualism" that appeared in David Leslie's *Among the Zulus*, published in

1875. Here the white hunter related how a Zulu ritual specialist had learned the fates of missing African assistants by lighting fires, ingesting an herb, and "opening the gates of distance."[71] But Lang's textual evidence also included the novels of Rider Haggard. In his earliest anthropological writings, Lang had drawn evidence from the novelist James Fenimore Cooper, whose *Last of the Mohicans* provided such vivid and compelling details of Native American life. Here he cited Haggard as providing anthropological data: " 'I am one of those,' says the Zulu medicine-man in Mr. Rider Haggard's *Allan's Wife* (1889), 'who can make men see what they do not see.' " The full passage from Haggard's novel finds the diviner Indaba-zimbi placing this Zulu psychic capacity in opposition to European knowledge: "You white people are very clever, but you don't quite know everything," the diviner asserts. "There are men in the world who can make people believe they see things which they do not see."[72] Although Haggard's hero Allan Quatermain was content to explain this phenomenon as mesmerism, Andrew Lang cited the psychic power of this fictional Zulu diviner as anthropological data, concluding, "[The] class of persons who are said to have possessed this power appear, now and then, in all human history, and have at least bequeathed to us a puzzle in anthropology."[73] For Lang, therefore, Haggard's fictional Zulu diviner was emblematic of the kind of evidence that savages could provide in posing and solving problems of anthropological theory.

As a close reader of Haggard's novels, Lang knew that the phrase "opening the gates of distance" appeared in *Nada the Lily* not only to refer to clairvoyance but also to represent the power of storytelling that "opened the gates of distance."[74] Haggard used the phrase throughout his career to refer to extraordinary psychic power. In a 1921 reprise of characters that had appeared in his earliest novels, She explained to Allan Quatermain that the mind can know all things "when the breath of vision or the fury of a soul distraught blows away the veils or burns through the gates of distance."[75] But he also linked the "gates of distance" with death, as when a wizard "opened the gates of Distance" to send a character "down among the dwellers of Death," or when a Dutch family found that "the hand of approaching Doom had opened the gates of Distance."[76] Zulu spiritualism, therefore, brought together the reality of death, the capacity of the mind, and the power of fiction for "opening the gates of distance" in exploring the unseen dimensions of the spiritual world.

John Buchan built his novel *Prester John* around Zulu spiritualism. But he emphasized spiritual conflict in the struggle between the spirit of African rebellion and the spirit of British technology, military superiority, and entitlement to the material as well as the spiritual resources of Africa. Recognizing the native ability for opening the gates of distance, the school teacher and linguist Wardlaw observed, "They are cunning fellows, and have arts that we know nothing about. You have heard of native telepathy. They can send news over a thousand miles as quick as the telegraph, and we have no means of tapping the wires."⁷⁷ Fearing that this "native telepathy" could be used in a native insurrection, the British nevertheless were confident that on the battlefield their technology would prevail. "We can't match their telepathy," Captain Arcoll observed, going into battle, "but the new type of field telegraph is not so bad, and may be a trifle more reliable."⁷⁸ The hero of the novel, the shopkeeper David Crawfurd, emerged victorious after the death of John Laputa, not only by gaining a fortune in gold and diamonds, but also by stopping the conflict when he convinced the natives that he was a medium for the spirit of the Zulu messiah:

> Your king is dead. He was a great king, as I who stand here bear witness, and you will never more see his like. His last words were that the Rising was over. Respect that word, my brothers. We come to you not in war but in peace, to offer a free pardon, and the redress of your wrongs. If you fight you fight with the certainty of failure, and against the wish of the heir of John. I have come here at the risk of my life to tell you his commands. His spirit approves my mission. Think well before you defy the mandate of the Snake, and risk the vengeance of the Terrible Ones.⁷⁹

By asserting himself as heir to both the material riches and spiritual authority of this great African king, the hero of Buchan's novel enacted a British imperial fantasy. The British were like Lang's supreme beings, eternal, moral, and powerful, but those features of divinity had to be locally demonstrated not only by the moral exhortations of respect, peace, and redress of wrongs but also by the spiritual appropriation of indigenous religion.

Wilhelm Bleek, in his philological research in South Africa, had distinguished between two kinds of religion, a sidereal religion of worshipping the sun, moon, and stars and an ancestral religion of venerating the spirits of the deceased. Adventure novelists appropriated both sidereal and ancestral religion. In a crucial incident in Haggard's *King Solomon's Mines*, the hero Allan Quatermain defeated the natives during a solar eclipse by claiming to be from the sky. "We come from another world," he declared, "with an imperial smile," having descended to earth "from the biggest star that shines at night."⁸⁰ Although human, these Europeans drew their power from their heavenly place of origin. As E. B. Tylor had observed in *Primitive*

Culture, such eclipse myths were common in savage religion, arising from the superstitious awe experienced by savages under the sun and the moon. In *Prester John*, the hero David Crawfurd drew his power from the original Zulu ancestor, uNkulunkulu, as embodied in the Zulu messiah whose spirit approved his mission. In *Primitive Culture*, E. B. Tylor had noted this savage tendency to regard Europeans as their ancestors, observing that black people, beholding the white man's "pallid deathly hue combined with powers that seem[ed] those of superhuman spiritual beings, [had] determined that the manes of their dead must have come back in this wondrous shape."[81] Within imperial comparative religion, therefore, the science of myth and the art of fiction were finding common cause in representing African religion.

In Lang's analysis, spiritualism was a distinctively material medium, causing people to see what they do not ordinarily see by means of a range of sensory and material phenomena—the movement of objects, levitation, the disappearance and reappearance of objects, the passage of matter through matter, a variety of sounds, scents, and lights, of hands touched, of objects "materialized."[82] Seeing and hearing spirits, therefore, was materially embodied. Spiritualism registered in material effects. Within the changing material conditions of colonial South Africa, the Zulu were finding difficulty in seeing, hearing, and entering into exchanges with ancestral spirits. As the ritual specialist Mkando observed in 1902, speaking of recent times, "We do not see *amadhlozi*; we do not know where they have gone to; they left us with death. And we have no cattle to kill for them as, according to our beliefs, we ought to do."[83] Here also spirituality registered in material terms, not as a means of access to a spirit world but as a measure of alienation. While imperial theorists and novelists might dispute whether gods or spirits, the sky or ancestors, came first in the evolution of religion, colonial situations were creating new terms and conditions for Zulu religious life in South Africa.

POLITICAL POWER

Since Andrew Lang was concerned with not only the mental but also the social conditions of myth and ritual, he developed an analysis of primitive politics in which he found that religion was politicized and politics was inevitably enveloped in a religious aura. Here again, reports about the Zulu religious polity served as Lang's model. Noting that the "social and political condition of the Zulu [was] well understood," he related that the Zulu society was based on herding and farming, with a "centralized government and a large army, somewhat on the German system." With no formally organized priesthood, Zulu society was nevertheless governed by a kind of sacerdotal politics in which "supernatural power [was] owned by the chiefs and the king, and by diviners and sorcerers."[84] Lang discerned a symbiotic relationship between chiefs and diviners in Zulu politics, with diviners supporting chiefs and chiefs authenticating diviners, sometimes by assuming their supernatural powers. "Among the Zulus," he noted, "we have seen that sorcery gives the sanction to the power of the chief."[85] Because chiefs needed to be consecrated by ritual specialists, the "political power of the diviners [was] very great."[86] In this respect, the religious resources of ritual specialists, of priests, diviners, or sorcerers, supported political authority. At the same time, political power itself carried a sacred aura. The chief derived sacred power from diviners but also exercised sacred power over diviners, including the ultimate power to have them executed. Political and religious power merged, as Lang recounted: "When the chief, as among the Zulus, absorbs supernatural power, then the same man becomes diviner and chief, and is a person of great and sacred influence."[87] Absorbing power that is simultaneously political and religious, the chief becomes ruler, "medicine-man," and "lord of the air."[88]

This symbiosis between political ruler and ritual specialist was emphasized by Rider Haggard in his report on South Africa titled *Cetywayo and His White Neighbours*, published in 1882. The Zulu *sangoma* or *isanusi* was rendered by Haggard, as in most colonial reports, as "witch-doctor." Regarding witch doctors, Haggard explained, "[They] are largely employed in Zululand to smell out witches who are supposed to have bewitched others, and are of course very useful as political agents. Any person denounced by them is at once executed." Haggard recounts how a friend told him about attending a "political smelling-out." According to his friend, the translator Fred Fynney, this horrifying event featured thousands of Zulu men sitting in a circle while the "witch-doctors" exclaimed wild incantations and singled out some unfortunate fellow to be led away for immediate execution. "These instances will show how dark and terrible is the Zulu superstition connected with witchcraft, and what a formidable weapon it becomes in the hands of the king or chief."[89]

Zulu religion, therefore, was a kind of political terror exercised by diviners and chiefs against internal enemies. According to Haggard, this terror was the sacred center of Zulu religion. "Even a Zulu," he observed, "must have some object in life, some shrine at which to worship." That "shrine," according to Haggard, was built on the "political smelling-out" of human sacrifice, since Zulu "religion," he insisted, was embodied in "the fierce denunciation of the *isanusi*" that underwrote the political power of chiefs.[90] Here Haggard was echoing a constant theme in Secretary for Native Affairs Theophilus Shepstone's depiction of Zulu religious politics. Working together, chiefs and diviners allegedly eliminated political rivals by exposing them as witches. Once exposed, the person identified as a witch, an *abatakathi*, a disruptive, antisocial agent, was subject to confiscation of property, banishment, and in some cases execution. As Shepstone submitted in 1863, the practice of identifying witches was a "political engine" to "overthrow the most powerful subject."[91] In 1881 he observed, "If the chief fears a strong member of his tribe, it is only necessary for him to induce the witchdoctor to point him out publicly as guilty of witchcraft to accomplish his ruin."[92] Consistently, Shepstone pointed to witch detection as the "political engine" of Zulu religious politics, the driving force that ensured loyalty by eliminating competition. "Take away the engine," he observed in 1892, "and nothing will be left to lean upon but the power of government."[93] By outlawing witch detection, Shepstone and other colonial administrators imagined that the power of chiefs and diviners would be weakened to such an extent that only the power of colonial government would remain.

Chiefs and diviners conspired not only in eliminating internal rivals but also in fighting external enemies. The Zulu object in life, Haggard claimed, was war, since their "affections were fixed on the sudden rush of battle, the red slaughter, and the spoils of the slain."[94] In support of this assertion, Haggard cited the authority of Theophilus Shepstone, who wrote just before the Anglo-Zulu War, "[Warfare] is the universal cry among the [Zulu] soldiers, who are anxious to live up to their traditions."[95] Zulu martial traditions, Haggard reported, were reinforced by the collective religious ritual of the "war dance." In one of his earliest publications, "A Zulu War Dance," which appeared in 1877 in the popular periodical *Gentleman's Magazine*, Haggard provided an account of such a ritual event that he witnessed at the homestead of Chief Phakade. This "powerful chief," as Haggard certainly realized, was not necessarily representative of Zulu religious politics, since he had fled the Zulu kingdom decades earlier to live under the authority of the secretary for native affairs and "under the protection of the Crown." Phakade (d. 1880) had come to terms with the changing religious and political terrain. During a meeting with Theophilus Shepstone and John William Colenso in 1854, Phakade had listened patiently to Colenso's account of uNkulunkulu, learning that the British apparently used this Zulu term for their God across the seas in England. When he was asked if he had any questions about uNkulunkulu, Phakade responded, "How do you make gunpowder?"[96] More than twenty years later, Chief Phakade convened the war dance for Shepstone and other government officials that Rider Haggard described for a British audience.

As the ceremony began, a woman approached, one like Macbeth's "weird sisters," rushing around in front of the "little group of white men," addressing them in frantic, spasmodic words that Haggard could not understand. But he nevertheless thought he could convey the spirit: "Ou, ou, ou, ai, ai, ai. Oh, ye warriors that shall dance before the great ones of the earth, come! Oh, ye dyers of spears, ye plumed suckers of blood, come! I, the Isanusi, I, the witch-finder, I, the wise woman, I, the seer of strange sights, I, the reader of dark thoughts, call ye! Come, ye fierce ones; come, ye brave ones, come, and do honour to the white lords! Ah, I hear ye! Ah, I smell ye! Ah, I see ye; ye come, ye come!"[97] This ecstatic performance by a wild woman, calling upon the assembly to honor the "white lords," was followed by the appearance of a young man, "arrayed in the full panoply of savage war." This warrior also addressed the group of white officials, singling out Shepstone for special praise as "father of Chiefs, son of the great Queen over the water." Following these opening speeches, five hundred warriors approached, intoning their "war-cry, a paean of power," which built into the hissing of ten thousand snakes, as they charged back and forth, as if entering battle, as if killing and being killed. As this "mimic" of war continued, individual warriors came forward to fight invisible foes. The ceremony concluded with the "royal war-salute of the Zulus," which Haggard noted was rarely heard.[98]

After the dance, Chief Phakade joined the government officials to take Shepstone's hand and address him as Sompseu, his Zulu title, which could be translated as "Father of Whiteness," but he also praised the secretary for native affairs as "holder of the Spirit of Chaka." Shepstone had earned that title during the coronation of the Zulu king Cetshwayo (1826–1884) in 1873, when he assumed the "mantle of Shaka" in presiding over the official enthronement ceremony. Although that official ceremony had been preceded by Zulu rituals, the colonial administration assumed that the Zulu king had been enthroned by the authority of both the original Zulu monarch, as embodied by Shepstone, and the prevailing colonial government. "I came as Chaka," Shepstone recounted, "I was commissioned by the Zulus, and by the Government that was superior to the Zulus."[99] On the colonized peripheries of empire, as the historian Terrence Ranger has observed, "the 'theology' of an omniscient, omnipotent and omnipresent monarchy [was] almost the sole ingredient of imperial ideology as it was represented to Africans."[100] Shepstone's appropriation of the sacred aura of the Zulu king Shaka, claiming indigenous religious resources, was the colonial side of this imperial theology of absolute sovereignty.

By the time Haggard accompanied Shepstone to witness Chief Phakade's war dance, colonial interests and imperial ambitions were conspiring against King Cetshwayo. Contributing to the propaganda against the Zulu king, Haggard observed that he had been fortunate to attend Phakade's ceremony instead of one of Cetshwayo's war dances, which featured thirty thousand instead of five hundred savage warriors. Those royal war dances served only as a political pretext for "smelling out" and executing political rivals. Although executing accused witches was actually against Cetshwayo's policy, such depictions of the savage Zulu tyrant were increasingly being sent to London. In 1878, the British high commissioner of South Africa, Henry Bartle Frere (1815–1884), presented Cetshwayo with an ultimatum: stop the executions, disband the army, and welcome Christian missionaries. Cetshwayo's refusal to comply with this ultimatum was the pretext for the Anglo-Zulu war of 1879, which resulted in the devastating British defeat at the Battle of Isandhlwana but the ultimate imperial victory over the Zulu kingdom.[101]

Captured and imprisoned in Cape Town, the Zulu king Cetshwayo was allowed in August 1882 to travel to London to meet with Queen Victoria and the Colonial Office to petition for his return to Zululand. Causing a sensation in the popular press, Cetshwayo's visit was the subject of editorials, cartoons, jokes, and regular newspaper reports. For his part, the Zulu king was apparently pleased with his visit to the imperial center, which he called "this great workshop of the Queen, my mother" and where he beheld "the wonders of the English nation." Although he did not entirely succeed in restoring his kingdom, Cetshwayo was apparently transformed by his initiation in London. "I feel I have grown up, so to speak, in a day," the king reportedly declared, "that from an intellectual childhood I have suddenly sprung to manhood."[102] Allowed to return to Zululand with limited sovereignty, King Cetshwayo died shortly afterward in 1884 during the Zulu civil wars that erupted in the political vacuum.

Bartle Frere also went to London, recalled in 1880 by the new Liberal government of Gladstone to answer charges that had been brought against him for mismanaging Anglo-Zulu relations. While preparing his defense until his death in 1884, Frere presented two papers about South Africa at meetings of the Anthropological Institute. Having served in India since 1834, including a term as governor of Bombay, Frere was interested in comparing India and South Africa, giving special attention to differences in religion. In his presentation, "On Systems of Land Tenure among Aboriginal Tribes in South Africa," Bartle Frere was an imperialist developing an imperial comparative religion. He quickly surveyed indigenous notions of the ownership of land. He reported that the Bushmen, "the least civilized," as nomads and thieves, were "an almost unique instance of a people without visible territorial rights, or even a shadow of land tenure." Like wild animals, the Bushmen had no idea of the ownership of land. As for the pastoralist Khoikhoi, who might have once had some system of land tenure, European law and Christian missions had supplanted any indigenous system of ownership. According to Bartle Frere, the case of the Khoikhoi revealed an "important truth" of colonial administration: the government had to adopt a "quasi-patriarchal authority" to replace the authority of traditional heads of families, clans, or tribes. Turning to Bantu-speaking Africans, Frere observed that the Zulu were adapting indigenous ideas of the ownership of land to their new roles as "colonial subjects and tax-payers." This colonial development was positive, he argued, because the indigenous Zulu system of land tenure was based entirely on force, with any owner of land constantly at risk from foreign invasion or from political dispossession by being "smelt out" as a witch. "A Zulu title," he insisted, "rests simply on force, whether the power to hold be that of the occupant, or of the chief who protects him."[103]

According to Bartle Frere, the British Empire had brought to South Africa not only a greater force but also a greater religion that would provide the foundation for a stable society. Religion, he argued, had provided the basis for social cohesion among "Aryans, either of Europe or of India," which was entirely lacking among Africans in South Africa. While Christianity had educated the European barbarians in religious laws of inheritance and land tenure, the Hindu religion, pervading every aspect of life in India, had given religious continuity and stability to land ownership. Among the natives of South Africa, Frere found the "total absence of this religious element of cohesion." Christian missions, however, were introducing religious values of monogamous marriage, private ownership, and inheritance of property that promised to "produce on South African soil results as permanent as those we find produced in Europe by Christianity, and in Rajpootana by Hinduism." Calling for further research into religion, law, and social cohesion, Frere urged his audience at the Anthropological Institute to adopt a practical perspective that was grounded in colonial realities instead of being based on "theories as to what imaginary men in imaginary situations might or ought to do."[104]

During the discussion of Bartle Frere's paper that followed, respondents examined his assumptions about the evolution of property, with Hyde Clarke focusing specifically on religion by observing that "there was a prominence given to the religious sentiment, which was not perhaps carried far enough," because the notion of property in Hindu, Christian, and other historical religions had to be traced back to the original primitive rites of taboo that had consecrated certain property for individual use "by excluding extraneous influences."[105] In his response to a paper in 1870 by E. B. Tylor, Hyde Clarke had accused Tylor of not going back far enough because he had not traced animism to the "animistic tendencies of animals."[106] Here he advocated beginning with primitive religious rites of taboo rather than with Frere's historical comparison of Europe, India, and Africa. From Bartle Frere's perspective, however, such theorizing was also about "imaginary men" in hypothetical primitive conditions of human prehistory. He was theorizing about religion on the frontlines of real colonial situations.

In Rider Haggard's African fiction about "imaginary men in imaginary situations," the intersection between savage religion and politics was arguably his central narrative theme; it definitely set the framework for dramatic action and interaction between Europeans and Africans, civilization and savagery, in his tales of African adventure. Frequently, priests ruled and rulers had the supernatural power of priests. In *Allan Quatermain*, Haggard invented a Zu-Vendi society in southern Africa in which priests held such political power that "it [was] scarcely too much to say that they really rule[d] the land."[107] In *King Solomon's Mines* (1885), an indigenous African diviner, the *isanusi* Gagool, played a central role, not as a religious dreamer with no basis in reality, but as a substantial political force, effectively the ruler of a people and a territory, even if she was cast as the "evil genius of the land."[108] The adventurers in this novel achieve success and acquire substantial wealth, but only after the death of the diviner Gagool. In this exchange between the center and the periphery of empire, Haggard's imaginary literature performed ideological work in the way it mediated imperial interests through the defeat of the evil diviner Gagool by the agents of Queen Victoria's empire, making the characters' acquisition of wealth also an imperial religious victory over African indigenous religious beliefs, practices, and polity.

In Buchan's *Prester John*, the African messiah John Laputa represented a kind of inverse British Empire, with his gospel of "Africa for Africans" promising "to lead the African race to conquest and empire."[109] Although the Europeans in the story found his religious syncretism of Christianity and heathenism to be a "bastard" religion, John Laputa galvanized his following by attacking the illegitimate civilization and oppressive religion of Europeans. " 'What have ye gained from the white man?' he cried. 'A bastard civilization which has sapped your manhood; a false religion which would rivet on you the chains of the slave.' "[110] Certainly this fictional account of an attack on the imperial mission echoed real British anxieties about rebellion in the colonies. The novel's hero David Crawfurd rails against the African messiah, "You are educated and have seen the world, what makes you try to put the clock back? You want to wipe out the civilization of a thousand years, and turn us all into savages."[111] The imperial British adventure novel, as Patrick Brantlinger has observed, "expresses anxieties about the waning of religious orthodoxy," thereby wrestling with the problem of religion as it "expresses anxieties about the ease with which civilization can revert to barbarism and savagery and thus about the weakening of Britain's imperial hegemony."[112] Haggard and Buchan captured different moments in the history of imperial anxiety. Haggard wrote about the Zulu "in all their superstitious madness and bloodstained grandeur" as he imagined they lived during a time when they were still "a reigning nation."[113] Buchan wrote about the Zulu as "bloodthirsty savages" without a nation, who were ready to follow a charismatic leader in rebelling against civilization. In different ways, therefore, these adventure novelists explored the relation between savagery and civilization that was crucial to imperial comparative religion.

SAVAGE SURVIVALS

Andrew Lang's academic research in the study of religion and South African adventure novels merged in a common project of juxtaposing, sometimes through ironic inversions, the binary opposition between savagery and civilization. Lang often found savagery within civilization, discovering echoes of the Zulu king Cetshwayo, for example, in the smelling out of witches and the washing of the spears in Scottish history. "Cetewayo's medicine-men, who 'smelt out' witches, were only some two centuries in the rear of our civilisation," he observed.[114] "Like Cetewayo," he noted, the Scottish hero "Marmion feels the imperative instinctive craving 'to wash his spears.' "[115] In his collection of satirical stories *In the Wrong Paradise* (1886), Lang's dedication to Haggard read: "We are all savages under our white skins; but you alone recall to us the delights and terrors of the world's nonage."[116] Haggard had his hero declare in *Allan Quatermain,* "Civilization is only savagery silver-gilt."[117] Although Haggard's engagement with savagery and civilization reflected imperial anxiety, it was complex. Variously, Haggard presented these crucial terms as absolute opposition, as degrees on a continuum, and as ironic inversion.

First, these key words marked a dramatic opposition, excluding one another, because, as Haggard wrote, "A savage is one thing, and a civilized man is another." But such a stark, binary opposition held little dramatic potential. It allowed for no narrative movement. So Haggard considered possible transformations from savagery to civility, which was, after all, the basic social-evolutionary assumption upon which much of the anthropology of religion was based, only to question its possibility. "Though civilized men may and do become savages," he observed, "I personally doubt if the converse is even possible."[118] As Haggard expressed anxiety about civilization reverting to savagery, he also undercut the developmental promise of evolutionary anthropology, let alone the "civilizing mission" of empire.

Second, Haggard immediately undermined this stark opposition by relativizing the terms. In the actual encounters between colonizers and indigenous people, *civilized* and *savage* became relative terms on the scale of human virtue. Civilized and savage might be opposites, "but whether the civilized man, with his gin, his greed, and his dynamite, is really so very superior to the savage is another question. . . . Savagery is only a question of degree."[119]

Third, by relativizing the terms *savagery* and *civilization,* Haggard allowed for the possibility of their ironic inversion. Zulu "savages" could display a higher degree of civility than civilized Europeans who had degenerated into savagery. In one of his Zulu novels, *Child of Storm* (1913), Haggard argued that there was no basis for designating the Zulu as savages. "To begin with," he wrote, "by what exact right do we call people like the Zulus savages?" "Setting aside the habit of polygamy, which, after all, is common among very highly civilised peoples in the East, they have a social system not unlike our own. They have, or had, their king, their nobles, and their commons. They have an ancient and elaborate law, and a system of morality in some ways as high as our own, and certainly more generally obeyed. They have their priests and their doctors; they are strictly upright, and observe the rites of hospitality."[120] Conversely, if the Zulu are civilized, then Europeans might very well be savages, their civility only "silver-gilt," a veneer covering the savage substance of European civilization. Haggard observed in his introduction to *Allan Quatermain* (1887), "Supposing for the sake of argument we divide ourselves into twenty parts, nineteen savage and one civilized, we must look to the nineteen savage portions of our nature, if we would really understand ourselves."[121] In this surprising inversion, the savage was not the alien other but the massive underlying substratum of civilization.

In his collection of short stories *In the Wrong Paradise* (1886), Andrew Lang made this ironic inversion of savagery and civilization a matter of both imaginative fiction and anthropological method. Framed by his dedication to H. Rider Haggard, two stories in particular playfully invert this opposition: "The Great Gladstone Myth," which exposes the learned ignorance of a professor in the future applying the philological methods of Friedrich Max Müller to understand the religion of "savage" Victorian Britain, and "The Romance of the First Radical," which recounts the travails of a savage skeptic by the name of Why-Why, a primitive John Stuart Mill, who applies enlightened reason to all inherited beliefs, customs, and traditions.

Lang's dedication to Haggard affirmed their friendship but also their collaboration in reading and writing relations between the savage and the civilized. Lang praised Haggard's knowledge of the savage but also his savage imagination. "You," he addressed Haggard, "who know the noble barbarian in his African retreats, appear to retain more than most men of his fresh natural imagination." Given his own accomplishments in scholarship as a literary critic and anthropologist, Lang describes himself as a "student" of Haggard's adventure novels, such as *King Solomon's Mines* and *The Witches Head*, which he ascribed with the power to transform even a scholar into a child again, a youthful vitality that the "barbarian wakens even in the weary person of letters."[122] This promise of youth resonated with other anthropologists, as R. R. Marett observed in his 1912 eulogy for Andrew Lang: "It is to the eternal schoolboy in us, I believe, that anthropology must speak, if it is to be a real science, and not a farrago of dreary trivialities."[123] In his dedication, Andrew Lang stated that Rider Haggard's adventure novels made him feel like a schoolboy.

In this dedication, Lang declared that his favorite "hero" of modern romance literature was not the adventurer, hunter, and sportsman Allan Quatermain, Haggard's hero, but the Zulu Umslopogaas, a recurring character in Haggard's novels. "Of all modern heroes of romance," Lang confessed, "the dearest to me is your faithful Zulu, and I own I cried when he bade farewell to his English master, in *The Witch's Head*." Why did Lang regard this Zulu character so dearly? Here was the "natural man," Lang explained, revealed not through the "civilized spectacles" of the anthropologist but "with the eyes of the sympathetic sportsman."[124] As R. R. Marett recalled, Lang once remarked, "The savage is an absurd fellow, but on the whole a sportsman."[125] In his sympathy with the savage sportsman, Lang implied, Haggard uncovered resources of youth, vitality, and sympathy that "civilized spectacles" obscured.

In the short stories that followed, Lang dwelled in the absurdity of the opposition between the savage and the civilized. His entertaining satire of the method of Max Müller, as applied by Professor Boscher in AD 3886 to interpret the myth of the "Great Gladstone," addressed the limits of "civilized" knowledge of the "savage" in Victorian anthropology. "In the post-Christian myths of the Teutonic race settled in England, no figure appears more frequently and more mysteriously than that of Gladstone or Mista Gladstone." Most documentary evidence had been destroyed; only fragments remained; so scholars had to develop methods to reconstruct the ancient history, mythology, and religion of Victorian Britain. Although some scholars in the fourth millennium mistakenly persisted in seeing Gladstone as a historical figure, Professor Boscher was able "to reconstruct the Gladstonian myth by the comparative method—that is, by comparing the relics of old Ritual treatises, hymns, imprecations, and similar religious texts, with works of art, altars, and statues, and with popular traditions and folklore. The results, again, [were] examined in the light of the Vedas, the Egyptian monuments, and generally of everything that, to the unscientific eye, [seemed] most turbidly obscure in itself, and most hopelessly remote from the subject in hand." Out of these disparate and arcane materials, Professor Boscher reconstructed the "Gladstonian myth."[126]

Professor Boscher was aware of objections to his philological method, recognizing that Longus, or Longinus, footnoted with the observation, "There must be some mistake here," since the critic was Andrew Lang, had "meanly argued that her services must be accepted with cautious diffidence." Rejecting this caution, Professor Boscher insisted, "Philology is the only real key to the labyrinths of post-Christian myth." By applying this philological key, Gladstone, of course, turns out to be the solar deity of Victorian Britain, the supreme solar deity who is not to be confused with [Charles] Spurgeon, a river god, or [David] Livingstone, "a mythical form of the midnight sun, now fabled to wander in the 'Dark Continent,' as Bishop of Natal, the land of the sun's birth place, now alluded to as lost in the cloud-land of comparative mythology." This reference to Natal, confusing the missionary David Livingstone with Bishop John William Colenso, nevertheless reinforced the importance of the Zulu who lived in a "cloud-land" for comparative studies in comparative mythology and comparative religion.[127]

In counterpoint to the civilized ignorance of Professor Boscher, Lang posed the savage enlightenment of Why-Why, the primitive skeptic, in the satire "The Romance of the First Radical." Here also, satirical fiction was an occasion for methodological reflection. Again, as in Professor Boscher's analysis of Victorian Britain, any reconstruction of a primitive past in which the first radical appeared could not be based on a textual record. "History tells us less about the first Radical—the first man who rebelled against the despotism of unintelligible customs, who asserted the rights of the individual against the claims of the tribal conscience, and who was eager to see society organized, off-hand, on what he thought a rational method." Accordingly, in the absence of texts, the history of the first radical had to be reconstructed through what Lang called "that branch of hypothetics which is known as prehistoric science." Hypothetically, but scientifically, the history of the first radical could be deduced "from the hints supplied by geology, and by the study of Radicals at large, and of contemporary savages among whom no Radical reformer has yet appeared."[128]

Based on these research methods, according to Lang, we can assume that Why-Why was inclined to ask many questions, especially about "metaphysical conundrums" such as "Who made men?" or "Why don't lobsters grow on trees?" His mother, who could draw upon the "store of traditional replies to inquisitive children, replies sanctioned by antiquity and by the authority of the medicine-men," must have explained to Why-Why that everything "came out of a plot of reeds and rushes." This hypothetical response to a question about origins recalled Zulu accounts of the bed of reeds, the *uhlanga*, as the source of life. But Why-Why was skeptical about this myth of origin; he "thought in his heart that the whole theory was "bosh-bosh," to use the early reduplicative language of these remote times."[129]

These rhetorical turns—stating, undermining, but also reinscribing the opposition between savagery and civility—were crucial to the comparative religion of Andrew Lang. Recently, the anthropologist Talal Asad has proposed that the secular "disenchantment" of the modern West was at least in part produced through efforts directed toward the "enchantment" of the premodern. Arguably, as Asad suggested, the secular "disenchantment of the world" was "a product of nineteenth-century romanticism, partly linked to the growing habit of reading imaginative literature—being enclosed within and by it—so that images of a 'pre-modern' past acquire in retrospect a quality of enchantment."[130] Romantic adventure novelists, such as H. Rider Haggard and John Buchan, were actively engaged in such a project. So was Andrew Lang. "The world is disenchanted," he wrote in 1887 in a sonnet that was incorporated in the novel *He*, which both satirized and paid tribute to Haggard's *She*.[131] However, Lang found that the disenchanted world was being reenchanted through the adventure novel's capacity for mediating savage and exotic worlds for the modern imagination. Lang declared that adventure novels were a medium through which "people have become alive to the strangeness and fascination of the world beyond the bounds of Europe."[132] Here, as throughout his career, Andrew Lang affirmed the intimate convergence of his literary and anthropological interests.

Was the increasingly widespread reading of popular romance and adventure novels a way of finding enchantment in other worlds, the premodern, the savage, or the exotic, while the modern world was becoming disenchanted? Imaginative literature certainly was a medium for transacting these relations. A modern, secular world could be disenchanted by creating and reinforcing stark contrasts between modern Britain and thoroughly enchanted others. Therefore, imaginative literature, especially imperial adventure novels, served a secularizing purpose, distancing the modern world from what Max Weber (1864–1920) in his 1918 lecture "Science as a Vocation" called "mysterious, incalculable forces" by locating them firmly in the premodern. By clearing the modern space of any trace of mystery, as Weber observed, "one can in principle master all things by calculation." In calling this feature of modernity "disenchantment," and observing that "the world is disenchanted," Weber was probably unaware that he was employing a term that also appeared in a sonnet by Andrew Lang composed in friendly tribute to H. Rider Haggard.[133]

In his literary criticism, however, Andrew Lang worked hard to bring an aura of enchantment home. Although he ultimately rejected E. B. Tylor's theory of animism as an explanation for primitive religion, Lang found animism operating in the modern novels of Charles Dickens (1812–1870) and proposed that the power of his prose resided in "what one may call his Animism." Adapting this term from the study of religion, Lang argued that Dickens exemplified this "mark of savage and popular invention, as displayed in myth and fairy tale." Dickens brought inanimate objects to life in his fiction, where doors and windows, fog and wind, were animated by impulses of their own. Accordingly, Lang identified Dickens's genius in his recovery of primitive animism, a reading of Dickens echoed recently by anthropologist of religion Stewart Guthrie, who observed, "The most striking animist is a Victorian, Charles Dickens."[134] Lang found this primitive religious capacity in the work of other creative authors, such as Wordsworth, Scott, and George Sand; there, he said, "The world is all animated and personal, everything in it has life and character." Found both in "early human thought" and the thought processes of childhood, this animistic "gleam," this "ancient mood," Lang argued, "with the associated difficulty of discerning between dreams and realities," stands as "the indispensable basis of poetry and mythology."[135] According to Lang, animism was alive and well in the imaginative capacity of modern secular literature.

Animism was also alive and well in the spiritual politics of British imperialism. As the literary theorist Laura Chrisman has argued, imperial political economy and spiritual enchantment cannot be easily separated in analyzing the literature produced by Rider Haggard.[136] Here was an imperialist advocating the empire, celebrating its economic and military interests, actively promoting the Shepstone system of indirect rule, and reinforcing all of the racialized, gendered, and sexualized tropes of empire through his best-selling novels. But here also was a spiritualist, of sorts, believing in reincarnation, even vaguely recalling his own past lives as a caveman, a black savage, an ancient Egyptian, and a medieval barbarian, while holding on to a romantic ideal of British pastoral life.[137] Was this myth, fiction, or scholarship?

As the historian Michael Saler has proposed, Sherlock Holmes demonstrated a rationality that can be called "animistic reason," which expanded the scope of rationality beyond instrumental reason, with its calculations of means and ends, to include an imaginative capacity for discerning meaning, motion, and even life in material objects. Holmes called this capacity "the scientific use of the imagination." According to Saler, it was "through this animistic reason that Holmes the private detective bested professional detectives."[138] Just as Sherlock Holmes was not a professional detective, Andrew Lang was not a professional anthropologist of religion. Yet he was actively involved in the production of knowledge about religion during the late Victorian era. In his exchanges with adventure novelists, Lang showed how knowledge about religion could be animated by complex mediations between imperial, colonial, and indigenous locations and by literary transactions, blurring genres, between myth, fiction, and scholarship. As we recover these mediations, transactions, and relations, we gain a richer portrait of how knowledge was produced about any specific religion, such as Zulu religion, as well as how religion emerged as a generic category during a formative period in the history of the academic study of religion.

Fiction and scholarship, the play of possibility and the discipline of factuality, merged in British imperial comparative religion. In Haggard's novel *She*, Ayesha, She Who Must Be Obeyed, both priestess and ruler, wielded imperial power that was simultaneously real and imaginary. "What was her real religion?" Haggard asks. Ultimately, her religion was the spiritual terror animating empire. "How thinkest thou that I rule these people?" Ayesha demands. "I have but a regiment of guards to do my bidding, therefore it is not by force. It is by terror. My empire is of the imagination."[139] Through a complex process of mediation—indigenous, colonial, and imperial—religion registered as imagination and terror not only on the colonized periphery, with its savage gods and spirits, its witch doctors and war dances, but also at the imperial center.

CHAPTER SIX

Ritual and Magic

If we define religion as the propitiation of natural and supernatural powers, and magic as the coercion of them, magic has everywhere preceded religion.

JAMES FRAZER

In January 1915, a European missionary and an African evangelist, both working among the rural Thonga, witnessed a ceremony at the urban residential hostels, or compounds, reserved for African mine workers in Johannesburg. At one of the compounds, men were dancing in celebration but also in anticipation, awaiting the arrival of a procession that, as the European missionary observed, included many women. Knowing that very few women lived around the mines, the European missionary asked his African colleague why so many women were participating in this ceremonial procession. The African evangelist explained: "They are not women! They are *tinkhontshana*, boys who have placed on their chests the breasts of women carved in wood, and who are going to the dance in order to play the part of women."[1]

What kind of ceremony was this? Was it expressive in saying something about life in the mines, or was it functional in compensating for living there? As an expressive ritual, the ceremony might have been enacting the importance of gendered relations in African religious life, in which structured relations between males and females were inscribed and sanctified in life-cycle rites, marriage contracts, family gatherings, healing practices, and sacrificial offerings for ancestral spirits. Alienated from these traditional structures, mine workers might have performed this ceremony as a functional equivalent, or functional substitute, for the familiar gendered relations of their rural homes. As a functional ritual, the ceremony might have been performed to maintain a sense of traditional order under modern conditions.

The African evangelist, however, offered a much more pragmatic analysis. The procession, the dance, and the entire ritual was effective in marking and making human relations—juniors and seniors, males and females, wives and husbands—in the life of the mining compound. "To-night," he explained, referring to the young men who were dressed up as women for the ceremony, "when they return to their dormitories, their 'husbands' will have to give them 10 [shillings], and only on that condition will the *tinkhont-shana* remove their breasts and comply with the desire of their husbands."[2] As a term referring to boys "used by another man to satisfy his lust," the *tinkhontshana* could be any young men who were courted by policemen, supervisors, and other elders in the mining compounds by formal proposals and even by the marriage rituals of *lobola*, which required a payment to the family of the "bride." The marriage ritual might even be sanctified by the sacrificial offering of a goat to the ancestral spirits. The boy became wife (*nsati*) and the man became husband (*numa*) in the formation of these ritualized but also intimate relations. The ceremony, therefore, whatever its expressive registers or functional compensations, was an integral part of ritually, actually making men and boys, males and females, and husbands and wives in the mining compounds of Johannesburg.

The missionary, linguist, and ethnographer Henri-Alexandre Junod, who described this ritual in the context of reporting on "unnatural vice in the Johannesburg compounds," had for many years provided meticulously detailed and theoretically informed accounts of African material, social, and cultural life, with special attention to African religion and magic.[3] Junod's interest in this ritual reflected a concern with sexual morality, a concern that had been the subject of a government commission of inquiry in 1907 into sexual practices in the mining compounds and prisons.[4] But Junod was also interested in rites of passage, not only life-cycle rituals that made men and women in traditional society, but also in the rites of passage between primitive society and civilization.

Henri-Alexandre Junod (1863–1934) had studied English and medicine at Edinburgh before taking up his work as missionary for the Mission Suisse Romande. He spent most of the years between 1893 and 1920 in southern Africa and later lived his last fourteen years in Switzerland lecturing and writing on primitive magic and ritual. Originally intent on studying entomology in southern Africa, Junod claimed that he was converted to ethnography by James Bryce (1838–1922), a historian, a politician, and a friend of James Frazer.[5] At their meeting in Lourenço Marques in 1895, Bryce urged Junod to document the customs of the natives. This research would be essential for their efficient colonial management, but Bryce thought it would also benefit the natives in the future by providing reliable knowledge about their primitive past. He compared the situation of nineteenth-century Europeans in Africa to the opportunities of ancient Romans among the barbaric tribes of Europe. "How thankful should we be," Bryce exclaimed, "if a Roman had taken the trouble fully to investigate the habits of our Celtic forefathers!" Following this analogy, Junod imagined that Africans of the future would be grateful for scientific efforts to preserve accounts of their savage life. Turning from entomology to ethnography, Junod found that "Man is infinitely more interesting than the insect!"[6]

Although Junod might have exaggerated the role of James Bryce in prompting his ethnographic research, Bryce did put him in touch with the metropolitan theorist James Frazer. As a result of that link, Junod employed Frazer's questionnaire in his ethnographic fieldwork.[7] Frazer quoted Junod's research findings in his publications. Junod's earliest ethnographic monograph, *Les Ba-Ronga* (1898), received Frazer's frequent citation, particularly where it provided ample evidence of the practices of primitive magic.[8] Occasionally, Frazer also deferred to Junod's analysis, observing at one point, for example, "[The] Swiss missionary who reports this strange superstition has also suggested what appears to be its true explanation."[9] More than merely providing raw materials, therefore, Junod represented a co-worker in the field. His research also drew the attention of Emile Durkheim and Marcel Mauss, leaders of French sociology and the study of religion; both of them reviewed *Les Ba-Ronga* in their journal *L'Année sociologique* during 1898, when Mauss was beginning to publish landmark texts in the study of sacrifice and magic and Durkheim was working on his major theoretical book on religion, *The Elementary Forms of the Religious Life*.[10]

"My documents are not books," Junod declared in his major work, *The Life of a South African Tribe*. "They are living witnesses."[11] Junod's principal witnesses or indigenous informants can be identified. In his research, Junod relied upon recent Christian converts, such as Elias "Spoon" Libombo, Mboza, Tobane, Viguet, and others, who, in providing accounts of traditional religion, advanced their own Christian critiques of a pagan, heathen past. Not only expressing their religious interests, these informants, who came from Lourenço Marques, also displayed political loyalties that affected their accounts of local African beliefs and customs. Elias Libombo, in particular, was highlighted as a diviner, a "fortune-teller," who revealed to Junod the indigenous, "ingenious system of divination."[12] Depicted in photographs as a "bone thrower" in 1894 and a "church elder" in 1907, Libombo mediated between ancestral traditions and Christian conversions in Junod's accounts of the life of a South African tribe. In addition to these Christian converts, Junod relied upon information from a ritual specialist, Mankhelu, a diviner and counselor to kings, whom Junod described as "a Bantu so steeped in the obscure conceptions of the Bantu mind that he could never get rid of them."[13] In conversing with Junod, Mankhelu also had to mediate between ancestral and Christian religion. But Mankhelu found himself in a different kind of mediation around 1888, when he was convicted and sentenced to death by a colonial court for presiding over a traditional trial for identifying a person as guilty of performing witchcraft.[14] Although he was reprieved from execution, Mankhelu underwent a different kind of conversion, not by becoming a Christian, but by passing through the ultimate power over life and death that was wielded by new colonial forces.

In his imperial reflections on ritual, James Frazer (1854–1941) distinguished between magical and religious rites, contrasting magical coercion with religious submission in ritual practices. However, as Edmund Leach observed, although Frazer focused on ritual, he was really interested in psychology, primitive mentality, and strange beliefs. "The customs Frazer records with such painstaking elaboration are all examples of ritual action," Leach noted. "Yet his ultimate interest was not in the ritual as such, but in the underlying beliefs."[15] Nevertheless, Frazer argued that beliefs had practical implications, informing dispositions toward the world. Magical beliefs, underwritten by principles of imitation and contagion, were essentially coercive, while religious beliefs, deferring to supernatural beings, led to a submissive disposition toward higher powers. In his reading of this distinction between magic and religion, R. R. Marett found that Frazer was arguing "in effect that humility is the differentia of religion."[16] Beliefs, attitudes, and dispositions, therefore, were the essential ingredients in Frazer's trajectory from magic, through religion, to modern science.

Guided by Frazer, Henri-Alexandre Junod nevertheless charted his own course in coming to terms with these key words—magic, religion, and science. Certain rituals, Junod found, were "inspired by the magic principles," the "axioms of primitive mentality," in which practitioners of magic assumed that "like acts on like and produces like," that a "portion of a complexus acts on the whole," or that "words in which a wish is emphatically expressed produce the desired result."[17] These magical axioms, according to Junod, were deployed in "all the rites, practices, and conceptions which aim at dealing with hostile, neutral, or favourable influences." Essentially pragmatic, magic was engaged in the contested arena of forces, from beneficial to hostile, that might be harnessed or averted. Religion, by contrast, he defined as "all the rites, practices, conceptions or feelings which presuppose the belief in personal or semi-personal spirits endowed with the attributes of Deity." Religion, like magic, was a matter of rites and practices, underwritten by conceptions, but was amplified by feelings absent in magic. Those feelings, Junod argued, were relational, since religion was marked by efforts "to enter into relation" with divine spirits, though not necessarily in a spirit of submission or humility, because religious actions could be performed "either to win their assistance or to avert their anger." Whatever the motive, religious acts were consistently identified by Junod in the formal features of prayers and offerings. Completing his definition of the three key words of an imperial study of religion, Junod proposed that science should be understood as "all the rites, practices, and conceptions which are inspired by a true observation of facts."[18] From this perspective of scientific truth, magic was "absolutely false," Junod insisted, because "we cannot assign any scientific value to any of these axioms of primitive mentality."[19]

These definitions of magic, religion, and science, which Junod adapted from Frazer, were modified by his missionary goals and his colonial context. Like Frazer, Junod placed magic in competition with religion, as contrasting dispositions, one coercing and the other deferring to supernatural powers, and he also placed magic in competition with science in the realm of facts. Departing from Frazer, however, Junod argued for the scientific value of religion, which was displayed in rites of offerings and prayers, and the religious value of science, as "rites, practices, and conceptions" that underwrote his project of Christianizing and civilizing the natives. Although he was clearly conversant with the most recent developments in European theory, Junod was also recasting those theoretical resources in mediating between metropolitan centers of theory production and his colonial situation in southern Africa.

Here again we find what I have called the triple mediation in the production of knowledge about religion within imperial comparative religion. James Frazer, mediating between a hypothetical primitive humanity and modern civilization, was in correspondence with Henri-Alexandre Junod's mediation between European theory and colonial projects of converting and civilizing, containing and controlling, the indigenous people of southern Africa. The third mediation, worked out by indigenous Africans, was crucial. Whether mediating between ancestral traditions and Christian conversion, as in the case of Elias "Spoon" Libombo, or mediating between indigenous and colonial legal systems, as in the case of the diviner Mankhelu,

Africans were struggling to move in and move through new religious and political terrains. Although they were Junod's informants, feeding into Frazer's global network of reports from "men on the spot," they were on the frontlines of mediating between ancestral traditions and new realities. Religion, in these mediations, was situated not in a primordial past but in the ordeals of military conquest, colonial subjugation, coercive taxation, migrant labor, and life in the cities, mining compounds, and prisons of South Africa.

IMPERIAL REFLECTIONS ON RITUAL

Although imperial comparative religion was primarily focused on beliefs, concentrating on distilling a primitive psychology, mentality, or "belief in spiritual beings," theorists also had to pay attention to religious practice. William Robertson Smith (1846–1894) was at the forefront of directing attention to ritual in the study of religion. Ritual came before myth, in Robertson Smith's analysis. In the social cohesion of ritual, people act together in concert and in community, especially when sharing the communal meal of a sacrifice. In *The Religion of the Semites*, originally published in 1889, William Robertson Smith advanced a theory of sacrificial ritual that placed the religion of ancient Israel, and the Hebrew Bible, firmly within the global context of imperial comparative religion.[20] Robertson Smith restricted his comparisons to the ancient Near East until roughly midway through his book, when he invoked the authority of E. B. Tylor to make the point that the belief that blood provides nourishment for the gods can be regarded as universal because the "same belief appears among early nations in all parts of the globe."[21] Suddenly shifting to a global scope, Robertson Smith cited evidence from the Indians of North America, the Tartars, and three African examples, including the report from South Africa that "among the Hottentots the pure blood of beasts is forbidden to women but not to men." "In the last case," Robertson Smith observed, "we see that the blood is sacred food."[22] In primitive sacrifice, therefore, the sacred appeared not as a gift to a spiritual being, as E. B. Tylor had argued, but as a communal meal that served as a religious marker of social cohesion and gendered divisions in the formation of society.

As the development of his argument shifted to the global perspective of imperial comparative religion, how did Robertson Smith propose to control the evidence that could be derived from different "nations" all over the world? In the theoretical centerpiece of *The Religion of the Semites*, its chapter on sacrifice, Robertson Smith advanced a socioeconomic principle of comparison, isolating the material basis, for example, that made pastoral societies comparable, whether they were in the ancient Near East or in contemporary Africa. "Similar institutions are found among all the purely pastoral African peoples," he observed "and have persisted with more or less modification down to our own time." To make his comparative case, Robertson Smith selected evidence from a region that, at first glance, must have appeared most distant and different from the ancient Near East. "Out of a multitude of proofs I cite these," he explained, juxtaposing the ancient Near East and South Africa, "as being drawn from the parts of the continent most remote from one another." In South Africa, Robertson Smith found pastoral people, living on a common diet of milk or game, who seldom killed their cattle, except on special ritual occasions—circumcisions, weddings, or ceremonial preparations for war. "So among the Caffres," he concluded; and so among the pastoralists of the ancient Near East. Drawing upon South African evidence, Robertson Smith found, "These examples may suffice to show the wide diffusion among rude pastoral peoples of a way of regarding sacred animals with which the Semitic facts and the inferences I have drawn from them exactly correspond."[23]

Objections to Robertson Smith's comparative inferences came from many quarters. In addition to theological scandal, Robertson Smith was subjected to the complaints from philologists that he had compared incompatible families of language. A. H. Sayce voiced this objection, saying, "I must enter a protest against the assumption that what holds good of Kaffirs or Australians held good also for the primitive Semite. The students of language have at last learnt that what is applicable to one family of speech is not necessarily applicable to another, and it would be well if the anthropologist would learn the same lesson."[24] His friend James Frazer, however, recognized that Robertson Smith had established a new principle for comparison. He had developed new terms and conditions for using evidence and drawing conclusions that were based, not on the classification of languages, the collection of mythic motifs, or the catalog of customs, but upon the comparability of similar socioeconomic systems. As Frazer observed in 1894, Robertson Smith's major contribution was his demonstration of the comparability of Semitic pastoral life, and its religion that revolved around animal sacrifice, with "pastoral life as observed among rude pastoral tribes in various parts of the world, especially in Africa."[25] Especially in South Africa, the pastoral religion and society of indigenous Africans could provide a template for rewriting the religion of the ancient Semites.

In his own work, James Frazer ignored this principle of sociological method, building his vast literary edifice upon the promiscuous collection and collation of data without any regard for socioeconomic context.[26] Frazer marked the apogee of imperial comparative religion by developing a truly global network of informants and information, which was assembled not only through his prodigious command of the literature, but also through his cultivation of direct contact with local experts all over the world, "men on the spot," such as Baldwin Spencer and F. J. Gillen in Australia, R. H. Codrington in Melanesia, and John Roscoe in Uganda, who mediated between colonized peripheries and the metropolitan center.[27] As his biographer Robert Ackerman has shown, Frazer's basic theoretical distinction between magic and religion, and his hypothetical evolutionary sequence from magic, through religion, to science, were developed not by reading Comte, but in conversation and collaboration with the Australian aboriginal researches of former zoologist Baldwin Spencer and colonial administrator F. J. Gillen. Their work in Australia led Frazer to conclude that "if we define religion as the propitiation of natural and supernatural powers, and magic as the coercion of them, magic has everywhere preceded religion."[28] However, as a manipulation of matter, which was effected by applying "one or other of two great fundamental laws of thought, namely, the association of ideas by similarity and the association of ideas by continuity in space and time," magic was more practical, realistic, and even scientific than religion.[29] Where religious ritual submitted before mysterious power, magic sought to control it. In either case, whether religious or magical, primitive thought and practice were about materiality. In this respect, perhaps, Frazer developed, in his own way, Robertson Smith's concluding observation in *The Religion of the Semites* that a "ritual system must always remain materialistic, even if its materialism is disguised under the cloak of mysticism."[30] While focusing on underlying beliefs, Frazer's imperial comparative religion documented the global distribution of an all-pervading mysticism of materiality.

Frazer's method was evident in 1885 in one of his earliest anthropological essays, an analysis of the sacred fire maintained by the vestal virgins in ancient Rome. This perpetual fire, tended by young women, was the central symbol of Roman religion and politics. If the fire went out, it was regarded not only as a religious disaster but also as a threat to the political stability of the empire. Special sacrifices were required to deal with this crisis. The fire had to be reignited by the most ancient method of rubbing two sticks together. Frazer posed the question, Why was maintaining this sacred fire so important in ancient Rome? Once the practice had started, Frazer casually observed, it inevitably became sacralized, or canonized, to ensure its continuation. But why did it start in the first place? Here the prescribed method of relighting the sacred fire suggested for Frazer the key to explaining the primitive origin of this ritual institution. "That its history goes back to the embryo state of human civilization seems proved by the fact that when the fire chanced to go out it was formally rekindled by the most primitive of all modes of lighting a fire, that of rubbing two sticks against each other. It is probable therefore that some light may be thrown on the Roman custom by comparing it with the customs of peoples in earlier stages of civilization."[31] This focus on the most primitive technique of fire-lighting led Frazer to inquire into the primitive customs of savages as they were reported by European travelers, missionaries, and colonial agents. "Turning to South Africa," Frazer observed, "we are told by a distinguished traveler that amongst the Damaras the chief's daughter 'is to the Damaras what the Vestal was amongst the ancient Romans; for, besides attending to the sacrifices, it is her duty to keep up the "holy fire."' "[32] This traveler's report about the savage Damara solved Frazer's comparative problem.

The distinguished traveler was Charles John Andersson (1827–1867), a Swedish explorer, hunter, and trader in South West Africa, now Namibia. Having traveled to Cape Town with Francis Galton in 1850, Andersson published his book *Lake Ngami* on the natural and cultural features of South West Africa in 1856. As an amateur ethnographer, Andersson paid considerable attention to religion, noting that useful "knowledge of the mental tendencies of the natives" could be gained "by attending to what many might call absurd superstitions." Focusing on the Damara (Bergdama), who were allegedly the most primitive people in the region, he found hints of religious sentiment in their sense of something beyond the visible world and their reluctance to speak about such matters. According to Andersson, whenever any questions about religion arose, his African guide would exclaim, "Hush!"[33] The nature of the people's religion, therefore, could be discerned only in observable ritual, such as the practices associated with preserving the sacred fire. Here Andersson highlighted the correlation between contemporary Damara and ancient Romans.

In its colonial context, this account of the primitive religion of the Damara held significance that Frazer would not have noticed. During the second half of the nineteenth century, reports by European travelers, traders, and missionaries depicted the Damara as the most primitive people in South West Africa. By contrast to the Herero and mixed-race Afrikaner groups who were competing with Europeans for dominance in the region, the Damara had no centralized political organization. The depiction of the Damara as "occupying extreme levels of primitivity," as the historian Marion Wallace has observed, justified capturing them in large numbers and taking them into forced labor in the Cape Colony. At the same time, European observers were interested in distinguishing these primitive people as a separate "tribe," even though, as Wallace has noted, the "Damara cannot be said to have formed a 'tribe' until the colonial authorities invented it."[34] The Roman model of social cohesion, revolving around the sacred fire, provided a convenient formula for representing this tribal solidarity. As an interested party in struggles for power in South West Africa, during the 1860s Charles John Andersson organized an army of European traders, with African allies, to defeat all the other "tribes" and establish European domination. In this colonial history, maintaining the sacred fire, a practice held in common by the Damara and the Herero, continued to hold political significance. Johannes Hangero, who had been taken prisoner during the genocidal war against the Herero beginning in 1904, recounted how the Germans had targeted the sacred fire in their campaign of destruction. "When the Germans took over South West Africa people were punished for having holy fires," he recalled. "Even the holy fires were extinguished."[35] Knowledge about African religion, therefore, marked out a site for colonial intervention and even for a military campaign of extermination.

James Frazer, however, used evidence from South West Africa to answer his question about the origin of the sacred fire in ancient Rome. Observing a "complete correspondence between Damaraland and ancient Italy," he highlighted the similar female roles, sacrificial rituals, and methods of rekindling the fire by rubbing sticks together. This correspondence enabled him to formulate an explanation for the origin of the ancient Roman ritual. "When we have thus tracked the custom of maintaining a perpetual fire to a savage tribe in Africa," Frazer declared, "a simple explanation of its origin is not far to seek." Indeed, Frazer's explanation was extremely simple: savages make fire by rubbing two sticks together; this process of making fire is difficult, especially in wet weather; therefore, it is convenient to keep a fire constantly burning. According to Frazer, the origin of the sacred fire, with all its attendant rituals, could thereby be reduced to practical necessity, a solution to a purely technical problem, which was only later "elevated into a religious obligation."[36] Here in embryo was James Frazer's method, which he later developed in his long-term, multivolume research project into the meaning of the Priest of Nemi. He set a problem in the study of classical religion, correlated that problem with evidence about savages from all over the world, and then identified a simple practical solution that had been obscured by magic and religion in the process of human evolution.

Frazer's theoretical mediation between savage religion and primitive origins was surprisingly popular. Celebrating Frazer's influence, R. R. Marett observed: "If our imperial race is beginning to know something about those people of rudimentary culture whose fate is in its hands, [it] is in no small part due to the wide circulation achieved by *The Golden Bough*."[37] As part of this imperial project, as noted, Frazer cultivated a wide-ranging network of local experts in the colonies, drawing new data by corresponding with colonial experts like Baldwin Spencer, R. H. Codrington, and John Roscoe. He also developed working relations with contemporary "men on the spot" in South Africa. While *The Golden Bough* grew from two volumes, to three volumes, to twelve volumes, it was clear that Frazer relied upon several key sources in the region, especially the historian George McCall Theal, the author Dudley Kidd, and the Swiss missionary-ethnographer Henri-Alexandre Junod. Although he was familiar with the earlier ethnographic work of Wilhelm Bleek, Henry Callaway, and Theophilus Hahn and had mastered the nineteenth-century reports of travelers and missionaries, Frazer preferred to engage these local experts directly as correspondents and collaborators in a common global project. Frazer made personal references to these scholars when he cited them in his published work. In providing a general explanation of Bantu totemism, for example, Frazer deferred to "Dr. Theal, the eminent historian of South Africa."[38] Praising Dudley Kidd as a "well-informed writer," a "writer who knows [the Bantu] well," Frazer made frequent reference to Kidd's popular works *The Essential Kafir* (1904) and *Savage Childhood* (1906).[39] And he singled out for special mention the missionary-ethnographer Henri-Alexandre Junod, noting that Baronga "customs and beliefs have been recorded with praiseworthy diligence by the Swiss missionary Mr. H. A. Junod" and citing Junod's "masterly account of his dusky flock."[40]

From his various African informants, Junod distilled a single, coherent religious system. As the historian Patrick Harries has demonstrated, Junod was instrumental in manufacturing a "Baronga" or "Thonga" linguistic, political, and tribal identity that never actually existed.[41] The term *Thonga* was not used by the people themselves; they had no traditions of common origin. Junod constructed a common tribal language, culture, and religious tradition for the Thonga. His attention to religion, ritual, and magic, which he covered extensively in *The Life of a South African Tribe* and other publications, underwrote that presumed homogeneity of a tribal unit. In the hands of James Frazer, the internal, systematic coherence that Junod had constructed was easily dissolved, as he deployed Junod's Baronga or Thonga, like other savages, as free-floating evidence of a magical mentality.

Back in South Africa, however, Frazerian categories assumed strange local forms in the colonial situation. For example, the sympathetic, homeopathic, or imitative magic that supposedly pervaded Bantu mentality took on a distinctive political cast in Junod's reading of the challenges of reconstruction after the South African War. Lacking any grasp of scientific causality, the Bantu held a magical conception of nature that was based, in Frazer's terms, on the principle of imitative magic. In political relations, Junod argued, this magical mentality drove blacks to imitate their white masters, as they followed "the imitative instinct" that was "natural to them as to all primitive natures," displaying an endemic "tendency to servile imitation." By demanding political independence or civil rights, therefore, black southern Africans, according to Junod, were merely engaging in Frazerian imitative magic. On the basis of science, rather than magic, Junod rejected the "principle of similarity" between blacks and whites in southern Africa. Insisting instead on a nonnegotiable principle of difference, Junod advised, "If we want to avoid the dangers which threaten us, let us encourage the Natives to remain as much as possible faithful to their own nature, to their traditions, to their mentality, and in view of all that, to their language." Rather than trying, by imitative magic, to be imitations of white people, Africans should maintain their "natural" place, "remaining Bantu tribes, keeping all they can of their old feudal system under the supervision of their white masters." If this course was adopted in southern Africa, Junod promised, then Africans "would be truly men, and not caricatures of white people, and they would not be so accessible to that spirit of dissatisfaction of which we see the traces growing amongst them."[42]

The Frazerian interest in fertility, like Frazer's theory of magic, also assumed strange local forms in southern Africa. In reviewing theoretical work on religion in nineteenth-century British social anthropology, Edmund Leach proposed that Frazer's attention to fertility ritual and magic should be read as an interest in sexuality, euphemistically disguised under the designation "fertility," in deference to late-Victorian sensibilities.[43] By contrast, in the context of southern Africa, Junod was less reticent about primitive sex, even though he observed, "[The] sexual life of the Bantus especially shocks our moral feelings."[44] He wrote freely, and directly, about sex in Thonga religion, culture, and social relations. A direct discourse about sexuality was necessary, for Junod, because keeping Africans "under the supervision of their white masters" depended upon authoritative scientific knowledge about the most intimate details of African personal and social life.

COLONIAL STRUGGLES WITH RITUAL

In an essay on the Thonga published in 1905, Henri-Alexandre Junod recapitulated basic themes of imperial comparative religion, beginning with animism as the savage philosophy underlying Thonga religion; considering savage supreme beings by speculating that the Thonga term for heaven, *Tilo*, bore traces of a forgotten monotheism; and asserting a fundamental distinction between religion and magic, with religion found in offerings and prayers and magic found in divination and rainmaking.[45] Clearly, Junod's research on religion was informed by imperial theory—E. B. Tylor's animism, Andrew Lang's primitive monotheism, and James Frazer's distinctions among magic, religion, and science. As noted, Junod carried Frazer's questions into the field, trying to provide local answers to these general questions about marriage or government.[46] Often, Junod's answers to Frazer's questions were negative: no, they do not practice primitive promiscuity; no, they do not periodically kill their kings. Nevertheless, Frazer's imperial anthropology of religion, with its scientific intent, was invoked by Junod in underwriting and legitimating his own scientific enterprise.

However, while he deferred to Frazer's broad framework for defining magic, religion, and science, Junod turned to the work of Arnold van Gennep (1873-1957), whose landmark study of rites of passage was published in 1909, to advance the analysis of ritual process.[47] Consistently and repeatedly, Junod employed Van Gennep's modeling of the three ritualized stages of social separation, marginality, and reaggregation in analyzing Thonga rituals of entering adulthood, dealing with death, moving a village, and engaging in warfare.[48] In all of these cases, from life-cycle rituals to national rituals, Junod followed Van Gennep in analyzing the social dynamics of change in ritual processes.

Junod might very well have felt a linguistic affinity with the author of *Les rites de passage*, since he was quite clear in his introduction to *The Life of a South African Tribe* that he would have preferred writing in French; he wrote in English only to reach a wider scientific audience. However, the distinction between scientific and practical spheres was crucial to Junod's work, as he self-consciously separated these concerns, reserving his "practical" recommendations for a series of appendices. Significantly, almost all of his practical advice had to do with intervening in African rites of passage—rites of infancy, male circumcision, polygamous marriage, and *lobola*—and civilizing Africans by breaking the hold of "communalism" and converting them to the "individualism" of civilization. Having applied science to the analysis of ritual, drawing on Frazer for defining terms and Van Gennep for analyzing process, Junod gave practical advice that was almost entirely focused on intervening in African rituals.

Sacrifice, the most "clearly established and typical ritual" of the Thonga, constituted "the most definite and settled element of the religious life of the tribe."[49] Junod distinguished between family sacrifices, on the one hand, which were performed to mark life-cycle transitions, to establish or leave a homestead, and to maintain ongoing relations with ancestors, and, on the other hand, national sacrifices of chiefly authority in celebrating the first fruits of a harvest, making rain, or preparing for war. In all these cases, sacrifices combined ritual speech and action, the uttering of prayers and a sound that Junod at one point called the "sacramental *tsu*," and the offering of a sanctified object, a *mhamba*. In his 1913 edition of *The Life of a South African Tribe*, Junod explained that material offerings were necessary, but it was "the famous *tsu* which makes them a *hahla*, a real sacrifice."[50] Revising this discussion in his 1927 edition, Junod repeated the importance of these two elements, the verbal and the material, but he deleted the phrase "a real sacrifice."[51] This revision, we will find, was consistent with Junod's eventual recasting of Thonga "mental life" as more magical than religious. Repeatedly, Junod redefined as magic practices that he had previously regarded as religious.

Junod's definitions of magic, religion, and science, which were broadly derived from Frazer's basic categories, remained constant in the two editions.[52] These definitions were not revised, but their applications to Thonga practices underwent a subtle transformation. For example, after describing ancestral sacrifice, Junod in 1913 observed that these "propitiatory rites very rarely bear a magical character: they are *religious acts*, viz., acts performed with the intention of influencing living, conscious and superior beings, and consist in most cases in gifts."[53] In the 1927 edition, in place of this assertion that sacrifices were essentially religious acts, with little trace of magic, Junod observed: "We shall often see such *magic acts* performed in the ancestor worship of the Thongas. This is in keeping with their general conception of Nature . . . and with the magic principles or axioms of primitive mentality."[54] His summation of the "general characteristics of ancestrolatry" in the two editions was almost identical. Ancestral observances were spiritualistic, animistic, particularistic, social, unsacerdotal, nonmoral, unphilosophical, and directed toward gaining specific material benefits in this life.[55] In the 1927 edition, however, Junod interpolated a sentence to amplify the magical character of ancestral sacrifice: "Though consisting essentially of offerings and prayers, which are distinctly religious acts, it is mingled with magic to a considerable extent."[56]

This mingling of religion and magic was a concern for Junod in both editions. But where he had previously seen essentially religious acts tainted by magic, by 1927 he was convinced that religious features had only been added on to basically magical acts. Where he had worried in 1913 that in Thonga ritual "religion [was] greatly disfigured by magic," in 1927 he revised this sentence to assert more decisively that "religion [was] largely adulterated by magic."[57] In principle, Junod was able to separate religion and magic, especially in sacrificial ritual, by distinguishing between objects that were given religiously and objects that were employed magically. He invoked Thonga terms—*mhamba* for sacrificial offerings, *miri* for magical charms—in reinforcing this distinction between religion and magic. In the 1913 edition, this distinction was simple and straightforward: "When the national priest 'sacrifices' with the great *mhamba*, he prays to the ancestor-gods of the country: this is Religion; but he also brandishes the sacred object containing their nails and hair, to influence them: this is Magic."[58] This passage, with its clear distinction between religion and magic, was deleted from the 1927 edition. Thus Thonga religious practices were redefined as magical practices.

Even his old friend the diviner Mankhelu suffered from this redefinition. Described by Junod as "the most distinguished medicine-man I ever met," Mankhelu was a diviner and herbalist, a rainmaker and counselor to chiefs, and a general of the army.[59] During the Sikororo war, Mankhelu entered a battle in November 1901 by first fashioning a *mhamba*, a sacred bundle of grass, to invoke ancestral protection. Recounting this event in 1913, Junod characterized the *mhamba* as "a prayer in action"; in 1927 he rendered it as "verbal magic."[60]

What happened? What happened between 1913 and 1927 to change Junod's analysis of the religious or magical character of Thonga ritual practices? Certainly his anthropological mentor, James Frazer, had changed his terms of reference, modifying the subtitle of his master work, *The Golden Bough*, from "A Study in Comparative Religion" in his first edition of 1890 to "A Study in Magic and Religion" in the second edition of 1900 and all subsequent editions.[61] For Frazer, this emphasis on magic allowed him to highlight "fundamental laws of thought" that distinguished magic from science. In Junod's case, however, we might consider several possible explanations.

First, according to Junod, during the intervening years he had acquired new information that enabled him to provide a more accurate account of the meaning of sacrificial offerings, the *mhamba*, in Thonga "mental life." Certainly almost all of the substantial revisions of his book between 1913 and 1927 related to the meaning of material objects used in ritual. Perhaps new conversations with informants or further fieldwork provided Junod with more information to discriminate between religious and magical practices. If so, he must have gathered this new information between 1913 and 1920, when he left South Africa for Switzerland. But the changes in his text seem less like new information than like simple editorial revisions, recasting the same ritual objects; for example, "gifts offered to the gods" became "the magical objects used in worship."[62] The 1927 edition did not provide new data; it reclassified old data.

Second, if Junod had adopted a new theoretical framing, this is not clear from his texts. As noted, his definitions of key terms—magic, religion, and science—remained constant in the two editions. Perhaps he had been influenced by Lucien Lévy-Bruhl, since he used the phrase "primitive mentality," but he was critical of Lévy-Bruhl, and his theoretical mentors remained Frazer and Van Gennep. Certainly he was testing their theories. In the case of Frazer, for example, Junod accepted his evolutionary scheme but adapted it to his Protestant missionary interests. Accordingly, Frazer's evolutionary progression from magic, through religion, to science was modified by Junod to anticipate an African evolution from magical manipulation, through symbolic representations, to a "perfectly spiritualized" religion "without any external and intermediary means."[63] Of course, that was not what Frazer had in mind. But Junod still considered himself to be faithful to both science and religion in charting this evolution from matter to spirit. Although this is purely speculation, Junod might have emphasized the magical character of African religious life after so many years as a missionary in Africa because he was frustrated that Africans had not participated in this evolutionary trajectory.

Finally, given this resistance to the civilizing process, Junod's use of the term *religion*, which could be a translatable, convertible, term, was supplanted by *magic*, a term of opposition, signifying an obstacle. Africans, with this magical mentality, stood in opposition to civilization. Nevertheless, Junod also documented the ambivalence of civilization. While it brought benefits, such as education, it also introduced "unnatural vice." Obstacles were everywhere, even at the heart of civilization. As Junod recognized, Africans were undergoing changes, requiring new rituals for mediating changing relations of colonial conquest, migrant labor, and urban life in the mining compounds of Johannesburg.

In what Junod called the "national" rituals of the Thonga, sacrifices were offered for harvest, rainmaking, and war. All of these collective rituals were reinforced by the "great *mhamba*," a ritual object associated with the authority and even incorporating the hair and fingernails of great chiefs of the past. These former chiefs, now powerful ancestral spirits, were all understood to reside in sacred forests. Junod recounted several stories demonstrating the statement "It is evident that, for the Thonga, the ancestor-gods dwell in the sacred woods."[64] These sacred groves, which must have recalled for Junod the sacred grove of Nemi that was the centerpiece of Frazer's *Golden Bough*, needed only the regular, periodic killing of a magician-king to conform to Frazer's archetypal model. "In many sacred woods," Junod maintained, without any supporting evidence, "a living *human victim* is offered to the gods."[65] But chiefs usually died natural deaths and were buried in the sacred woods. According to Junod, these sacred woods were sites of national significance.

Following the war with the Portuguese between 1894 and 1895, any "national" sovereignty was subsumed under the establishment of a colonial administration. As Junod recounted, this administration also intervened directly, even if unconsciously, in traditional Thonga sacred space. Building a camp and then a town near one of the sacred woods, the Portuguese authorities undertook the construction of a twenty-kilometer road to the port city of Lourenço Marques, widening an existing trail by cutting down the trees of this forest. One of Junod's informants, an elder by the name of Nkolele, described how he was horrified by witnessing this desecration of a chiefly ancestral site. In response, Nkolele performed a new kind of sacrificial ritual, presenting an offering to the ancestral chiefs of the sacred woods to ask their forgiveness for this colonial violation. Clearly, Junod was moved by this account, rising to Frazerian rhetoric in his florid evocation of the significance of this ritual encounter between the primitive and civilization: "Is there not something significant and touching about this tale? Civilization penetrates irresistibly, crushing everything in its way, and cutting remorselessly, perhaps unwittingly, through the edge of the sacred wood! And there, under the mahogany tree, the aged priest, the guardian of its traditions, swoons away and asks forgiveness for having been an involuntary witness of the sacrilege!"[66] Civilization, in the lexicon of imperial comparative religion, generally held positive valence, either as a term in structural opposition to savagery or as the destination of evolutionary progression from savagery. Here, although Junod adopted Frazer's florid rhetorical style, he countered these assumptions by depicting civilization as "penetrating," perhaps raping, but certainly desecrating a sacred space that was associated with African political sovereignty.

Another violation of African sovereignty can be seen in new colonial interventions in the regulation of native labor. As in other colonial regimes of labor extraction, the Portuguese coerced men into wage labor by imposing new forms of taxation, while justifying this coercion with rhetoric about the idleness of African males under the traditional gendered division of labor and the civilizing (and even Christianizing) influence of a "gospel of work" in which African laborers would be placed under colonial tutelage. In his 1905 essay on the Thonga, Junod relied on the colonial wisdom of a "Johannesburg labour agent, who had thousands of labourers under his daily notice," to identify the "intellectual traits" of Africans in this new labor market. According to this expert, while the Sotho were good for farm work and the Zulu for housework, the Thonga or Shangaan "can be put into a post requiring more intelligence; for example, he can be trusted with engines, as he seems to have some natural bent for mechanics." Junod cited the authority of an "old resident in the low country" to establish that in "mining operations the Thonga is better."[67] These migrant workers accounted for the majority—at least 70 percent—of the labor force in the mines.[68]

As Junod observed in *The Life of a South African Tribe*, the Thonga no longer lived in the primitive isolation of rural villages or sacred woods: "Now practically every grown-up Thonga has been to Johannesburg."[69] New rites of passage were necessary to mediate the movement between the home and the city. Junod documented the sacrifice performed for a young man leaving home for Johannesburg. Preparing protective medicines, the diviner took a little of the concoction in his mouth to spit at the young man while uttering "the sacramental *tsu*." Then the diviner prayed: "Death does not come to him for whom prayer is made; death only comes to him who trusts in his own strength! Let misfortune part [to far-off places]. Let him travel safely; let him trample on his enemies; let thorns sleep, let lions sleep; let him drink water wherever he goes, and let that water make him happy, by the strength of this leaf (viz., of my medicinal herbs)." Invoking the ancestral spirits, asking the diviner's ancestors to meet the traveler's ancestors, the diviner concluded the ritual of departure by washing the young man's body in the medicinal liquid.[70]

In this rite of separation, the traditional payment of the diviner was suspended, Junod noted, because the young man would "pay the fee on his return home." This deferral was certainly part of the ritual trust in ancestral protection during the journey. It anticipated the corresponding rite of reincorporation, "the sacrifice on behalf of the son who has just returned from Johannesburg."[71] In these new rites of separation and aggregation, migrant labor and reintegration in the homestead, the liminal space of working in the mines held the greatest danger. However, as we have seen, life in the mines and in the mining compounds also held the potential for creating new rituals, perhaps marginal rituals, perhaps even counter-rituals, for mediating the in-between space of life in an alien, alienating environment. As Junod had reported, ritual processions, marriage payments, and sacrificial offerings made "brides" and "husbands" in the mining compounds.

Junod struggled to propose practical methods for stopping this "unnatural vice." The mining compounds should prohibit curtains, prevent beds from touching each other, introduce guards, and install electric lights, he suggested, although he was not confident that any of these measures would provide a "remedy for this terrible evil." The corruption, as Junod saw it, resulted from contact with civilization, because "white civilization is responsible for the introduction and the frightful development of this vice amongst the Natives." Although ancient Greek heathenism, the font of European civilization, had celebrated this "refinement of immorality," Junod insisted that "Bantu heathenism, whatever may be its corruption, never dreamed of it." Sex between males, Junod insisted, was an alien intervention in Africa, coming with European civilization. He declared, "Unnatural vice was taught to the South African Bantus by men of a foreign race; it first invaded the prisons; now it is raging in these big Native miners' settlements, where it is deflouring [sic] the Bantu youth." Same-sex relations between African men in the prisons and mining compounds of Johannesburg, Junod concluded, represented "an iniquity which threaten[ed] the very life of the South African Tribe."[72] Junod's concern reflected a certain ambivalence about the beneficial effects of European civilization. While his anthropological mentor, James Frazer, was tracing "the gradual evolution of thought from savagery to civilization,"[73] Henri-Alexandre Junod was entangled in the colonial contradictions of civilization.

For African mine workers, who were mediating between urban and rural realities, the rituals of gender and sexuality, which marked males and females, making husbands and wives in the mining compounds, might have been antithetical to conventional practices of the rural homestead, even if they retained traditional forms of ritual exchange and sacrifice. Nevertheless, as historians of migrant labor have found, the rural homestead was increasingly dependent upon such contradictions, requiring the income from urban wage labor to sustain traditional relations of social reproduction. Certainly in the mining compounds, marriages between men were sexual relations, but they were also ritual relations that reflected back on relations of gender, families, and ancestors that built up a home. For example, young men who became "wives" in the mining compounds could accumulate resources to return home and become husbands of their own households.[74] Accordingly, as Junod found, rituals in the homestead paid special attention to the rites of passage for young men leaving and returning from working in Johannesburg.

MINES, COMPOUNDS, AND PRISONS

For migrant laborers, working in Johannesburg required entering a liminal space. Following Van Gennep's formula for rites of passage, rituals of separation and rituals of incorporation could mediate the process of leaving and returning home. But what rituals were being developed for dealing with the potential and the danger of the in-between space of liminality?

Carrying on his father's ethnographic work, Junod's son Henri-Philippe Junod (1897–1987) became an expert on African life in the mines, compounds, and prisons. As an anthropological consultant for the Transvaal Chamber of Mines, during 1936 and 1937 the younger Junod gave lectures to mining officials and compound managers on the "Bantu Heritage." In 1938 these lectures were published as a book, complete with a preface by mining-industry spokesman William Gemmill, who recommended the volume because it explained "the races whose work [made] European life in South Africa, as we know it, possible."[75] Reviewing Henri-Philippe Junod's *Bantu Heritage*, the American anthropologist William R. Bascom observed that it offered a "sketchy outline of Bantu life used as a basis for demonstrating that Africans are human beings and that some of their customs are worth preserving." Displaying confused ideas about race, language, and psychology, Henri-Philippe Junod explored and explained Bantu mentality by "discussing baskets, xylophones, bark cloth, totemism, magic, possession, ancestor worship, and the supreme deity entitled 'The Bantu Mind.'"[76]

Although Henri-Philippe Junod described the Bantu mentality, particularly as it was manifested through ritual and magic, it was probably what he had to say about the sex life of the Bantu that was most relevant to the interests of the mining industry. Unlike other human beings, he claimed, a black migrant worker in the mines was perfectly suited to have sexual relations with his wife once a year when he returned home to his family in the reserves, because his "sexual life [was] more seasonal, more natural, than other people." In other words, according to Henri-Philippe Junod, the Bantu had a sexuality more animal than human, which was entirely fit for migrant labor, the single-sex hostel, and the closed compound of the mines. In this respect, black southern Africans were supposedly unique: "One only needs to remember the 330,000 Bantu men working on the mines, most of them segregated in compounds, to visualize what the conditions would be from a sexual point of view if they belonged to other races." Other people might present a problem, Henri-Philippe Junod concluded, but black workers—more seasonal, more natural, and, by implication, more animal than human—were supposedly suited to the subhuman working and living conditions on the mines. Well into the mid-twentieth century, these arguments about magical mentality and seasonal cycles of primitive sexuality continued to be used by the mining industry to justify the exploitation of African labor.[77]

As Henri-Alexandre Junod recognized, new rituals were being enacted in the mining compounds of Johannesburg. These rituals might have echoed ancestral exchanges by sacrificing a goat or interfamily relations by the paying of *lobola*, but they effectively remade males and females, husbands and wives, within the liminal space of life on the mines.

An African innovator in ritual, Mzuzephi Mathebula (1867–1948), who came to be known as Nongoloza, left Zululand in 1888 to look for work in Johannesburg. He found employment with a group of white criminals, highwaymen, which opened up new possibilities. Nongoloza later recounted, "I decided to start a band of robbers on my own."[78] Inspired by the biblical account of the people of ancient Nineveh, who had rebelled against the Lord, Nongoloza determined that his band of robbers would be the Ninevites fighting against government and industry that had set themselves up as lords over Africans. Within ten years, Nongoloza's army of criminals, the Ninevite army, had grown to more than a thousand. Through the concerted efforts of the South African army and police during the period 1910–20, the Ninevites were eventually defeated and Nongoloza imprisoned.[79]

Although the historical Nongoloza, Mzuzephi Mathebula, became a prison warder, the mythical Nongoloza, as the journalist Jonny Steinberg has recently documented, became "the God of South African prisoners."[80] This deification of Nongoloza developed against the background of a mythic horizon, a sacred narrative familiar to every prisoner, in which an old wise man, variously known as Nkulukut or Po, initiated Nongoloza into the sacred secret of the gold-mining industry. "I have been to the mines," the wise man revealed. "The gold of the white man is good. You must take it, but not from the ground. You must rob it from the white man himself."[81] In this myth, historical details were modified temporally by placing the foundational event in 1812, seventy-four years before gold was discovered on the Witwatersrand, and they were modified spatially by placing the gold mines in Portuguese-controlled East Africa, at Delagoa Bay, in Lourenço Marques rather than in Johannesburg. Nevertheless, this narrative provided a mythic warrant for criminal activity.

Myth also underwrote ritual. Stealing a bull from a white farmer, Nongoloza and his colleagues performed a ritual sacrifice, killing and consuming the bull but preserving the hide of the sacrificial animal as a parchment for transcribing all of the sacred laws of their criminal confederation. Dissension broke out, however, over the lawfulness of sex between men. Invoking the authority of the sacred laws inscribed on the hide of their original sacrificial victim, Nongoloza insisted that women were poison, so soldiers in his criminal army had to choose wives from among the young men. Others disagreed. The ancient wise man intervened in this dispute by saying, "Go to the mines." But he died before this dispute could be resolved. In the myth, this question of sex between men was not resolved, because the criminals drew different conclusions from what they observed in the residential compounds of the mining industry. Seeing men engaging in sexual relations, some felt vindicated, and others opposed what they regarded as an alien practice that had been introduced by foreigners, echoing, in this respect, Henri-Alexandre Junod's insistence that "unnatural vice" was alien to Africans. In this dispute, however, what was at stake was the process of making and remaking human relations, under dehumanizing conditions, in which ritual marked elders and juniors, males and females, in new rites of passage within the civilized institutions of the mining industry, residential compounds, and prisons.

These rituals of making soldiers and subordinates, adults and children, and men and women have been central to prison life in South Africa. Nongoloza, "the God of South African prisoners," lives on through the men, the *ndotas*, who can divine the sacred law and enforce the sacred rituals of violence. In their studies of ritual, James Frazer and Henri-Alexandre Junod attended to such intersections of divinity, divination, and politics. According to Frazer, there were two types of "human gods," the religious and the magical, one receiving offerings, the other asserting control.[82] In Junod's research, ancestral spirits and diviners represented the two types of "human gods" in this calculus of religion and magic. Since Frazer objected to any deification of human beings, he was uncomfortable with Junod's practice of referring to Thonga ancestral spirits, *shikwemba*, as "ancestral gods" or sometimes simply as "gods."[83] He was also uncomfortable with any suggestion that diviners might know what they were doing.

Diviners, according to Frazer, were magicians, setting themselves up as "human gods" in asserting control over nature. "Among the objects of public utility which magic may be employed to secure," Frazer asserted, "the most essential is an adequate supply of food."[84] Claiming magical authority over public access to food, whether in hunting, fishing, or farming, diviners, Frazer argued, performed magical rites to control what was beyond their control. Among his illustrations, Frazer cited Junod's account of diviners engaged in "the magical control of rain."[85] Such diviners, Frazer concluded, were clever frauds, "men of the keenest intelligence and the most unscrupulous character."[86] Echoing Frazer, Junod observed, "One of the greatest curses of native life, perhaps the greatest obstacle to the enlightenment and true progress of the Thonga, is the little basket of *divinatory bones*"; yet he also echoed Frazer's paradox by observing, "These bones are the most clever thing they possess."[87] Acknowledging this "keenest intelligence" in divination, Junod sought to learn its system. But he also saw diviners as crucial mediators between ancestral religion and Christianity, as in the case of Elias Libombo, or between ancestral tradition and civilization, as in the case of Mankhelu, on the frontlines of new rites of passage into modernity.

Frazer imagined an evolutionary trajectory in which magicians became kings. In Frazer's politics of magic, the public magician rose to political power by inspiring fear and accumulating wealth. Then, Frazer maintained, magic eventually gave way to religion as "the king, starting as a magician, tend[ed] gradually to exchange the practice of magic for the priestly functions of prayer and sacrifice." In this argument, circling back to his analysis of "human gods" as either magical or religious, Frazer concluded, "No class of the community has benefitted so much as kings by this belief in the possible incarnation of a god in human form."[88] Junod's magicians, however, were neither gods nor kings. They were converts or criminals, as can be seen in the case of the diviner Elias Libombo who became a church elder and in the case of the diviner Mankhelu who became a reprieved convict. Although he attempted to apply the basic principles of Frazer's imperial theory, which defined magic in opposition to religion and posed magic as a prelude to religion, Junod also struggled to make sense of the role of ritual in colonial situations. Here ritual was being redefined, not only through changes in the primordial practices of ancestral homesteads or sacred woods, but also in the modern mediations of labor, industry, and disciplinary institutions.

Within the mining compounds and prisons, new gods and kings were emerging, with new rituals of sacrifice and new rites of passage. Their rituals, which appropriated the military discipline and insignias of rank associated with what the anthropologist Michael Taussig has called the "magic of the state," became deeply embedded in the culture of South African prisons and urban criminal gangs.[89] James Frazer, from the imperial center, could not comprehend these new ritual transactions, and Henri-Alexandre Junod, from within the colonial context, could not control them. In a changing South Africa, ritual took on a life of its own.

Under changing colonial conditions, Junod felt a sense of urgency to document savage culture before it disappeared in the wake of civilization's advance in South Africa. Clearly, African life was changing through colonial interventions, Christian conversions, and the ongoing incorporation of people in networks of excessive taxation, labor extraction, and political exclusion. In his introduction to *The Life of a South African Tribe*, Junod seemed more concerned that Africans were abandoning traditional ways for new forms of political mobilization. To illustrate the urgency of collecting information about savage life before it was distorted beyond recognition, Junod related his "sad experience" of trying to pursue his research questions about ritual and magic with three African political leaders he met in 1909 while traveling on a Union-Castle steamship to England. These three "well known Native gentlemen," Junod understood, were going to London "for political reasons." One was the editor of a native newspaper, another a Christian chief, and the third the head of an education and training institution that he had founded. Junod enjoyed their shipboard meetings and conversations. But he also wanted to take the opportunity of their mutual confinement on the ship to advance his research by gathering "ethnographic facts from them." Since they "were Zulus," he recalled, "I wanted to know for purposes of comparison what were the precise ideas of their tribe about witchcraft." Imagining that these Zulu gentlemen would cooperate with his research just as his Thonga informants had, Junod was shocked when they either refused to answer his questions or turned the tables by questioning him. Junod exclaimed, "Never in my scientific career did I meet with a more complete failure!"[90]

These three gentlemen were, in fact, traveling to England for political reasons, since they were petitioning the British Parliament against the injustice of the color bar in the South Africa Act that excluded Africans from citizenship and other rights in the Union of South Africa that was to be established in 1910. They were part of a larger delegation led by W. P. Schreiner, former prime minister of the Cape Colony, which included president of the Cape Native Convention John Tengo Jabavu, president of the African Peoples Organization Abdullah Abdurahman, and various other political leaders. Although Junod did not identify them by name, these three gentle-men were prominent figures in the emerging South African Native National Congress, which eventually became the African National Congress. Junod reported only that they were uncooperative subjects in a failed ethnographic experiment. The editor, Walter Rubusana, was not only a minister of the Congregational Church but also an educator, with a PhD from McKinley University, and president of the South African Native Convention. From a Xhosa-speaking rather than a Zulu-speaking background, editing a "na-tive paper" that was published in isiXhosa, Rubusana might not have been able to help in Junod's comparative research into Zulu ritual and magic. Nevertheless, Junod expressed disappointment that the editor, born into a Christian family, had "never lived amongst heathen" and therefore could not provide authentic responses to questions concerning Zulu heathenism. While concluding that the Christian editor was unable to help, Junod was surprised that the Christian chief was unwilling to help. This chief, Daniel Dwanya, like Rubusana, was an elected representative of the South Af-rican Native Convention. Also like Rubusana, he did not represent a Zulu-speaking constituency. In their conversations, Junod found that the chief knew much more about the subject of witchcraft than the editor "but, for some obscure reason, was not inclined to disclose his knowledge."[91]

For all of his efforts to reinforce the notion of tribalism in South Africa, emphasizing the unity of language, culture, and religion in his Thonga tribe, Junod seemed strangely unaware of the linguistic or ethnic backgrounds of his conversation partners. He also seemed oblivious to their political work to cut across such boundaries as they opposed injustice in South Africa. However, during his failed shipboard experiment, Junod experienced his greatest frustration in conversation with the head of the native educational institution, John Dube, who actually was from a Zulu-speaking back-ground. As we recall, this American-educated Christian minister was ac-tively involved in African education, politics, and international exchanges, even raising money for his school from the international academic visitors of the British Association for the Advancement of Science in 1905. Finding him to be a "very clever man," Junod was shocked when Dube disrupted his scientific experiment in comparison, first by asserting his own com-parison between Africans and Europeans and then by recasting Junod in the role of the informant. Although Junod was trying to gather informa-tion for a comparison of Thonga and Zulu notions about witchcraft, John Dube "declared that witchcraft was met with amongst white people just the same as amongst South African Natives." Accordingly, beliefs and practices associated with witchcraft could not be regarded as uniquely African nor understood by comparing Africans. Proposing an explanation that embraced both Africans and Europeans, Dube argued that in both cases what Junod was calling "witchcraft" was really "only a form of mesmerism." As both an aspiring science and a public performance, mesmerism had a long and popular career in Europe that Dube thought might explain a wider range of spiritual beliefs and practices in Europe and Africa. Saying that he was "always anxious to get more knowledge himself," Junod recalled, Dube "proceeded to question me about mesmerism." Forced to shift roles from scientific investigator to indigenous informant, Junod complained, "The whole interview ended therefore in a lesson which I was obliged to give him on that mysterious subject."[92]

In a "melancholy mood" as a result of this failed experiment, this "sad experience" in which he learned nothing from his new Zulu friends on the ship, Junod exclaimed, "How different it was with my Thonga informants, Mboza, Tobane, and even Elias!" Certainly those three Thonga friends were different because they answered his questions. But they were also different from the native gentlemen on the ship, according to Junod, because they supposedly had not been affected by any outside European influences. Of course, this was not the case, since European colonization had affected everything in their lives. But Junod persisted in asserting that the Thonga provided the perfect setting for his research, the "most favourable imaginable for such an investigation," because the "great bulk of the tribe is still absolutely savage."[93]

Perhaps Junod used the term *savage* in this case to distinguish his authentic Africans from the African politicians who were protesting their exclusion from the Union of South Africa. For the study of religion, however, Junod's claim that his Thonga were still "absolutely savage" was framed in the light of the criteria set by James Frazer for reliable information about savage religion. First, European researchers had to be present, basing their reports on what they had personally observed. According to Frazer, "What we want, therefore, in this branch of science is, first and foremost, full, true, and precise accounts of savage and barbarous peoples based on personal observation."[94] Second, however, European researchers had to pretend that they were not present. In producing their accounts about savages, observers were urged to render reports that erased not only their own presence but also the colonial conditions and intercultural exchanges in which they were working. Frazer advised, "Every observer of a savage or barbarous people should describe it as if no other people existed on the face of the earth."[95]

Although Junod knew that most of his Thonga had been to Johannesburg, if not on the ship to England, and were increasingly drawn into migrant labor, mining compounds, and prisons in South Africa, Frazer's methodological mandate required him to represent his "absolutely savage" Thonga as if no other people on the face of the earth were part of their lives.

ELEMENTARY FORMS OF THE STUDY OF RELIGION

In the history of anthropology, Henri-Alexandre Junod has often been celebrated for producing the first modern ethnographic monograph, *The Life of a South African Tribe*. Relying on his African informants, such as the Christian convert Elias Libombo and the indigenous diviner Mankhelu, for his primary religious data, Junod depended upon the latest developments in imperial theory to organize this data into scientific findings about Thonga religion. Writing both in English and in French, Junod was a mediator in the study of religion between two imperial centers, with the additional complexity that his homeland of Switzerland also placed him between French and German interests. On the British side, while claiming James Bryce as his British imperial patron and adapting James Frazer's key terms—magic, religion, and science—in his research, Junod identified with British social anthropology. But he also looked to contemporary developments in the academic study of religion in France, where the sociologist Emile Durkheim (1858–1917) had turned his attention to religion around 1895 and created a community of scholars in the sociological study of religion. As the historian Patrick Harries wryly observed, "Informants ranging from Elias Libombo to Emile Durkheim inspired Junod to uncover a strongly religious element in the spirituality of the Thonga."[96] Strangely, Junod never mentioned Durkheim in print. Nor did he acknowledge the work of Durkheim's nephew, student, and eventual successor in the sociology of religion, Marcel Mauss, who, with Henri Hubert, was publishing landmark studies on ritual sacrifice in 1898 and on magic in 1902–3, the very terms that Junod used to organize the spirituality of the Thonga.

In reviewing Junod's first ethnographic book, *Les Ba-Ronga*, published in 1898, Emile Durkheim and Marcel Mauss were both appreciative of the effort but critical of the results. According to Durkheim, Junod was ignorant of comparative ethnography, so he provided a wealth of descriptive detail about a savage tribe with no attention to explanation. Without answering any theoretically informed question, all of this detail only amounted to a wasted opportunity for studying primitive society. In his review, which was generally more positive, Marcel Mauss raised a different problem by observing that Junod's "tribe" was not primitive at all because it was involved in processes of social change brought on by European colonization and Christian missions. Accordingly, Junod's research could not be expected to uncover anything useful about the elementary forms of social or religious life.[97] Junod seems to have taken these criticisms seriously. He embarked upon an intensive study of the comparative ethnography of religion and religions.

Junod certainly must have read the contemporary Durkheimian research on ritual and magic. In the same issue of Durkheim's journal, *L'Année sociologique*, in which Junod's *Les Ba-Ronga* was reviewed by Durkheim and by Mauss, Marcel Mauss and Henri Hubert published their landmark study on sacrificial ritual. Rejecting earlier theories of sacrifice, such as E. B. Tylor's "gift theory" and William Robertson Smith's "communion theory," they introduced a new theory of sacrifice as the dynamic mediation between the sacred and the profane. To sacrifice was to consecrate, to make sacred, to "set apart," which entailed transforming the social status of the performers, the participants, the beneficiaries, and the sacrificial objects from the ordinary, profane realm of social life. According to Mauss and Hubert, sacrifice was not a bribe to the gods, an act of giving something of value to spiritual beings so they would give in return, nor was sacrifice merely a meal shared with the gods, an occasion for participating in a communal meal by sharing the sacrificial victim. As a social process, sacrificial ritual mediated between ordinary, everyday life and the sacred, enabling participants to enter the sacred realm and then to exit transformed, as the sacrificial victim was transformed by being destroyed in the ritual.[98]

By contrast to this social mediation of the sacred and profane in sacrificial ritual, Mauss and Hubert defined magic as essentially antisocial. In their essay on magic, they found both religion and magic to be ways of gaining access to supernatural power, so they could not easily be differentiated. Rejecting the intellectualist orientation of British anthropology, which was evident in E. B. Tylor's notion that religion was a prescientific way of explaining things or James Frazer's notion that magic was a prescientific way of controlling things, they located the distinction between ritual and magic in society. While religious practices were "public, obligatory, [and] regular," reinforcing a public sense of social solidarity, magical practices were "mysterious, isolated, furtive, scattered and broken up," often performed in woods, away from dwellings, in some out-of-the-way place that was remote or hidden from public space. Religion, ritual, and sacrifice were all public, building up social solidarity, but magic was private, asserting individual claims on supernatural power, and therefore it was essentially antisocial.[99] In his *Elementary Forms of the Religious Life*, published in 1912, Emile Durkheim certified this social distinction between religious ritual and magic, defining religion as beliefs and practices in relation to the sacred that unified people into a community and identifying magic as individual claims to sacred power that were inherently contrary to the formation of any social solidarity or institutionalized religion.[100]

In his study of comparative ethnography, Junod could have adopted these terms of reference. But he did not. Instead, he turned to the work of Arnold van Gennep, a personal friend, whose book on rites of passage, published in 1909, guided much of Junod's analysis of life-cycle rituals of birth, adolescence, marriage, and death in Thonga religion. As both a folklorist and an anthropologist, Arnold van Gennep (1873-1957) had a very difficult career.[101] In his first ethnographic book, *Tabou et Totémisme à Madagascar* of 1904, he tested various anthropological theories about totemism in relation to evidence that could be gained from travelers' reports about Madagascar, France's most recent colony, while also hoping to provide knowledge about religion and society that would be useful for the "durable colonization" of that African island.[102] His next book, on Australian totemism, brought him directly into conflict with Emile Durkheim, who was building his theory of religion on the premise that the indigenous Arunta of Australia represented the most primitive form of religious organization. According to Van Gennep, the aboriginal Arunta were not primitive fossils from human prehistory but a more complex society with developed institutions.[103] Therefore, directing Mauss's criticism of Junod back on Durkheim, these aboriginal Australians could not reveal the elementary forms of religious and social life. For his part, when Van Gennep's *Les rites des passage* appeared in 1909, Mauss turned Durkheim's criticism of Junod onto Van Gennep, observing that the book just collected disparate descriptive details without any explanation that was grounded in social context.[104]

Arnold van Gennep was ostracized, even exiled, from the sociological study of religion that was developing around Emile Durkheim and his colleagues in Paris. But he had a friend in Junod, who helped arrange the only academic position that Van Gennep ever held, a professorial chair in ethnography at the University of Neuchâtel, Junod's home in Switzerland, which he occupied from 1912 to 1915. During his tenure, Van Gennep convened an international conference on ethnographic research. Junod spoke at this conference, the only time he directly addressed the Durkheimian approach to the study of religion. He appreciated its attention to society but criticized its neglect of the personal character of religion.[105] Van Gennep's professorship was short-lived. He was forced to leave on account of his publications that questioned Swiss neutrality by criticizing what he saw as the country's pro-German policies at the beginning of World War I. Returning to France to breed chickens, Van Gennep also returned to his studies of European folklore, abandoning the ethnographic study of religion that had rejected him. As a folklorist, he wrote and lectured—including a tour of the United States in 1922 during which he suffered a cerebral hemorrhage—until his death in 1957. Long neglected by the study of religion, his work on rites of passage was eventually recovered in the 1960s by the Africanist anthropologist Victor Turner, who discovered Arnold van Gennep as a student at the University of Chicago by reading Junod's *Life of a South African Tribe*.[106]

Within South Africa, Junod's book was the central text in the training of a new generation of social anthropologists. Occupying the first chair in social anthropology at the University of Cape Town in 1921, A. R. Radcliffe-Brown was critical of some of Junod's conclusions, especially with respect to his analysis of kinship, but he nevertheless made his *Life of a South African Tribe* a required textbook for his lectures on anthropology. Bronislaw Malinowski, who had developed his own fieldwork-based theoretical reflections on religion, magic, and science, admired Junod's book, using it as background for his consultations in South Africa with the Swazi king Sobhuza in the 1930s and a baseline for understanding social and cultural change. Moving between South Africa and Britain, social anthropologists such as Isaac Schapera, Max Gluckman, and Monica (Hunter) Wilson built on Junod's legacy. New approaches in the anthropology of religion—functionalist, structural-functionalist, and eventually structuralist—drew on the pioneering efforts of Junod. Increasingly, however, social anthropologists in South Africa situated religion within the social fields of intercultural exchange and conflict.[107]

Even Marcel Mauss (1872–1950), a critic, used Junod's *Life of a South African Tribe* as a textbook in his courses at the Ecole Pratique des Hautes Etudes in Paris. As a historian of religions with wide-ranging interests and rigorous theoretical insight, Mauss had an abiding concern for Africa. Not only looking for elementary forms of social and religious life in Africa, Mauss attended to contemporary conflicts, such as the South African War (1899–1902). At the beginning of the war, while Friedrich Max Müller in Oxford was defending British sovereignty over South Africa, Marcel Mauss published an article in the journal *Mouvement Socialiste* attacking British aggression; at the end of the war, in the same journal, he attacked British capitalists, who had emerged as the only victors from the war by mining gold and diamonds and effectively enslaving African workers. Out of the South African War, Mauss drew a larger lesson for the international socialist movement: "For socialism," he wrote, "human solidarity is a sort of vague formula; it is not yet a traditional and active faith on the part of the universal proletariat."[108] Social solidarity, as the essence of religious faith, was the formula for a Durkheimian theory of religion. Here Mauss applied this theory of religion and society to the socialist movement, which could not achieve the human solidarity of a religion until it identified with the plight of African workers in South Africa.

However, even for a socialist such as Marcel Mauss, imperial pressures shaped relations with Africa. For example, during 1906 and 1907, his courses at the Ecole Pratique dealt primarily with Africa and the study of African religious systems, but they were specifically designed to establish "ethnographic instructions for observing the populations of French colonies in Western Africa and the Congo."[109] In 1925, along with the physical anthropologist Paul Rivet (1876–1958) and the philosopher Lucien Lévy-Bruhl (1857–1939), Mauss founded the Institute for Ethnology to train students for colonial service, with special attention to French colonies in Africa. His colleague Lévy-Bruhl explained that the institute would train colonial officers to advance "more rational and human modes of colonization."[110] For Lévy-Bruhl, the term *rational* held a specific significance, since he had argued in a series of books—*How Natives Think, Primitive Mentality*, and *The "Soul" of the Primitive*—that Africans and other savages had a "pre-logical mentality," based on mystical participation with the world, which was radically different from civilized rationality. "Primitives see with eyes like ours," he argued, "but they do not perceive with the same minds."[111] Junod objected to this great divide between two different types of mind, primitive and civilized, perhaps because it seemed to deny the possibility that Africans might not only hear but also understand his missionary gospel. But it also contradicted his own experience with African colleagues in his scientific research. Nevertheless, Junod's objection did not stop Lévy-Bruhl from combing through his publications for evidence of primitive mentality.

In the Durkheimian tradition, scholars of religion in France during the 1930s were interested in Junod not as a source for evidence of primitive mentality but for his relatively open discussion of sexuality. Following the translation of *Life of a South African Tribe* into French in 1936, Roger Caillois (1913–1978) devoted a substantial appendix in his book *Man and the Sacred*, originally published in 1939, to the topic "Sex and the Sacred," relying on Junod's research in South Africa for a detailed analysis of the role of the sacred in the "Sexual Purification Rites among the Thonga." Along with two other unconventional Durkheimians, Georges Bataille and Michael Leiris, Caillois was working at the time in the Collège de Sociologie, which they established between 1937 and 1939 to pursue themes in religion and the "dark side of humanity" that had been opened up by Durkheim's student Robert Hertz in his research on the asymmetrical opposition between right and left hands, religious rituals of death and mourning, and religious conceptions of sin and expiation. In his reading of Junod's account of Thonga sexuality and rituals of sexual purification, Caillois found that the Swiss missionary had provided the most precise and thorough description of savage life. For his theoretical purposes, Caillois used Junod's *Life of a South African Tribe* in two ways, to argue against Freudian psychoanalysts who had "too quickly projected the complexes of the 'civilized' upon 'savages'" and to broaden the notion of the sacred as not only the opposite of the profane but also an efficacious force, evident in human sexuality, which was "contagious, fleeting, ambiguous, and virulent."[112] The sacred, according to Caillois, "emanates from the dark world of sex and death, but it is the principle essential to life and the source of all efficacy." As Junod demonstrated in the case of the Thonga, religious rituals are enacted to harness this dangerous potency, attempting to "capture, domesticate, and engage it in beneficial ways, and if need be, to neutralize its excessive acidity."[113] Henri-Alexandre Junod, who had been frustrated in his attempts to capture and neutralize "illicit sex" among African migrant laborers, would have been surprised if he had lived long enough to discover that he had finally been accepted by Durkheimian students of religion as an expert on the rituals of sexuality at the heart of the sacred.

As a colonial middleman in the triple mediation that generated knowledge in the empire of religion, Henri-Alexandre Junod interacted with imperial theorists, both British and French, and engaged with indigenous Africans who were undergoing dramatic social change. Although he preferred his Thonga informants, who could provide him with primary data for constructing the religious system of an African tribe, the African political leaders who were his shipboard conversation partners in 1909 were emblematic of emerging intellectuals refusing to be data and seeking to alter the terms of engagement in producing knowledge about African life. In the early twentieth century, African intellectuals in South Africa drew inspiration from African Americans. While John Dube adhered to the educational philosophy of Booker T. Washington, other intellectuals, such as S. M. Molema and H. I. E. Dhlomo, were drawn to the more radical philosophy, sociology, and historical research of W. E. B. Du Bois, who was also a scholar of African religion. Turning imperial theorists into informants for their own projects, these intellectuals made significant interventions in the flow of knowledge production in the study of religion.

CHAPTER SEVEN

Humanity and Divinity

The idea of the "barbarous Negro" is a European invention.

LEO FROBENIUS

In *Souls of Black Folk*, published in 1903, W. E. B. Du Bois (1868–1963) insisted that the religious life of African Americans did not begin in America, because it was built on "definite historical foundations," the religious heritage of Africa. Characterizing indigenous African religion as "nature worship," with its incantations, sacrifices, and attention to good and evil spiritual influences, Du Bois invoked the African priest as both the guardian of African religious tradition and the mediator of religious change under slavery in America. As a result of colonization, passage, and enslavement, African social formations were destroyed, "yet some traces were retained of the former group life," Du Bois observed, "and the chief remaining institution was the Priest or Medicine-man." With the destruction of established African social relations of kinship and political sovereignty, which bore their own religious significance in Africa, the African priest represented a relatively mobile, transportable focus of religious life. Assuming multiple roles, operating as bard, physician, judge, and priest, the African ritual specialist "early appeared on the plantation and found his function as the healer of the sick, the interpreter of the Unknown, the comforter of the sorrowing, the supernatural avenger of wrong, and the one who rudely but picturesquely expressed the longing, disappointment, and resentment of a stolen and oppressed people."[1] In these evocative terms, Du Bois recalled the creativity of the African priest, who deployed indigenous African religious resources under radically altered conditions.

Although the religion of the African priest came to be known by different names, such as "Voodooism" (Vodou) or "Obe Worship" (Obeah), Du Bois provocatively proposed that another name eventually adopted in America for indigenous African religion was "Christianity." Within the limits of the slave system, but also within the space opened by the African priest, "rose the Negro preacher, and under him the first Afro-American institution, the Negro Church." According to Du Bois, this church, in the first instance, was not Christian but African, since it only placed a "veneer of Christianity" upon the ongoing adaptation of indigenous African beliefs and practices under slavery. Suggesting that the Christianization of indigenous African religion should be regarded as a gradual process of religious transformation, Du Bois observed that "after the lapse of many generations the Negro church became Christian." In reviewing the "faith of the fathers" in *Souls of Black Folk*, Du Bois sought to establish a basic continuity in religious life from Africa to African America. The "study of Negro religion," he insisted, had to carefully track a transatlantic process of religious development "through its gradual changes from the heathenism of the Gold Coast to the institutional Negro Church of Chicago," which began with indigenous African religion.[2]

Among his many interests, Du Bois was an African historian. During the long course of his life, he took up the challenge of providing general historical overviews of Africa and the African diaspora in five books, *The Negro* (1915), *Africa: Its Place in Modern History* (1930), *Black Folk: Then and Now* (1939), *The World and Africa* (1947), and *Africa: An Essay toward a History of the Continent of Africa and Its Inhabitants* (1963). Du Bois's interest in writing these books was certainly not strictly or merely historical, although his wide reading enabled him to synthesize a diverse range of historical and ethnographic sources into coherent narratives. In the process of providing accounts of African history, Du Bois engaged the African past as a basis for forging a pan-African future. Looking back in order to look forward, he concluded his earliest account of African history in *The Negro* with the promise, "[The] future world will, in all reasonable probability, be what colored men make it."[3] All of his histories of Africa were similarly focused on the African future.

In reconstructing the religious history of Africa, Du Bois had to have been tempted by prevailing forms of racial, ethnic, territorial, or geopolitical essentialism about Africans, African Americans, and the "dark continent" of Africa. He seems to have given in to those temptations occasionally. In *Souls of Black Folk*, he suggested that African Americans could essentially be defined by their inherent religiosity, because the Negro is "a religious animal."[4] In his earliest historical overview of Africa, *The Negro*, he suggested that Africa is essentially a religious continent, the "refuge of the gods."[5]

Reinforcing assumptions about wild Africans—the "religious animal" who came from the "refuge of the gods"—he proposed that when their religion was transposed to America, it inspired a "spirit of revolt."[6] But Du Bois's efforts to understand the role of indigenous African religion in Africa and the African diaspora went beyond such essentialist stereotypes. By wrestling with the dilemma of representing indigenous African religion, Du Bois raised crucial issues for the study of religion.

In his academic training at Harvard and in Germany, W. E. B. Du Bois established expertise in sociology, but he had wide interests in philosophy, psychology, and history as well. Studying with William James (1842-1910) at Harvard, Du Bois had explored both philosophy and psychology, influenced by the philosophical pragmatism and the psychology of will that James was developing. In his *Varieties of Religious Experience*, published in 1902, James highlighted the profound struggles of the divided soul, the "sick soul," in ways that have sometimes been compared to Du Bois's insights into the "double consciousness" of African Americans.[7] But Du Bois was more interested in sociology than psychology. In this regard, his experience in Germany was more influential, leading him into empirical sociology. By his own account, it was the German-American anthropologist Franz Boas (1858-1942) who inspired Du Bois to study African history. He invited Boas to Atlanta University, where he was lecturing in history, to speak at a commencement ceremony in 1906, and Du Bois was impressed by the anthropologist's lecture on African history. Having been taught in high school and at two universities that "the Negro has no history," Du Bois heard Franz Boas tell the students, "You need not be ashamed of your African past" and then proceed to recount the history of black kingdoms in Africa over the past thousand years. "I was too astonished to speak," Du Bois recalled. "All of this I had never heard and I came then and afterwards to realize how the silence and neglect of science can let truth utterly disappear or even be unconsciously distorted."[8] Recovering African history, therefore, was also a recovery of science from its own history of suppression.

As members of the U.S. delegation to the Universal Races Conference in London in 1911, Boas and Du Bois spoke on race, with Boas challenging the scientific validity of race and Du Bois providing detailed statistical analysis of the sociology of African Americans.[9] Neither was particularly interested in religion. But other speakers addressed indigenous religion in Du Bois's section, "The Modern Conscience in Relation to Racial Questions (the Negro and the American Indian)." A delegate from South Africa, John Tengo Jabavu (1859-1921), offered a quick sketch of the indigenous religious life of Africans: "In regard to religion they had a deep veneration for a Great Omnipresent, Omnipotent Unknown, and the spirits of their departed fathers were supposed to plead in their behalf concerning all the circumstances of their life. No temples were consequently reared. They neither worshipped the spirits of their fathers, as is commonly supposed, nor was their faith pinned to creatures 'in the heaven above, or that are in the earth below, or that are in the water under the earth.' In their customs may be discerned much of what one reads in the Pentateuch."[10] With its traces of Christian theology and a biblical framework for comparison, this account of African indigenous religion could not have been regarded by either Boas or Du Bois as a scientific rendering of African history. Clearly, Jabavu was following in a long line of European travelers, missionaries, settlers, and colonial administrators in looking for the unknown God and finding comparisons with ancient Israel in the religious beliefs and practices of Africans. As he dealt with indigenous African religion in many subsequent publications, Du Bois sought to place its beliefs and practices in African history.

African history, however, also included the history of Africans in America. Du Bois was particularly concerned with tracking the continuities and disruptions in that transatlantic history. According to the prevailing popular discourse, missionary propaganda, and academic research in the United States, African Americans had inherited a range of superstitious beliefs and magical practices from Africa. Superstition and magic, which were supposedly evident in African Vodou, Obeah, juju, or "mumbo-jumbo," allegedly characterized the spiritual inheritance from Africa. Any scientific recovery of African religious history, therefore, had to first confront that denial of the validity of African religion.

Native Americans had also confronted such denials of their religion in the United States. For example, the legislation banning religious ceremonies such as the Sun Dance in 1883 did not use the word "religion" but instead referred to "savage rites and heathenish customs" that had to be outlawed as contrary to civilization.[11] Gradually, however, as their sovereignty was destroyed and they were contained in reservations, Native Americans were acknowledged to have "religions." Researchers for the Smithsonian Institution's Bureau of American Ethnology advocated the performance of rituals that had been outlawed because John Wesley Powell wanted to study the Kiowa Medicine Dance and James Mooney wanted to stage a Ghost Dance at the Columbian Exposition in 1893.[12] As Native Americans increasingly began to use the term *religion*, some worked to radically spiritualize indigenous traditions. David Murray has observed in comparing perceptions of the religious life of Native Americans and African Americans in the United States, "While African Americans were restricted to magic the Indians were elevated above it into the realms of spirituality."[13] At the Universal Races Conference in 1911, a spokesperson for Native Americans, Charles A. Eastman (1858–1939), representing the Sioux, promoted this indigenous spirituality. "The religion of the American Indian," he explained, had been "generally misunderstood"; the misunderstanding had arisen from Native American secrecy as well as from "the intolerance and prejudice of the outsider." Revealing the secret of Native American religion, Eastman explained that every Indian embraced a natural spirituality: "He was trained from infancy to hold the 'Great Mystery' sacred and unspeakable. That Spirit which pervades the universe in its every phase and form was not to be trifled with by him in express terms. The Indian cultivated his mind and soul so as to feel, hear and see God in Nature. He distinguished clearly between intellect and spirit, and while conceding to man superior intelligence, as evidenced by the gift of articulate speech, he perceived in the unerring instinct of the dumb creation something mysterious and divine."[14] Such an account of natural spirituality would not have been regarded by Boas or Du Bois as a scientific finding. Like Jabavu's Great Unknown, Eastman's Great Mystery seemed more like theosophy than history. While Boas developed the science of anthropology in the United States, with special attention to the cultures of Native Americans, Du Bois kept returning to the challenge of recovering African history that Boas had inspired.

Although religion was not his primary focus, Du Bois attempted to represent indigenous African religion in his histories of Africa. In the process, he wrestled with three enduring problems—African humanity, African divinity, and transatlantic continuity between Africa and African America. First, the problem of African humanity, which had been denigrated in the study of religion by representing Africans as fetishists, as less than human because they allegedly worshipped objects that were less than human, required a historical critique of the conditions under which the fetish had emerged in European discourse about Africans. Second, the problem of African divinity, which had been formulated by European travelers and missionaries as the search for the unknown God, also had to be subjected to historical review. Africans, Du Bois argued, knew about God, but that religious knowledge was not a question of theology; it was an issue of political sovereignty. Third, the problem of transatlantic continuity, connecting African Americans with an African religious heritage, was an academic problem; Melville J. Herskovits argued for continuity and E. Franklin Frazier argued for radical disruption in this relation.[15] For Du Bois, however, this question was not merely an academic problem, since he sought to forge in African America and the African diaspora a pan-African unity. By tracing the shifts in his historical representations of indigenous African religion from 1915 to 1947, we can see how Du Bois struggled with these problems of humanity, divinity, and transatlantic continuity.

RECOVERING THE FETISH

As a significant part of African cultural heritage, the indigenous religious life of Africa featured in *The Negro*. In his discussion of African religion in 1915, Du Bois was concerned with three things: the meaning of the fetish, the belief in God, and the continuity between the indigenous religion of Africa and African American religion across the Atlantic.

Initially, Du Bois adopted a social evolutionary framework to account for African religious development. Borrowing familiar terms from the scientific study of savage or primitive religion, he maintained that African religion followed an evolutionary trajectory. Du Bois observed, "The religion of Africa is the universal animism or fetishism of primitive peoples, rising to polytheism and approaching monotheism chiefly, but not wholly, as a result of Christian and Islamic missions."[16] By adopting the terms *animism* and *fetishism*, Du Bois seemed to align his inquiry into African religion with the interests of European theorists who had been searching for the origin of religion in the fetishist's worship of material objects or the animist's attribution of spiritual life, agency, and power to material objects. A variety of evolutionary schemes, whether derived from the positivist philosophy of Auguste Comte or the scientific anthropology of E. B. Tylor, had identified this primitive religious materialism as the origin of religion. Whether identified as fetishism, animism, or totemism, that origin provided a baseline for tracking the evolutionary development of religion.[17] In his initial formulation of African indigenous religion, Du Bois seemed to be subscribing to this evolutionary model.

For evidence of the primitive origin of religion, as we have seen, European theorists looked to reports by European travelers, traders, missionaries, and colonial agents about savages in Africa, the Americas, Asia, Australia, and the Pacific Islands. Through a remarkable intellectual sleight-of-hand, European theorists used reports about their living contemporaries, these savages on the colonized peripheries, as if they were evidence of the original primitive ancestors of all humanity. In the process, they speculated about an evolutionary trajectory, beginning in fetishism, which left both the original primitives and contemporary savages behind in the developmental advance of human progress.[18] In *The Negro*, Du Bois also relied upon such European reports about the African fetish, citing a missionary, an explorer, and even an imperial bureaucrat, James Bryce. Du Bois cited Bryce's account of the religion of Bantu-speaking people in South Africa as evidence of the primitive baseline of fetishism or animism out of which all other forms of religion had developed. For indigenous Africans in South Africa, as for "most savage races," Bryce reported, "the world was full of spirits—spirits of the rivers, the mountains, and the woods."[19] This fetishism or animism, according to Bryce, had developed into the ancestor worship, the propitiation of "ghosts of the dead," that characterized the religious life of Africans in South Africa. In the process of religious evolution that began with primitive fetishism or animism, African ancestor worship could gradually evolve into polytheism and monotheism, as ancestral spirits were transformed into many gods and many gods were synthesized into one. Employing this developmental scheme, Du Bois's formulation of African religion clearly bore traces of evolutionary assumptions to which European theorists of religion such as John Lubbock, E. B. Tylor, Herbert Spencer, and James Frazer would have subscribed. He seemed to be making their case in his account of African religion.

However, Du Bois was also making a different case by arguing against any association of the fetish with cultural degeneration. Running contrary to the discourse of prominent European theorists, popular accounts of fetishism did not always place the fetish at the origin of evolutionary progress. By stark contrast, European politicians, journalists, and especially Christian missionaries often represented fetishism not as the beginning of human evolution but as the end of human degeneration. For example, one of Du Bois's sources, the American Presbyterian missionary Robert Hamill Nassau (1835–1921), who had spent forty years in West Africa, insisted that fetishism was the primary cause of African degradation. In his monograph *Fetichism of West Africa*, published in 1904, Nassau maintained that the fetish stood at the center of indigenous African religion. However, for Nassau, the fetish was not the origin but the loss of religion. Fetishism, in Nassau's rendering, was a superstitious regard for the power of insignificant material objects that wove witchcraft and sorcery into every aspect of African thought, government, family, work, and daily life. Although essentially meaningless, according to Nassau, the fetish nevertheless produced disastrous practical effects in African society, leading to distrust, poisoning, secret societies, cannibalism, and depopulation, which effectively degraded Africans.[20]

In the light of these allegations, Du Bois's embrace of evolutionary theory was not necessarily designed to make common cause with European theorists of religion; it was more immediately deployed against any link between fetishism and degeneration. Although he briefly deferred to an evolutionary theory of religion with the fetish at its origin, Du Bois seemed more concerned with countering this missionary account of Africa's fetishistic degradation. As if he were responding directly to Nassau's accusation, Du Bois sought to rehabilitate the fetish. "It is not mere senseless degradation," he insisted. "It is a philosophy of life."[21] Instead of rendering fetishism as superstitious regard for material objects, he recast the fetish as the material focus of an indigenous African philosophy. According to Du Bois, the fetish represented both a logical and a practical recognition of the dynamic forces of life, the positive and negative spiritual conditions within which Africans lived. "Fetish is a severely logical way of accounting for the world in terms of good and malignant spirits," he asserted.[22] The fetish, therefore, was at the center of a moral philosophy in practice.

Du Bois's recovery of the African fetish can be seen against the deep background of nineteenth-century European efforts to position fetishism at the center of civilized life. Under the term *fetish*, some European theorists of modernity referred to primitive religion in their struggles to make sense of the animating relations of human psychology, sexuality, and political economy. Whereas Karl Marx found fetishism in the logic of capitalist economy, Alfred Binet identified fetishism in the psychology of sexual perversion. Following these recoveries of the fetish, a range of European inquiries into psychology and society attended to different forms of fetishism operating in modern society. As the anthropologist William Pietz has observed, "Both the new scientists of sex and the new critics of political economics turned an idea used by the civilized to distinguish themselves from primitives back onto those who identified themselves as nonfetishists."[23] However, these European theoretical reversals in finding the primitive fetish at the heart of civilization were not quite what Du Bois was doing in recovering the African fetish. After all, the European scientists of psychology, sociology, and economy who were focusing on fetishism still saw the fetish as a problem. Du Bois's account of African fetishism placed the fetish in a positive light. According to Du Bois, the African fetish was not misdirected desire for material objects, whether bodies or commodities. Rather, in African religion, the fetish was the material basis for a logical apprehension and moral appreciation of the good and evil forces impinging on human beings. In re-covering the fetish in African religious history, therefore, Du Bois implicitly worked on two fronts—against European theorists who saw the fetish as an original problem and against European missionaries, such as Robert Hamill Nassau, who saw the fetish as the depths of degradation. Recovering the fetish as the center of a material philosophy, Du Bois proposed that African fetishism was not superstitious ignorance or moral depravity but a coherent material philosophy of the spiritual dynamics of life.

But reinterpreting the fetish was not sufficient to demonstrate that in-digenous Africans had their own religion. Africans also believed in God. In this respect, Du Bois found the Yoruba as his privileged example of Africans who not only believed in God but also made that divinity the foundation of organized political life and state building. In *The Negro*, however, Du Bois deferred to the testimony of European reporters to establish indigenous African belief in God. "The African has a Great Over God," the explorer Mary Kingsley observed.[24] No matter how superstitious Africans might be, the missionary Robert Hamill Nassau found, "I do not need to begin by tell-ing them that there is a God."[25] In Du Bois's account of indigenous African religion, European observers—the explorer, the missionary—were invoked as authorities on the indigenous theology of Africa. Effectively, they certi-fied that Africans believed in God.

In the light of the evolutionary theory of religion that Du Bois had cited, this assertion that Africans were not merely fetishists or animists but also theists was surprising. Supposedly representing a more advanced stage in the development of religion, belief in God should not have mixed so easily with the earlier stage of religion's supposed origin. Perhaps, by juxtaposing fetishism and theism, not in opposition but in counterpoint, Du Bois was working to undermine the developmental premises of religious evolution. As both material philosophy and spiritual theology, African religion could not so easily be claimed as the point of origin for the evolutionary progres-sion of all humanity. Instead, African religion could be recovered as a dif-ferent kind of origin, for the development of the material and spiritual life of Africans in America.

Nevertheless, in *The Negro*, Du Bois clearly relied upon the reports of outsiders—the European explorer, the Euro-American missionary—to cer-tify the existence of an indigenous African God. Certainly such witnesses were problematic, since they were entangled in a complex history of repres-sion, translation, and representation. Although searching for the "unknown God" all over the world, they often reported that such a deity was absent in Africa. In southern Africa, for example, explorers and missionaries frequently testified to the absence of any belief in God among the Khoisan, the Xhosa, the Zulu, the Sotho-Tswana, and other people in the region.[26] The lack of African belief in God, as well as the absence of any trace of indigenous African religion, was reported by Richard Burton in the lake regions of central Africa, by James Grant on his "walk across Africa," and by René Caillié on his "travels to Timbuctoo."[27] In citing the authority of James Bryce in his account of the African material spirituality of the fetish, Du Bois neglected to quote Bryce's assertion that for Africans in South Africa, "religion did not mean the worship of any deity, for there was no deity."[28] Arguably, these insistent denials, these recurring discoveries of religious absence, fit with broader colonial projects in representing Africa as an empty space for conquest and colonization. With no God, these denials seemed to suggest, Africans lacked any transcendent claim to political sovereignty.

In his handling of belief in God in *The Negro*, Du Bois seemed to recognize this link between theology and polity, observing briefly, in passing, that the Yoruba believed in a God who established the basis for royalty, sovereignty, and independent statehood. Nevertheless, he emphasized the authority of Kingsley and Nassau, the independent witnesses, in certifying indigenous African understandings of deity. Relying upon these reports, Du Bois was able to establish that belief in God was an indigenous feature of African religion that was not necessarily introduced by Muslim or Christian missions. Although he reviewed the importance of these missionizing religions in Africa, Du Bois appeared to regard them primarily as a disruption of African life, noting, for example, that the modern slave trade coincided with "the greatest expansion of two of the world's most pretentious religions."[29] Between the practical philosophy of the fetish and belief in God, however, African religion had its own integrity.

Crossing the Atlantic, Du Bois argued in *The Negro* for a basic continuity between African indigenous religion and African American religion. In the transportation from Africa, the indigenous priest, responsible for religion and healing, carried that continuity. As he had proposed in *Souls of Black Folk*, Du Bois asserted in his account of African religion in *The Negro* that the African priest, even within the alien, alienating environment of the plantation system, continued to function as "the interpreter of the supernatural, the comforter of the sorrowing, and as the one who expressed, rudely but picturesquely, the longing and disappointment and resentment of a stolen people." Not only transporting African religion across the middle passage, the priest created a free space for transposing indigenous religious resources, even translating them into Christian terms.

Again, Du Bois held that the Black Church, "the first distinctively Negro American social institution," emerged directly from these indigenous African religious resources. "It was not at first by any means a Christian church," Du Bois insisted, "but a mere adaptation of those rites of fetish which in America is termed obe worship, or 'voodooism.'" Similar arguments of African continuity had been advanced. For example, the missionary Robert Hamill Nassau, in his analysis of the fetish, had also proposed a direct continuity between Africa and America, but he complained that the religion of the fetish, "the evil thing that the slave brought with him," not only endured but actually grew under slavery. Against the background of his rehabilitation of the fetish, however, Du Bois proposed that fetishism was not an "evil thing" but the authentic religious inheritance from Africa. The philosophy of fetishism, with its attention to material signs of good and evil forces, provided the solid foundation for African religious life. Although eventually covered by a "veneer of Christianity," Du Bois argued, "the Negro church . . . base[d] itself upon the sole surviving institution of the African fatherland," the indigenous religion of the fetish.[30]

Clearly, this formulation of transatlantic African religious continuity was important to Du Bois. With slight modification of phrasing, but almost word for word, the same account appeared in Souls of Black Folk (1903), in The Negro Church (1903), and even in a section on historical background for a Carnegie-funded report, Economic Co-operation among Negro Americans (1907).[31] When he came to writing his first history of Africa in The Negro in 1915, Du Bois integrated this same account of African religion, tracing the essential religious continuity from African fetishism to African Christianity.

Although he certainly was not trying to advance a general theory of religion, Du Bois's intervention in representations of indigenous African religion carried significant implications for the history of religions. Poised between the evolutionary theory of religious progress and the missionary theory of religious degeneration, Du Bois's handling of the history of African religion could not be contained within either theoretical model. Implicitly, he challenged both the scientific evolutionists and the Christian missiologists. On the one hand, by attempting to rehabilitate fetishism as a viable material philosophy, he challenged the social evolutionary model that postulated a developmental trajectory from primitive fetishism to the modern material philosophy of science. On the other hand, by representing the Christian conversion of Africans in America as a superficial covering placed over the indigenous African religion of the fetish, he suggested that Christianization represented not progress but degeneration of authentic African religion. In either case, Du Bois placed indigenous African religion in a different kind of history—neither a speculative evolutionary history nor a missionary faith history—which he outlined in *The Negro* as a basic continuity, despite the radical disruption of slavery, in fetishism, the material philosophy of spiritual influences.

DISCOVERING GOD

Nearly twenty-five years later, Du Bois substantially revised and expanded his earlier account of African history in *The Negro* for publication as *Black Folk: Then and Now*, which was published in 1939. With respect to African indigenous religion, his discussion in *Black Folk* remained largely unchanged from his treatment of African fetishism and belief in God in *The Negro*, except for two dramatic alterations. First, he removed any reference to the explorer Mary Kingsley or the missionary Robert Hamill Nassau, who had reported on West African beliefs in God. They were erased from his new history of Africa. Their authority was no longer necessary. Second, Du Bois introduced the Yoruba God Shango as a powerful African supreme being, a God of indigenous political sovereignty. Through these subtle but substantial changes in his account of African religious history, Du Bois in the text of *Black Folk* effectively dismissed the authority of alien observers, however much they might have served his interests earlier, in preference for a direct appearance, almost a theophany, of an indigenous African deity. No European explorer or Euro-American missionary, Du Bois seemed to be saying in this erasure of Kingsley and Nassau, was necessary to certify the meaning and power of an indigenous African God. Shango, as he appears in *Black Folk*, is sufficiently powerful to display his own meaning in indigenous African religion. In place of alien authority, therefore, Du Bois in this new account of African indigenous religion presented Shango.

In Yoruba religion, Shango is God of thunder and lightning. As the deity of such awesome heavenly power, Shango has been recognized as comparable to other West African Gods, such as Hebieso among the Ewe or Gua among the Ga, but in Yoruba tradition Shango has also been regarded as a historical figure, the fourth king of Oyo, ruling an extensive kingdom in West Africa. As king, Shango discovered a ritual technique to summon lightning, but when he deployed this technique, the lightning destroyed his house and killed his family. In the aftermath of that destruction, Shango left the world, according to different accounts killing himself, ascending to the heavens, or descending under the earth, to control the spiritual forces of thunder and lightning. Besides exercising this heavenly power, Shango reinforced political authority in the world. Yoruba kings of Oyo, according to this tradition, could be traced back through a royal lineage to Shango. Within the priesthood of Shango, the head priest was responsible for initiating kings into the mysteries of this tradition. Synchronizing religion and politics, Shango stood as a transcendent deity of power among the Yoruba.[32]

In *Black Folk*, Du Bois introduced Shango as an African God of thunder who "soars above the legend of Thor and Jahweh," thereby transcending the power of the European and Semitic thunder Gods. This assertion of the preeminence of an African God over and above the deities of Indo-European and Semitic traditions was a remarkable claim. During the nineteenth-century debates over what should be regarded as the original language, culture, and religion, biblically based assumptions about the preeminence of ancient Israel had contended with new scholarly formulations of the priority of ancient Indo-European societies. Stretching from ancient Ireland to India, the Indo-European, Indo-Iranian, or Aryan represented a cultural zone that could be recovered in direct opposition to the Semitic culture of the Bible. As Maurice Olender has shown, defenders of Indo-European and Semitic origins asserted competing claims not only about human prehistory but also about establishing access to the original "language of Paradise."[33] Almost casually, Du Bois dismissed this entire controversy by introducing Shango. Soaring above the Indo-European Thor and the Semitic Yahweh, this indigenous African God left them far behind. By bringing Shango into the revised history of Africa that formed the text of *Black Folk*, Du Bois dismissed not only alien authorities such as Kingsley and Nassau but also alien deities like Thor and Yahweh from his account of indigenous African religion.

As a textual effect, the introduction of Shango in *Black Folk* is startling. Seeming to appear from nowhere, inserted as an unreferenced quotation, Shango simply registers as a force. Bringing death, giving life, causing fear, inspiring love—Shango is devastating and invigorating. Without providing any indication of the source of this profile of Shango, Du Bois announced the transcendent power of the African God: "He is the Hurler of thunderbolts, the Lord of the Storm, the God who burns down compounds and cities, the Render of trees and the Slayer of men; cruel and savage, yet splendid and beneficent in his unbridled action. For the floods which he pours from the lowering welkin give life to the soil that is parched and gladden the fields with fertility. And, therefore, mankind fear him, yet love him."[34] Having dispensed with the European explorer and the Christian missionary, Du Bois replaced their testimony with the awesome indigenous power of Shango, the violent destroyer of cities and compounds, sites of destruction that it is tempting to read as colonial cities and native compounds. More powerful than alien Gods, Shango—the destroyer, the source of life— registers as the most important indigenous divinity of Africa.

Du Bois's description of this African deity recalls Rudolph Otto's classic formula for the religious experience of "the holy" as the *mysterium tremendum* that inspires overwhelming awe, fear, and even terror, but also as the *mysterium fascinans* that evokes love and devotion. Clearly, Shango embodied this dual mystery of fear and love. In his landmark book *Das Heilige*, which was published in 1917 and translated into English in 1923, the German theologian Rudolf Otto (1869-1937) analyzed religion in terms of the experience of the *numinous*, the awe and love in relation to divinity that was "wholly other" than ordinary, everyday human experience.[35] Although he developed his analysis of religious experience in line with certain trends in German Protestant theology, most obviously building on Friedrich Schleiermacher's early-nineteenth-century emphasis on religious feeling, Otto also was situated in the social context of the changing political fortunes of German nationalism and colonialism.

As the historian of religions Gregory D. Alles has shown, Rudolph Otto's discovery of the holy was deeply embedded in German imperial ambitions, which were poised in competition with the ambitions of other European nations, and in increasing German colonial expansion. By his own account, which was repeated by colleagues, Otto first recognized the numinous experience of the holy during his travels in North Africa in 1911. Entering a synagogue in Morocco, he heard the Jewish prayer "Holy, holy, holy, Lord God of hosts, Heaven and earth are full of your glory!" Otto wrote that he had not only understood the import but more importantly had also felt the impact of these "most sublime words" that "seize one in the deepest ground of the soul, arousing and stirring with a mighty shudder the mystery of the other-worldly that sleeps therein."[36] But Otto framed his experience of the holy in this Moroccan synagogue between the imperial struggles of European nations and the degradation of the colonized. By contrast to what he saw as the base materialism of British or French colonialism, Otto promoted a German colonial mission, which he formulated in an article, "Germany's Cultural Tasks Overseas," that was based on a distinctive spirituality of culture. Unlike the materialistic French colonizers in North Africa, the German colonial project would recognize and understand the spiritual aspirations of the colonized.[37] In his discovery of the holy in Morocco, however, Otto did not necessarily display this spiritual sympathy with the Jews he encountered in what he described as their dark and filthy synagogue. Instead, he echoed Schleiermacher in condemning Judaism as a dead religion, paraphrasing his depiction of Jewish religion as an "undecaying mummy."[38] While claiming to have experienced the numinous mystery of the other-worldly in this synagogue, Otto also claimed that the Jewish congregation did not understand or feel what they were hearing because they had "discarded the highest and most genuine product of their nation and spirit and now [sat] lamenting by the side of the undecaying mummy of 'their religion,' standing guard over its casing and its trappings."[39] Although Rudolph Otto located the experience of the holy in the deepest ground of the soul, thereby making this numinous experience a universal human capacity, his discovery of the holy in a Moroccan synagogue was entangled with assumptions and assertions about German imperial spirituality and the spiritual degradation of Jews living under colonial conditions.

During the period when Du Bois was reworking his history of Africa, Rudolph Otto's idea of the holy had become widely absorbed into the study of religion, providing a basis for focusing on religious experience that was in principle, if not in practice, independent of any specific theology. Certainly Du Bois was not primarily interested in working out an indigenous African theology. In revising his earlier account of African history, however, he inserted Shango as an African deity to be loved and feared. As a deity of destruction, Shango was a divinity that recalled the devastating destruction of African life under slavery but also suggested the potential for the liberating destruction of the enclosures of colonialism and racist oppression. While Europeans were debating the racial superiority of Aryans or Semites, a debate disguised by deliberations over the history of language, culture, and religion, Du Bois simply asserted the transcendent power of the African deity Shango, who soared above their pretensions.

Embedded in African history, with a specific Yoruba biography, Shango could not easily be equated with Rudolph Otto's universal "wholly other" that evoked numinous experience. Shango did not live in the depths of every human soul but in Yoruba historical experience. Likewise, Shango could not be easily assimilated into the romantic recasting of indigenous spirituality proposed by John Tengo Jabavu and Charles A. Eastman at the Universal Races Conference in 1911. Shango was not the "Great Omnipresent, Omnipotent Unknown" of Jabavu's version of Xhosa religion nor the sacred and unspeakable "Great Mystery" of Eastman's version of Sioux religion. In his account of Shango, Du Bois avoided such generic spiritualizing of this African God, who appeared in his text as the deity not of a universal spirituality but of a specific history. At the same time, he avoided the imperial impulse, best exemplified by James Frazer, to collate deities under generic categories, such as "dying gods" or "gods of thunder." Recognizing that Thor and Yahweh were also associated with thunder, Du Bois compared them with Shango only to assert their disadvantage in relation to this African God.

Although he highlighted the local and transcendent power of an African deity, Du Bois was less confident in *Black Folk* about the historical development of African religion across the Atlantic. He retreated from his earlier conviction that indigenous African religious resources had successfully survived the crossing. Turning to America, he revised his earlier account of transatlantic religious continuity. While he had observed in *The Negro* that slavery had not destroyed the religion of the fetish or the religious role of African priests, in *Black Folk* Du Bois stressed the radical disruption of kinship, community, and religion under slavery.

> The African family and clan life were disrupted in this transplantation; the communal life and free use of land were impossible; the power of the chief was transferred to the master, bereft of the usual blood ties and ancient reverence. The African language survived only in occasional words and phrases. African religion, both fetish and Islam, was transformed. Fetish survived in certain rites and even here and there in blood sacrifice, carried out secretly and at night; but more often in open celebration which gradually became transmuted into Catholic and Protestant Christian rites. The slave preacher replaced the African medicine man and gradually, after a century or more, the Negro Church arose as the center and almost the only expression of Negro life in America.[40]

In this revised version, by changing a few words, Du Bois charted the transatlantic crossing not as gradual continuity but as radical change. The cumulative effect of his key terms—disruption, impossibility, transference, bereavement, transformation, transmutation, and replacement—created a sense of complete disjuncture between Africa and African America. His earlier accounts, from 1902 to 1915, had tried to outline a continuous historical development, from the indigenous religion of West Africa to the institutionalized church of Chicago, in which an underlying persistence of religious currents could be discerned. In *Black Folk*, a revised version of the same story in 1939 emphasized loss.

As a revision of *The Negro*, the text of *Black Folk* showed substantial erasures with respect to African religion. Besides deleting the testimony of Kingsley and Nassau, the alien explorer and missionary, as authoritative witnesses to African deity, Du Bois removed any reference to the persistence of Vodou or Obeah in America. Although "Voodooism" and "Obe Worship" had featured prominently in his earlier accounts of the continuity of African indigenous religion in America, they disappeared entirely in 1939. Traces of African heritage, he acknowledged, might be found in customs, literature, art, music, and dance, but further study would be required to establish historical connections. In *Black Folk*, Du Bois no longer seemed confident that the persistence of cultural resources, let alone religious resources, could be established. His language evoked a radical break between Africa and America.

In the case of the Black Church, which he had earlier identified as the "sole surviving institution of the African fatherland," Du Bois in *Black Folk* characterized the Black Church as an American institution that had become "almost the only expression of Negro life in America."[41] Again, Du Bois's language involved a subtle editorial change, but the shift from "sole surviving" to "almost the only," from "African fatherland" to "Negro life in America," hints at a broader shift in his structuring of the historical narrative. Instead of surviving the crossing from Africa, as the "sole surviving institution," animated by the African priest, the fetish, and the material philosophy of Africa, indigenous African religion, whether it is called Vodou, Obeah, or even Christianity, failed to take root in America. In *Black Folk*, Du Bois represented the Black Church not as a historical, developmental, or gradual continuity with indigenous African religion but as an American institution, almost the only one that had emerged in America, for the "expression of Negro life."

In his treatment of African religion in 1939, therefore, Du Bois highlighted destruction and discontinuity, the awesome destructive power of the Yoruba God Shango, and the radical discontinuity between indigenous African religious life and the Black Church in America. Nevertheless, his treatment of African fetishism, which he had developed in *The Negro*, remained entirely unchanged in his account of indigenous African religion in *Black Folk*. Surrounded by ongoing disputes about whether it represented the absence, origin, or degeneration of religion, the fetish presented a persistent problem in Du Bois's attempts to provide a historical account of indigenous African religion. The fetish also posed a dilemma in his thinking about continuity or disjuncture between African religion and the African American religion of the Black Church. After celebrating the material philosophy of the fetish in his earlier accounts of African religious history, by 1939 Du Bois seems to have become reluctant to assert fetishism as the basis of African religion in America, removing any reference to fetish, Vodou, or Obeah in the emergence of slave religion or the Black Church in America.

DECONSTRUCTING THE FETISH

In 1947, following the destruction of World War II, which signaled the "collapse of Europe," Du Bois returned to the challenge of writing a comprehensive history of Africa. In *The World and Africa*, he certainly devoted less attention to religion than he did in his previous histories of Africa. He focused more directly on identifying the basis for pan-African unity that he saw emerging in a postwar and postcolonial world. African history was central to world history. The slave trade, he argued, was "the prime and effective cause of the contradictions in European civilization and the illogic in modern thought and the collapse of human culture."[42] Postcolonial liberation in Africa and the African diaspora promised to free thought, culture, and civilization from the legacy of slavery. Du Bois did not focus on the role of religion in liberation. Nevertheless, if read against the background of his earlier accounts of African history, Du Bois's interventions in the analysis of fetishism, divinity, and transatlantic connections are important for his historical reconstruction of African religion.

Most decisively, in *The World and Africa* Du Bois demolished the fetish as a representation of African religion. By contrast to his earlier attempts in rehabilitating the fetish, Du Bois in 1947 vigorously denounced fetishism as an account of African indigenous religion. Citing the German anthropologist Leo Frobenius, who had observed, "I have seen in no part of Africa the Negroes worship a fetish," Du Bois rejected fetishism, identifying it as a foreign, alien, and ultimately denigrating and dehumanizing characterization of African religion.[43]

Certainly Leo Frobenius (1873–1938) was a controversial authority. He was an anthropologist, entrepreneur, and advocate of Africa whose theories and methods were not always accepted by his anthropological colleagues. As Du Bois realized, Frobenius was not popular with conventional anthropologists and historians because he "indulged his imagination," but Du Bois nevertheless found that his unprejudiced vision of Africa and his interpretations of Africans were of unparalleled value.[44] In retrospect, Frobenius has often been criticized for harboring a Germanic romanticism for the purity of languages, cultures, and religions in Africa. He has also been exposed as an entrepreneur in the international trade in African artifacts, benefiting from the economic exploitation and colonial brutality of the Belgian

Congo. During his years as an ethnological collector, Frobenius reportedly set fire to a village, tested a new rifle by shooting Africans, and "robbed the natives of their most sacred relics."[45] Praising colonial initiatives in providing education for Africans, he observed that such "experiments can be conducted only when the European has complete control of the Negro."[46] Clearly, Frobenius relied upon local colonial coercion in collecting African artifacts to sell to the Ethnological Museum in Berlin and other buyers in the expanding international market for primitive and exotic objects.

As an anthropological theorist, Leo Frobenius divided languages, cultures, and religions into distinct cultural circles, each with its own spiritual essence or soul or what Frobenius called *paideuma*. Known as "culture circle theory" (*Kulturkreislehre*), this essentially romantic approach to ethnology saw cultural traits emanating or diffusing from an originating cultural center. This diffusionist theory was developed during the 1930s by the Austrian anthropologist Wilhelm Schmidt, who, like Andrew Lang, sought evidence for an original monotheism in the history of religions, and it was embraced much later in the United States as the theoretical basis for the work of the popular mythographer Joseph Campbell.[47] Drawing his basic categories of analysis from Africa, Frobenius proposed that within each culture could be discerned two basic tendencies, which he called the Hamitic and the Ethiopian, one developing a "mechanistic" approach to interpreting reality, the other displaying an "intuitive" approach. Although he held that every culture oscillated between these two basic tendencies, Frobenius was personally drawn to the intuitive, even calling for "the revival of an intuitive attitude" that would usher in a new cultural era in the world.[48]

With respect to the fetish, Leo Frobenius displayed a capacity for critical analysis of material relations under colonial conditions. Explicitly, he linked colonial conquest, dispossession, and enslavement of Africans with the representation of Africans as fetishists. As part of the larger colonial, capitalist project of turning Africans into objects for the slave trade, Frobenius suggested, Europeans claimed that Africans were already less than objects since they were subject to fetishism, the worship of objects. According to Frobenius, therefore, the very term *fetishism* was implicated in European representations of Africans as commodities for the slave trade. The market in African slaves, Frobenius argued, "exacted a justification; hence one made of the Negro a half-animal, an article of merchandise. And in the same way the notion of fetish (Portuguese, *feticeiro* [*feitiço*]) was invented as a symbol of African religion." Besides challenging the empirical validity of the concept by insisting that he had never witnessed Africans worshipping

a fetish, Frobenius observed that European discourse about African fetishism was an integral part of colonizing projects in subjugating, dehumanizing, and commodifying Africans. Under the sign of fetishism, he concluded,
"The idea of the 'barbarous Negro' is a European invention."[49]

By embracing and advancing this critique of fetishism, Du Bois recast
African indigenous religion as a site of struggle over conflicting representations of materiality and humanity. As recent research on the history of the
fetish has shown, the term emerged in West Africa around 1470 within intercultural trading zones.[50] In these mercantile trading networks, Portuguese,
Dutch, and English traders in West Africa dealt with African Christians,
Muslims, and "fetishists," who, according to the English trader William
Smith, had "no religion at all."[51] From this European Christian perspective,
fetishists, allegedly lacking any trace of religion, had no stable system of
value to assess material objects. They overvalued trifling objects—a bird's
feather, a pebble, a piece of rag, or a dog's leg—by treating them as "fetishes"
for ritual attention, but they undervalued trade goods, showing a lack of
interest in acquiring what European traders were interested in selling.
Fetishism, therefore, emerged in the eighteenth century as a European mercantile theory not of the origin but of the absence of religion. In the context of incommensurable values in these intercultural trading relations,
Europeans developed the stereotype of "fetishism" to characterize Africans
who had no religion to organize the necessary relations of meaning, power,
and value between human beings and material objects and thereby to organize relations among human beings in the exchange of objects. The
discourse of fetishism, which cast Africans as incapable of properly valu-
ing objects, Frobenius suggested, could also be deployed to turn Africans
themselves into objects, rendering them suitable commodities for the slave
trade.

Other theorists were rejecting the viability of the fetish as a category in
the study of religion. Felix von Luschan, for example, who had assembled
a large collection of objects from Benin in the Ethnological Museum of
Berlin, questioned the European category of "fetish" by insisting that he
had collected not religious objects but objects of art. As an entrepreneur,
Luschan raised the value of these artifacts by transposing them from objects
of religious worship to objects of aesthetic appreciation. While influencing
European aesthetics by stimulating the rise of primitivism in European art,
Luschan's collection also inspired a new pride in Africa among the poets,
novelists, and artists of the Harlem Renaissance in the United States.[52] More
decisively for the study of religion, the Durkheimians were replacing the

term *fetish* with "the sacred," which was seen not only in opposition to the profane but also as a source of power. Reviewing Nassau's *Fetishism in West Africa*, Robert Hertz argued against focusing on the fetish, whether it was regarded as the beginning of religious evolution or the depths of human degradation. Instead, drawing on R. R. Marett's notion of *mana*, Hertz argued that religious objects should be understood as features of religious power, as aspects of an "inexhaustible reservoir of spiritual energy."[53] Dismissing the term entirely, Marcel Mauss argued that the term *fetish* referred to nothing but "an immense misunderstanding between two civilizations, African and European."[54] Following Frobenius, however, Du Bois insisted that the term *fetish* arose out of more than merely a misunderstanding between Europeans and Africans; it arose out of a history of Europeans enslaving Africans. Instead of representing the authentic origin of indigenous African religion, the notion of "fetishism" was implicated in the dehumanizing representations of Africans that had legitimated their colonization and enslavement. Du Bois took this insight seriously. Although he referred to the fetish briefly in passing, perhaps accidentally, at one other point in *The World and Africa*, he erased all of his previous observations about African fetishism. Neither the basis of indigenous African religion nor the link between religious life in Africa and African America, the fetish was a European invention. When he considered African indigenous religion as an aspect of African history in 1947, therefore, he removed not only the European explorer and missionary but also the European category "fetishism" that had been deployed as an ideological instrument of African dehumanization and enslavement.

Within the limited scope that Du Bois gave in *The World and Africa* to reconstructing the indigenous religion of Africa, only Shango remained. Invoking, once again, the power of Shango, Du Bois also revealed the source of his quotation about how this African God of thunder inspired fear and awe, which had been omitted in *Black Folk*, as the German anthropologist Leo Frobenius. In the earlier volume, Shango seemed to appear from nowhere, the African God, more powerful than the Gods of ancient Israel or Europe, but also the God who needed no source, citation, reference, or footnote. In *The World and Africa*, however, the source is duly cited, but the citation gains force by being linked to the critique of fetishism as a dehumanizing representation of Africans and African religion. Against this background, Du Bois expanded upon the divinity and power of the Yoruba God. In addition to highlighting Shango's destructive force and creative capacity, he emphasized the Yoruba deity's indigenous political role, which had been alluded to in previous accounts, by asserting that Shango was the supreme source of political power, authority, and sovereignty, father of royal rulers, whose "posterity still [had] the right to give the country its kings."⁵⁵ Having rejected the alien construction of fetishism, Du Bois reinforced the indigenous African religious resources supporting independent and autonomous political sovereignty in Africa.

In his African history of 1947, Du Bois seems to have lost interest in the question of continuity or discontinuity with America. Besides the rejection of fetishism and the celebration of Shango, no other reflections on indigenous African religion or African American religion remained. The text of *The World and Africa* did not contain any reprise or revision of the formulations of religious development from Africa to America that had featured in his early historical accounts. Instead, he devoted his attention in *The World and Africa* to actively building a pan-African solidarity.

Du Bois's reconstructions of indigenous African religion were part of a larger pan-African project, which developed, however, in unexpected ways. For example, the problem of African fetishism, which Du Bois had wrestled with from 1915 to 1947, moving from imaginative rehabilitation of the fetish in *The Negro* to critical rejection of the fetish in *The World and Africa*, became a point of departure for the anticolonial work of scholars, poets, and artists associated with the Négritude movement in Paris. One of the movement's leaders, the Martinican poet Aimé Césaire (1913–2008), drew inspiration for his *Discourse on Colonialism* from the same passage by Frobenius that Du Bois cited to reject fetishism: "The idea of the barbaric Negro is a European invention."⁵⁶ Likewise, the Senegalese poet Léopold Senghor (1906–2001) was inspired by the work of Frobenius, regarding his *Histoire de la civilisation africaine* (*History of African Civilization*) and *Le destin des civilisations* (*The Destiny of Civilizations*) as "sacred" texts.⁵⁷ For these artists and activists within the Négritude movement, Leo Frobenius defined such key words as emotion, art, and myth in African culture. But Frobenius also validated intuition, or "intuitive reason," as an essential African capacity in ways that Senghor and other advocates of Négritude could enthusiastically embrace as their own.⁵⁸ According to Léopold Senghor, they had learned the value of intuition from the philosophy of Henri Bergson, with its emphasis on vitality, feeling, and even mysticism, but from Leo Frobenius they learned that intuitive reason was essentially African.⁵⁹

Providing terms for recovering African identity, Frobenius also offered a global perspective on the role of African people in human history. Contradicting Hegel's assertion that Africans were without history, which

Du Bois called Hegel's "ancient lie," Frobenius elaborated Africa's important place in human history. According to Senghor, Frobenius's new ethnographic history, which identified and distinguished the different cultural areas in the world, had established the cultural unity of African people on all continents. Like every other culture, African culture had a soul, a *paideuma*, which Senghor followed Frobenius in defining as "a psychological notion which designates the spiritual structure of a people to the extent that it is manifested in cultural behavior." Although each cultural circle had its own spiritual structure, Senghor and other leaders of the Négritude movement were impressed that Frobenius drew his key terms for comparing cultures from Africa. Applying his distinction between "mechanical" Hamitic cultures and "intuitive" Ethiopian cultures, Senghor found that Frobenius had established a spiritual affinity between Germany and Africa by placing "the Germans, along with the Negro-Africans, into Ethiopian civilization, whereas the French, the English, and the Americans are placed into the Hamitic civilization."[60] Senghor recalled the effect of this German connection on the Négritude movement: "We had to wait for Leo Frobenius before the affinities between the 'Ethiopian,' that is the Negro African, and the German soul could be made manifest and before certain stubborn preconceptions of the 17th and 18th centuries could be removed." While this link with the German soul supposedly overcame European prejudices against Africans as people without history, culture, or rationality, it also represented a promise for the future. Following Frobenius, they could anticipate a global meeting of the cultures of Europe, Asia, and Africa, all centered in Germany, as Senghor quoted Frobenius: "The West created English realism and French rationalism. The East created German mysticism. . . . The agreement with the corresponding civilizations in Africa is complete."[61]

In this global vision of the spiritual structures of cultures, Frobenius contrasted the German mystical soul with the materialism of the other imperial nations in Europe and then posited the German soul as the central meeting place of Europe, Asia, and Africa. The Négritude movement embraced this German imperial vision as a revitalization of the African soul in world history. Here, of course, was an irony: Leo Frobenius, who had been directly complicit in colonial violence, was the inspiration for anticolonial activists. A similar irony was unfolding in America, where Felix von Luschan, who had collected not only African skulls but also African art, was inspiring African American artists and activists in Harlem. Although Du Bois shared with these movements an interest in deconstructing the fetish, he did not necessarily identify with their spiritual mysticism or aesthetic primitivism

that turned fetishes into works of art. After all, he had already tried to rehabilitate the fetish as a material philosophy in 1915; he was not interested at
this point in recasting the fetish as the essential African embodiment of art,
emotion, or intuition. He rejected the fetish as a defining feature of African
indigenous religion. Finding common cause with these cultural movements
in rejecting the fetish as a sign of African inhumanity, Du Bois nevertheless differed by insisting that the fetish was not a spiritual problem or an
aesthetic problem but a political problem.

Nevertheless, as an admirer of Frobenius, Du Bois sometimes proposed
a global vision of Africa, Asia, and Europe that was based on contrasting
spiritual structures. In *The World and Africa* in 1947, Du Bois sketched those
contrasts as a kind of global comparative religion. According to Du Bois,
Africans, who had so often been represented as having an absence of religion, allegedly worshipping material objects instead of God, looked into the
sky and "saw the stars of God," while Asians, looking within, "saw the soul
of man." By contrast to the religions of Africa and Asia, the spiritual structure
of Europe was gross materialism. Du Bois concluded, "Europe saw and sees
only man's body, which it feeds and polishes until it is fat, gross, and cruel."[62]
In this comparative account of spiritual structures, the absence of religion
was found not in Africa or Asia but in the material heart of Europe.

WRITING RELIGION

It is tempting to locate Du Bois's changing representations of indigenous
African religion in relation to his broader intellectual biography, linking his
shift from rehabilitating to rejecting fetishism, for example, to his transition
from a racialized to a radicalized pan-Africanism. Although such connections might be established, we can focus here on the methodological rather
than the biographical considerations arising from this brief review of Du
Bois's handling of three features of indigenous African religion—fetishism,
God, and transatlantic continuity—in his historical writings about Africa.

First, with respect to fetishism, we have seen that Du Bois consistently
rejected the two standard accounts that placed the fetish either at the origin of religious evolution or at the end of religious degeneration. He emphatically countered the missionary slander of degradation, but he initially
seemed to adopt the evolutionary model that emerged in late-nineteenth-
century anthropology of religion. Although in *The Negro* he seemed to defer
briefly to an evolutionary progression of religious development from fetishism, through polytheism, to monotheism, and he repeated that formulation
in *Black Folk*, Du Bois actually did not accept that model's primary premise,

which asserted that the origin of religion, fetishism, was essentially a mentality, a primitive psychology, which mistakenly attributed life to inanimate objects. In social evolutionary theories of religion, fetishism was defined as a "frame of mind," as John Lubbock put it in the 1870s, which induced dogs, children, and savages to think that objects were alive.[63] As a primitive mentality, according to Edward Clodd, fetishism was the "confusion inherent in the savage mind between things living and not living."[64] Standard evolutionary theories of religion repeated this premise that fetishism was a primitive, childish, or uncultured psychology, a "low grade of consciousness," as Alfred C. Haddon proposed in 1906 in *Magic and Fetishism*, because it was based on imagining that material objects were alive.[65]

Understandably, Du Bois wanted to reverse this rendering, countering the anthropologist's assumption that Africans were children and the missionary's allegation that Africans were degenerates. Both charges focused on the materiality of the African fetish. Certainly a response could be formulated by celebrating African spirituality, as we find in African accounts of indigenous religion from John Tengo Jabavu's invocation of the Great Unknown at the Universal Races Conference in 1911 to the Négritude movement's adoption of "intuitive reason" as Africa's spiritual structure in Paris during the 1930s. In these countermaneuvers against any association with the fetish, Africans were spiritual rather than material, a designation that was recast against the materialism of the West. But celebrating an idealized African spirituality was not adequate to the task. Representations of African religion as spirituality remained embedded in the opposition between pure spirit and material fetish.

Representations of African spirituality also remained entangled with assertions of European imperial authority. Drawing inspiration from Bergson and Frobenius, the influential account of African religion provided in 1945 by the Belgian missionary Placide Tempels (1906–1977), with its spirituality of "vitalism," continued the tendency to cast indigenous African religion as a mentality, psychology, or spirituality that attributed life to inanimate material objects. Tempels certainly represented African religion as a psychology, a spiritual way of knowing, which he hoped to be able to explain to a philosophical audience but also to Africans themselves. Insisting that Africans were incapable of formulating their own philosophy, Tempels proposed, "It is we who will be able to tell them, in precise terms, what their innermost concept of being is." Hoping that Africans would recognize themselves in his systematic presentation of their spiritual psychology, Tempels imagined that Africans would "acquiesce saying, 'You understand us; you know us completely; you "know" in the way we know.'"[66]

By contrast, Du Bois refused to render fetishism as a primitive psychology. Consistently, he wrestled with fetishism as a "material philosophy," from his early attempt to validate an indigenous African logic of material signs of spiritual forces to his later rejection of fetishism as an alien European logic for turning spiritual beings into material commodities. Du Bois seemed to recognize, in William Pietz's phrase, the fetish's "irreducible materiality."[67] Instead of seeing the fetish as the symptom of a primitive African mentality, he focused on material conditions, from an indigenous African "material philosophy" to the alien forces of slavery, colonization, and capitalism. Capitalism had its own fetishism of commodities, "abounding in metaphysical subtleties and theological niceties," as Marx insisted, in which the meaning and value of being human were at stake.[68] By 1947, therefore, Du Bois had realized that fetishism, far from representing a primitive mentality that turned dead objects into living beings, was a term that provided ideological cover for capitalist transformations of living beings into objects. For the study of indigenous African religion, this focus on materiality, rather than spirituality, advanced a critical perspective on the contingent, contested relations in which knowledge about religion was produced and deployed.

Second, with respect to God, Du Bois dealt with African divinity not as a theological but as a political problem. By stark contrast to the prevailing religious interests of Christian missionaries, Du Bois was not concerned with establishing theological principles of translation between African and Christian concepts of God.[69] In his early historical work in 1915, he invoked missionary testimony for the existence of an African God, which was supposedly just like the Christian God, but that Christian assertion of translatability was eventually erased. In place of the missionary's claims about the inherent familiarity of the Christian God in Africa, Du Bois inserted Shango, an African deity with at least three features—locality, specificity, and sovereignty—that could not be easily subsumed within the missionary concept of the Christian deity. Instead of representing the vague, generalized "Great Over God," in the explorer Mary Kingsley's phrase, Shango was the God of a definite place, with a specific identity, even a biography, which reinforced the claims of a royal lineage to political sovereignty. By 1939, asserting that Shango was greater than the deities of either European paganism or the Hebrew Bible, Du Bois suggested that such a deity could not easily be translated or assimilated into the God of Christianity.

In the missionary literature on indigenous African concepts of God, the overriding concern was the theological translation of the "unknown God" of Africa into the Christian God. A leader in this work of translation, Edwin W. Smith (1876–1957), who was born in South Africa, was a prominent missionary and anthropologist; an active participant from 1909 in the Royal Anthropological Institute, serving as president between 1933 and 1935; and in 1926 a founding member of the International Institute of African Languages and Cultures, along with Frederick Lugard, Lucien Lévy-Bruhl, C. G. Seligman, and other prominent scholars. In a series of publications, Edwin W. Smith analyzed African religion as a progression from Friedrich Schleiermacher's feeling of dependence, through R. R. Marett's religious dynamism, to Rudolph Otto's numinous sense of the holy.[70] Accordingly, Smith represented the indigenous religion of Africa as an intrinsic trajectory toward theism, a developmental process leading Africans to God as Otto's "wholly other." Formulated in the proceedings of a conference, *African Ideas of God*, edited by Edwin W. Smith, this theological interest continued to be developed in accounts of the African God such as John S. Mbiti's *Concepts of God in Africa* (1970) and Malcolm J. McVeigh's *God in Africa: Conceptions of God in African Traditional Religion and Christianity* (1974).[71] Even in sociological formulations of the problem of God in Africa, such as the anthropologist Robin Horton's analysis of the conversion from local African "microcosmic" worldviews to global Christian or Islamic "macrocosmic" worldviews, the question of theological translatability from local spirits to the translocal deities of "world religions" has been prominent in academic analysis of the history of African understandings of God.[72]

By invoking Shango, however, Du Bois effectively asserted that the problem of God in Africa was political rather than theological. Not a primitive high god, a Christian-like supreme being, or a world religion's macrocosmic deity, Shango was a local deity of political sovereignty, bearing the "right to give the country its kings," who "soar[ed] above the legend of Thor and Jahweh," not by transcending the world but by being imminent, situated, and forceful in a specific African world. This refusal to translate an African deity into Christian theology broke with conventional missionary practice. But it also challenged the emerging inventions and constructions of "African Traditional Religion."[73] Just as Shango could not be easily translated into the "wholly other" of Rudolph Otto's Protestant theology, this Yoruba deity could not be conveniently assimilated into the profile of African ideas of God in a generic traditional religion in Africa. By invoking Shango as a specific, historically situated claim on indigenous political rights, Du Bois implicitly countered both missionary and academic constructions of African traditional religion.

Third, the question of transatlantic continuity between Africa and African America also raised the problem of translatability, but with an entirely different valence. This transatlantic history did not reveal a universal, macrocosmic worldview, such as Christianity, assimilating all Africans. Instead, the transatlantic passage entailed the challenges of translation posed by transportation, enslavement, and alienation in America. In his earliest formulations, Du Bois identified the indigenous African priest as the nexus of transatlantic translation. Generally, under colonial conditions within Africa, indigenous ritual specialists, with specialized knowledge and techniques of healing, divining, and gaining access to sacred power, were best equipped to survive the displacements of the religion of the home and the destruction of the religion of the polity that dramatically altered the terrain of indigenous African religion. As Du Bois suggested, the knowledge and power of African religious specialists had a kind of portability that could even cross the Atlantic. By focusing on the African priest, along with the indigenous religious resources of Vodou or Obeah, Du Bois advanced the challenging assertion that Christianity did not convert Africans but was actually converted by Africans in the Americas into indigenous African religion.

Although Du Bois seems to have lost confidence in this formula for the African conversion of Christianity by 1947, when he was no longer showing an interest in tracing African religion "from the heathenism of the Gold Coast to the institutional Negro Church in Chicago," the second half of the twentieth century witnessed a dramatic vitality of African American religion with explicitly African roots. Shango, for example, was alive and well in America, flourishing in Haitian Vodou, Cuban Santeria, Brazilian Candomblé, and the Shango movement in Trinidad. Although these religious movements certainly involved translation, identifying Shango with the Christian Saint Barbara in Cuba or with the Christian Saint John in Trinidad, such interreligious translations were obviously not controlled by any Christian orthodoxy.[74] These translations arose, as Du Bois had suggested, out of the portable resources of the African priest, with the priest's capacity to heal the sick, interpret the unknown, comfort the sorrowing, and avenge wrongs, but also out of the locality, specificity, and contested sovereignty of an African, American, and transatlantic politics of religion. That religious politics, as Du Bois proposed, operated within the symbols, myths, and rituals that configured the "longing, disappointment, and resentment of a stolen and oppressed people."

Du Bois's decreasing interest in transatlantic African religious continuity was perhaps connected to his failing confidence in the efficacy of indigenous African religion, or any religion, in serving the goals of an emancipatory political project. Certainly this political problem of the role of an indigenous African religious heritage was inherited by other African political activists. In *Wretched of the Earth*, for example, Frantz Fanon (1925–1961) largely ignored religion, whether Islam in Algeria or Christianity, Islam, and indigenous African religion in West Africa, but he did reflect on recurring revivals in Africa of wild religion, with its "terrifying myths," populated by maleficent spirits, the "leopardmen, serpent-men, six-legged dogs, zombies," that generated an imaginary world of spiritual powers and prohibitions that were "far more terrifying than the world of the settler."[75] As both psychological displacement and political distraction, however, this wild religion could not be coordinated with a revolutionary political project. In *Souls of Black Folk*, Du Bois touched briefly on the capacity of this kind of wild religion for rebellion. Drawing on an indigenous African religious inheritance, with its gods and devils, elves and witches, and other spiritual influences, the African in bondage in America could only conclude that evil had triumphed. "All the hateful powers of the Under-world were striving against him," Du Bois wrote, "and a spirit of revolt and revenge filled his heart." Acting out that spirit of revolt, Africans "called up all the resources of heathenism," Du Bois related, but those religious resources were rituals, sacrifices, spells, "weird midnight orgies and mystic conjurations."[76] Certainly these religious practices gave expression to living under oppressive conditions, perhaps even expressing a religious "spirit of revolt" against oppression, but they did not provide the basis for any viable political revolution against oppression.

"At the intersection of religious practices and the interrogation of human tragedy," as the political philosopher Achille Mbembe has recently observed, "a distinctively African philosophy has emerged."[77] But that African philosophy of tragedy, with its roots in slavery, colonization, and apartheid, has engaged religion in different ways, from radical rejection to nativist romanticism. As Mbembe has suggested, indigenous African religion, which has not been adequately captured by either radical dismissals or nativist reconstructions, has to be regarded as a modality of self-writing, self-styling, and self-practice. In writing about the history of Africa, Du Bois was engaged in precisely such a struggle of self-formation. But he was also trying to make sense out of a political project, initially located in the United States but increasingly global in scope. Writing about indigenous African religion, in this context, was a way of writing not only about a religious heritage but also about a changing world.

CHAPTER EIGHT

Thinking Black

We are told on all sides that "man is a religious being."

S. M. MOLEMA

On December 15, 1900, in room 12 of the Royal Hotel in Ladysmith, the colonial administrator James Stuart was engaged in a vigorous discussion about religion with John Kumalo, Solomon Mabaso, and Stuart's longtime assistant, Ndukwana kaMbengwana. John Kumalo, a Christian convert, defended Christianity as *ukukanya*, "light, illumination." During an earlier conversation in October, Kumalo had argued that the Christian *ukukanya* had enabled Africans to learn not only the light of the gospel but also their own history, in which they had "descended from Jews."[1] Kumalo held that the Zulu people "follow[ed] the laws of Moses; their laws and customs to a great extent [were] similar to those of the Jews."[2] Like the ancient Israelites, the Zulu observed strict laws, with the death penalty imposed for adultery and other offenses; they practiced circumcision; they made offerings of incense; and they worshipped spirits in the form of snakes like the biblical "serpent set up in the wilderness."[3] In all of these respects, the Zulu could recognize through the Christian *ukukanya* that they were descendants of ancient Jews.

Ndukwana, a traditionalist, defended indigenous religion, arguing that Zulu life and civilization was already *ukukanya*, because "life was more clearly apprehended by the natives than the ins and outs of European life, which had Christianity for its basis."[4] Zulu people did not need to be illuminated by the Christian gospel, he argued, because they already had a traditional light to live by. Mabaso, who held that "all people from time immemorial believe[d] in the existence of a God," reinforced Ndukwana's position on religion by observing that among the Zulu the Christian "*ukukanya* was the cause of the mischief," although he revealed that he could also engage in religious mischief by recounting how he had once pretended to be a sangoma.[5] Trying to mediate in this argument, James Stuart proposed that perhaps Christianity should be regarded not as *the* light but rather as *a* light, as one *ukukanya* among many, but possibly better than the traditional veneration of ancestral spirits, the *iDhlozi*, in the Dhloziism of Zulu tradition.

How can we know? Although knowing which religion was better, the *ukukanya* of Christianity or the *ukukanya* of Dhloziism, was a normative question that came up in this discussion, a more basic descriptive question was at play: How do we know anything about Christianity, Dhloziism, or any other religion? As an intervention in this problem, Stuart tried to link empirical knowledge to empire, which provided the context for thinking, the stability for securing knowledge. Observing that civilizations come and go in the long course of human history, Stuart assumed that authoritative knowledge was embedded in imperial civilizations. For Stuart, reliable knowledge was imperial knowledge. Although he was afraid to admit it, he acknowledged that "the British Empire, that great *dhlozi*, I called it, which is in the act of swallowing the Zulus and other nations, is itself doomed one day to come to an end." In the absence of that great spirit of empire, with its power to swallow all nations, how can knowledge about religion and religions be secured? If the British Empire came to an end, Stuart worried, "to what is thought to be anchored?"[6]

Fluent in Zulu, James Stuart (1868–1942) conducted such conversations for over two decades, taking meticulous notes, creating a monumental archive not only of Zulu traditions but also of Zulu voices. Converting Stuart's research into Zulu idiom, John Kumalo called room 12 of the Royal Hotel *Kwa sogekle*, referring to a special place and an important occasion in which men engage in serious discussions while smoking hemp.[7] Under law, Stuart could talk to only three Africans at a time in his hotel room, which suggested that these conversations were not only important but also risky. Why did Stuart engage in these discussions? In an entry in his notebook of 1902, he revealed: "My object is to collect native custom so universally and thoroughly as to become an authority on it." By becoming an authority, Stuart hoped, he would be able to contribute to colonial policy and legislation, aiding the work of governing natives. He would be a local expert. But his aspirations were broader, even global, because he asserted, "Such work has never been done in any country." In the international enterprise of producing knowledge about indigenous beliefs and customs, Stuart imagined, "All will then be bound to come to my well to drink."[8]

Although James Stuart devoted considerable attention to questions of Zulu religion, there is no suggestion in his monumental archive that he knew anything about the imperial theorists of religion we have considered, except for his exchanges with H. Rider Haggard. Stuart hosted Haggard in South Africa and went to London to consult on Zulu authenticity for a stage production of one of Haggard's novels. If he needed general theory, Stuart referred to Jean-Jacques Rousseau.[9] In return, the imperial theorists in the study of religion never quoted him. Yet his work embodied the triple mediation—imperial, colonial, and indigenous—at the heart of knowledge production in the study of religion. While empire secured knowledge, indigenous informants provided evidence that could only be collected, translated, and transmitted by a local colonial expert. James Stuart enacted a mediation that unfortunately did not circulate in the study of religion. Like Henry Callaway, Stuart transcribed Zulu voices, often speaking about religion, but he did not distill a religious system that could be engaged by metropolitan theorists. Instead, his archive preserved the sound of voices, the struggle of memory, the wrestling with unresolved arguments, and even the smell of smoke. Returning to London in 1922, Stuart published readers in Zulu, recounting traditions for children, which were used as textbooks in Natal schools.

While James Stuart was pursuing his colonial research, E. Sidney Hartland emerged as the leading imperial theorist of indigenous religion in South Africa. He summarized the state of the art in his presidential address to the Folklore Society in 1901, led the anthropological delegation of the British Association for the Advancement of Science, along with Alfred C. Haddon, during the visit to South Africa in 1905, and wrote the entry "Bantu and South Africa" in the Hastings *Encyclopedia of Religion and Ethics* in 1909.[10] In his collection of essays published in 1914, *Ritual and Belief*, Hartland reviewed the history of the academic study of religion, from Max Müller to Emile Durkheim, as a prelude to what he proposed as its key, "Learning to 'Think Black.'" Observing that E. B. Tylor had long ago dismissed the notion that there were tribes without religion, he repeated Tylor's suspicion that savages were reluctant to reveal their religious beliefs and practices to superior white people, disclosing "to the prying and contemptuous foreigner their worship of gods who seem to shrink, like their worshippers, before the white man and his mightier Deity."[11] Hartland quickly cited examples from South Africa: Peter Kolb had reported that the Hottentots were secretive; Charles John Andersson had reported that every time he asked the Damara about religion, he was told, "Hush!" According to the South African author Dudley Kidd, the African "dislikes to find Europeans investigating his customs, and he usually hides all he can from them and takes a sportive pleasure in baffling and misleading them."[12] The solution to this problem of gaining knowledge about African religion in the un-equal power relations of intercultural contact, Hartland proposed, was for Europeans to learn how to think black.

Acknowledging his source for this notion of thinking black, Hartland invoked the work of the explorer, journalist, and anthropologist Mary Kingsley (1862–1900), who had used this phrase in describing her research in West Africa. In her efforts to understand fetishism, Kingsley wrote, "It can only be thoroughly done by a white whose mind is not a highly civilized one, and who is able to think black." Joking, perhaps, that as a woman her mentality might also register as primitive in imperial anthropology, she stressed the risk in thinking black. It required entering a field of relations but also entailed hardship and danger. "I beg you will not think from my claiming this power I am making an idle boast," she noted, "for I have risked my life for months at a time on this one chance of my being able to know the way people were thinking round me, and of my being able to speak to them in a way that they would recognise as just, true and logical."[13] As Hartland translated this risk, thinking black required a "considerable apprenticeship," whether in the field or in critically reflecting in the study, informed by anthropological theory, on the reports from the field. The rela-tive comfort of the study, Hartland maintained, was "an advantage perhaps not un-accompanied by dangers of its own."[14]

In thinking black, Hartland advocated sympathetic inquiry, without prejudice, in order to grasp the "protean ideas and half-formulated specula-tions of savage minds." To think black the researcher would have to empa-thetically and imaginatively enter the mind of the savage but also enter the mind of a child, because, as Hartland remarked, "[The savage] is a child, but a child familiar only with what we deem a topsy-turvy world, though it is the same world from which we ourselves emerged long ago."[15] By in-voking this cliché, Hartland showed that he did not understand what Mary Kingsley had meant by thinking black. Kingsley had observed in 1897, "My capacity to think in black comes from my not regarding the native form of mind as 'low,' or 'inferior,' or 'childlike,' or anything like that, but as a form of mind of a different sort to white men's—yet a very good form of mind too, in its way."[16] By self-description, Kingsley was an imperialist, "a hardened, unreformed, imperial expansionist," but she argued against the denigra-tion of blacks and women in imperial administration and scholarship.[17] As Sidney Hartland reported in his presidential address to the Folklore Society in 1901, one of the great casualties of the Anglo-Boer War in South Africa was the loss of Mary Kingsley, who had gone to serve as a nurse to Boer prisoners and had died of typhoid at age thirty-eight in Cape Town, South Africa.[18]

Reviewing the work of key figures in the history of imperial comparative religion, this chapter focuses on African producers of knowledge who were thinking black and writing back to empire. We will meet the Zulu philologist uNemo, the Manyika diviner John Chavafambira, the Sotho novelist Thomas Mofolo, the Tswana historian S. M. Molema, and the Zulu scholar of religion, ritual, magic, and drama H. I. E. Dhlomo. In different ways, sometimes destabilizing, sometimes enabling, and sometimes refashioning, they engaged in the production of knowledge about religion in imperial comparative religion.

PHILOLOGY

In developing his science of religion, Friedrich Max Müller relied upon colonial middlemen, such as Henry Callaway, to provide data. Callaway's account of Zulu religion was important to Max Müller's theory of religion. Callaway provided primary evidence for theorizing not only about savage religion but also about the origin of religion in the sense of the infinite displayed by the veneration of the Zulu for ancestors, leading back to the first ancestor, uNkulunkulu, the "Great, Great One."[19] Featured in Max Müller's preface to *The Sacred Books of the East,* uNkulunkulu played an important role in the study of religion. In 1897, however, Max Müller reported that he had recently received a disturbing account in a series of newspaper articles from Zululand, "from the hand, as it would seem, of a native," that contradicted the version of uNkulunkulu given by Callaway. According to this native account, uNkulunkulu was not the primordial ancestor but the supreme being of the Zulu. Accusing Callaway of becoming "bogged in a philological mess," the author of these articles, "our Zulu informant," presented a threat to Max Müller's entire theoretical enterprise, which was built on the "boggy foundations" of evidence from colonial experts such as Henry Callaway. "If we can no longer quote Callaway on Zulus," Max Müller bemoaned, "whom shall we quote?"[20]

The articles that caused this crisis, "Zig Zag Notes for Zulu Scholars," were published during 1895 in six issues of the newspaper *Inkanyiso yase Natal,* which ran articles in both Zulu and English. In a section of the paper called "Native Thoughts," the author, uNemo, wrote in English about "our Zulu language." He invoked "our Zulu ancestors," used the term "we Zulus," complained about the "whiteman," and celebrated the original, creative, and cognitive capacity of the Zulu language. uNemo explained, "Each and every one of the noun-prefixes in Zulu had originally a certain 'idea,' or quality of thought, inherent in it."[21] Arguing for the originality of Zulu tradition, uNemo insisted that biblical narratives—Adam and Eve, the Tree of Life, and Noah's Flood, which was prefigured by the Zulu *uhlanga*, the bed of reeds—were stories already familiar to the Zulu. Accordingly, he argued, "We might by a stretch succeed in proving that the ancient Hebrews plagiarized all they had from our own Kaffir ancestors."[22] With respect to uNkulunkulu, uNemo was "inclined to differ *toto coelo* from Dr. Callaway," because this term was "the exact Native counterpart of our Creator and God."[23]

If Max Müller had read these articles carefully, he must have noticed the slippage between subject positions, the shift from "our Zulu language" to "our Creator and God." In the latter position, uNemo observed, "The Natives, as we know, are a people not yet educated to reason penetratingly on any problem of life."[24] As a result, the Zulu could not think through the analogies between their bed of reeds and the biblical creation, their original ancestor, uNkulunkulu, and the Christian God. Neither, apparently, could Henry Callaway, who had coined the term *uDio* for his mission. While Methodists had imported the Xhosa term *uTixo*, derived from the Khoisan, into Zulu missions, Anglicans and Roman Catholics had appropriated *uNkulunkulu*. Against this background, the argument of the "Zulu informant" uNemo was not with Max Müller over philology or theory-building in the academic study of religion but with Henry Callaway over the name that should be used for God in Christian missions to the Zulu.

Certainly uNemo had no intention of destabilizing Max Müller's theoretical project. As a Zulu philologist, recalling his pleasure in studying philological texts in the British Museum in London, uNemo laced his analysis of the Zulu language with examples not only from other African languages but also from German, Latin, and Sanskrit. Insisting on the originality of Zulu, uNemo was convinced that the study of African languages would lead to a revolution in knowledge similar to the one that had resulted from Oriental studies. In his article in *Inkanyiso yase Natal* of April 5, 1895, uNemo quoted Max Müller quoting Wilhelm Bleek:

> There are many reasons for believing that the South African dialects have preserved more of their primitive form than almost any other living languages

in the world; for these nations have, less than any other, come into contact with foreign influence. Max Müller, in his *Science of Language*, quoting Bleek, says, "It is perhaps not too much to say that similar results may at present be expected from a deeper study of such primitive forms of language as the Kaffir and Hottentot exhibit, as followed at the beginning of the century, the discovery of Sanscrit and the comparative researches of Oriental scholars."[25]

At this point, Max Müller certainly must have been suspicious of this "native" uNemo, "our Zulu informant." He must have wondered how this Zulu knew so much about him. How could this Zulu informant be quoting Max Müller quoting a local colonial expert such as Wilhelm Bleek, when Max Müller built his theories of language, myth, and religion on quoting such colonial experts? Perhaps Max Müller was in on the joke, since no one reading these articles could mistake uNemo, "No One," for an authentic Zulu informant.

Our Zulu author in this case was the Roman Catholic missionary Alfred T. Bryant (1865–1953). He had used the pseudonym uNemo in a book published around the same time; he was temporarily stationed in the Eastern Cape, where uNemo located his submissions; and he was emerging as the leading philologist of the Zulu language, if not a Zulu philologist, by preparing his *Zulu-English Dictionary*, which would be published in 1905.[26] In the introduction to the dictionary, Bryant repeated the same citation of Max Müller quoting Wilhelm Bleek to the effect that in the future African studies would generate new knowledge about language, culture, and religion in the same way that Oriental studies had in the past.[27] In the case of uNemo, the triple mediation—imperial, colonial, and indigenous—in the production of knowledge about religion and religions was strangely scrambled, as the local colonial expert assumed an indigenous Zulu disguise to reveal the "boggy foundations" of imperial knowledge.

As an interested party in the colonial mission, Bryant defined uNkulunkulu in his dictionary by both what the term had meant and what the term had become in the hands of Anglican and Roman Catholic missionaries. In the relevant entry, he defined uNkulunkulu as "the Great-great-ancestor or ancestral-spirit (of mankind), the first man who is supposed to have made most of the things round about; hence, adopted by missionaries to express God, Creator."[28] As uNemo had argued, the analogy between original ancestor and supreme being, both creators, made uNkulunkulu an appropriate term to be appropriated by Christian missionaries. However, as uNemo was well aware, this strategy of translation had not been adopted by the Wesleyan Methodists or the American Board for Foreign Missions. It was vigorously opposed by Henry Callaway. Translation, therefore, was entangled in conflicts within the colonial mission in Natal and Zululand.[29]

Turning to the entry *iDhlozi*, ancestral spirit, in his dictionary, Bryant indulged in a long digression on Zulu indigenous religion. Ancestors were the heart of Zulu religion:

> *N.B.* The *i-dhlozi* is the nearest approach the Zulus have to the idea of a "God." The *u-Nkulunkulu* (q. v.) or "first man" who is said to have "made the world," is nowadays merely a nursery-myth, neither trusted in nor cared for. He seems to have created mankind and vanished altogether from their further experience; for the government today is certainly not in his hands, but entirely in those of the *ama-dhlozi*. These spiritual beings are the benevolent or malevolent "Providence" of the Zulu, according as they be pleased or displeased with the conduct of the living. They are the supreme feature of whatever religion he still retains—all his faith is founded on them; all his worship is directed towards them; all his hopes and fears are centred in them.[30]

While his definitions were situated in the colonial context, Bryant also aspired to knowledge that could be acquired only by the comparative philology practiced by metropolitan theorists such as Max Müller. "It would be interesting to know," Bryant observed, "whether there is really no relationship traceable between the Zulu word *i-dhlozi* and the Skr. *dyaus*, sky (Z = *i-zulu*); Gr. *theos*, god; and L. *deus*, god."[31] In this interest, Bryant suggested that Zulu could be inserted into the imperial study of Indo-European languages. Zulu ancestral spirits, therefore, played multiple roles in Bryant's *Zulu-English Dictionary*. They were the center of an indigenous religion retained under colonial conditions; they provided a key term, *uNkulunkulu*, used by the colonial mission; and they could be drawn into the Indo-European philology of imperial comparative religion.

Eventually, A. T. Bryant emerged as the leading historian of the Zulu. His *Olden Times in Zululand and Natal*, published in 1929, set the model for recounting Zulu history.[32] In recent years, that model has been generally rejected by historians. Although he claimed to draw on oral traditions, Bryant's version of tribal history reproduced the colonial accounts of Zulu-speaking tribes distilled by Theophilus Shepstone for his administrative system of indirect rule. In his last book, *Zulu People as They Were before the Whiteman Came*, which was completed in 1935, Bryant used philology and the study of religion to trace the prehistory of the Zulu back to the Uganda-Kenya region of East Africa. Affinities of language, pointing to an ur-Bantu language, suggested for Bryant that the Zulu shared the same mother tongue as people of East Africa. A common language suggested a shared religion. Comparing the Zulu to the Kavirondo of Uganda, Bryant found, "Just as the Zulus have their *uNkulunkulu* (or Great-great-One, the creator of mankind), the Kavirondos likewise have their *Nyasi* (or Supreme One)." Establishing what he concluded was "the practical identity of Kavirondo and Zulu life customs and beliefs," Bryant found that the Zulu had originated in the North, in East Africa, before migrating three thousand miles over half a millennium to end up in the South around 1600, when their migration was "blocked by the Whiteman" who was arriving at roughly the same time.[33] By this account, the precolonial history of Africans was a saga of migrations, with Bantu groups moving from the North into the "empty land" of South Africa.[34] As the historian Norman Etherington has observed, such accounts of Bantu migrations "drew inspiration from the language-based theories of Aryan migrations developed in the mid-Victorian period by Max Müller and other Sanskritic scholars," indicating that Max Müller and his Indo-European philology had an unexpected afterlife in the development of the study of history in South Africa.[35]

In addition to his interest in philology, Bryant read widely in the imperial anthropology of religion. Entering the debate about totemism, he found that the scholarship of leaders in the field such as Andrew Lang, James Frazer, and E. Sidney Hartland was incoherent. For Bryant, the problem of totemism was simple. The term was being used in imperial scholarship to refer to a commonplace mix of personal clan names, religious ancestor worship, and social taboo in indigenous life. European scholars were mystifying this commonplace. Responding to Andrew Lang's account of Zulu totemism, Bryant complained, "Now, if a writer of Lang's repute can write such ignorant twaddle, what confidence can we place in the statements of less celebrated 'arm-chair' ethnological authorities." Turning to James Frazer, he remarked, "One feels it almost profanity to criticize anything great Frazer wrote. Yet even a Jove could nod." As for E. Sidney Hartland, he found it amusing to watch the anthropologist grope in the dark searching for an imaginary "totem," only to catch an ancestor.[36] Claiming to be standing in the light because he was on the ground with the Zulu, Bryant dismissed the speculations of these imperial scholars. Like the Zulu philologist uNemo, who had destabilized the theoretical project of Max Müller, the philologist Alfred T. Bryant sought to unsettle the theoretical industry of definition, interpretation, explanation, and analysis in the imperial study of religion.

PSYCHOLOGY

In 1917, A. T. Bryant published two articles in British academic journals. While his article "The Zulu Cult of the Dead," in *Man*, the journal of the Royal Anthropological Institute, outlined his understanding of the role of ancestral spirits in Zulu religion,[37] his article in the *Eugenic Review*, "Mental Development of the South African Native," reduced indigenous religion, culture, and personality to a relatively undeveloped primitive mentality. Echoing uNemo's criticism of the native's reasoning, Bryant asserted, "The African intellect, as exemplified in its manhood, is simply incapable of reaching the brilliance or of attaining the range of that of the European." Although African intellect was incapable of rational conceptions, comprehensions, or judgments, it did display certain primitive capacities, such as memory and intuition, which had supposedly atrophied among Europeans in the course of their advanced mental development. Intuition, in particular, was strong in the African mentality, which was "endowed with some peculiar sense of sympathy or telepathy." This capacity explained the existence of "witch-doctors or sorcerers," who do not understand "clairvoyance" but "attribute their powers to the inspiration of ancestral spirits."[38]

E. B. Tylor, as we recall, defined religion as a mentality, as a "belief in spiritual beings," which was a kind of dream-world in which believers could not distinguish between subjectivity and objectivity, between psychological experiences and external reality. Animism, as exemplified by the aspiring Zulu diviner James, was a "house of dreams."[39]

One student of dreams, the psychoanalyst Sigmund Freud (1856–1939), was an avid reader of the anthropology of religion. From E. B. Tylor, Freud adopted the analogy between savages and children, who both "believe they can alter the external world by mere thinking."[40] But he extended that analogy to include neurotics. The mental development of savages, bearing the stamp of the primitive, could elucidate the psychology of modern neurotics, just as the psychology of neurotics could explain primitive mentality. Freud proposed in *Totem and Taboo* that the anthropology of savages and the psychology of neurotics could be joined in a common cause:

> There are men still living who, as we believe, stand very near to primitive man, and whom we therefore regard as his direct heirs and representatives. Such is our view of those whom we describe as savages—or half-savages—and their mental life must have a peculiar interest for us if we are right in seeing in it a well-preserved picture of an early stage of our own development. If that supposition is correct, a comparison between the psychology of primitive peoples,

as it is taught by social anthropology, and a psychology of neurotics, as it has been revealed by psychoanalysis will be bound to show numerous points of agreement and will throw new light upon familiar facts in both sciences.[41]

Freud developed this analogy between the savage and the neurotic, which both supposedly exemplified the primitive, in his major psychoanalytical works on religion—*Totem and Taboo* (1913), *Future of an Illusion* (1927), *Civilization and Its Discontents* (1930), and *Moses and Monotheism* (1939). As the anthropologist T. O. Beidelman observed, Freud transposed the comparative method of nineteenth-century anthropology, which had been developed in imperial comparative religion, "from culture to the mind itself."[42] Freud's student C. G. Jung (1875-1961), despite the differences between him and Freud, developed a similar fascination with the primitive, especially as it was preserved in the "Dark Continent" of Africa, which provided a window into the collective unconscious of humanity.[43]

During the 1930s, the Freudian Wulf Sachs (1893-1949), who had immigrated to South Africa in 1922 to practice medicine, emerged as the leading psychoanalyst in the country. His textbook on the subject, *Psycho-Analysis: Its Meaning and Practical Applications*, published in 1934, carried a foreword by Sigmund Freud.[44] Investigating Freud's analogy between savagery and neurosis, the heart of primitive psychology, Sachs embarked upon a long-term research project among Africans living in the slums around Johannesburg. Through the social anthropologist Ellen Hellmann, who was conducting research in "Roiiyard," Sachs met the primary subject for his analysis, John Chavafambira.[45] Born in Zimbabwe, he was an initiated diviner, herbalist, and healer, a doctor in his own right. For Sachs, however, "John" was both psychoanalytic patient and research subject. Sachs's account of this project, *Black Hamlet*, originally published in 1937, embodied the triple mediation of an imperial theory, in this case a universal theory of human psychology, a local expert in that theory operating within a colonial situation, and an indigenous informant. Like uNemo, John Chavafambira had a voice in this mediated production of knowledge for a psychology of religion, although Wulf Sachs, like A. T. Bryant, might have engaged in a kind of ventriloquism in relating John's story.

Introduced by Sachs as "an ordinary native man, a witch-doctor," John Chavafambira agreed to submit to the Freudian doctor's psychoanalytic therapy, lying on a sofa for one hour every day for two and a half years, engaging in free association, saying whatever came into his mind. Because he was "ordinary," John allowed Sachs to explore whether psychology, both abnormal and normal, was identical in blacks and whites. As a witch doctor, however, John took Sachs into an extraordinary world of religious beliefs and practices. On both his father's and mother's sides, John came from distinguished Manyika lineages of *ngangas*, indigenous doctors, diviners, and herbalists, which provided his own rationale for agreeing to participate in the Freudian talking cure. "We doctors," John said, "can know everything through the bones, or through talking with our *midzimu* (ancestral spirits). But it is true that I cannot throw the bones for myself."[46] Drawing his own analogy between divination and psychoanalysis, John agreed to tell his dreams, visions, and religious experiences to the Freudian analyst.

John related dreams. But he had to provide his own interpretations. Dreaming of eggs and hens signaled good fortune; dreaming of fishing without catching fish presaged bad fortune. More important than the hermeneutics of dreams, however, was the energetics of dreams, the ways in which dreams were not only texts to be interpreted but also calls for action. In response to his dreams of many hens and abundant eggs, John sacrificed a black chicken for his ancestors, reinforcing relations of communication and exchange. Misfortune resulted from neglecting such relations. Reflecting upon a village suffering from drought, he observed: "Perhaps they prayed to the wrong god, maybe they are Christians and forgot their dead people. Were they at peace with their *midzimu*? Had they killed the goats to them?"[47] Dreams, therefore, were vital media for ongoing relations with ancestral spirits.

In John's case, his deceased father, who had been a powerful *nganga*, communicated in dreams and visions, asserting his presence as John's "protector and guide, whose life and spirit he was destined to perpetuate."[48] Sachs found that this relation with the dead was the key to African psychology: "For John, as for all Africans, there is no rigid dividing-line between the living and the dead; he has no conception of 'another world.' The dead continue to exist in this world in the form of *midzimu*, the spirits of the ancestors; and John believes implicitly that the *midzimu* come and speak to him, giving him advice and help." John lived in the "house of dreams," where spirits come and speak, which had served as E. B. Tylor's defining illustration of animism. For Sachs, however, this engagement with ancestral spirits enabled John to retain his lost father and mother, illustrating what psychoanalysis could diagnose as the "introjection of an object."[49] By internalizing his parents in the beliefs and practices of ancestral religion, according to Sachs, "Father and mother, though dead, remained accessible to him whenever he was in need of them." Introjection, however, was matched by projection, as parents assumed divine status, "as omniscient as God, but in a concrete and tangible form." Here Sachs was deploying fundamental themes in Freud's psychology of religion. Divine beings were projections of parents into an imaginary realm; religious sensibilities were an introjection of the authority of parents. According to Sachs, invoking the Freudian theme of infantile regression through religion, John "remained an infant throughout his life" as a result of communicating with the ancestral spirits of his father and mother.[50]

The narrative arc of *Black Hamlet* was structured by totem and taboo. In the early stages of the book, John reveals the importance of his clan totem, his *mutopo*, inherited through the father's line, which is "the animal who protects the man." In John's case, his totem was Soko, the monkey. From childhood, he was warned by his elders not to make love to a woman of the same *mutopo*, which would be "like sleeping with your own sister."[51] The totem, therefore, entailed taboo. As Sachs reinforced this point in the second edition, "marriage in John's society was governed by endless taboos," the most important being the incest taboo against sexual relations with a partner of the same totemic clan.[52] At the end of the book, returning home to what was then Rhodesia, John makes love with a woman without asking her about her *mutopo*, only to learn later that she was also Soko, the monkey, making their sexual intercourse a violation of the incest taboo. Although this violation should have entailed serious punishment from ancestral spirits, at the very least requiring sacrifices of goats or chickens to appease their wrath, Sachs suggests that this crisis provided the occasion for John to resolve his oedipal dilemma. On his way back to Johannesburg, he fought with three white men who were attacking monkeys, thereby reconciling himself with his ancestral spirits. At peace with his ancestors, John resolved to be a father to his own son, guiding him through the contradictions of black and white, tradition and modernity, in South Africa. According to Sachs, John realized that "the black and the white people must work together. Given that, the future of his son was assured. But, without it, it would be bare and purposeless indeed."[53] Psychological resolution, therefore, required overcoming infantilization by reconciling with parents and becoming an adult.

Wulf Sachs was a mediator of Freudian theory in a colonial situation, using a universal theory to explain the local natives. In the psychoanalytic transfer between therapist and patient, Sachs's Jewish background provided one frame for mutual recognition. John Chavafambira recognized a common bond between African traditionalists and Jews. "I read in the Bible that Jews also refused to have Jesus and believe in God," John observed.

"We are also the same."[54] As we have seen, an African identification with Jews had been internalized by Zulu Christians interviewed by James Stuart. As we will see, an African genealogy leading back to ancient Israel also came to be developed by African historians such as Magema Fuze, Petros Lamula, and John Henderson Soga. For John Chavafambira, however, this identification with Jews was based not on a shared origin in the distant past but on a similar situation of religious alienation from contemporary South Africa. In exchange, Sachs reinforced this identification of Africans with Jews. "Didn't I myself, a Jew," he demanded, "belong to a people ceaselessly driven from pillar to post?"[55]

As a socialist, Wulf Sachs was attentive to the intersections of psychology and South African politics. Although he applied basic principles of psychoanalysis to religion, finding that his subject had psychologically internalized his parents as ancestral spirits, projected his parents as omniscient deities, and regressed to an infantile state in the process, Sachs was also aware of the broader political context. In the revised edition of *Black Hamlet* published in 1947 as *Black Anger*, the political analysis was intensified. Although the oedipal drama in African childhood produced a "retarding effect" that constrained "every African child in his fight for independence," this psychological obstacle was relatively insignificant when compared to the overwhelming political, social, and economic disabilities enforced upon Africans. Sachs observed, "Today this important psychological factor counts little compared with the poverty and starvation, the economic exploitation, and the severe racial discrimination to which black people are subjected in South Africa."[56] The merger of psychology and politics was further emphasized as psychological resolution involved a new political consciousness. As the historian Saul Dubow has noted, an extended political speech at the end of *Black Anger* seems to be drawn from an article published in a journal edited by Sachs. The article, by the African intellectual and political activist H. I. E. Dhlomo, celebrates the "New African" in South Africa who was "awakening to the issue at stake and to the power of organised intelligently led mass action and progressive thinking African intellectuals and leaders."[57] In this awakening, simultaneously psychological and political, a new definition of African adulthood was being formulated.

HISTORY

In building his psychoanalytic account of John Chavafambira, Wulf Sachs complained that he did not know how many of John's stories were fiction.

Experimenting with fiction himself, Sachs wrote a draft of his research as a novel, *African Tragedy*, but opted in the end for a more scientific presentation. Observing that it was "difficult to tell truth from fiction," Sachs concluded that the distinction did not matter, because John's stories, whether they reflected actual or imagined events, revealed "a psychological reality."[58] As we recall, novels featured in imperial comparative religion, from Max Müller's *German Love* to Andrew Lang's collaborations with the adventure novelists H. Rider Haggard and John Buchan. In South Africa, the missionary and ethnographer Henri-Alexander Junod wrote a novel, *Zidji*, which incorporated his ethnographic research into a morality tale about a young man leaving his traditional homestead, migrating to the city, and ultimately becoming a Christian.[59] Framed as a kind of pilgrim's progress, this novel nevertheless presented what Junod regarded as ethnographic reality, including profiles of indigenous religion. Fiction, therefore, could be a medium for conveying fact. As for history, the preeminent South African historian George McCall Theal (1837–1919) created the most authoritative archival record and historical interpretation of the history of South Africa. In his account of African religion, however, which he glossed as "the supposition of the existence of spirits," he repeated the colonial fantasy of African ignorance and childishness. "The Bantu power of reasoning in such matters did not extend so far," Theal asserted. "Their minds in this respect were like those of little children."[60] In many ways, the scholarly study of the history of religion in South Africa was a mix of myth, fiction, and history.

The earliest history of the Zulu written by a Zulu author was *Abantu Abamnyama Lapa Bavela Ngakona (The Black People and Whence They Came)*, published in 1922, by Magema Fuze (c. 1840–1922). As an early convert of John Colenso, Fuze had absorbed the promise of the mission. With regard to religion, he adopted the genealogy of Zulu religion from ancient Israel. Introducing his history, Fuze stated, "I feel strongly that our people should know that we did not originate here in Southern Africa." In contrast to the philological and historical accounts of Bantu migrations from the North, which also suggested that the Zulu came from elsewhere, Fuze turned to the Bible as a template for inserting the Zulu into a universal history. Familiar with the colonial analogies between Zulu practices and the rituals of ancient Israel, Fuze agreed with the conjecture "We black people came from the people of Israel."[61] Likewise, the historian Petros Lamula (c. 1881–1948), who once described himself as "The Professor of the Hidden Sciences," saw Zulu history through "the great 'telescope'—the Bible." In *UZulukaMalandela: A Most Practical and Concise Compendium of African*

History, published in 1924, Lamula used the Bible to establish the common origin of all nations but also to locate the Zulu at the beginning of human history. According to Lamula, Zulu traditions echoed biblical stories. God's creation of Adam and Eve was like the folktale told by old people about uMvelinqangi creating people in the original bed of reeds. God telling Adam and Eve about death was like the traditional tale about uNkulunkulu sending a chameleon to tell people that they would die. "The folk tales agree with the Bible," Lamula concluded, proving that the religion of ancient Israel had been preserved in Zulu tradition.[62] This theme of African origin in ancient Israel was also implicit in the historical work of the Xhosa historian John Henderson Soga (1860–1941), who framed his account of Xhosa religion by establishing similarities between Jewish and Xhosa sacrifice "purely in the interests of truth and scientific research."[63] For African historians, African history flowed from the Bible and could be interpreted in the light of the Bible.

If they accepted this biblical history as fact, African authors might have felt greater freedom to tell stories outside of any Christian orthodoxy in the medium of fiction. In his novel about precolonial Zulu society, *Jeqe the Bodyservant of King Tshaka*, the Christian educator John Dube did not trace Zulu language, culture, and religion back to ancient Israel. Instead, he related a dramatic story of an attendant to King Shaka, who should have been killed along with the king but became a powerful and wealthy diviner in Swaziland.[64] For African Christian authors, we might suspect, history was Christian history, while fiction gave scope for narratives about indigenous tradition.

In the case of Thomas Mofolo (1876–1948), who is often celebrated as the first African novelist in South Africa, Christianity and tradition, history and fiction, merged in his creative work. His first novel, *The Traveller of the East* (*Moeti oa Bochabela*), was an African pilgrim's progress, a story of Fekisi leaving his traditional home, which was a world of darkness, to journey to the East, toward the rising sun. He met Christians and, ultimately, Christ, as his journey ended in leaving his body behind.[65] Turning from Christianity to tradition, Mofolo's historical novel *Chaka* traced the career of King Shaka through the intervention of a traditional diviner, Isanusi, who enabled Shaka's rise to power.[66] There is an inverse parallel in the spiritual journeys of Fekisi and Shaka: In *Traveller of the East*, the novel culminates as Fekisi rises to heaven, with only his flesh remaining behind. In *Chaka*, after the aspiring king has been initiated by Isanusi, he returns to his people to assume power, but "only his flesh is coming back," because his soul remained in the wilderness.[67]

Mofolo's *Chaka* was caught up in the mediations of imperial, colonial, and indigenous interests. Mofolo explained in 1928, "I am not writing a history, I am writing a tale."[68] Nevertheless, he relied on previous historical accounts to write his tale. As a Basotho, he also engaged in a kind of ethnography, studying others by visiting Natal to interview Zulu people about their traditions relating to Shaka and other matters of belief and custom. Accordingly, this tale, informed by history and ethnography, was not entirely fiction.

In the colonial exchange, the Protestant missionaries of the Paris Evangelical Missionary Society in Lesotho were concerned that this fiction, because it was not entirely fiction, would have a real impact on Africans by glorifying indigenous religion. One missionary warned that publication of *Chaka* could "do nothing but harm to its readers, because it [was] an apology for pagan superstitions."[69] Although some missionaries defended the book for its literary merit, others sought to block its publication.

In the imperial exchange, a local translator, Frederick Hugh Dutton, rendered an English version that attracted the attention of the International Institute of African Languages and Cultures in London. Submitting the manuscript for publication to Longmans, the institute received a reply from J. W. Allen, one of directors of the press, which echoed concerns raised by the missionaries in Lesotho. "I do not think it would be wise to publish it," Allen wrote. "There is so much stress laid on the power of witchcraft, and any book that shows the enormous influence witchcraft has on the native would be likely to do more harm than good."[70]

In the end, Thomas Mofolo's *Chaka* was published and no harm was done. As the literary analyst Daniel P. Kunene has observed, Longmans in London did not have to worry about harming Africans with this novel, since not many would read the English translation. However, the exchange between imperial, colonial, and indigenous interests in producing this novel is instructive. In placing the indigenous diviner Isanusi at the center of his novel about Shaka, Thomas Mofolo might very well have been advancing a Christian critique of the Zulu polity. According to Kunene, the whole novel, revolving around the controlling figure of Isanusi, who gave Shaka his power and took his reward at Shaka's death, rendered the Zulu king as evil.[71] For some of the missionaries, however, any attention to indigenous tradition in fiction was a harmful "apology for pagan superstitions." Certainly they did not feel the same way about history or ethnography, since missionaries of the Paris Evangelical Missionary Society were distinguished authors of factual accounts of indigenous traditions, from Eugène Casalis to David-Frédéric Ellenberger.[72] The fact that Longmans absorbed this missionary concern that a novel about indigenous religious life in South Africa would be harmful suggests again that colonial interests could also feed back into knowledge production at the center of empire.

In these multiple exchanges, Mofolo's *Chaka* could also register as new "data" about indigenous Zulu history, culture, and religion. Reviewing the novel in *American Anthropologist*, the Africanist Wilfrid Dyson Hambly recommended *Chaka* as a textbook for students of South African history and ethnology. According to Hambly, "All is perfectly sound ethnological fact skilfully woven into the thread of the story." *Chaka* provided new data not only for anthropology and history but also for psychology, especially for the psychology of dreams in Africa, which had been pioneered by C. G. Seligman.[73] "The dreams of Chaka," Hambly asserted, "give some new material for the study of oneiromancy." For the study of African religion, Hambly found that the novel "seem[ed] to touch the core of ancestor worship," but that core turned out to be human sacrifice, as the fictional Isanusi revealed that the "highest form of witchcraft" was killing children or parents to gain the support of powerful spirits. Just as Andrew Lang had used data from the novels of H. Rider Haggard, Hambly found "perfectly sound ethnological fact" in the novel *Chaka*. As a result, Mofolo's fictional account of the Zulu king and diviner, underwritten by his Christian critique, was embraced by this Africanist as primary data for understanding the essence of African religion.[74]

Silas Modiri Molema (1891–1965) was the first African South African to write a general history of Africans in South Africa. Published in 1920, *The Bantu, Past and Present* was a comprehensive history. From a Tswana background with a missionary education, Molema left South Africa in 1914 to study medicine in Glasgow. Remaining in Scotland during the World War, Molema researched and wrote his account of the past, present, and future of Africans.[75] While touching on religion in his profiles of the various African "ethnical groups," he demonstrated a remarkable innovation by proposing a generic definition of religion that was situated not only in Africa but also in conversation with the academic study of religion. Molema's bibliography included many of the major authors of imperial comparative religion—Friedrich Max Müller, John Lubbock, Herbert Spencer, Andrew Lang, and James Frazer—in the section on "books referring indirectly to Africa." Curiously, E. B. Tylor was missing, but Molema had clearly engaged key texts in the history of imperial theorizing about religion. He had also seriously reflected on W. E. B. Du Bois's *Souls of Black Folk* and quoted from Du Bois, especially when looking to the future of Africa. In a chapter on the future of religion in Africa, "Religious Outlook," Molema introduced another innovation by including Islam as an African religion and anticipating the expansion of Islam in Africa. For the study of religion in South Africa, therefore, S. M. Molema can be regarded as an indigenous innovator in defining religion as a generic term and engaging religious diversity.

Introducing the "ethnical groups" of Bushmen, Hottentots, and Bantu, Molema referred to the work of Max Müller and Wilhelm Bleek in classifying languages, but his accounts of the religions of these groupings preserved colonial stereotypes. "The religion of the Bushmen was the fear of ghosts and evil spirits," he recounted. "They had a strong faith in charms and witchcraft."[76] The religion of the Hottentots, who "were given to merrymaking, singing and dancing," especially at the new moon, was some form of "Lunar worship." Although they venerated the mantis, the "Hottentot god," their supreme being was Gounza Ticquva, "an undefined sort of deity, who left the immediate care of the Hottentots in the hands of the spirits and insects."[77] Arriving at the religion of the Bantu, Molema deferred to the authority of the Scottish evangelist Henry Drummond, author of *Tropical Africa*. "What was their religion?" Molema asked. "The question is answered accurately by Mr. Drummond: 'They had a national religion—the fear of evil spirits.'"[78] Accordingly, Molema found that Bantu religion could be characterized as spiritism, spiritualism, or animism, concluding that "the religion, if religion it is, of the Bantu, was Animism."[79] Colonial stereotypes of Africans worshipping evil spirits, therefore, could be reproduced; but they also could be translated into E. B. Tylor's imperial theory of religion as animism, "belief in spiritual beings."[80]

Molema's transactions with imperial theory led him to reflect on the definition of religion. Although he repeated colonial stereotypes about the religious beliefs of "ethnical groups," he pushed his analysis forward by asking, "How far do they agree with the usual definitions of religion?" Observing that scholars had produced many definitions, all different, Molema concluded from a review of the literature that three terms—the supernatural, the human, and the adjustment of the relationship between the supernatural and the human—were the essential ingredients in any generic definition of religion.

To illustrate the variety of definitions, Molema invoked three authorities—Friedrich Max Müller, James Frazer, and William James. Beginning with the putative founder of the academic study of religion, Molema observed: "Professor Max Müller thus vigorously defines it: 'Religion is the outcome of desire to explain all things—physical, metaphysical, and moral—by analogies drawn from human society, imaginatively and symbolically considered. In short, it is a universal sociological hypothesis, mythical in form.'" Unfortunately, this definition was not actually provided by Max Müller but by the French philosopher Jean-Marie Guyau (1854–1888), whose *Irréligion de l'avenir* (1886), which was translated into English in 1897 as *The Non-religion of the Future*, advanced a sociology of religion around this definition.[81] This text was mistakenly attributed to Max Müller in Molema's bibliography. Certainly Guyau's sociological definition was inconsistent with Max Müller's definition of religion as a sense of the infinite. How did Molema confuse Guyau with Max Müller? In *A Psychological Study of Religion*, published in 1912, James H. Leuba (1867–1946) collected forty-eight definitions of religion, classifying them into three categories—intellectualistic, affectivistic, and voluntaristic—on the basis of their primary emphasis on thought, emotion, or will. In a section of the book in which he criticized definitions based on emotion, Leuba observed, "A similar criticism is applicable to Max Müller and to Guyau."[82] Proceeding to analyze the latter's definition of religion, Leuba provided the definition and reference to *The Non-religion of the Future* exactly as it was cited by Molema in *Bantu, Past and Present*. Although Leuba does not appear in his bibliography, Molema must have read him. Besides accounting for the confusion about Max Müller, Leuba provided all three of the definitions of religion cited by Molema. If he had read James H. Leuba, then S. M. Molema was familiar with a text that has been used as a reference point in the academic study of religion to argue for both the futility and the possibility of defining religion.[83]

While the definition Molema cited from Max Müller (or Guyau) illustrated the human side of religion, as religion was "drawn from human society," the definition by James Frazer emphasized the supernatural side. As Molema noted, "In the Golden Bough, p. 63, Frazer thus defines religion: 'It is a propitiation or conciliation of powers supreme to man, which are believed to direct and control the course of nature and human life.'"[84] Again, this definition appears in Leuba's catalog, although Molema might also have consulted the *Golden Bough*. As we will see in a moment, a contemporary South African scholar, H. I. E. Dhlomo, was familiar with the work of James Frazer, relying on him for his understanding of indigenous ritual and sympathetic magic. For Molema, however, Frazer's definition captured the supernatural dimension of religion that had to be placed in relationship with the human.

Situated between the human and the supernatural, the third definition, by William James, focused on the adjustment of relationship between the two that was crucial to Molema's understanding of religion. As Molema quoted James, "Religious life consists in the beliefs that there is an un-seen order, and that our supreme good lies in harmoniously adjusting our-selves thereto. The belief and the adjustment are the religious attitude of the soul."[85] Mediating between the supernatural and the human, adjustment was the pivot around which Molema's generic definition of religion turned. Distilling his definition of religion from a review of imperial comparative religion, he deployed that definition to refute a colonial legacy of denying African religion. "If then the three elements—supernatural, man, and the adjustment of relationship between the two by the latter—constitute reli-gion," Molema concluded, "it seems that the Bantu had a religion, primitive and unevolved certainly, but none the less a religion."[86]

At this juncture in his work, Molema achieved something remarkable. As an African scholar, he altered the terms, reversing the flow, in the triple mediation in which knowledge about religion had been produced in impe-rial comparative religion. Instead of acting as an indigenous informant in the colonial exchange with metropolitan theorists, he transformed imperial theorists into "informants" about defining religion in order to solve a colo-nial problem, the recognition of African indigenous religion as religion.

Having established that the Bantu had an indigenous religion, Molema countered the colonial stereotype that Africans were subject to a savage re-ligion. For understanding the religion of savages, he suggested, we would have to look not to the religion of Africans but to the religion of the German savages of pre-Christian Europe. In an extended quotation from Edward Gibbon's *Decline and Fall of the Roman Empire*, Molema profiled the religion of German savages:

> The religious system of the Germans (if the wild opinions of savages can de-serve that name) was dictated by their wants, their fears, and their ignorance. They adored the great visible objects and agents of Nature—the sun and the moon, the fire and the earth—together with those imaginary deities who were supposed to preside over the most important occupations of human life. They were persuaded that, by some ridiculous arts of divination, they could discover the will of the superior beings—such was the situation, and such were the man-ners, of the ancient Germans.[87]

He provided a similar profile of the savage religion of the English in pre-Christian Britain. While identifying the enduring template that had been used by Europeans in representing African religion as savage religion, Molema's invocation of Gibbon effectively put Europeans in the "savage slot," rendering their ancestors as wild savages with a religion driven by ig-norance, fear, and desire, enveloped in imaginary delusions, and displayed in ridiculous rituals.[88] However, Molema rejected the notion that savagery and civilization were fixed terms of reference, a permanent opposition, by quoting W. E. B. Du Bois to the effect that such an assumption "would have made it difficult for the Teuton to prove his right to life." Molema quoted Du Bois from *Souls of Black Folk*: "The silently growing assumption of the age is that the probation of races is past, and that the backward races of to-day are of proven inefficiency and are not worth saving. Such an assumption is the arrogance of peoples irreverent towards time, and ignorant of the deeds of men."[89]

Writing about the African past and present, Molema was also looking to the future, inspired by Du Bois to imagine a pan-African future in which the categories of savagery and civilization would be transcended. In his analysis of religion, Molema engaged in a complex dialectic—repeating the colonial stereotypes about the religions of "ethnical groups," engaging the imperial study of religion for a generic definition of religion, and then challenging the imperial assumption of a fixed racial hierarchy of religions. Molema observed, "We are told from all sides that 'man is a religious being.'"[90] Quite possibly, Molema was quoting Henry Callaway, who had made that assertion in 1876 in a widely distributed pamphlet, *Religious Sentiment amongst the Tribes of South Africa*.[91] But Molema was intervening in the study of religion by challenging both colonial and imperial assumptions about African religion. His sustained attention to the problem of religion distinguished S. M. Molema as a significant scholar of religion in South Africa.

ANTHROPOLOGY

As Bronislaw Malinowski replaced James Frazer as the center of gravity in anthropology, South Africa emerged as a training ground for a new generation of anthropologists. Generally regarded as the founder of modern fieldwork methods in anthropology, Malinowski (1884–1942) developed the theoretical framework of functionalism for linking kinship, economy, and religion in the analysis of any functioning social system. Although Malinowski eventually visited South Africa in 1934, his competitor, A. R. Radcliffe-Brown (1881–1944), served between 1921 and 1925 as professor of anthropology at the University of Cape Town. Radcliffe-Brown's structural-functionalism also departed from the theory and method of an earlier generation of anthropologists, although some of the key figures in imperial anthropology—James Frazer, R. R. Marett, and especially Alfred C. Haddon, who wrote to South African prime minister Jan Smuts—were instrumental in securing his appointment in Cape Town.[92] Radcliffe-Brown's successor, Isaac Schapera (1905–2003), emerged as the leader of English-speaking social anthropology in South Africa. Developing intensive fieldwork methods, Schapera and other social anthropologists participated in an ongoing exchange between the South African field and Malinowski's seminars at the London School of Economics. Max Gluckman (1911–1975), who earned a doctorate from Oxford for a thesis on Zulu religion, also engaged in this anthropological exchange.[93] Moving away from the study of tribes, social anthropologists eventually focused on culture contact and social change in a unified social field.

By contrast, *volkekunde*, the anthropology of Afrikaans-speakers, emphasized the linguistic, cultural, and religious differentiation of tribal groups. Appointed to the first post in anthropology at the University of Stellenbosch in 1925, Werner Eiselen (1899–1977) emerged as the leading Afrikaans-speaking anthropologist and later as one of the architects of apartheid. Schapera recalled in an interview during the 1980s, "Eiselen [was] the son of a missionary in the civil service. He became Secretary for Native Affairs and drafted the original blueprint of apartheid."[94] Fifty years earlier, however, Schapera had praised Eiselen for his in-depth knowledge of the indigenous religious beliefs and practices of Africans in South Africa. Schapera remarked in 1932, "Eiselen is now engaged in writing a book on the religious life of the Southern Bantu which . . . should make this aspect of Bantu life one of the best known."[95] Although this book was never written, Eiselen wrote extensively on African religious life, trying to recover its primitive forms and endeavoring to assess the impact of Christianity and civilization.[96]

These two streams of anthropology—British social anthropology and Afrikaner *volkekunde*—have usually been depicted in opposition, but during the 1920s and 1930s they shared an interest in the study of African religion.[97] In the landmark compendium *Bantu-Speaking Tribes in South Africa*, published by the South African Inter-University Committee for African Studies in 1937, Isaac Schapera and Werner Eiselen coauthored the chapter "Religious Beliefs and Practices." Two features of this introductory survey of African religion are worth noting. First, Schapera and Eiselen made no reference to imperial theorists of religion. Not only James Frazer, but also every other metropolitan theorist in the academic study of religion was absent. Without reflecting on a general theory of religion, the authors were content to rely upon the reports of local experts among the natives. Second, in focusing on local knowledge, Schapera and Eiselen relied almost entirely on texts. Although they mentioned their own unpublished fieldwork, their account of African religion was derived from the texts of local experts, such as those produced by Henry Callaway, Henri-Alexandre Junod, and W. C. Willoughby, which they synthesized into a general profile.[98] In South African anthropology of the 1930s, the study of African religion was still text-based but had broken from imperial theory. It was based solely on the findings of local experts.

While James Frazer was disappearing from theory and method in anthropology, his influence diffused through a variety of creative arts, most notably in the work of the poets T. S. Eliot and W. B. Yeats and the novelists James Joyce and D. H. Lawrence.[99] In South Africa, the primary artist to embrace the legacy of Frazer was the journalist, poet, and dramatist Herbert Isaac Ernest Dhlomo (1903–1956). During the 1930s, hoping to advance a new African National Dramatic Movement, Dhlomo traced the origin of African dramatic art back to indigenous religion. "The origin of African drama," he explained, "was a combination of religious or magical ritual [with] rhythmic dances and the song."[100] Picking up themes from Frazer, such as the notion of sympathetic magic, a pragmatic theory of religious ritual, and the need to relate magic, religion, and science, Dhlomo created his own synthesis. Although he annotated his copy of *The Golden Bough*, his primary textual source for reflecting on these Frazerian themes was provided by the feminist, classicist, and student of comparative religion Jane Ellen Harrison (1850–1928), whose *Ancient Art and Ritual*, published in 1913, gave Dhlomo key terms for tracing the religious origin of African drama. Harrison had revealed ancient Greek religion as savage, just as Robertson Smith had unearthed the savage in the religion of ancient Israel. As Harrison observed in the bibliography of *Ancient Art and Ritual*, her understanding of the religious origins of ancient Egyptian, Greek, and Roman drama had been derived from the study of primitive religion advanced by William Robertson Smith and James Frazer. She singled out the importance of Robertson's Smith's *Lectures on the Religion of the Semites*, "an epoch-making book," for clarifying "fundamental ritual notions," while she identified Frazer's *Golden Bough* as the best general reference for the study of ancient and primitive ritual, especially the section devoted to Adonis, Attis, and Osiris, "from which," she said, "most of the instances in the present manual are taken."[101]

In a series of articles on African drama in the 1930s, H. I. E. Dhlomo showed that he had undertaken a careful reading of Jane Harrison's *Ancient Art and Ritual*. He invoked her authority to support not only the ritual origin of drama but also the dramatic character of ritual. In his article "Nature and

Variety of Tribal Drama," published in 1939 in *Bantu Studies*, the journal of the South African Inter-University Committee for African Studies, Dhlomo quoted Harrison on ancient Egyptian rituals of Osiris to reinforce the relationship between religion and drama: "In Egypt, then, we have clearly an instance—only one of many—where art and ritual go hand in hand. Ancient art and ritual are not only closely connected, not only do they mutually explain and illustrate each other, but . . . they actually arise out of a common human impulse."[102] If Harrison's research proved the link between religious ritual and art, Dhlomo argued that indigenous Zulu rituals could be seen "to contain the germs of a great art such as drama."[103] However, by developing his own theoretical synthesis, he was not merely applying imperial theory. Like S. M. Molema, H. I. E. Dhlomo reversed the flow in the production of knowledge in imperial comparative religion, turning theorists such as Robertson Smith, Frazer, and Harrison into "informants" about ancient religion in order to pursue his own project, in this case the advancement of African drama under colonial conditions in South Africa.

In Dhlomo's analysis, the religious rituals that gave rise to drama were "based on what anthropologists call Sympathetic Magic." Invoking this classic Frazerian category, which was based on the belief that "like always and everywhere produced like," he found that sympathetic magic in both ritual and drama was not only imitation but also anticipation. Observing that imitation was central to indigenous African ritual, he argued that this mimetic acting did not represent the past. It anticipated the future. "There are also what one may call anticipatory dances or ceremonies based on the principle of sympathetic magic," he noted. "In these ceremonies the people 'Acted', not what had happened, but what they wished to happen."[104] In this respect, he focused on what Jane Harrison had called the ritual "fore-done for magical purposes," the "dance that anticipates by pre-presenting."[105] Harrison outlined the anticipatory character of imitation in savage ritual:

> If we consider the occasions when a savage dances, it will soon appear that it is not only after a battle or a hunt that he dances in order to commemorate it, but before. Once the commemorative dance has got abstracted or generalized it becomes material for the magical dance, the dance pre-done. A tribe about to go to war will work itself up by a war dance; about to start out hunting they will catch their game in pantomime. Here clearly the main emphasis is on the practical, the active, doing-element in the cycle. The dance is, as it were, a sort of precipitated desire, a discharge of pent-up emotion into action.[106]

As Dhlomo adopted Harrison's profile of anticipatory ritual, he agreed that it should be understood as acting out desires. Instead of adapting to the conditions of life, tribal Africans acted through ritual to bend its course to their desires, which "gave birth to what anthropologists call Sympathetic Magic." However, by contrast to Harrison's reduction of this anticipatory performance to an emotional discharge, Dhlomo regarded indigenous ritual drama as revelatory, insisting that "anticipatory ceremonies were psychological and imaginative, revealing the thoughts, the feelings and the desires of the people, and giving full play to the faculty to imagine and conceive."[107] In Dhlomo's understanding of indigenous ritual, imitation and anticipation held a wider range of intellectual and emotional significance.

Nevertheless, like James Frazer, H. I. E. Dhlomo developed a pragmatic theory of ritual. The purpose of most rituals, he suggested, is "a utilitarian, a practical one."[108] While rituals served such practical ends as cleansing, protection, and appeasement of ancestors, they primarily addressed human desires for food, children, and success. "Many of these tribal, magical dramatic representations," he observed, "sprang from the desire to have much food, many children, and to conquer in battle."[109] Here Dhlomo was certainly referring to the pragmatic theory of ritual advanced by Frazer. Jane Harrison summarized, "The two great interests of primitive man are food and children. As Dr. Frazer has well said, if man the individual is to live he must have food; if his race is to persist he must have children. 'To live and to cause to live, to eat food and to beget children, these were the primary wants of man in the past, and they will be the primary wants of men in the future so long as the world lasts.'"[110] Although he added conquering in battle as a practical objective, Dhlomo shared this pragmatic theory of ritual. However, he blurred Frazer's distinctions among magic, religion, and science. For the tribal African, religion was magic, ritual was "magico-religious representation," and "Magic was his science."[111] Modern science could also be based on magico-religious representation. "Many European historians worship at the shrine of Colour and 'Science,'" he observed, "and succeed only to produce colourful and pseudo-scientific race doctrines."[112] As a kind of sympathetic magic, the enactment of these race doctrines also sought control over resources, reproduction, and power.

Looking back to sympathetic magic, Dhlomo also looked forward to modern drama in his analysis of ritual. In his vision for African drama, Dhlomo was not a primitivist, calling for a return to pure tradition. "The development of African drama cannot purely be from African roots," he proposed. "It must borrow from, be inspired by, shoot from European dramatic art forms, and be tainted by exotic influences."[113] Dhlomo mediated between traditional and modern. If Africans were totemists, feeling kinship with animals, Darwinism might show they were not wrong in understanding humans as animals.[114] If Africans were spiritualists, psycho-analysis might show they were not wrong in exploring the subconscious mind.[115] Likewise, in the study of ritual, Dhlomo used a modern European dramatic structure, the five-act play, to analyze the indigenous Zulu ritual of death. "In this great ceremony," he observed, "there are five divisions or five 'acts': Death, Burial, Mourning, Ihlambo (Cleansing), and Ukubuyisa (the bringing back of the spirit of the deceased)."[116] Proceeding to outline the "great, tragic performance," he identified the crucial elements in each of the five acts of this ritual drama. By developing a performance theory of ritual, Dhlomo showed how indigenous Zulu religion employed basic patterns and processes that were also evident in modern dramatic art. While drama originated in religion, religion was already drama.

As a scholar of drama, but also as a scholar of religion, Dhlomo announced a research program. He called for historical and anthropological research on the "dramatic elements in Bantu ritual ceremony," while urging the "comparative study of African life and literature, and Greek, Hebrew and Egyptian life and literature."[117] Here again, we must detect the influence of the comparative research of Jane Harrison. But Dhlomo's research program in the history and anthropology of religion was addressed specifically to African scholars. "The European historian was handicapped by preconceived ideas and existing prejudices," Dhlomo observed. "He could not enter into the mind and the aspirations and the feelings of the black people of whom he wrote."[118] Trusting that African scholars would not suffer from such a handicap in studying indigenous religion, Dhlomo imagined that they would also have greater insight into ancient religion, since they would be able, as the rhetorician Giambattista Vico had advised, to look "at the world with primitive eyes" in order "to recapture the ancient point of view."[119] Since he was primarily interested in the revitalization of African drama in South Africa, Dhlomo's research goals also included collecting indigenous praise poetry and traditions of African kings and heroes, translating Shakespeare into African languages, and studying new developments in African American theater in the United States. In all of these enterprises, his sustained attention to the religious roots of drama distinguished H. I. E. Dhlomo as a significant scholar of religion in South Africa.

PRODUCING KNOWLEDGE

In his skepticism about the ability of European scholars to enter the minds of black people, H. I. E. Dhlomo implicitly challenged E. Sidney Hartland's proposal that the key to the study of religion was to "think black." Hartland made thinking black sound too easy, as if it were a kind of telepathy. This easy empathy was an imperial conceit, which we recall from John Buchan's claim that the British were "the only race on earth that [could] produce men capable of getting inside the skin of remote people."[120] While Mary Kingsley earned this skill in the field, Hartland claimed that he had learned to think black in the study by reviewing reports from observers such as Kingsley. As an example of what Dhlomo called handicapping prejudice, Hartland explained that thinking black was thinking like a child in two senses—as the opposite of an adult and as the childhood of humanity. Countering this assumption that Africans were permanent children and primitive survivals, S. M. Molema invoked W. E. B. Du Bois: "Such an assumption is the arrogance of peoples irreverent towards time, and ignorant of the deeds of men."[121]

This same passage from Du Bois was cited by Dudley Kidd (1863-1921), the South African missionary author of *The Essential Kafir* (1904), *Savage Childhood* (1906), and *Kafir Socialism and the Dawn of Individualism* (1908), an author read by Sidney Hartland in the quiet space of his study. Referring to Du Bois, Kidd dismissed "what an American negro has to say on the latent capacity of the black races to rise in the scale of civilization." Revealing that an old friend of Du Bois had told him that this American Negro was more white than black, Kidd wondered why Du Bois identified with his African ancestry rather than with his European heritage. More white than black, according to Kidd, Du Bois was not a good model for what Africans in South Africa might achieve. According to "colonists in South Africa," Kidd explained, Africans came from bad stock, inheriting no civilized traits, and thereby suffered a "hopeless handicap."[122]

How was knowledge produced in the imperial study of religion? As we have seen, over and over again, knowledge was produced by quotation. As an engine for producing knowledge, quotation was central to the triple mediation—imperial, colonial, and indigenous—in the production of knowledge about religion and religions in the British Empire. When Max Müller quoted Wilhelm Bleek quoting Max Müller, this production of knowledge was circular, feeding back into itself, reinforcing the imperial theorist. However, when uNemo quoted Max Müller and Wilhelm Bleek, the effect was destabilizing, suggesting an alternative basis for generating knowledge about religion and religions.

In the production of knowledge, raw materials were required. Collecting, therefore, would seem to be the primary point of production. Instead of collecting skulls, as Felix von Luschan did, James Stuart collected oral testimonies, meticulously recorded in an archive, of Zulu traditions. Even if this archive was only a collection of fragments, it provided a wealth of raw materials to be processed. However, while Stuart hoped that all would come to drink from his well, no imperial theorist knew about his collection. Instead, they kept returning to the well of Henry Callaway, who had also assembled a chaotic archive, because he had actively positioned himself as a mediator between imperial theory and the Zulu. As a result, the transmission of Callaway's archive was ensured through its quotation by Max Müller, E. B. Tylor, Andrew Lang, James Frazer, and other imperial theorists of comparative religion. For all of these theorists, the quotation of indigenous voices, made available by colonial mediators, was the primary source of knowledge production for any theory of religion.

Combining telepathy and ventriloquism, Alfred T. Bryant, thinking black and talking black as uNemo, would seem to represent the perfect middleman in the exchange between indigenous Africans and imperial theorists. However, while his indigenous voice unsettled the theorizing of Max Müller, his attacks on imperial theorists completely dismissed the knowledge they had produced in the quiet of the study. Nevertheless, although he claimed to be gaining knowledge on the ground, Bryant's knowledge about the mentality of the native was infused with the racial theories of empire.

As Wulf Sachs demonstrated, new raw materials could be generated out of psychoanalysis. Under analysis, John Chavafambira told his stories, whether factual or fictional, about African religion. Collecting, in the psychoanalytic encounter, clearly produced new data for the study of religion, but its method of collection raised the question of transference: How did the analytic subject alter his stories in the psychoanalytic transfer between patient and therapist? How did the analyst alter the subject's stories in the process of turning them into psychological narratives? Although we cannot easily answer these questions with respect to Wulf Sachs and John Chavafambira, the new data about African religion produced in their exchanges was certainly transacted in the triple mediation between an imperial theory, a colonial mediator, and an indigenous informant struggling with his own dilemmas of mediation. In this particular exchange, Wulf Sachs—Jew, doctor, and socialist—forged a bond with John Chavafambira, who identified with Jews and was himself a healer, in the dream of moving into the full adulthood that H. I. E. Dhlomo represented as a "New African."

While new data could be produced through dreams, it could also be produced through fiction. Outside of the biblical framework that structured the sense of history for African Christians, African novelists experimented with the narrative recovery of indigenous traditions. In the case of Thomas Mofolo, the novelist was able to distinguish between fact and fiction, between recounting history and telling a tale, even if the distinction was blurred by a London publisher worrying about the religious impact and an American anthropologist finding new data for the study of religion in his fiction. At stake in these transactions was the question, What counts as evidence in the production of knowledge about religion? As we have seen, fiction competed with ethnography in generating evidence.

As theorists in their own right, the historian S. M. Molema and the dramatist H. I. E. Dhlomo reversed the flow in the triple mediation of knowledge production in the study of religion. Instead of providing evidence like the testimonies collected by Callaway or Stuart, where indigenous voices served as raw material for theory building, they interrogated the theorists of imperial comparative religion. In that inquiry, they found resources they could use in refashioning knowledge about African religion. While Molema cited imperial theorists in distilling his own generic definition of religion, which demonstrated that the Bantu actually had a religion, Dhlomo invoked imperial theory to reveal the religious roots of African drama. In both cases, they were not serving imperial theory. Imperial theory was serving them in their thinking about religion.

Still, the question of race remained, looming over the entire history of imperial comparative religion. Living, working, and thinking within a racist regime, theorists such as Molema and Dhlomo made knowledge, but not under conditions of their own making.

Looking to the future of religion in Africa in his chapter "Religious Outlook," Molema reflected on the three faiths—Paganism, Christianity, and Islam—on the continent. Taking Islam seriously, he quoted from the Qur'an and referred to an academic history of the tradition. As Molema noted, in *The Conflict of Colour* B. L. Putnam Weale had argued that in Africa "the black man [would] be superficially civilized and either Christianised or Islamized."[123] Although Weale had proposed that Africans would be attracted to Islam because that religion was better suited to their militant nature than Christianity, Molema focused on the nonracial character of Islam, its "practical spirit of equality and fraternity." Molema observed, "The strength and vigour of Mohammedanism is in its 'assimilation,' racial barriers and distinctions being swept off between co-believers." Since the link between race and social class in South Africa had been thoroughly entrenched, Molema called attention to the fraternity in Islam between rich and poor, citing G. W. Leitner's chapter, "Muhammadanism," in *Religious Systems of the World*: "The rich man is considered to be the natural protector of the poor, and the poor man takes his place at the table of the rich."[124] In looking to the future of religion in Africa, therefore, Molema was interested in the nonracial character of Islam. Although he concluded that the European presence in South Africa, which would not go away, strengthened the prospects of Christianity, Molema was clearly thinking black about Islam.

Thinking about religion under the same racial regime, H. I. E. Dhlomo turned to imperial theorists of religion James Frazer and Jane Harrison to recover tradition and invigorate his own projects. Like Molema, he was using them instead of being used by them. He found in their theoretical vocabulary key terms for rethinking black religion, culture, and art. However, under the shadow of a thoroughly racialized imperial theory, with its presupposition that Africans were incapable of thinking, of engaging "matters of abstract thought and metaphysics," of performing "intellectual work," Dhlomo had to deal with race. Although the imperial theorists had helped his thinking, he also had to think otherwise about the denigration of Africans in imperial theory. Shifting from the academic study of religion to religious invocation, Dhlomo asserted that in imaginative art, "the Universal Mind can and does express itself actively through primitive men and humble."[125] Insisting that African art, like any other great art, was not racial or national, he proposed that the Universal Mind, the All-Creative Being, transcended race. "Great art or thought (art is thought-feeling) is more than racial and national," Dhlomo insisted. "It is universal, reflecting the image, the spirit, of the All-Creative Being who knows neither East nor West, Black nor White, Jew nor Gentile, time nor space, life nor death. The tragedy of a Job, an Oedipus, a Hamlet, a Joan, a Shaka, a Nongqawuse, is the tragedy of all countries, all times, all races."[126] Thinking black, for H. I. E. Dhlomo, was thinking beyond race, even while thinking within the racialized categories advanced in imperial theory and entrenched in South Africa.

In recovering the centrality of African religion in the history of the academic study of religion, the work of A. T. Bryant is emblematic of racist scholarship, not only in his reduction of African religion to a primitive mentality, but also in his erasure of Africans from the land in which their religion might be recognized as indigenous in South Africa. As painful as it might be to rehearse this racial legacy in scholarship, Bryant's work, whether as uNemo or under his own name, can be recovered as providing alternative points of engagement with the centralizing and universalizing aspirations of imperial scholarship. As we have seen, Bryant vigorously challenged the pretensions of imperial scholars of religion on the grounds that they were not on the ground with the Zulu. This warrant for authentic knowledge, of course, came to underwrite the entire enterprise of ethnography, which was based on the opposition between the armchair theorizing of the study, which E. Sidney Hartland thought entailed its own dangers, and the dangers of the field. Studying religion, in either case, was a dangerous business. But it was also a circulating enterprise, circulating throughout an expanding empire of relations, contacts, and exchanges in which religion registered as an index to persons and places, identities and geographies, essential or enduring stabilities and shifting or transient migrations in the world.

In these circulations of knowledge about religion, A. T. Bryant drew upon the latest research on Indo-European linguistic, cultural, and religious migrations without realizing that those theories were based upon ideas of racial segregation that had been developed and enforced in South Africa and the American South. "In this fantastic back-projection of systems of racial segregation in the American South and in South Africa onto early Indian history," the historian Thomas R. Trautmann has observed, "the relations of the British 'new invader from Europe' with the peoples of India is prefigured thousands of years before by the invading Aryans."[127] Circulating and circling back on itself, racialist theorizing of religion in South Africa lies exposed in the work of Bryant as a fraud, as a carnival sideshow of telepathy and ventriloquism, which was nevertheless engaged with the global circulation of imperial comparative religion. Whatever his failings, Bryant highlights the dynamics of the imperial circulation of knowledge in the study of African religions and the general study of religions.

For S. M. Molema and H. I. E. Dhlomo, the circulation of knowledge about African religions entailed simultaneously working within and struggling against racist scholarship. In solidarity with W. E. B. Du Bois, they worked toward a pan-African study of African religions. Refusing to be data and declining the role of "native informant," they theorized religion in relation to imperial scholarship. But they also theorized religion within their own situations. As a result, Molema found that African indigenous religion in South Africa actually was religion. Given recent criticisms of the term *religion* as an illegitimate Western, Christian, and imperial imposition on the world, we might wonder why he would want to do that. Despite its imperial pedigree, of which he was well aware, *religion* provided Molema an opening, a range of possibilities, to negotiate a space for Africans in South Africa. Accordingly, he made strategic use of the term. Although he deferred to colonial constructions of the religions of "ethnical groups," he focused on distilling a generic definition of religion, which effectively obliterated those stereotypes, and tried to imagine a nonracial future for religion in Africa. For his part, H. I. E. Dhlomo found that African indigenous religion was a basis for dramatic creativity. Although he drew upon theories of religion advanced by James Frazer and Jane Harrison, Dhlomo turned those theorists into informants, quoting them as any imperial theorist might have done, for evidence in support of his own project, which in his case was the project of revitalizing African drama in South Africa. Subsequently, Dhlomo developed other projects, such as the emergence of the "New African," but his activist assertions of political independence resonated with his refusal to be merely data in any imperial theory of religion. In the work of both Molema and Dhlomo, imperial theorists of religion, from Friedrich Max Müller through James Frazer, were engaged not as monuments to thinking about religion and religions but as openings in a field of strategic possibilities for another kind of study of religion.

CHAPTER NINE

Spirit of Empire

The genius of the Empire is to make every nation that you conquer feel that
you bring them into the Imperial Family.

ANNIE BESANT

In August 1907, hoping to revive the manly and military spirit of the British
Empire, Robert Baden-Powell (1857–1941) founded the Boy Scouts. As a
professional soldier in the British imperial army, Baden-Powell drew upon
his military experience in India, West Africa, and South Africa in creating a movement that imitated military discipline, particularly imitating the
khaki uniforms, green and gold colors, and motto, "Be Prepared," of the
South African Constabulary that came under his command after the South
African War.[1] As an amateur ethnographic enthusiast, Baden-Powell derived songs, myths, and rituals from his experience in British imperial wars
against the Zulu, calling upon all Boy Scouts to imitate the Zulu war song
and war dance as a ritual for instilling military discipline and martial cour-
age among British boys. Introduced in Baden-Powell's scouting manual of
1908, *Scouting for Boys*, the Zulu war song, recast as the "Scout's Chorus,"
was to be performed in a formalized war dance:

> LEADER: Een gonyâma-gonyâma.
> CHORUS: Invooboo.
> Yah bôbô! Yah bô!
> Invooboo.
> The meaning is—
> LEADER: "He is a lion!"
> CHORUS: "Yes! He is better than that; he is a hippopotamus!"[2]

This appropriation by the Boy Scouts of a Zulu war song, however, required an authenticating original. Baden-Powell accounted for that original

in describing how he had first heard this Zulu song in 1888 while serving in a British regiment that sought to contain the resistance of the Zulu king Dinizulu. His column was joined by two thousand Zulu warriors under the leadership of John Dunn, a white Zulu chief. Baden-Powell told of his original encounter with the Zulu war chant: "I heard a sound in the distance which at first I thought was an organ playing in Church. . . . But when we topped the rise we saw moving up towards us from the valley below three long lines of men marching in single file and singing a wonderful anthem as they marched. Both the sight and the sound were intensely impressive."[3] Like a church organ, this sacred anthem, with its wonderful polyphony, its immense roar of sound, exhibited authentic intensity, but it was also part of a structure of authentication based on subordination to a chief, even if the authentic Zulu chief in this case was John Dunn, the appointed chief of Scottish background, because this was the song that the Zulu warriors used to sing to their chief. In appropriating this Zulu war song, Baden-Powell reinforced the very notion of an authenticating original, certifying the authenticity of his imitation.

However, the question of the authenticity of any Zulu war dance poses a problem that can be easily resolved by recalling the research findings of South African historian Jeff Guy: there was no such thing.[4] Although delegates of the British Association for the Advancement of Science in 1905 were convinced they had witnessed a genuine Zulu war dance, even if assegais had been replaced by sticks, the original notion of a Zulu war dance was a British colonial construction, built out of a mix of misunderstanding, paranoia, and propaganda, which has no originating authenticity. Rituals of purification, for example, could be rendered in colonial reports as war dances. As the anthropologist Charles Lindholm has argued, claims to authenticity tend to be based on an alignment with either a genealogical origin or an essential content.[5] If there never was any such thing as a Zulu war dance, then no one could possibly include it in their genealogy or faithfully reproduce its essence in the present. They would have no historical ground on which to stand. However, the Boy Scouts, informed by the Zulu war song and war dance, circulated throughout the British Empire.

In 1921, the president of the Theosophical Society and founder of the Indian Boy Scout Movement, Annie Besant (1847–1933), recited the Scout Promise before Chief Scout Robert Baden-Powell at a ceremony in India. Designated as the "Honorary Commissioner for All India of the Boy Scout Movement," in 1932 she received "The Silver Wolf" in recognition of her service to scouting.[6] Having been a prominent feminist, socialist, and activist for Irish home rule, Besant discovered Theosophy and moved to India to work for Indian independence. How did she reconcile her anti-imperialist campaigns in Ireland and India with the implicit imperialism of the Boy Scouts? Ashis Nandy and Shiv Visvanathan have proposed that she rejected Baden-Powell's imperialism and appropriated from the Boy Scouts themes that matched her own interests, highlighting love of nature, skill in woodcraft, and kindness to animals; the last theme resonated with her opposition to vivisection and promotion of vegetarianism.[7] However, from her theosophical perspective, Annie Besant also had a vision of the spirit of empire. "The genius of the Empire," she observed, "is to make every nation that you conquer feel that you bring them into the Imperial Family, that they and you from that time forward are brothers, and not conquered and conquerors."[8] In the Theosophical Society, the notion of brotherhood had a specific resonance, since the ancient wisdom upon which the society was based had been derived from the spiritual adepts of Tibet, the Great White Brotherhood. As the unseen governors and administrators of the universe, this ancient brotherhood maintained the spiritual empire of theosophy. However, in theosophical terms, Besant affirmed the unifying power of the British Empire, observing that in the cycle of reincarnation, the ancient Egyptians had been reborn as ancient Romans and had been reborn again as modern Anglo-Saxons in London, "again Empire-building."[9] Although she imagined an imperial system in the future that was "not an Empire made by force but a commonwealth made by mutual goodwill and friendliness," Great Britain remained the center of Besant's theosophical world order.[10] In this respect, she could easily make common cause with Chief Scout Baden-Powell in working to revitalize the spirit of empire.

As a theosophist, Annie Besant directly engaged imperial comparative religion, since one of the guiding principles of the Theosophical Society was to advance the study of comparative religion, philosophy, and science. In *The Ancient Wisdom*, she observed that anyone could recognize the similarities among the religions of the world. How should those similarities be explained? According to eminent scholars of comparative religion, the unity of religions could be explained as the product of primitive human origins, savage origins in which "religions have grown up on the soil of human ignorance tilled by imagination," evolving from fear or desire, fetishism or animism, as "fear, desire, ignorance, and wonder led the savage to personify the powers of nature, and priests played upon his terrors and hopes, his misty fancies and his bewildered questionings." Whether they preferred a solar theory or a phallic theory, the Doctors of Comparative Mythology traced religion to this savage origin. In opposition, Besant demanded: "Are all man's dearest hopes and loftiest imaginings really nothing more than the outcome of savage fancies and of groping ignorance?" Rejecting the findings of the doctors of imperial comparative religion, Annie Besant proposed an alternative explanation for the unity of religions: all religions originated in the teachings of a universal brotherhood of spiritual masters. Besant argued, "The second explanation of the common property in the religions of the world asserts the existence of an original teaching in the custody of a Brotherhood of great spiritual Teachers, who—Themselves the outcome of past cycles of evolution—acted as the instructors and guides of the child-humanity of our planet, imparting to its races and nations in turn the fundamental truths of religion in the form most adapted to the idiosyncrasies of the recipients."[11] Contradicting the evolutionary assumptions held by the authorities of imperial comparative religion, Besant insisted that religion had been imparted, in its original purity, by a spiritual brotherhood. Although that pure revelation might have been distorted, its essence could be recovered. Comparative religion, as practiced by the Theosophical Society, was a project of recovery.

Developing an alternative approach to the study of religion, theosophical comparative religion rejected the findings of scholars such as Friedrich Max Müller, E. B. Tylor, Andrew Lang, and James Frazer, even if the "savage" remained a crucial reference point. In Annie Besant's account of the ancient wisdom, the savage featured as both opposition to theosophy and the point of departure for the theosophical version of evolution. On the one hand, savagery was opposed to theosophy. Besant stressed "the immense differences that separate the lowest savage and the noblest human type in mental and moral capacities."[12] In this respect, theosophical attention to race, with its seven root races, placed savages at the bottom of the human hierarchy. Their minds, Besant insisted, were radically different from the mind of a philosopher or a saint. On the other hand, savagery was posited as the beginning of the evolution of human souls, through many lifetimes, in what Besant described as "the stages of man's ascent, from the lowest savagery to the divine manhood."[13] Convinced that a secret brotherhood governed the universe like an imperial bureaucracy, Besant held that each soul proceeded on a long evolutionary trajectory from savagery to theosophy. In their understanding of savagery, theosophists and imperialists found common ground.

Focusing on savagery, this chapter reviews three versions of imperial comparative religion—interfaith, theosophical, and critical. First, interfaith

comparative religion was on display during 1924 at an imperial conference in London that featured religious adherents speaking about their own
faiths, including a presentation by an African from South Africa, Albert
Thoka, who outlined the indigenous nature mysticism of the Bantu. While
interfaith comparative religion relied upon the authentic voices of religious
adherents, nature provided a common ground for religious unity. The unifying force of nature was a conviction firmly held by Francis Younghusband,
who was a leader of the conference, an explorer, a soldier, a spy, and the
founder of the World Congress of Faiths. Revisiting this conference at the
British Empire Exhibition in 1924, we will see how savagery was incorporated in interfaith comparative religion. Second, theosophical comparative religion, which was central to the mission of the Theosophical Society,
was evident in the report in 1927 by Patrick Bowen, who, by his own account, was also a soldier, an explorer, and a secret agent; he reported on
a secret African brotherhood that had preserved the ancient wisdom in
Africa. While the Great White Brotherhood of the Himalayas taught the
ancient wisdom in Sanskrit, identifying the Universal Spirit as the *Atma*,
the African Brotherhood used the Zulu language to convey the same truth
of the Universal Spirit as the *Itongo*. Although Bowen's discovery might
be unbelievable, it recovered African savagery for theosophy. Finally, in
counterpoint to interfaith and theosophical comparative religion, we will
review the theoretical work of imperial theorists of religion—Friedrich Max
Müller, E. B. Tylor, Andrew Lang, and James Frazer—by looking back at
how they dealt with the *Itongo*, the Zulu term for spirit, in theorizing religion. As simple as it might sound, these theorists advanced a critical comparative religion by providing footnotes.

INTERFAITH COMPARATIVE RELIGION

From September 22 to October 3, 1924, under the auspices of the School
of Oriental Studies, University of London, and the Sociological Society,
the Imperial Institute in London hosted an interfaith event, "Religions of
the Empire: A Conference on Some Living Religions within the Empire."
Linked with the British Empire Exhibition of 1924–25, this conference
featured representatives of the ancient religious traditions and new religious movements that had been encompassed within the vast scope of the
British Empire. Speakers explained the tenets of Hindu, Buddhist, Muslim,
Zoroastrian, Jain, and Sikh traditions as well as those of more recent religious movements such as Brâhmo Samâj, Ârya Samâj, and the Bahâ'i Cause.

The organizers explained that the "spokesman of each religion should be one who professed such religion."[14] By inviting presentations from religious adherents, the Religions of the Empire conference looked back to the precedent of the World's Parliament of Religions held in Chicago during the Columbian Exposition of 1893, which provided a model for interreligious dialogue.[15] The organizers hoped that interreligious understanding would form the basis for the peaceful coexistence of all the religions under imperial rule. This aspiration was shared by the speakers. For example, in his presentation, "The Spirit of Islam," Mustafa Khan expressed his ambition for the conference by declaring: "Let us hope that it will lead to a better understanding among the apparently conflicting religions of the British Empire; and will thus bring about a permanent peace and tranquility in humanity."[16] Representatives of Christianity and Judaism were not included in the program on the grounds that these religions should already be familiar to the audience in London. By excluding familiar religions, however, the conference gave the impression that it was gathering together representatives of strange foreign religions, "queer religions," as the *Times* reported, perhaps because they were perceived as potentially threatening to peace within the empire.

In addition to the precedent of the World's Parliament of Religions, the organizers invoked the series of conferences in the history of religions that began in Paris in 1900 and convened at Basel in 1904, Oxford in 1908, and Leiden in 1912.[17] Although claiming this academic lineage, the Religions of the Empire conference clearly departed from the principle that had been established in Paris as a fundamental rule: All presentations and discussions about religion must be historical rather than confessional. At the imperial conference in 1924, religious adherents confessed their faith not only in their own religions but also in the unity of religions and the peace of the British Empire. For some speakers, the unity of religions was evident in the meeting of East and West. While Mustafa Khan proclaimed the East as the source of religious light for the West, G. P. Malalasekera observed that the Buddhist revival in Ceylon, under British rule, was "combining all that is best in both the East and West."[18] New movements, in particular, stressed interreligious unity, such as the Brâhmo Samâj understanding of the "harmony of religions" and the Bahâ'i commitment to "religious unity."[19] In summarizing the entire proceedings, Rev. Tyssul Davis of the Theistic Church observed that the conference had demonstrated the central finding of the study of religion, the unity of religions. "Every student of comparative religion knows," he asserted, "that the same truths are taught in the great religions."[20] According to many speakers, religious unity was ensured by the peace of empire, which Pandit Shyam Shankar identified as the "grand lesson of religious toleration given by the Imperial Government." Although the spokesperson for Jainism employed a minimal definition of peace by insisting that "the Jains are a law-abiding people; their criminal record is marvelously white," most participants embraced a larger vision of religious toleration, harmony, and unity under British imperial rule.[21]

Religious unity and imperial peace were ideals fervently held by a driving force behind the Religions of the Empire conference, the soldier, explorer, and mystic Sir Francis Younghusband (1863–1942). Over a long career in the British military and colonial administration, Younghusband served imperial interests in China, India, and Tibet. He also acted as a *Times* correspondent in South Africa, reporting on the intensifying conflict between Boers and British *uitlanders*.[22] While leading the British invasion of Tibet in 1903–4, Younghusband had a mystical experience of union with the entire world. Combining a "deep inner-soul satisfaction" with a sense of "being literally in love with the world," as he later described this transformative experience, Younghusband's mysticism was also a kind of imperial patriotism, a "patriotism extended to the whole universe."[23] As his mystical interests developed, Younghusband saw the unity of religions, blending East and West, manifest in reverence for nature and devotion to empire. Just as humans must find themselves in nature, he held, the English could "only attain their full personality in an England which has personality," a personality revealed in the spirit of empire.[24]

Giving the opening address at the Religions of the Empire conference, Francis Younghusband observed that the rationale for the gathering was to highlight the spiritual development of empire. While the empire's material development was obvious, the conference demonstrated that the British took "count also of its spiritual development." Inviting representatives to describe their religious views, Younghusband asserted that their different religious perspectives could all be drawn into providing a spiritual foundation for imperial unity. "Our conference," he declared, "will be a potent means of advancing that sacred cause of religion." But he also suggested that the empire itself was a sacred cause. Invoking the imperial spirit of Queen Victoria, he maintained that she was worshipped by her subjects, citing the imperial faith of "one of the great Chiefs of India," who reportedly declared, "To be in her presence was like being in a temple: she was divine."[25] For Younghusband, therefore, the unity of religions within the empire was underwritten by a spiritual recognition of the religion of empire. Recalling Max Müller's vision of the entire empire extending out from Queen Victoria's throne, Francis Younghusband expanded this imperial vision by reporting that colonized subjects also beheld the divinity of the British Empire.

These religious transactions between empire and subjects were spiritual but also natural. In his presentation at the end of the conference, "Man and Nature," Francis Younghusband celebrated a natural mysticism that communed with the "soul of nature" and established "fellowship with Nature." Discerning divinity in nature, he asserted, "Nature and God are one and the same."[26] Attention to nature as a common ground for adherents of all the religions of the empire was a recurring theme in the last section of the conference, which was devoted to social and psychological reflections on religion. While the sociologist Victor Branford observed that "man and nature must balance," the naturalist J. Arthur Thomson proposed that nature reveals "a glimpse of a continued divine creation."[27] However, the most detailed exposition of the religion of nature was presented in the section devoted to primitive religions by Albert Thoka of Pietersburg, South Africa. In his exposition, "The Bantu Religious Ideas," Thoka explained how his people, the Bapedi, adhered to a nature mysticism that understood God as He was revealed through nature and nature as providing glimpses of God.

In her introductory note to this section, Alice Werner, who served on the organizing committee for the conference, pointed to the recurring themes—animism and ancestor-worship—that ran through the four presentations on primitive religion. Here the principle of religious adherents speaking on behalf of their own faiths broke down. The Anglican Archdeacon of New Zealand, the venerable H. W. Williams, provided an account of the indigenous religion of the Maori. Richard St. Barbe Baker, the former assistant conservator of forests, Kenya Colony, and founder-in-chief of the African Forest Scouts, described the religious beliefs and practices of East Africa. Captain L. W. G. Malcolm, who had served in the West African Frontier Force before securing a position in the Department of Archaeology and Ethnology, Bristol Museum, described the religions of West Africa. These lectures differed in style, with Baker's personal observations and anecdotes about the Kikuyu, "my friends," contrasting with Malcolm's ethnographic description, supported by relevant literature, and systematic analysis with reference to imperial theorists such as E. B. Tylor and James Frazer.[28] Nevertheless, all three departed from the principle that speakers should describe their own religions. In this context, the presentation by Albert Thoka was particularly striking for featuring an African explaining

African religion. As Alice Werner observed, his presentation was also strik-ing for its spiritual sophistication. "His paper may surprise some readers," she warned, "who are not prepared to find so spiritual a view of the uni-verse taken by people whom they are accustomed to regard as savages."[29] Speculating that his contact with Europeans and an English education might have led him to insert alien religious ideas into his account of Bantu religion, Werner defended its authenticity, maintaining that Albert Thoka was articulating themes that were implicit in his tradition.

There are other striking features of this presentation, "The Bantu Religious Ideas." Although Thoka is a common surname in Pietersburg (now Polokwane), South Africa, Albert Thoka does not seem to feature any-where else in the historical record. *The African Yearly Register*, a "Who's Who" of Africans in South Africa, published by Mweli T. D. Skota in 1930, includes C. Thoka of Pietersburg, "General Dealer and Fresh Produce," but makes no mention of Albert Thoka, evidently an accomplished African in-tellectual, who represented African religion at a major international confer-ence.[30] Unlike his contemporary, S. M. Molema, who also emerged as an African intellectual, historian, and scholar of religion while in the United Kingdom, Albert Thoka left no trace of his education or accomplishments. In his paper for the Religions of the Empire conference, Thoka certainly employed a self-effacing style by referring to Africans in the third person, describing what "they," "the natives," or "the Bantu" believe about God and nature. Although he was ostensibly speaking on behalf of his own people, Thoka used "we" to refer to humanity in general, declaring, for example, "We are all one in nature."[31] Most surprising, however, is the remarkable resemblance between Thoka's account of Bantu religion and the nature mysticism advanced by Francis Younghusband. In both cases, God and na-ture are one and humanity knows God through nature.

According to Albert Thoka, Bantu religion is based on belief in God, "the native belief in a certain Supreme Being whom they regard as exercis-ing divine dispensations over the whole universe." Although this supreme being is known by different names, such as *Modimo*, *Utixo*, *Unkulunkulu*, and *Chikewe'vu*, all Bantu understand God as the "Supernatural Power" who "ordained the universe." As Thoka explained this theology, the Bantu understand God as being both above nature, as a supernatural power, and within nature, as "an indwelling being within the universe." Since God is the "essence of all attributes," the Bantu find God dwelling in every aspect of the natural world. According to Thoka, "they believe that, all attributes being inherent in God, He is capable of residing in every element of Nature, be it organic or inorganic." Accordingly, to know nature is to know God. The supreme being is gradually revealed, "unfolded to mankind," through the "study and apprehension of natural phenomena." God lives in perfect knowledge; God reveals that knowledge through "the operation of phenomena"; God reveals his Will in the "laws of Nature"; God's knowledge, character, and will can be known through studying the "phenomena of the universe." In phrasing reminiscent of an aphorism attributed to the geologist Louis Agassiz, Thoka observed, "To understand God, therefore, we must study His works in Nature."[32] Certainly Francis Younghusband must have welcomed this exposition of Bantu nature mysticism, which so obviously resonated with his own understanding of God as a spiritual power, supernatural in determining, directing, and controlling the universe but also indwelling in nature, since "physical nature is merely the outward manifestation of this inward spirit." In his conference presentation on the unity of God, nature, and humanity, perhaps Younghusband was thinking of this Bantu religion when he remarked, "The most cultured European feels affinity with the most primitive savage in the farthest wilds."[33] Bantu religion, as recast by Albert Thoka, provided a primitive analogue for Francis Youngblood's modern European religion of nature.

In his account of Bantu religion, Albert Thoka challenged basic categories of imperial comparative religion. Implicitly redefining animism as knowing God in nature, Thoka explained ancestor worship as insight into the "infinite continuity of life," in which human beings develop "to a higher plane of existence in the growth of human intelligence." Animism and ancestor worship, which Alice Werner had identified as the two basic themes in the conference presentations on primitive religion, were translated by Thoka into a modern religion of nature mysticism and spiritual evolution. Turning to the vexed problem of totemism in imperial comparative religion, Thoka proposed that the role of animal emblems in Bantu religion had been misunderstood. Instead of serving as markers of clans, ancestors, or taboos, the totems were communication media between God and humanity. On the one hand, totems were media for addressing God. Totems were "emblems to praise God for His wondrous works of creation." On the other hand, totems were media for understanding God, as "one object, or totem, was in each case chosen as symbolic of the whole universe of God." While God was present in every element of nature, the entire universe, animated by God's indwelling spirit, was present in each totem of Bantu religion. Supporting this analysis, Thoka provided an example of totemic praise poetry of the Bakwena, the people of the crocodile: "*Mokwena moila*

lethlaka, Moroka' metse a pula, Modheana modhalabetji, 'Mina tjeka la boroka."
Although he provided an English translation, "Hail, you that revere the
reed," Thoka cautioned that the meaning of the praises remained hidden
by their "philosophical frame." Concluding with this secret significance of
totemic praises, Albert Thoka nevertheless hoped that during his presentation "the pure significance of Totemism [had] been clearly explained, and
that any misapprehension of the native point of view regarding it [had] now
been obviated."[34]

So much is curious about this presentation of Bantu religious ideas at an
imperial conference. The spiritualist turns of phrase, the invocation of laws
of nature, and the echoes of nature mysticism all seem strange. Certainly, as
Alice Werner proposed, Albert Thoka might have been influenced in his interpretations of African religion by his English education and interreligious
contacts. Under similar conditions, Africans were reinterpreting tradition
not only in the light of the Christian gospel but also in the idiom of a universal spirituality, which John Tengo Jabavu formulated for the Universal
Races Conference in London in 1911 as the indigenous African "veneration
for a Great Omnipresent, Omnipotent Unknown."[35] Accordingly, Thoka
might have been advancing a similar reinterpretation of indigenous African
religion as a spirituality of the Great Unknown for an imperial conference.
However, Albert Thoka's translation of African indigenous religion into
a universal nature mysticism, in which God is not unknown but known
through the study of natural phenomena, was so specific, with numerous
echoes of the imperial spirituality of Francis Younghusband, that we must
begin to suspect a ventriloquism reminiscent of the missionary Alfred T.
Bryant, who pretended to be the Zulu philologist uNemo in order to address
Max Müller and attack Henry Callaway, thereby intervening in the ongoing
mediation between imperial theorist and colonial expert in the production
of knowledge about Zulu religion. As an indigenous voice, asserting indigenous authenticity, uNemo was able to disrupt that mediation. Of course,
as we now know, uNemo was a mask for a Catholic missionary. Was Albert
Thoka a mask for a nature mystic? Although this question cannot be resolved as easily as in the case of uNemo, since Albert Thoka might very well
have been a real person participating in the interreligious exchanges of the
religions of the empire, his account of God and nature clearly coincided
with the religious interests of Francis Younghusband.

Nevertheless, like uNemo, Albert Thoka contradicted imperial theory, in
this case dismissing established academic constructions of animism, ancestor worship, and totemism in the anthropology and history of religions.

Here also he served an aim of the conference. Liberated from academic theory, adherents of the religions of the empire, speaking for themselves, were the primary adjudicators of knowledge. However, as we find in the presentation by Albert Thoka and so many other participants in the conference, that knowledge was formulated in ways that could be easily assimilated into the unity of religions and the peace of empire.

Following the Religions of the Empire conference, Francis Younghusband and other organizers established the Society for Promoting the Study of Religions, which published a journal dedicated to advancing interreligious understanding. After attending a reprise of the World's Parliament of Religions in Chicago during 1933, Younghusband convened another interfaith conference in London in 1936 to mark the formation of a new organization, the World Congress of Faiths.[36] Featuring prominent Asian scholars such as D. T. Suzuki and Sarvepalli Radhakrishnan, this conference also highlighted unity and peace, with so much sweetness and light that one reviewer of the proceedings described the experience as like "dieting on pure honey."[37] Younghusband organized annual conferences of the World Congress of Faiths until his death in 1942. Surviving its founder, the organization continued to promote interfaith understanding through dialogue, meetings, and publications into the twenty-first century. Although the Religions of the Empire conference had explicitly claimed the lineage of international congresses for the history of religions going back to Paris in 1900, the aims of the World Congress of Faiths were clearly confessional rather than historical, a crucial difference highlighted by the International Association for the History of Religions (IAHR), which also traced its lineage to 1900 in Paris. Committed to producing knowledge about religion and religions through philological and historical methods, the IAHR was not a forum for religious adherents working toward mutual understanding, world peace, or a new religion suited to modern conditions. As the historian of religions C. J. Bleeker insisted, "A sharp, clearly-defined line separates the purely scientific work of the historian of religions from those who labour on behalf of the Ecumenical movement or the World Congress of Faiths."[38] Although sometimes blurred in the work of the historian of religions, this sharp line challenged the special privilege of religious insiders, such as those featured at the Religions of the Empire conference who spoke about the religions they professed, as the most authentic and authoritative producers of knowledge about religion and religions.

As we have seen in the case of Albert Thoka, the religious representative, speaking as an insider, is not always representative of a religious community. If not a mask, then Thoka was an indigenous African intellectual who was thoroughly informed by contemporary international productions and circulations of knowledge about religion within interfaith comparative religion. He represented the privilege of a religious adherent, the commitment to nature as a common ground for humanity, and the hope that interfaith dialogue, in obviating misapprehensions, would lead to mutual understanding. Many other religious adherents, like Albert Thoka, have been similarly informed by interfaith comparative religion in drawing religious resources into campaigns for world peace or global ethics. Even when they are explicitly anti-imperial, these campaigns have their roots in the interfaith comparative religion of the empire of religion.

THEOSOPHICAL COMPARATIVE RELIGION

Although the interfaith movement might include mystics, its notion of comparative religion was essentially public, drawing religious adherents into public dialogue about social ethics and world peace. Based on the assumption that all religions teach the same truths, interfaith comparative religion found that those truths were immediately available to the general public. In a parliament, congress, or league of world religions, interfaith comparative religion could generate knowledge about the role of religion in personal and social ethics that could be shared globally. By contrast, the Theosophical Society, founded in 1875 by Helena Petrovna Blavatsky (1831–1891) and Henry Steel Olcott (1832–1907), developed a theosophical comparative religion that was essentially secret, mysterious, and obscured from public view. Representing what Peter van der Veer has called an "anti-Christian comparative religion," centered in the ancient wisdom of the East, Theosophy based its knowledge of religion and religions on secrets, thereby exemplifying, as Wouter J. Hanegraaff has observed, "Comparative Religion on occultist premises."[39] In *Isis Unveiled* (1877), *The Secret Doctrine* (1888), and other publications, Helena Blavatsky documented the secrets of the ancient wisdom of the East.

While employing mysterious means for gaining knowledge, including spiritual correspondence with Buddhist masters of Tibet, Blavatsky also worked along lines that resembled philological and historical research in the comparative study of religion. As a philologist, she had gained access to the ancient language of Senzar, which enabled her to translate ancient Asian texts, such as the *Secret Book of Dzyan*, that formed the basis for her extended commentaries, explications, and elaborations of theosophy in *The Secret Doctrine*. Looking to Friedrich Max Müller as the leading nineteenth-century philologist in the study of religion, Blavatsky saw him as a model for her research, citing his account of Emperor Akbar, Max Müller's candidate for the founder of the comparative study of religion, who was not able to obtain, even by threats and bribes, the complete texts of the Vedas. Max Müller boasted that under the British Empire scholars had gained access to the Vedic texts that Emperor Akbar could not acquire, but Madame Blavatsky was able to trump his boast by insisting that she could discern their secret meaning. Having outdone Max Müller in the philology and history of religions, Blavatsky nevertheless invoked his authority as a warrant for Theosophy, even if she misquoted his paraphrase of a participant in the debates about religion at the court of Akbar as if it was his own assertion. She informed her readers that Max Müller agreed with Theosophy that there is "only one true religion—the worship of God's spirit."[40] Following Blavatsky's lead, other prominent theosophists invoked Max Müller's authority and imitated his philological methods but ultimately dismissed his science of religion as hopelessly ignorant of the secrets of religion.

Taking an interest in Madame Blavatsky in 1879, Max Müller developed a friendship with Henry Steel Olcott and included him among his correspondents. An issue of the *Theosophist* in 1889, on the assumption that he was a regular reader since he had mentioned to Olcott that he had been a subscriber since the beginning, extended an invitation to Max Müller to visit India.[41] Although he welcomed attention to ancient texts of the East, Max Müller attacked Theosophy's version of "Esoteric Buddhism" as "Buddhism misunderstood, distorted, caricatured."[42] For his 1892 Gifford Lectures, published the following year as *Theosophy or Psychological Religion*, he explained that he used the term *theosophy* to mean the highest knowledge about God in order to rescue it from its recent misappropriation and from any association "with spirit-rappings, table-turnings, or any other occult science or black art."[43] In these interventions he was more temperate than his colleague Edward Clodd, who complained in his presidential address to the Folklore Society in 1896 about "that colossal old liar, Madame Blavatsky."[44] Nevertheless, Max Müller's engagement with Theosophy resulted in a vigorous polemic in both mainstream and theosophical journals. Although they were also happy to distance Theosophy from common spiritualism, theosophists objected to his academic contempt for their secret wisdom, which displayed the ignorance of learned men. Max Müller insisted that there was nothing secret in Hinduism or Buddhism. Sacred texts and relevant commentaries for learning about these religions were available for open inquiry. In the ensuing polemic, theosophists dismissed Max Müller's construction of the science of religion. An unsigned commentator in *Lucifer: A Theosophical Magazine* in 1893 observed, "Any man with brains and leisure can do what Mr. Max Müller has done; only a pupil of Occultists and an Occultist can do the work of H. P. Blavatsky." Accusing Max Müller of being jealous of the accomplishments of Madame Blavatsky, this commentator alleged that he was a sexist academic elitist who resented a woman who could not decline Sanskrit nouns but knew more than he did about "hidden Sanskrit literature."[45] Although one of the founding aims of Theosophy was to encourage the study of comparative religion, philosophy, and science, theosophical comparative religion was pursued on the premise that the ancient wisdom at the root of all religions could be acquired only by mysterious means from the sacred texts of the East.

Proceeding in secrecy and mystery, the Theosophical Society neverthe-less had a profound public role in India. Annie Besant, who assumed the presidency of the society in 1907, played a crucial role in anti-imperialist politics. She campaigned for Indian independence, formed the Home Rule League, and briefly served as president of the Indian National Congress.[46] Besant eventually gave way to the leadership of Mohandas K. Gandhi, who had learned his Hinduism from the Theosophical Society in London, when he returned from South Africa to take up the struggle for India. South Africa and India, which Max Müller had identified as the twin poles of the British Empire in his last publication, *The Question of Right between England and the Transvaal,* were also linked by the Theosophical Society. As we re-call, Gandhi had presented a series of lectures on religion to the society in Johannesburg in 1905. Although his audience would probably have pre-ferred more of the "gleam" of ancient wisdom, he focused on the solidarity between the Indians and the British, certified by Max Müller, in a common empire. However, Gandhi also found Max Müller useful in public confron-tations with British imperialists, invoking his authority in arguing for the glory of India and the solidarity of Aryans in the context of fighting for Indian rights in South Africa. Committed to the British Empire, arguing that the English could "retire from South Africa as little as from India," Max Müller might have agreed with Gandhi's construction of the unifying spirit of empire while opposing his political campaign against British colo-nialism. Founder of the study of religion Max Müller left an ambiguous po-litical heritage, providing the Indo-Aryan model for colonial constructions of Bantu migrations that were used to justify European possession of the "empty land" of South Africa, while offering a reference point in Gandhi's anticolonial struggles for human rights in South Africa and political inde-pendence in India.

In August 1927, the *Theosophist* featured an article by Patrick Bowen (1882-1940), "The Ancient Wisdom in Africa." In a section of the periodical devoted to comparative religion, philosophy, and science, which was headed by a graphic montage featuring the Buddha, the Star of David, the Sanskrit Om, an eternal flame, and the pyramids of ancient Egypt at the rising sun, this article reported on the author's discovery of the secret wisdom that had been preserved among African tribes in South Africa. In his meetings with remarkable men among the Zulu, Bowen learned that a secret brotherhood—the *Bonabakulu Abasekhemu*, the Brotherhood of the Higher Ones of Egypt—were custodians of a tradition of ancient wisdom going back to the founder of the brotherhood, a priest of Isis during the reign of the Pharaoh Cheops in ancient Egypt. Acknowledging the theosophical principle that Asia was the source of all philosophy, Bowen proposed to demonstrate that Africa, the "Dark Continent," also held the ancient wisdom. Bowen's text was a remarkable instance of theosophical comparative religion in South Africa.

An extraordinary traveler's account of indigenous religion in Africa, Bowen's article was structured by two episodes, his meeting with the Zulu Isanusi Mankanyezi (the Starry One) and his yearlong apprenticeship with the Berber spiritual master Mandhlalanga (the Strength of the Sun), who lived among the Zulu. In the first episode, young Patrick Bowen, ten or twelve years old, by his recollection, accompanied his father on a wagon trip through the "wild Bushlands" of southern Africa. Meeting many so-called witch doctors, who he knew should be addressed by the Zulu term *Isanusi*, Bowen gained the confidence of the Isanusi Mankanyezi, a "pure Zulu, of the royal blood," with physical features that were "of a distinctly Jewish cast." When young Bowen told the Zulu Isanusi that his father wanted to place him in a missionary school, Mankanyezi attacked Christian missionaries for trying to force their religious beliefs on Africans without understanding African beliefs, complaining that not even Sobantu, referring to Bishop John William Colenso, knew anything about the real religion of Africa. "They think we worship the spirits of our ancestors," Mankanyezi told the boy, but the missionaries did not understand the true meaning of the *Itongo*. Not the ancestral spirit of a family, clan, or tribe, the *Itongo* is "the Spirit within and above all men." As the source and end of all life, the *Itongo* dwells in each human, as a spark, while every soul struggles through a cycle of birth, death, and rebirth to eventually become "one with that from which it came—the *Itongo*." During the time he spent with Mankanyezi, young Patrick witnessed the Isanusi's powers of telepathy, mental travel, and extrasensory exchanges with members of his brotherhood as far away as Kenya. His brotherhood extended throughout Africa, with at least one representative in every tribe. The leaders of the brotherhood, the Brothers, Elders, Masters, and Higher Ones, "whose names may not be spoken," were "the guardians of the *Wisdom-which-comes-from-of-old*," the ancient wisdom of the *Itongo*.[47]

In the second episode, sometime after the Anglo-Boer War, Patrick Bowen entered government service in Natal, on a secret mission "in a certain large Native Reserve," where his work's "confidential nature" made it necessary for him "to be vague concerning dates and places." While he was on this secret government assignment, Bowen discovered a small community, living in a remote, inaccessible valley, of people who appeared to him as Europeans. Although they had adopted Zulu names, customs, and lifestyles, these people had physical features that "were of pure European type, more classical indeed than is usual among Europeans." Their leader, Mandhlalanga, had features that were "almost pure Greek." Although he had adopted a Zulu name and lived among the Zulu, acquiring the "reputation of being a supernatural being," Mandhlalanga was a Berber from North Africa. Having traveled widely through Europe, Asia, and America, speaking English and other European languages fluently, Mandhlalanga was a Master in the secret brotherhood of Africa. Accepting Patrick Bowen as a pupil, the Master taught him "the secret Bantu tongue," the language of instruction in his lectures on African ancient wisdom, which had been lost to most Africans and undiscovered by European scholars. From his course of study over one year, Bowen was able to translate Mandhlalanga's essential teachings of the ancient wisdom in Africa.[48]

Although he claimed to know nothing at the time about the Theosophical Society, Patrick Bowen outlined the ancient wisdom of Africa as if it were a summary of Theosophy. Like Blavatsky, Bowen gained his knowledge by mastering a sacred language, in this case the secret ur-Bantu language Isinzu; he gained access to secret texts, which in Africa were written on parchment or the entrails of a hippopotamus in hieroglyphic symbols; and he received instruction from a spiritual master representing an occult brotherhood. In Bowen's translation of the discourse of the master on "The Riddle of Existence," Mandhlalanga declared,

> The *Itongo* (Universal Spirit) is ALL that ever was, is, or ever shall be, conceivable or inconceivable. The *Itongo* is ALL things, all things are of IT; but the sum of all things is not the *Itongo*. The *Itongo* is ALL the power there is, all power is

of it; but all power, perceivable or conceivable, is not the *Itongo*. The *Itongo* is ALL the wisdom there is, all wisdom is of IT; but all wisdom conceivable is not the *Itongo*. ALL substance, ALL power, ALL wisdom is of IT, and IT is in them and manifest through them, but IT is also above them and beyond them, eternally unmanifest.[49]

The notion of life as a riddle with a theosophical solution was familiar to theosophists not only from the proverbial riddle of the Sphinx but also from Annie Besant's *The Riddle of Life and How Theosophy Answers It*. In Africa, the Zulu *Itongo* seems to have taken the place of the Sanskrit *Atma* that was used in Theosophy to designate the divine source and ultimate destiny of human existence. In *The Occult Way*, published in 1933, Patrick Bowen presented a version of Mandhlalanga's formulation of the riddle of existence, almost word for word, as an ancient Hermetic text, "An Asservation (Hermetic Ritual)," removing both the African Master and the Zulu term *Itongo*.[50] For theosophical comparative religion, the recurrence of similar religious themes, formulas, and even phrases did not necessarily raise the question of plagiarism. Instead, such coincidences could confirm the theosophical truth that the same ancient wisdom was being preserved by secret brotherhoods in Asia and Africa. While the Great White Brotherhood of the Himalayas taught that the goal of life was union with the *Atma*, the African Brotherhood of the Higher Ones of Egypt taught that the goal for every human is "union with the source of his being—the *Itongo*.[51] Only years later, by Bowen's account, after he had moved to London in 1927, did he learn that the African teachings about the *Itongo* "were, in one word, THEOSOPHY."[52]

Unacknowledged by Patrick Bowen, other parallels with Theosophy were obvious in the teachings of the African brotherhood. Mandhlalanga outlined the Seven Principles of Man in Zulu: (1) the Physical Body (*Umzimba*), (2) the Etheric Body (*Isitunzi*), (3) the Lower Mind (*Amandhla*), (4) the Animal Mind (*Utiwesilo*), (5) the Human Mind (*Utiwomuntu*), (6) the Spiritual Mind (*Utiwetongo*), and (7) the *Itongo*, the "Ray, or spark of Universal Spirit which informs all lower manifestations."[53] These seven principles, representing man's "sevenfold being," or "septenary foundation," were familiar to theosophists, although they were designated not by Zulu but by Sanskrit terms: (1) *sthula sharira*, (2) *linga sharira*, (3) *prana*, (4) *kama*, (5) *manas*, (6) *buddhi*, and (7) *atma*, the "direct ray of the Universal Spirit," the "Spark of the Universal Spirit."[54] Eventually shifting from Zulu to Sanskrit, in 1933 Bowen presented these Seven Principles under their Sanskrit designations, with no reference to the Zulu terms or the African brotherhood.[55]

Like Theosophy, the African brotherhood observed seven grades of initiation, from pupils, under probation, to "perfect ones." As Bowen learned from Mandhlalanga, the various grades displayed spiritual powers—the Disciple, mesmerism; the Brother, astral consciousness; the Master, clairvoyance and clairaudience on the Etheric Plane—that built toward the knowledge of the *Isangoma*, "Those who Know," who "have attained consciousness on the Plane of the Real Self."[56] Only those who had been Masters in a previous life could achieve this higher level of consciousness of what Bowen called *Isangomaship*. The highest grade, however, was the *Abakulubantu*—the Supreme Ones, the Perfect Men—who were liberated from the cycle of rebirth and appeared in physical form only as they chose. In its stages of spiritual development to perfection, the African brotherhood clearly resembled Theosophy's understanding of what Annie Besant called "the steps by which a man may climb to the status of the Super-man."[57]

Patrick Bowen's account of the African brotherhood must seem like fiction, especially given his reference to the romances of H. Rider Haggard as a precedent for his discovery of a white race in Africa.[58] Nevertheless, he rose in prominence in the London Theosophical Society, partly because he published extracts from notes taken by his father, Robert Bowen, at secret seminars with Helena Blavatsky forty years earlier in 1890 and 1891. Although he claimed to have never heard of the society, his father turned out to be a member of Blavatsky's inner circle, providing material for guidelines on how to study Theosophy.[59] Patrick Bowen, therefore, discovered not only a secret theosophical brotherhood in remote Africa but also a lost text at the center of Theosophy. Continuing to publish on the ancient wisdom, including a book-length translation from a secret Isinzu text, *The Sayings of the Ancient One*, Patrick Bowen eventually became president of the Dublin Hermetic Society.[60]

Patrick Bowen's unbelievable discovery of the secret African wisdom of the *Itongo* was authenticated by its circulation through publications in India, South Africa, and England. In *The Essential Unity of All Religions*, published in 1932, the Indian theosophist and politician Bhagavan Das reproduced almost all of Bowen's "Ancient Wisdom in Africa." Bowen's discovery was valuable, according to Bhagavan Das, as evidence of the nearly universal belief in the cycle of rebirth and the evolution of the soul.[61] In 1951, the general secretary of the Theosophical Society in Southern Africa, Eleanor Stakesby-Lewis, revived interest in Bowen's African wisdom in *The Sayings of the Ancient One*, repeating its claims in her own article, "The Mystery Tradition of Africa," to assert the importance of a local theosophical tradition in Africa.[62] In 1969, the former spiritualist Francis Clive-Ross, editor of *Studies in Comparative Religion*, a London-based journal devoted to "traditional studies," republished Bowen's "Ancient Wisdom in Africa" in its entirety, presumably as evidence of the "perennial philosophy" that the editor found at the heart of all religions.[63] Through these and other circulations, Bowen's discovery acquired a certain kind of credibility, or at least weight, merely by being reproduced in different sites of knowledge production about the mystical essence of religion. Although his own evidence for discovering a secret brotherhood in Africa was suspect, Bowen's text could nevertheless be cited as evidence for a theory of religion that was localized in Africa but also perennial and universal, always and everywhere, because it was being reproduced in these circuits.

As a significant feature of the empire of religion, theosophical comparative religion discovered the mystical essence of humanity and the spiritual government of the entire universe. Combining myth, fiction, and scholarship, Patrick Bowen's discovery of the secret of the *Itongo* can be cited here as evidence for how knowledge was produced in theosophical comparative religion. Although his account of the secret wisdom in South Africa must seem more like invention than discovery, it nevertheless resonates with the search for spiritual essences and eternal returns of ancient wisdom that has been a recurring theme in theosophical scholarship within the study of religion. Often neglected in histories of the study of religion, this theosophical current was evident in the work of scholars such as Mircea Eliade, Henry Corbin, and Joseph Campbell, who participated in the Eranos conferences, beginning in 1933, under the guiding influence C. G. Jung.[64] By explicating secret wisdom, these scholars were part of a broader imperial quest for theosophical authenticity in which Patrick Bowen was also a participant.

CRITICAL COMPARATIVE RELIGION

How do we distinguish among religion, fiction, and scholarship about religion? During the early 1980s, the scholar of religion W. Richard Comstock proposed a framework, as a "thought experiment," for distinguishing religion, fiction, and scholarship as three different logical modalities. Adopting his basic terms from Immanuel Kant, Comstock proposed that we should understand these domains not in terms of any essential content but by the ways in which they are perceived. They are conventionally perceived as three different modes—possibility, necessity, and factuality. Imaginative literature is generally regarded as the play of possibility, religion as a domain of necessity, and scholarship as a discipline of factuality. Having proposed these distinctions, Comstock complicated his framework by insisting that these three modes are in dialectical tension with each other and that in any particular work of fiction or formation of religion, these modes "combine, coalesce and interfuse with one another in diverse ways."[65] Distinct but not separate, these three logical modes—possibility, necessity, and factuality—defined for Comstock the basic relations among fiction, religion, and scholarship.

Twenty years later, the historian of religions Bruce Lincoln examined these terms in theorizing myth. Power relations, rather than logical relations, were most prominent in his analysis. Defining myth as ideology in narrative form, Lincoln returned to Greek epic poetry to distinguish between two kinds of poetic discourse, the speech of *mythos* asserting the authority of the strong and the speech of *logos* demonstrating the cunning of the weak, which effectively embedded fiction in structural relations of power. Turning to academic research, Lincoln provocatively defined scholarship as myth with footnotes, inevitably displaying (or concealing) ideology in narrative form, but necessarily anchored in factual evidence that is publicly accessible, subject to review, and open to disputation. For these reasons, footnotes were crucial to authenticating scholarship.

Although he developed a very different approach to Comstock's key terms, Lincoln was also attentive to the ways in which they might combine, coalesce, and interfuse with each other. For example, he called attention to James Macpherson's *Ossian*, a work of imaginative fiction published between 1760 and 1763, which was presented by the author and generally accepted by readers as an ancient sacred myth of Ireland, inspiring a nationalist ideology in narrative form. But its assertion of strong authority depended upon the cunning of an author who relied on the myth of scholarship to fashion himself as an author not of fiction but of serious factual research.[66] Myth, fiction, and scholarship, therefore, can be distinguished but not always separated in any particular cultural production.

As a cultural production of empire, imperial comparative religion combined myth, fiction, and scholarship. Footnotes were crucial to the production, authentication, and circulation of knowledge about religion and religions in imperial comparative religion. Its leading figures, such as Friedrich Max Müller, E. B. Tylor, Andrew Lang, and James Frazer, were masters of the footnote. Not merely a referencing device, the footnote was an engine of production, a means for extracting raw religious materials, mediated by colonial middlemen, into the centralized manufacture of imperial theory.

At the same time, footnotes exposed any imperial theory to critique, making it vulnerable to critical disputation over the relation between theory and evidence.

Take the Zulu term *Itongo*, for example, as an entry into reviewing imperial theory in critical comparative religion. In his inaugural lectures in the science of religion, Max Müller announced an imperial theory of religion as a sense of the infinite, which could be positioned against a long colonial history of European travelers, explorers, missionaries, and government agents finding indigenous people who had no religion. Against this colonial denial of indigenous religion, Max Müller invoked the Zulu term *Itongo*, a word used by Africans who had been described as people lacking religion. Citing the research of Henry Callaway, Max Müller reported that the Zulu had an indigenous name for the Creator, *Itongo*, which Mpengula Mbande explained should be understood not as a man who had died and risen again but as "the up-bearer of the earth."[67] In the colonial context, as we have seen, missionaries engaged in an intense contest over appropriating Zulu terms to designate their Christian God. African converts at the Wesleyan Methodist mission station of James Allison, as John William Colenso found in 1855, were familiar with the use of *Itongo* for the Christian God. "The proper word for God, they said, was *iTongo*, which meant with them a Power of Universal Influence—a Being under whom all around were placed." Disagreeing, Colenso insisted that "Mr. Allison's [Africans] were in error as to the universal comprehension of the name *iTongo*." He found instead that the Zulu terms *uNkulunkulu* and *uMvelinqangi* more closely approximated the Christian God.[68] Disagreeing with Colenso, Henry Callaway acknowledged that Christians had appropriated the Zulu term *Itongo*, which "probably means a sleep-ghost or a dream ghost," as "a word to designate the Supreme," because it was the closest word the missionaries could find to "the idea of the impalpable and immaterial."[69] In citing Henry Callaway, Max Müller was apparently unaware of this missionary controversy. Nevertheless, this footnote enabled Max Müller to extend his theory of the religious sense of the infinite to all of humanity. In the case of the Zulu, he observed, "Thus we find among a people who were said to be without any religious life, without any idea of a Divine power, that some of the most essential elements of religion are fully developed."[70] Revolving around the *Itongo*, the Zulu had a religion featuring an invisible God, the creator of the universe, who caused storms, punished the wicked, and required sacrifices. Therefore, Max Müller concluded, we must be careful with evidence before finding that anyone has no religion.

While Max Müller invoked the *Itongo* as evidence of the universality of religion, E. B. Tylor was interested in Zulu data that might support his theory of the religious psychology of animism. In this respect, the *Itongo* appeared twice in Tylor's *Primitive Culture*. First, in analyzing the theology of sneezing, "best shown among the Zulus," Tylor cited the "native statements" provided by Henry Callaway. "Sneezing reminds a man that he should name the *Itongo* (ancestral spirit) of his people without delay," as one of Callaway's informants reported, "because it is the *Itongo* which causes him to sneeze, that he may perceive by sneezing that the *Itongo* is with him."[71] In this case, the *Itongo* was evidence of primitive animism, the "savage doctrine of pervading and invading spirits," a survival of the "theological stage" of sneezing in human evolution. Second, more important for Tylor's analysis, the *Itongo* appeared in Zulu dreaming. "So the Zulu may be visited in a dream by the shade of an ancestor, the *itongo*, who comes to warn him of danger, or he may himself be taken by the *itongo* in a dream to visit his distant people, and see that they are in trouble." Here the *Itongo*, as an ancestral spirit, is also a psychological phenomenon, an insubstantial apparition of primitive dream-life that generated religion. Although an ordinary feature of Zulu dreaming, available to everyone, ancestral spirits were also the specialized field of the diviner, the "professional seer," who becomes "a house of dreams."[72] In this reading of the *Itongo*, Tylor suggested that the psychological origin of religion in dreaming developed into the professionalized role of the diviner. As we recall, this particular Zulu diviner, James, was caught up in the crisis of dreaming under colonial conditions of dispossession, displacement, and interreligious relations. For Tylor, however, the *Itongo* was significant not in the here and now of a colonial situation but as evidence for reconstructing the evolution of religion from sneezing, through dreaming, into the emergence of religious professionals who mediated the evolution of religion from beliefs in spirits to beliefs in God.

Andrew Lang, arguing against Tylor's evolutionary theory of supreme beings, invoked the *Itongo* in support of his own theory that gods came first, spirits later, in the development of religion. Turning to the Zulu for evidence of ancestral spirits, Lang noted that although they revered their *amatongo*, they did not remember the names or praises of specific ancestors beyond one or two generations. "Thus," he observed, "each new generation of Zulus must have a new first worshipful object—its own father's *Itongo*." Since any memory of that paternal spirit would be lost in the future, the *Itongo* cannot provide the basis for the evolution of a deity. "The name of such a man," Lang concluded, "cannot survive as that of the God or Supreme Being from age to age."[73] Although the ancestral spirit could not be the germ of a deity, the *Itongo* could reveal the role of religion in establishing social rank. Criticizing Max Müller for ignoring the role of religion in politics, Lang invoked the Zulu, citing Callaway: "The *Itongo* (spirit) dwells with the great man; he who dreams is the chief of the village." By possessing the *Itongo*, the Zulu chief ruled the present from the past, drawing upon the ancestral spirit for political power. Such a link between spirits and power, Lang proposed, had been instrumental in the emergence of social status, hereditary aristocracy, inherited property, and political authority. The *Itongo*, in this case, was not the germ of a deity but the focus of spiritual forces that provided the "germs of rank" in human society.[74] Although Lang was interested in the poetics of the *Itongo*, noting that "Zulu *Inyanga* or diviners learn magical couplets from the *Itongo*," he was more concerned with the politics of the *Itongo*, the ways in which religious and political power intersected.[75]

Finally, for James Frazer, Zulu transactions with the *Itongo* confirmed his pragmatic theory of ritual. Focusing on children and food, ancestral ritual ensured that the dead would provide. When they felt afflicted by ancestral neglect or punishment, the Zulu enacted a kind of ritual ultimatum by warning the ancestral spirit that if his children died he would have no food. Citing Callaway, Frazer noted that the Zulu "suggest to the *Itongo*, by whose ill-will or want of care they are afflicted, that if they should all die in consequence, and thus his worshippers come to an end, he would have none to worship him; and therefore for his own sake, as well as for theirs, he had better preserve his people, that there may be a village for him to enter, and meat of the sacrifices for him to eat."[76] The *Itongo*, therefore, provided Frazer with further evidence that practical concerns about food and children were central to the practice of religious ritual.

In his ongoing reflections on dying and rising gods in the history of religions, Frazer invoked the *Itongo* as an illustration of the worship of the dead in Africa, especially when he explained the ancient Egyptian deity Osiris as having been a man, ruling as king, who was transformed into a god by being worshipped after death. As powerful ancestral spirits, Zulu kings were offered prayers and sacrifices. Although he knew that the Zulu reportedly forgot their remote ancestors, Frazer nevertheless found that the widespread African worship of the dead, especially dead chiefs and kings, provided a model for concluding that the myths and rituals of Osiris grew up around the memory of a dead man. Of course, he also drew an analogy between Osiris and Christ, implying that both could be understood in the light of African worship of the dead. Presenting his conclusion tentatively, or evasively, Frazer suggested that Osiris and Isis, although they might be purely imaginary beings, could also be unveiled as "originally a real man and woman about whom after death the myth-making fancy wove its gossamer rainbow-tinted web."[77] For James Frazer, therefore, the *Itongo* was a nexus of human interests and human gods.

By using the *Itongo* to cut a cross-section through imperial theory, we can see different theorists drawing upon the same body of evidence. Recalling Patrick Bowen's *Itongo*, the "spark of the Universal Spirit which informs all lower manifestations," the Zulu ancestral spirit, especially as it appeared in the oral testimonies collected by Henry Callaway, was cited as evidence informing all theories of religion. Max Müller's claim for the universality of religion, E. B. Tylor's explanation of the evolution of religion, Andrew Lang's arguments for the priority of "savage supreme beings" and the formative role of religion in politics, and James Frazer's suggestions that religion was the mystification of human interests and the deification of the dead—all of these theories of religion, at one point or another, drew upon the *Itongo* in their theoretical manifestations. Struck by the diversity of their findings, we might conclude that these theorists were simply forcing data into theory, kidnapping the *Itongo* to serve their own theoretical projects. However, ambiguity was inherent in the data. As we have seen, what Callaway collected was not a coherent religious system but a chaos of voices, a variety of indigenous positions, all influenced, in one way or another, by colonial disruptions and missionary incursions, which could be mined for evidence in support of almost any theory. Unlike interfaith or theosophical comparative religion, however, these theorists made their mining of data transparent through the revealing window of the footnote.

AUTHENTICATING KNOWLEDGE

In the preceding discussion, we have seen different ways of authenticating knowledge about religion. First, in interfaith comparative religion, the religious adherent, speaking from within a community of faith, was vested with authoritative knowledge. By insisting on speakers describing religions they personally professed, the Religions of the Empire conference was an instance of what has been called the insider-outsider problem in the study of religion.[78] If insiders provide authoritative accounts, then scholars of religion, as outsiders, can only faithfully reproduce believers' versions of their own religions. Authentic knowledge is premised on the adherent's assertion

"I am a believer." As many recent critics have argued, this privileging of insider accounts of religion raises epistemological problems by assuming that adherents possess a true subjective knowledge, innate or acquired, simply by virtue of affiliation. This assumption, as Jeppe Sinding Jensen has argued, is a "mystical postulate" that cannot be supported by any theory of mind or language.[79] However, the privileging of the insider can serve a politics of knowledge. As we have seen, at the Religions of the Empire conference this mystical postulate of the authenticity of insider knowledge served the political project of imperial peace. Accordingly, the privileged position of the insider was a politics of knowledge, authenticating the insider but also appropriating that aura of authenticity for an interfaith understanding that would form the basis for peaceful coexistence in the British Empire.

By violating the privilege of religious adherents when it came to primitive religions, the conference perpetuated the division of the empire of religion into citizens of world religions and subjects of savage religions. As we recall, Alfred C. Haddon found that South Africa was on the frontline of that division, a perfect site for studying the sociology of the religions of the higher races and the ethnology of the religions of the lower races. Breaking through this barrier, South African Albert Thoka claimed full citizenship in the empire of religion. This religious adherent, speaking on behalf of the indigenous religion of his own people, carried the authenticity of the insider into the conference. However, he also carried traces of the nature mysticism advanced by the organizers of the conference. In this transaction between inside knowledge and outside influence, his account of indigenous African religion recalled other indigenous accounts. If Magema Fuze could find the roots of African tradition in the Bible or John Tengo Jabavu could find them in the Great Unknown, Albert Thoka could certainly locate them in Nature. Although proponents of interfaith comparative religion might want to hear a pure indigenous voice, an authentic expression of indigenous religion by an insider, no indigenous speech about religion was possible without such mediations.

Like other religious adherents at the conference, Albert Thoka was informed by imperial constructions of religion—religion was a belief system; religion was a practical system; religion was a system that linked belief and practice with a social system. In the empire of religion, from the religious system of the Zulu to the religious systems of the world, religious adherents could only speak, not for themselves but for a collectivity, on behalf of a religious system that ostensibly validated their voices. The mystical postulate of authentic subjectivity, therefore, was underwritten by an imperial politics of *divide et impera*—"classify and conquer," as Max Müller translated this imperative in 1870, or "classify and understand," as he revised his rendering in 1882—in which representatives of the many religions of empire could all speak freely at the same table as long as it was clear who owned the table.

Second, in theosophical comparative religion, knowledge about religion and religions was authenticated by claiming access to secret wisdom. As we have seen, that secret wisdom, which could never be achieved by ordinary methods of philological analysis, textual exegesis, or historical research, nevertheless imitated these methods in discovering new languages, sacred texts, and hidden histories of religion. In creating an aura of authenticity, theosophical comparative religion depended upon what the historian of religions Paul Christopher Johnson has called *secretism*, which is not the keeping of secrets but the "divulgence of a reputation of secret knowledge."[80] Instead of being silent about secrets, secretism openly declares the possession of secrets. Even in the absence of real secrets, secretism generates an aura of authenticity for those who develop a reputation for knowing things that no one else knows. As a strategy for authenticating knowledge about religion, secretism was certainly practiced by the Theosophical Society, but it has also been evident in proponents of the mystical, spiritual, or perennial essence of all religions. In these cases, knowledge about religion is authenticated not by the testimony of religious adherents but by an underlying secret hidden from most religious adherents. In this respect, theosophical comparative religion represents a kind of conspiracy theory of religion, in which the essential truth of religion has been hidden from the world. Accordingly, not even religious adherents, if they were not in on the secret, would be able to speak authentically about their own particular religious traditions.

As we recall, the Theosophical Society invoked an imperial government—as above, so below—that ruled the spiritual universe and reincarnated on earth from the ancient Egyptians, through the Romans, to the British in empire building. By this account, an esoteric tradition was institutionalized in the world, secretly, by a spiritual brotherhood that acted like imperial rulers, governing everything, even if their day-to-day operations, as Gauri Viswanathan has observed, resulted in secret correspondence with Madame Blavatsky that often resembled the work of lower-level colonial bureaucrats.[81] Nevertheless, as exemplified by Mohandas Gandhi's political mobilization of a Hinduism he initially learned from Theosophy and by Annie Besant's role in the Indian National Congress, this esoteric tradition had a profound public impact on the long struggle for independence in India.

Patrick Bowen, who discovered the theosophical secret of the *Itongo* in South Africa, was also participating in a wider imperial exchange linking South Africa and India. Great Britain, as Max Müller insisted in his defense of English sovereignty over its colonies, depended upon securing the twin poles of India and South Africa. As we have seen, Gandhi was not the only one to move between these two poles. Henry Bartle Frere, Baden-Powell, and many others in the imperial military moved between India and South Africa, while the South African missionary A. T. Bryant drew upon academic research on India to construct a history of migrations of the Bantu into South Africa that mirrored contemporary historical speculations about the migrations of the Aryans. Bowen's discovery of the ancient wisdom in Africa, however, was secretism. He built a reputation for gaining access to secrets previously unnoticed in the exchanges between India and South Africa, even if what he revealed about these secrets mirrored the wisdom of the Theosophical Society by transposing its Sanskrit vocabulary into Zulu. In the circulations of his account, this mirroring registered not as plagiarism but as authentication, confirming that the same ancient wisdom was preserved all over the world. As above, so below; as in India, so in South Africa—the perennial wisdom was authenticated by its replication.

Finally, in critical comparative religion, we find traces of these strategies of authentication—insider purity and multiple replication—in the work of imperial theorists. With respect to the authenticity of insiders, as we recall, E. B. Tylor erased the social contexts of data collection to distill pure accounts of savage religion. Since his data were drawn from colonial situations, this distillation required the theorist "to separate the genuine developments of native theology from the effects of intercourse with civilized foreigners."[82] Likewise, James Frazer insisted that "every observer of a savage or barbarous people should describe it as if no other people existed on the face of the earth."[83] Savage insiders, in this respect, were social isolates, rendered as if they had been unaffected by the colonial relations, contacts, and exchanges within which data about religion were being produced.

With respect to the authenticity of replication, Andrew Lang established repetition as a principle of verification, a way of validating evidence by cross-checking colonial accounts from all over the world to see if they said the same thing. If local experts tell the same stories, "then we may presume that the inquirers have managed to extract true accounts from some of their native informants."[84] As in theosophical comparative religion, the recurrence of a religious theme was not evidence of plagiarism—or diffusion—but confirmation that replicating accounts were authentic.

For critical comparative religion, however, these strategies of authentication depended upon colonial middlemen who were mediating the global exchange between indigenous insiders and imperial theorists. Genuine knowledge, as Frazer observed, relied upon local experts providing "full, true, and precise accounts of savage and barbarous peoples based on personal observation."[85] By stressing personal observation, this strategy of authentication invoked the modern primacy of sight in verifying knowledge.[86] As opposed to hearsay, seeing is believable. Being there, which was eventually developed in ethnographic methods of participant observation, was essential for genuine knowledge, even if the claim to being there could be abused by the fabrications of a theosophist or confused by the fictions of a novelist. Being there could also be problematic for anthropologists, as we recall from the responses of the British scientists to witnessing a Zulu war dance in 1905, which they validated as genuine even though it had been staged to display the contrast between savagery and civilization. Although subsequent generations of ethnographers rejected the speculations of armchair anthropology, imperial theorists also invoked personal observation as validation. Without being there themselves, they relied upon the personal observations of local experts such as Henry Callaway or Henri-Alexandre Junod, who were crucial in verifying genuine knowledge about indigenous religion and religions. Even if they never left the comfort (and, according to Hartland, the dangers) of the study, imperial theorists relied upon local observation to authenticate knowledge about religion.

However, as we have seen, authentication of knowledge in the imperial study of religion was thoroughly intertextual. As imperial texts were built out of colonial texts, they also referenced each other in relation to the same colonial texts. The validity of the entire industry depended upon footnotes. Quotation of local experts, which was necessary for producing knowledge, was verified by textual citation, a procedure, as the historian Carlo Ginzburg has observed, designed "to communicate an effect of authenticity."[87] As imperial theorists provided footnotes, they opened their work to public review, to collegial confirmation or disputation, to a collective enterprise of verification or falsification in the production of knowledge about religion and religions. At the same time, they deployed footnotes as a kind of spiritual capital in an intellectual economy, using citations as a means not only for accumulating raw materials but also for certifying their provenance. Acknowledging their debt to local experts, imperial theorists transformed that debt into credit in a global exchange and credibility in a global study of religion. The footnote was the warrant for both credit and credibility. Transcending time and space, the footnote was just like being there in verifying the precise point of production, but better than being there by invoking the absent spirits of the empire of religion.

CHAPTER TEN

Enduring Empire

A pure race, if it exists at all outside of the brain of some ethnologists, is a
barren race. Mixed races, and mixed races alone, bring forth the fruit that we
term civilisation,—with social, religious, and intellectual progress.

MORRIS JASTROW JR.

While studying at Crozer Theological Seminary in Chester, Pennsylvania,
in February 1951 Martin Luther King Jr. wrote an essay, "The Origin of
Religion in the Race." Submitted for a course in the philosophy of religion, the essay outlined theories of the origin of religion not within any
particular race, as the term *race* was generally used in 1950s America, but
within the human race. King's essay was a summary of theories of religion
that had been developed primarily within British imperial comparative religion between 1870 and 1920. Although King omitted the putative founder
of comparative religion, Friedrich Max Müller, he reviewed the classic theories: the animism of E. B. Tylor; the ghost theory of Herbert Spencer;
the totemism of William Robertson Smith, Emile Durkheim, and E. Sidney
Hartland; and the preanimism or *mana* of R. R. Marett. Concluding with
a discussion of the relation between religion and magic, King contrasted
three positions: Andrew Lang's proposal that religion, which was grounded
in spiritual intuition and primitive monotheism, was prior to magic; James
Frazer's evolutionary scheme that placed magic as prior to religion on a
trajectory toward science; and R. R. Marett's contention, which King found
"quite valid," that magic and religion shared a common root in the human
sense of the mystery of life. Receiving an A grade for his "thoughtful, critical analysis," King showed that he could reproduce the standard narrative
of theoretical developments in imperial comparative religion.[1]

Here in the United States, we find the history of the imperial study of
religion being reproduced by an African American student, demonstrating
that its circulation of knowledge about religion and religions extended far

and wide, even as far as the young Martin Luther King Jr. in 1951, who recited this genealogy of European thinking about the origin and development of religion. The United States, of course, was not an empire, but it displayed the same imperial engines—competition with rival European powers over trading and financial interests, dominion over foreign territories, and a civilizing mission that justified proclaiming liberty while practicing coercion—that were the hallmarks of European empires. The poet of empire, Rudyard Kipling, recognized this imperial kinship in "The White Man's Burden: An Address to the United States," which he composed in 1899 to urge Americans to annex the Philippines.[2] Proceeding to build an empire of islands, which has been characterized as a networked empire, the United States became an imperial or neoimperial force in the twentieth century.[3] But the United States had already been constituted by an internal imperialism in North America that was based on conquering Native Americans for their territory and enslaving Africans for their labor.

How does the study of religion fit into this imperial mix? Superficially, the study of religion might be seen as an adjunct of power politics. In the middle of the nineteenth century, as Great Britain was expanding its empire, the British theologian F. D. Maurice undertook a study of world religions, which he justified on the grounds that knowledge about religions would be useful for a nation that was "engaged in trading with other countries, or in conquering them, or in keeping possession of them."[4] In the middle of the twentieth century, as the United States was assuming an imperial role in the wake of the collapse of European empires, American scholar of religion Huston Smith undertook a study of world religions, which he justified in 1958, based on his experience of lecturing to officers of the U.S. Air Force, as providing useful knowledge for military personnel because "someday they were likely to be dealing with the peoples they were studying as allies, antagonists, or subjects of military occupation."[5]

These recommendations for the study of religion suggest a remarkable continuity from British imperialism to American neoimperialism in justifying the field of study as an intellectual instrument of international trade, military conquest, and political administration of alien subjects. Such strategic justifications for the study of religion and religions have persisted, as we find in the introductory course "Religious Factors in Special Operations" offered in the 1990s by Chaplain Ken Stice at the U.S. Army John F. Kennedy Special Warfare Center and School. In the syllabus for this course, Chaplain Stice identified the "terminal learning objective" as enabling Special Operations soldiers to brief their commanders on the impact of religion and religions on a mission and its forces. "Why do Special Operations soldiers need to study religion at all?" Chaplain Stice asked. "Primarily, because of the truth of Special Operations Imperative #1: Understand the Operational Environment!" As an adjunct to military strategy and tactics, therefore, the study of religion and religions could be useful in gaining the cooperation or submission of adherents of foreign, unfamiliar religions that Chaplain Stice characterized as "different from our own."[6] More recently, Eric Patterson has advocated studying religions to produce a baseline of knowledge about religion and religions, what Stephen Prothero has called "religious literacy," because "U.S foreign policy must engage the world as it is, including its vibrant religiosity."[7] From the battlefield to international diplomacy, the study of religion might be useful for advancing U.S. economic, political, and military interests in the world.

But the history of the study of religion in the United States drew together many other motives. Although the encyclopedic collection by Hannah Adams originally appearing in 1784 might represent deep background,[8] the study of religions in the United States became formalized and institutionalized during the same era, from Max Müller's lectures to the eve of World War I, in which British imperial comparative religion developed. Within this time frame in the United States, we find different motivations for studying religion and religions: Christian apologetics in James Freeman Clarke, *Ten Great Religions: An Essay in Comparative Theology* (1871), which earned the author a professorship at Harvard; the theosophical quest for a "universal religion" in Samuel Johnson, *Oriental Religions and Their Relation to Universal Religion* (1872–1885); and the promotion of liberal sympathy in Morris Jastrow Jr., *The Study of Religion* (1901), which provided a profile of the entire field.[9] While Harvard appointed George Foot Moore as chair of the history of religions in 1892 and the University of Chicago appointed George Stephen Goodspeed as the chair of the Department of Comparative Religion in 1892, the academic study of religion was being gradually institutionalized in the United States.[10] On the initiative of Morris Jastrow, in 1895 a consortium of universities on the East Coast formed "The American Lectures on the History of Religions," with the first series of lectures delivered on Buddhism by the British scholar T. W. Rhys Davids.[11] Against the background of imperial comparative religion, the problem with these American initiatives in the study of religion was not merely their easy relationship with Protestant theology, their assumptions about liberal ecumenism, or their aspirations for sympathetic interfaith understanding. The central problem in America, as in South Africa, was race.

In an essay on the development of the scholarly study of religion in the United States, the historian James Turner has proposed that "the discipline of religious studies was born from a felt need to measure Christianity against alternatives. Such comparison aimed either to make Christianity more persuasive to the 'heathens' or to perfect Christianity by locating the elements of a universal religion common to all people."[12] Although Christian theological aspirations were certainly evident, the enduring opposition between the primitive and the civilized structured the birth of religious studies in America. Alfred C. Haddon's racialized division of academic labor between "the ethnology of the lower races and the sociology of the higher" persisted in the United States, with Native Americans and African Americans occupying the "savage slot" of lower races.[13] However, although the imperial structure of lower and higher races endured, the academic division of labor was modified, as the historian of anthropology Lee D. Baker has observed, to deal with "out of the way" Native Americans through methods of ethnology and "in the way" African Americans through methods of sociology and psychology.[14] For the study of religion in the United States, this division of labor in dealing with internally colonized people was crucial to the birth of an academic field of inquiry that was distinct from but located within the European empire of religion.

At the turn of the twentieth century, a key figure in the study of religion in the United States was Morris Jastrow Jr. (1861-1921). Having considered becoming a rabbi, Jastrow studied in Germany to become expert on the religion of ancient Mesopotamia—he published *The Religion of Babylonia and Assyria* in 1898—as well as on biblical literature and the religion of ancient Israel.[15] Recent archaeological excavations had uncovered Mesopotamia as the "cradle of civilization"; it was one end of the "Fertile Crescent" extending from Iraq to Egypt that emerged in scholarship as the ancient source of advanced religion, culture, and civilization. While Jastrow was a leading researcher in this history of civilization, he was also active in advancing a general study of religion in which the study of savage or primitive religion was foundational. In an article promoting the historical study of religions in American universities and colleges, Jastrow observed, "The religion of savages and of people living in a primitive condition of culture are the more special concern of the student of religions."[16] Among scholars of religion in the United States, there were differences on this point. Identified by Jastrow as "the most distinguished of American scholars within this field," Crawford Howell Toy devoted his introduction to the study of religion to primitive religion as the basis for studying "the more general problems connected with the unfolding of religious thought."[17] By contrast, George Foot Moore, in his introduction to the history of religions, insisted on covering "only the religions of civilized peoples," because he considered "'primitive' religions . . . a subject for themselves, demanding another method."[18] In both cases, the distinction between primitive and civilized persisted as the great divide in the academic study of religion in the United States.

Like Max Müller, Jastrow saw the scientific study of religion as a science of classification. Here he was more directly influenced by C. P. Tiele (1830-1902), to whom he dedicated *The Study of Religion,* who held that the "final result" of comparative study was "a morphological classification of religions."[19] As formulated in his article "Religions" in the *Encyclopaedia Britannica,* Tiele's system of classification, which Jastrow found "the most satisfactory," set up an ascending scale of five categories—primitive naturalism, animism, national polytheistic religions, nomistic religions, and universal religions. The great divide, in this scheme, is marked by nomistic religions, which merge religious belief with religious law (*nomos*) as a basis for personal morality and social ethics. In the classification of religions proposed by Jastrow, this merger of religion with law, morality, or ethics was the highest stage of religion, religions "which aim at a consistent accord between religious doctrine and religious practice."[20] Preceded by religions of advanced culture, this highest stage of intellectual and moral development could be contrasted with the religions of savages and the religions of primitive culture. Jastrow's distinction between savage and primitive is not always clear. As a purely hypothetical category, savage religion is "sharply differentiated from the religion of primitive culture," but because of the gradual development of culture, "a sharp dividing line between the religion of savages and the religion corresponding to the period of primitive culture cannot be drawn."[21] The sharp dividing line, sharply differentiated, was the gulf between the amoral religion of savage or primitive cultures and the law-governed religion of advanced cultures and civilizations.

For the genuine student, as opposed to the dilettante, studying religion required going directly to the sources. While the study of civilized religions demands the study of texts, the study of primitive religions requires the direct study of people. As a model, Jastrow cited the work of the pioneering American ethnographer Frank Hamilton Cushing (1857-1900), "who lived with the Zuni Indians, acquired their language, took part in their daily occupations, [and] shared their festivals and ceremonies."[22] Noting that the Columbian Exposition in Chicago of 1893 had provided exhibitions of primitive people, Jastrow observed that access to the sources of the religions of primitive culture required journeying, like Cushing, to "the native haunts of primitive man." However, the influence of Christian missions and Western civilization had extended all over the world to such an extent that "there [was] no district, unless it be the remote interior of Africa, where one [could] . . . encounter primitive culture in its pristine state."[23] Fortunately for American students of religion, it was not necessary to journey to the interior of Africa for direct observation of "the working of the primitive mind." Instead, they could study Africans in America. "In the United States," Jastrow observed, "students are fortunately placed in having, in the case of a large portion of the negro population, persons only two or three generations removed from the stage of primitive culture, and the large mass of negro folk-lore still extant in the south shows the abiding character of former influences."[24] For the study of religion in the United States, therefore, Native Americans and African Americans were the proximate primitives in a science based on the great divide between primitive and civilized religions.

PRIMITIVE RELIGIONS

During the winter of 1896-97, the second series of American Lectures on the History of Religions, "Religions of Primitive Peoples," was delivered by Daniel G. Brinton (1837-1899). The lectures were presented to audiences at Boston's Lowell Institute, the Brooklyn Institute, Cornell University, Yale University, New York University, Brown University, and the University of Pennsylvania, where Brinton, like Jastrow, held a professorship. A scholar of Native American languages, cultures, and religions, Brinton produced his landmark compendium, *Myths of the New World*, originally published in 1868, to explain the identity of American Indians "by an analysis of the simple faiths of a savage race."[25] In addition to his scholarly expertise on Native Americans, Brinton gained recognition for his contribution to the general science of religion, *The Religious Sentiment* (1876), and his contribution to the science of race, *Races and Peoples* (1890), in which he argued for a racial hierarchy in which the "European or white race stands at the head of the list, the African or negro at its foot."[26] Developing a political interest in anarchism toward the end of his life, Brinton also identified with American imperialism and became an instant expert on the "strange and varied population" of the Philippines. "Now that the Philippine islands are definitely ours," he observed in 1899, "it behooves us to give them that scientific investigation which alone can afford a true guide to their proper management."[27] In the work of Daniel G. Brinton, therefore, we find an explicit mix of religion, race, and imperialism.

As an introductory overview, his *Religions of Primitive Peoples* attended to theory, which must be scientific rather than theological, and method in the study of religion. Brinton identified methods that he termed the historic method, the comparative method, and the psychologic method, and he claimed that the psychologic method could uncover in primitive religions the "laws of human thought."[28] Acknowledging that Charles Darwin had traced religion back to the thoughts and feelings of his dog, Brinton focused on the human species. Drawing on his own field of research, he derived illustrations from the indigenous religions of North America. "Here, if anywhere," he observed, "we should find the religious sentiment, if it exists at all, in its simplest elements." At the same time, Brinton drew evidence from "Africa, with its countless dusky hordes." The "most primitive features" of African religion, he maintained, had been "best preserved in the extreme South, among the Hottentots, Bushmen, and Zulus."[29] Recirculating Henry Callaway's *Religious System of the Amazulu* (despite misspelling Callaway's name), Brinton invoked the Zulu for seeing things that are not there, experiencing waking visions, imagining the soul as a shadow, uttering ritual speech composed of meaningless syllables, and believing in Unkululu [*sic*] as "the means of helping the race into being."[30] In this use of Zulu evidence, Brinton engaged in the same procedure of turning Callaway's text into raw material for the production of theory that had been practiced by British imperial theorists of religion.

Brinton himself, however, had been subject to this same procedure when the material he collected and organized in his *Myths of the New World* had been used extensively by E. B. Tylor in composing *Primitive Culture*, as Tylor extracted illustrations of myths of the four winds, the identification of soul and breath, souls entering animals, bodily resurrection, and other motifs.[31] Like Callaway's Africans, Brinton's Indians fed into Tylor's development of his theory of primitive religion as animism.[32] In raising a perennial problem in imperial comparative religion, Tylor referred to Brinton in worrying about how to distinguish truly primitive religion from the influence of missionizing Christianity or Islam and from the impact of the culture of advanced civilizations.[33] Perhaps Tylor had a personal interest in Brinton's Native American researches, because he was certainly struck by this problem of discerning pure primitive religion during his 1856 travels through Mexico. He suspected that Indians, while practicing Christianity, were "keeping their ancient superstitious rites in secret." He expressed surprise to discover that a popular English music-hall song, "The King of the Cannibal Islands," was performed before the altar in Mexican worship.[34] Such religious circulations, for Tylor, raised the question of religious purity, which he resolved by distilling the pristine primitive religion of animism. Likewise, Brinton represented primitive religion as both a timeless present and a lost origin.

For the study of Native American religion in the United States, this quest for precontact purity continued, seeking to determine, as the ethnographer James Mooney observed in 1891, "the state of the aboriginal religion before its contamination by contact with whites."[35] In the classic study by Lewis H. Morgan (1818-1881), *Ancient Society* (1877), precontact Native Americans represented a stage of barbarism, between savagery and civilization, that revealed "the history and experience of our own remote ancestors when in corresponding conditions." This chapter of the human record, which had been disappearing for three centuries, had to be preserved for its wealth of ethnological, philological, and archaeological materials that "possess[ed] a high and special value reaching far beyond the Indian race itself."[36] Observing that American Indians were a religious people, Morgan provided a brief profile of myths, rituals, festivals, and ceremonies, focusing specifically on the Iroquois. Dancing was the heart of Native American religion. "In no part of the earth, among barbarians, has the dance received a more studied development." While each tribe had developed its own repertoire of dances, "some of them, as the war-dance, were common to all the tribes." Representing the barbaric stage in social evolution, the religious beliefs and practices of Native Americans had to be preserved because these "facts [would] hold an important place in the science of comparative religion."[37]

By contrast to this preservationist motive, others advocated the study of Native American religion in the interest of its elimination. John Wesley Powell (1834-1902), director of the Bureau of American Ethnology of the Smithsonian Institution, exemplified the eliminationist motive in the study of Native American religion. Like E. B. Tylor formulating an anthropological reformer's science that marked out primitive superstitions for destruction, Powell argued that knowledge of Indian culture was necessary because it "must necessarily be overthrown before new institutions, customs, philosophy, and religion can be introduced."[38] Such an approach to the study of Native Americans was backed up by the force of law in the Indian Religious Crimes Code of 1883, which outlawed indigenous dances, rites, and ceremonies as part of a project of civilizing Indians.[39] "It is a long way from savagery to civilization," Powell observed.[40] Civilization had been advanced only by "one great stock of people—the Aryan race."[41] Vestiges of savagery, which Powell found in Native American religion, had to be marked out for destruction in the continuing advance of Aryan civilization.

The widespread Ghost Dance religion, which was revived by the Paiute prophet Wovoka in 1890, proclaimed peace in expectation of a spiritually transformed world. Identified by the U.S. military as a war dance, the Ghost Dance became associated with Sioux resistance, which culminated in the massacre of Wounded Knee. On behalf of the Bureau of American Ethnology of the Smithsonian Institution, James Mooney (1861-1921) produced a detailed and broadly sympathetic account of the Ghost Dance movement. Attributing the cause of Indian resistance to colonial oppression, Mooney argued that the Ghost Dance represented a radical departure from the martial religion of Native Americans, evident in "the war dance, the scalp dance, and even the bloody torture of the sun dance," so it was remarkable that teachings of peace were "obeyed by four-fifths of all the warlike predatory tribes of the mountains and the great plains."[42] For an explanation, however, Mooney turned to hypnotism, which he found to be the only theory that could account for the trance-states achieved by the dancers. According to Mooney, "The Indian messiah religion is the inspiration of a dream. Its ritual is the dance, the ecstasy, and the trance. Its priests are hypnotics and cataleptics. All these have formed a part of every great religious development of which we have knowledge from the beginning of history."[43] Accordingly, this visionary complex was not a primitive survival but a recurring feature of the history of religions, evident in parallels Mooney cited from the Bible, the visions of Muhammad, the medieval flagellants, the French prophets, evangelical revivals, and other examples, including an extended extract on whirling dervishes, to show how hypnotism, trance, and visionary experience had been a prominent feature of the history of religions. Powell objected to these comparisons with civilized religion, especially with Christianity, even though he had once compared Native American "primitive institutions" with Buddhist social organization.[44] Nevertheless, in Mooney's account of the Ghost Dance, Native American religion was formulated as a visionary religion.

"The essence of Crow religion," the anthropologist Robert H. Lowie (1883-1957) wrote in *Primitive Religion*, originally published in 1924, "was found in the visionary experience." Lowie, one of a new generation of ethnographers trained by Franz Boas, who, according to the standard history of American anthropology, broke the hold of the racist science advanced by Brinton, based his account of Native American religion on his own intensive fieldwork among the Crow. Beginning his introduction to primitive religion with a profile of Crow religion, Lowie proceeded in the next chapter to contrast the visionary religion of Native Americans with the emotional religion of Africans. He focused on the Ekoi of West Africa and found the essence of their religion in "an emotional undertone that somehow penetrates the whole of their religion." The essence of Ekoi religion, according to Lowie, was found in the emotional experience of terror. "Theirs is a land full of mystery and terror," he wrote, "of magic plants, of rivers of good and ill fortune, of trees and rocks ever lowering to engulf unwary wayfarers; where the terror of witchcraft stalks abroad, and where, against this dread, the most devoted love or faithful service counts as naught."[45] Certainly this contrast between vision and emotion, between ecstasy and fear, was drawn for dramatic effect. Lowie had a lot more to say about the study of primitive religion, taking E. B. Tylor's side against Emile Durkheim, for example, in adopting psychological against sociological explanation. Furthermore, he was able to situate indigenous religions in contact zones, comparing South African prophetic movements with the Ghost Dance and finding that the "sudden contact of an aboriginal and a Caucasian population in South Africa produced results there roughly comparable to the Messiah cults of the North American Indians."[46] Nevertheless, his representation of African religion as essentially emotional replicated the ways in which African American religion was being represented in an emerging sociology and psychology of religion.

In the study of African American religion, the founding of the American Folk-Lore Society in 1888 represented a beginning. Under the direction of William Wells Newell (1839–1907), the society focused on "Negro Folk Lore," which included "old-fashioned religious beliefs" of African Americans that were "brought with them from Africa." Aligned with anthropological race science, with Brinton serving as president of the society in 1889, the American Folk-Lore Society also displayed an eliminationist motive for the study of the "body of songs, tales, old-fashioned religious beliefs, superstitions, customs, ways of expression, proverbs, and dialect, of American Negroes." Newell explained, "All this body of thought belongs to the past." Vanishing with the progress of civilization and the racial uplift of African Americans, these African traditions were being "superseded by more advanced ideas, habits, morals, and theology."[47] Studying African American religion, according to Newell, was a reformer's science, based on the assumption that "the best way to correct superstitious notions is to collect and study them."[48] Collecting and studying African American traditions resulted in the emergence of a professional discipline of black religion in psychology and sociology.[49] Recalling landmarks in that racist academic discipline, we find influential authors, such as Joseph Alexander Tillinghast, Frederick Morgan Davenport, and George Barton Cutten, outlining a racial science of religion in the United States.

In *The Negro in Africa and America* (1902), Joseph Alexander Tillinghast (1871–1944) insisted that African religion displayed a "lack of relation between religion and morality."[50] Divorced from morality, African religion, whether in Africa or America, was purely emotional. Developing this theme in *Primitive Traits in Religious Revivals* (1905), Frederick Morgan Davenport (1866–1956) highlighted the emotionality of African American religion in his chapter "The Religion of the American Negro."[51] Although he examined religious enthusiasm more generally, seeking "to segregate the primitive and baser elements," Davenport clearly was thinking about African Americans throughout his research on religious imagination. "In its early period it is very crude," he observed, "as it is to-day among the negroes of the United States, whose religious thinking, both lay and clerical, is very frequently one long stretch of most astounding images."[52] Characterizing African Americans as a "child race," Davenport traced that race back to Africa, noting that it displayed all the features of African religion: "Dense ignorance and superstition, a vivid imagination, volatile emotion, a weak will power, small sense of morality" that were "universally regarded as the most prominent traits of the negro in those sections of the country . . . where he appears in his primitive simplicity."[53] All of these denigrations, according to Davenport, were evident in African American religion. He explained, "The most prominent activity of the negro race in America is religion. Of course I mean religion of a certain type, which can only be understood when viewed historically and in the light of the mental development which this people has attained. A little time ago, comparatively speaking, their ancestors were practising primitive rites on the African west coast. And the slave ships brought to the West Indian sugar fields, and to the Southern states ultimately, a people who were saturated with superstition."[54] Citing W. E. B. Du Bois in support of his contention that the middle passage of slavery brought the African medicine man and his religion to America, Davenport made something else out of this continuity between Africa and African America by finding that as a result the Negro was "a primitive man with primitive traits in a modern environment," practicing a religion, with roots in Africa, that was "emotional and hypnotic to the core."[55]

As a purely emotional religion, hypnotic and hysterical, African American religion allegedly had no relation to morality. In this regard, Davenport could rely on the most recent findings of the academic study of religions, which identified the great divide between amoral primitive religions and the moral religions of advanced cultures and civilizations. "A very certain though unsavoury bit of evidence of the negro's primitive state," Davenport insisted, "is found in the great gulf still fixed in his consciousness between religion and morality," a "great gulf that is revealed by the absence of sexual virtue," to such an extent that the "wide prevalence of the crime of lynching among the whites of the South testifies eloquently to the reign of lust among the blacks."[56] As Ann Taves has observed, Frederick Morgan Davenport's emphasis on emotion in African American religion, with its racist undertones and overtones, was reproduced in subsequent scholarship in an emerging American psychology of religion.[57] In *The Psychological Phenomena of Christianity*, published in 1908, George Barton Cutten (1874–1962) characterized the religion of "ignorant and primitive negroes of the southern United States" as devoid of morality and full of volatile emotion, vivid imagination, and psychic contagion due to roots in Africa. "Thus we find the negro to-day," Cutten asserted, "the most religious and the most immoral of men, the present paradoxical condition being a survival of his former beliefs."[58]

In *Folk Beliefs of the Southern Negro* (1926), Newbell Niles Puckett (1898–1967) drew on interviews with more than four hundred informants to distinguish between the primitive and the civilized in African American religion. As the frontispiece to his book, he featured a photograph of "A Negro Conjure-Doctor," who was not a visionary shaman but a superstitious magician, suggesting the fundamental difference emerging in representations of primitive religions in America. Like Powell in the case of Native Americans, however, Puckett focused on identifying Negro folk beliefs in the hope of eliminating African superstitions. "Regarding the feelings, emotions, and the spiritual life of the Negro," Puckett observed, "the average white man knows little. Should some weird, archaic Negro doctrine be brought to his attention he almost invariably considers it a 'relic of African heathenism.' "[59] However, as Puckett observed, most often such weird doctrines are a mix of African and European superstitions that have been confused. Intending to disentangle such confusion, Puckett adopted an eliminationist strategy, seeking to eliminate superstition in the interest of improving race relations in the United States.[60] The African American anthropologist Zora Neale Hurston (1891–1960), having studied with Franz Boas and Ruth Benedict at Columbia University between 1925 and 1927, developed a very different perspective on the relations between primitive conjuring and civilized Christianity. Writing to Langston Hughes in 1929, she said she had found that Christianity, with all of its magic and mystery, was full of conjuring, "sympathetic magic pure and simple." Why, she wondered, did white Christians worry about conjure?[61]

The anthropologist Paul Radin (1883-1959), who had conducted his fieldwork among the Winnebago, signaled a radical departure from the racialized study of primitive religion in America. In *Primitive Man as Philosopher* (1927), Radin countered the racial notions of primitive superstition or primitive mentality by arguing that so-called primitive people could produce thinkers who were capable not only of rational reflection about religion but also of sustained skepticism and critique of religious ideas worthy of any European philosopher. For his primary evidence of skepticism and critique, Radin cited at length the "disquisition on Unkulunkulu, the supreme deity of the Amazulu of East Africa," which he found in the testimony of Mpengula Mbande as recorded in Henry Callaway, *The Religious System of the Amazulu*. As a Christian convert, catechist, and eventually deacon, Mbande had observed that what black men say about uNkulunkulu "has no point; it is altogether blunt. For there is not one among black men, not even the chiefs themselves, who can so interpret such accounts as those about Unkulunkulu to bring about the truth."[62] Over six pages in the culmination of his argument that primitive peoples could produce primitive philosophers, Radin quoted Mpengula Mbande's Christian invective against Zulu ancestral religion. As an exemplar of primitive man as philosopher, Mbande was certainly a strange choice, since he had been enlisted in a Christian campaign against primitive religion. Despite good intentions, which in Radin's case involved rescuing so-called primitive people from their denigration that had been entrenched in the study of religion in Europe and America, any invocation of primitive religion was entangled in the mediations—imperial, colonial, and indigenous—that produced and circulated knowledge about religion.

RELIGIONS OF CIVILIZATIONS

Although the study of primitive religion, according to Morris Jastrow, was the special concern of the student of religion, the earliest professorships in religion at American universities were held by experts in the religion, history, and literature of ancient civilizations. At Harvard University, George Foot Moore (1851-1931), who focused his introduction to the history of religions on civilized religions, was an expert on biblical literature and early Judaism.[63] At the University of Chicago, George Stephen Goodspeed

(1860-1905) was an expert on the religions of ancient Mesopotamia; he provided not only a history of the Babylonians and the Assyrians but also a history of the ancient world that began in the "Fertile Crescent" extending from the Euphrates and Tigris Rivers of Mesopotamia to the Nile River of Egypt.[64] Participating in the intellectual ferment generated by recent archaeological discoveries in Mesopotamia, scholars of religion were engaged in recasting civilization as beginning not in Greco-Roman antiquity but in the ancient Near East. Although the American military historian and naval strategist Alfred Thayer Mahan coined the term *Middle East* in 1902, the terms *Orient, Near Orient,* and *Near East* persisted in scholarship.[65] A colleague of Goodspeed at Chicago, the Egyptologist James Henry Breasted (1865-1935), sought to popularize the importance of the Fertile Crescent in a high school textbook, *Ancient Times: A History of the Early World,* with more than seven hundred pages of text beginning with the ancient Near East.[66] For Breasted, this ancient history held religious, cultural, and racial significance. The ancient Near East of Mesopotamia and Egypt, according to Breasted, was "the keystone of the arch, with prehistoric man on one side and civilized Europe on the other."[67] As the pivot in the evolutionary transition of Europeans from primitive to civilized, the ancient Near East was a racial inheritance because, Breasted asserted, "the evolution of civilization has been the achievement of this Great White Race."[68]

Morris Jastrow was also a specialist in the religion of the ancient Near East. For the American Lectures on the History of Religions in 1911, he titled his presentation "Aspects of Religious Belief and Practice in Babylonia and Assyria." By sharp contrast to Breasted's racial civilization, Jastrow argued that the civilization of ancient Mesopotamia, like any civilization, was the product not of racial purity but of interracial mixture. According to Jastrow, "Civilisation, like the spark emitted by the striking of steel on flint, is everywhere the result of the stimulus evoked by the friction of one ethnic group upon another." As he examined in detail the relations between Semitic Akkadians and non-Semitic Sumerians in the civilization of ancient Mesopotamia, Jastrow noted quickly that ancient Egyptian civilization mixed Semitic and Hamitic cultures, ancient Greek civilization mixed Aryan and non-Aryan cultures, and ancient Roman civilization mixed Aryan with Etruscan cultures. In modern Europe, the advanced civilizations of England, France, and Germany depended upon "the commingling of diverse ethnic elements." Turning to the United States, he invoked *The Melting Pot,* the title of a recent play, to promise "a new type of culture springing from the mixture of almost innumerable elements." For Jastrow, therefore, civilization was not carried by a race, not even by the "Great White Race," because civilization was a product of interracial mixture. "A pure race, if it exists at all outside of the brain of some ethnologists, is a barren race," Jastrow maintained. "Mixed races, and mixed races alone, bring forth the fruit that we term civilisation,—with social, religious, and intellectual progress."[69]

In the historical emergence of the modern notion of religion, with its attendant and complementary realm of the secular, as Gil Anidjar has observed, "religion and race are *contemporary*, indeed, coextensive and, moreover, co-concealing categories."[70] For imperial comparative religion, as we recall, religion often intersected with race. Certainly race marked the great divide between lower and higher races, between the savage and the civilized. But race also differentiated among the civilized, especially in distinguishing between the Aryan and the Semitic. Although Matthew Arnold proposed that this distinction was essentially cultural rather than racial, with both Hellenic and Hebraic cultural streams flowing into the culture of England, and Max Müller insisted that the distinction was only linguistic and not racial, the racial division between Aryan and Semitic persisted in structuring the study of religious civilizations. As we have seen, subjects of empire could intervene in this racial division. In South Africa, Mohandas Gandhi identified Indians with the Aryan race as part of an imperial family; Zulu Christians identified themselves with the Semitic race as lost tribes of ancient Israel. Through such interventions, the racial distinction between Aryan and Semitic circulated through the empire of religion in ways that were not necessarily controlled by any imperial center. As Morris Jastrow took up this problem in the study of ancient religion in Mesopotamia, he also employed these terms, although his primary distinction between Semitic and non-Semitic races might have subtly given greater weight to Semites as the key term in the history of religions within the cradle of civilization. Nevertheless, by insisting on racial mixtures, whether in friction or in merger, as the key to civilization, Jastrow disrupted any simple equation of race with religion.

Nevertheless, like S. M. Molema and H. I. E. Dhlomo in South Africa, who in their own ways were also scholars of religion, Morris Jastrow had to think against race within a thoroughly racialized domain. Although he was an expert in the religions of ancient Mesopotamia, as well as a leader in theory and method in the general study of religion, his professorship at the University of Pennsylvania was in Semitic languages. As a result, he attended to the religions of the Semites, but along the lines pioneered by

William Robertson Smith, as a nexus of comparison in the play of similarities and differences with other religions, both primitive and civilized. In his lectures on aspects of Babylonian and Assyrian religions, Jastrow emphasized continuities, observing that the religions of Mesopotamia began with "animistic conceptions of nature," enacted in ceremonies of "Taboo and Totemism," before developing beliefs in supernatural beings.[71] Embodying the evolutionary trajectory from primitive to civilized religion, the religion of ancient Mesopotamia also bestowed certain religious structures on Judaism, Christianity, and Islam. For example, the Babylonian *zikkurat*, a tower of both religious and political power, was developed in the Christian cathedral and the Muslim minaret. The Babylonian rituals of mourning for the dying and rising god Tammuz, which were transmitted to the Greeks in similar rituals for Adonis, were inherited by Christianity, at least according to the theory advanced by James Frazer, which held that "the story of the crucifixion and resurrection of the Christ embodies a late echo of the Tammuz-Adonis myth."[72] Reluctant to reduce the central Christian story to an inheritance from ancient Mesopotamia, Jastrow noted that this theory had been subjected to extensive criticism by Andrew Lang.[73] Nevertheless, Jastrow was interested in establishing a range of continuities between the religions of the ancient Near East and Judaism, Christianity, and Islam.

At the same time, as a matter of method, Jastrow was also interested in the differences. A critical analysis of the evidence, he argued, suggests that "resemblances in myths and traditions are frequently as deceptive as resemblances in the words of different languages." Lacking a "complete chain of evidence," we cannot assume that an apparently similar myth, ritual, or tradition is the same thing or derived from the same source.[74] In his Haskell Lectures of 1913 on Babylonian and Hebrew religions, Jastrow highlighted difference as his principle of comparison, analyzing how apparently similar motifs, such as creation myths or deluge myths, were actually not the same. Comparison of Hebrew with Babylonian traditions, he proposed, was not an exercise in solving an equation. Instead, the challenge was to document the long history of intercultural contact and analyze religious differences. Jastrow explained, "It is through these differences that the specific quality of the Hebrew civilisation as distinguished from the Babylonian-Assyrian is revealed. The resemblances are of value chiefly in pointing to a common ethnic stock to which both Babylonians and Assyrians and Hebrews belong—though it must always be borne in mind that Babylonians and Assyrians represent a mixture of non-Semitic elements with Semites, and that the Hebrews are far from being a pure, unmixed Semitic race."[75] Here again, the Semitic was a mixture, not a pure race, which was both continuous with and distinct from other religious formations in the ancient Near East. In his area of academic specialization, Jastrow attended to the dynamics of similarity and difference, while always locating his analysis within the broader field of the study of religion.

When war erupted in Europe in 1914, Morris Jastrow turned his attention to analyzing its causes, assessing the moral issues at stake, and proposing terms for a just peace. During the last years of his life, he published a series of books—*The War and the Bagdad Railway* (1914; reprinted 1917), *The War and the Coming Peace* (1918), *Zionism and the Future of Palestine* (1919), and *The Eastern Question and Its Solution* (1920)—in which he sought to put his expertise in the study of religion to work in the interest of peace in the Middle East and the world.

In his analysis of the causes of war, Jastrow focused on his field of academic expertise, the Near East. Since the earliest empires, he argued, the key to dominating the entire region was gaining control over the trade route from Asia Minor to the Persian Gulf. In the early twentieth century, with a concession from Turkey, Germany was building a railway from Istanbul to Baghdad that would secure regional domination in the Near East. Providing a review of the entire history of the region going back to ancient Babylonia and Assyria, Jastrow argued that the German empire had threatened to shut out all other European nations as effectively as the Muslim conquest of Constantinople, which was renamed Istanbul, in 1453. By securing this route, "Germany would be in a position to follow in the wake of ancient Persia, Greece, Rome and the Arabs, and to have Mesopotamia, Syria, Palestine and Egypt fall into her lap."[76] In this diagnosis, Jastrow employed historical analysis, reviewing a history of empires and insisting on the pivotal importance of the Near East. After all, he reminded his American readers, the Muslim conquest of Constantinople and the capture of the trade route from Istanbul to Baghdad had sent Columbus off to find an alternative route to the East. The primary cause of the war, Jastrow insisted, was the attempt by German imperialists to dominate the Near East as Muslim imperialists had in the past.

As a scholar of religion, Jastrow highlighted the religious significance of the Near East. In his publications on the war, he repeatedly observed, "It is to the East that we owe three-fourths of all the religion that there is in the world."[77] Having provided the world with most of its religion, the Near East was also a region of religious conflict. Palestine, in particular, would require special attention in any peace settlement after the war,

"because of the sacred character of the land, [which was] further compli-
cated by the unfriendly feelings between Christians, Mohammedans and
Jews."[78] Arguing against European mandates that would divide up the region in the interests of Great Britain and France, Jastrow proposed international commissions that could oversee local transitions to self-government.
With such a commission in Palestine, he argued, "the fear of the native
Mohammedans that Palestine would some day be converted into a Jewish
State with the approval of Western powers would disappear."[79] Guided by
the fundamental democratic principle "that a country belongs to all the
people who live in it," an international commission would facilitate the
emergence of a democratic Palestine.

As a Jew, aligned with Reformed Judaism, Morris Jastrow opposed political Zionism. In *Zionism and the Future of Palestine*, he distinguished three
forms of Zionism—religious, economic, and political.[80] In Orthodox Judaism, religious Zionism was a promise of redemption in Jerusalem, which
would restore the temple, with its "primitive rituals of sacrifice," with the
advent of the Messiah. This religious Zionism, which Jastrow found as a
scholar of religion to be entirely understandable but as a political analyst to
be "innocuous," was distinct from the economic Zionism that had enabled
Jews suffering persecution in Russia, Poland, Romania, and elsewhere to
migrate to Palestine.[81] Jastrow noted that by 1920 approximately ten thousand migrants, in as many as forty settlements, were engaged in agricul-
tural, industrial, and educational projects in Palestine. While understanding religious Zionism and supporting economic Zionism, Jastrow opposed
political Zionism, with its aspiration for a Jewish state in Palestine; he saw
political Zionism as a formula for disaster. Besides contradicting the democratic principle that a state should belong to all who live in it, political
Zionism, he warned, was "a veritable firebrand in its capability for mischief
and for keeping alive religious hostilities."[82] An international commission,
he hoped, would resolve religious hostility in a negotiated political resolution for a Palestinian state.

In his opposition to political Zionism, Jastrow was speaking as a political
analyst and a historian of religions. He argued in *The War and the Coming
Peace* that the war against Germany had been dedicated to "fighting an unholy alliance between power and national ambitions."[83] Political Zionism,
he worried, ran the risk of forming another unholy alliance of military
power and national expansion in the Near East. However, by aligning with
Great Britain against Germany, had the United States not merely supported
one imperial power, one unholy alliance, against another European impe-

rialism? According to Jastrow, "Imperialism as it actually appears in the world's history is not all of one color. Its shades vary from the dark hue of the Assyrian-Babylonian policy, to dominate the world by crushing the independent life of the nations subdued, to the brighter shade of the humane policy of the Persian kings led by Cyrus." Against this historical template, German imperialism was as dark as that of the Assyrians and Babylonians, while British imperialism was brighter, like the liberal policy of Cyrus that allowed Jews in exile to return to their homeland, in being willing "to preserve the national life of those who came under her domination."[84] Acknowledging that British imperialists had made some mistakes, such as Britain's loss of the North American colonies and its oppression of Ireland, Jastrow called attention to recent successes—the sound financial management of Egypt and the good faith shown in South Africa "by according to the Boers the fullest measure of political liberty."[85] In this benign imperialism, Great Britain had developed "a great Federalized Empire, allowing fullest scope for the development of the various states and divisions, and with no thought of subjugation of dependent peoples."[86] Like Max Müller, Morris Jastrow was a scholar of religion who admired the global ideals of the British Empire.

"Civilization," Morris Jastrow observed, "is essentially a struggle against nature."[87] In the history of religions, the great divide between natural, savage, or primitive religions and civilized religions was the basic principle of classification. But it also represented a historical struggle in which the civilized savagery of pan-Germanism, like pan-Islamism, could threaten the very existence of civilization. Reflecting on the moral meaning of the war, Jastrow explicitly drew this parallel between Germanic and Islamic empires, focusing on their fusion of spiritual aspirations with territorial expansion. "Therein lies Germany's fatal error, her sin against the moral law which presides over mankind's efforts to overcome the hostile forces of nature. The alliance between militarism and civilization is an unholy one. It forms a parallel to the combination of the Sword with the Koran as the means of propagating Islam, and which has similarly been the fatal moral error of that great religion."[88] If German imperialists were the new Muslims threatening Christian civilization, how did Morris Jastrow, as a Jew, as an American, and as a historian of religions, fit into this complex mix? Certainly his position was complicated. Educated in Germany and pursuing his research in conversation with German scholarship, translating his own research into German, Jastrow might have been sympathetic to Walter Benjamin's observation, "Every document of civilization is also a document of barbarism."[89] As a citizen of the United States, having endured discrimination as a Jew in America, he nevertheless advocated American civilization and what he understood to be American ideals of democracy as a "spirit" of America that was needed in the Near East.

As a historian of religions, however, Jastrow referred back to the ancient religion of Zoroastrianism, founded by the Persian prophet Zoroaster, or Zarathustra, as a benchmark for understanding the struggle between civilization and nature as an enduring conflict between good and evil. Jastrow revealed, "It has always seemed to me, in my studies of the religious evolution of mankind, that in one respect at least the religion founded by Zoroaster, in the sixth century before our era, penetrated more deeply in the struggle of man against nature than any other, by positing two forces in control of the world, a power of good, and a power of evil."[90] In this cosmic dualism of two powers, in which the power of good, Ahura Mazda, contended against the evil power of Ahriman, Jastrow found an analogy for the war in Europe, which was a battle, like all human history, between the higher principles of civilization and the forces of nature. However, he was also well aware of German nationalists and imperialists who read or misread Nietzsche's *Thus Spoke Zarathustra*, which had appropriated the Persian prophet to speak on behalf of an *übermensch*, a superman, beyond good and evil, as a warrant for merging military power with national ambition. As a historian of religions, Jastrow found a template in ancient Persia for understanding the war as a contest of good and evil, of civilization against nature, but he also had to argue, in detail, against imperialist German readings of Nietzsche.

In the empire of religion, Morris Jastrow exemplifies the complex situations of scholarship. Master of his trade, he was also subject to his locations. In his profile of the entire field of the study of religion in 1901, *The Study of Religion*, he invoked European founders—Friedrich Max Müller in Great Britain, C. P. Tiele in the Netherlands, and Albert Réville in France—while his own specialized research in ancient Babylonia and Assyria was conducted under the auspices of German scholars working in the Middle East. Although the study of religion had European origins, Jastrow was effectively bringing it home to America. Given the structuring of the entire field of study by the great divide between the primitive and the civilized, within the United States Jastrow looked to Native Americans and African Americans, to Indians in their "primitive haunts" and "the large portion of the negro population," as primary sources for students of religion to examine the primitive side of the great divide. Although this rendering of the primitive in the United States was definitely racial, we have seen that Jastrow argued against any notion of racial purity. Primitive races were an ethnographic fantasy; civilizations were the product of racial mixtures. The primitive and the civilized, therefore, could not be so easily reproduced as racial categories in the study of religion.

With civilization at risk in a world at war, Morris Jastrow devoted the last years of his life to arguing for peace, which had to include a just peace in the Middle East, in ways that drew upon what he had learned from a lifetime of studying religions. Although he had argued that the study of religion should produce a spirit of sympathy based on an informed understanding of religion and religions, his intervention in the politics of the Middle East highlighted the modern problem of religious antipathy. Assuming that Great Britain was a good empire—it had even bestowed liberty in South Africa—his comparison of pan-Germanism with Islam, which displayed the "spirit of fanaticism," rendered both imperialist Germans and Muslims as enemies of civilization in the Middle East.[91] At the same time, by opposing political Zionism, he sought to protect Muslims in the region from an imposition of a Jewish state, backed up by European powers, which would disable them from participating in any democratic resolution. In his struggle with war and peace, Morris Jastrow pursued a study of religion that was politically engaged but also politically situated within the empire of religion.

CIRCULATING KNOWLEDGE

Knowledge about religion and religions has circulated through imperial, colonial, and indigenous mediations, through information circuits and communication networks that extended all over the globe. Spinning out of the control of any imperial center, these circulations nevertheless bore traces of a genealogy, which could be reproduced by a seminary student in America such as Martin Luther King Jr., for thinking about the origin and development of religion. In reciting this genealogy of European theorists of religion, King participated, in a small way, in the circulation of knowledge about religion from European empires to the United States. At the same time, these circulations of knowledge carried a fundamental structure, the great divide between the primitive and the civilized, which in the United States relegated African Americans such as King to the primitive side of the divide, exemplifying savage Africa, as Morris Jastrow observed, "only two or three generations removed from the stage of primitive culture."[92] As the study of religion developed in America, it was structured by this great divide and the methodological division of labor between sciences for studying the primitive and sciences for studying the civilized.

With respect to this genealogy, the American anthropologist Clifford

Geertz (1926–2006) displayed an ambivalent affiliation. At a conference in 1963, Geertz presented a paper on religion, "Religion as a Cultural System," arguing that religion must be understood as a symbolic system of beliefs and practices that generates powerful moods and motivations—shaping desire, directing agency—and clothes these dispositions in an aura of factuality to make them seem uniquely real. In this paper, Geertz sought to advance a theory of religion, but he also claimed European ancestors, in an ironic mode, by noting that since the time of the ancestors in the study of religion—Tylor, Durkheim, Weber, Freud, and Malinowski—there had been "no theoretical advances of any importance."[93] Toward the end of his life, however, reviewing the genealogy of the anthropology of religion, Geertz recalled the ancestors, such as James Frazer, but was skeptical about any ancestral inheritance. Geertz asked, "Are we, after all, Frazer and I, in the same business? Is he in my genealogy, am I in his? Does an aim connect us? A history run through us? A field embrace us?"[94]

Talal Asad (b. 1933), who edited a collection of essays in the early 1970s that marked a first blast against the European colonialism of anthropology, entered the anthropology of religion by taking on Clifford Geertz's essay "Religion as a Cultural System."[95] In terms of genealogy, Asad argued that Geertz's definition inherited and perpetuated a legacy of Western, Christian, and especially Protestant theological constructions of religion as essentially a matter of belief, a private interiority that can be separated from the public sphere. Although Geertz contested this characterization of his essay, a distinctively Protestant rendering of religion, defining religion as separate from and independent of the power of the state, has been crucial in the history of Euro-American negotiations over the relation between religious meaning and political power. But Asad went further by suggesting that this notion of religion as an autonomous cultural system converged with the contemporary interests of secular liberals in confining religion and liberal Christians in defending religion within modern societies. Asad's critique, therefore, was not merely about the validity of Geertz's definition; it was also about the politics of defining religion as an autonomous cultural system.

As the structural divide between primitive and civilized religion circulated to the United States, Native Americans and African Americans became the proximate primitives, while the primary location of ancient civilized religion shifted from the British interest in India to the American interest in the languages, cultures, and religions of the ancient Near East. What happened to the Aryans? As we have seen, the term continued to be used for a civilization, whether based on linguistic or racial grounds, which could be invoked to mark the divide between primitive and civilized, as when the scholar of Native Americans John Wesley Powell insisted that civilization was carried by "one great stock of people—the Aryan race," or could be used to represent the ancient origin of civilization. At Yale University, the linguist William Dwight Whitney (1827-1894) specialized in Sanskrit and directed scathing attacks against the philology of Friedrich Max Müller, even contending that Max Müller lacked sufficient competence in Sanskrit to translate the *Rig Veda*.[96] As another contributing factor in the decline of Max Müller's academic reputation, this attack from across the Atlantic Ocean undermined his standing as an authority on Aryan religion. As we have seen, however, in the United States the concentration of academic expertise in the study of religion was not in Aryan but in Semitic religions. Although attention to civilized religion shifted from India to the Near East, the racialized construction of the origin and development of the religion of civilization was evident in James Henry Breasted's claim that it was the singular "achievement of this Great White Race."[97] Although Morris Jastrow argued against such a racialized construction by insisting that any civilization, even the American "Melting Pot," was racially mixed, in the study of religion in the United States the Fertile Crescent nevertheless displaced India as the origin of Euro-American civilization.

All of this points to the contingent character of knowledge about religion and religions. In imperial comparative religion, we can see a predilection for religions of empires. While ancient religions were the religions of Egyptian, Babylonian, Persian, Greek, and Roman empires, the major religions of the world were associated with imperial rule—Solomon's palace and temple, Constantine's *in hoc signo*, Muhammad's conquests, the Hindu world-ruler, the Buddhist emperor Ashoka, and the Confucian court of the emperor of China. Reclassified from an indigenous animism to a religion, Shinto gained admittance to the world of world religions in the wake of the expansion of the Japanese empire. In a kind of circular gesture of self-recognition, imperial comparative religion found that world religions were imperial religions.

However, as we have seen, circulations of knowledge about religion and religions were not always controlled by any imperial center. Looking back to South Africa, we can recall how world religions, Semitic and Aryan, were locally imagined. For African theorists, knowledge about the Semitic religions—Judaism, Christianity, and Islam—assumed a distinctive character. Judaism, as the religion of ancient Israel, was a religion of the past, a religious heritage that had been preserved in many features of indigenous African tradition. Under the influence of the Christian mission, African Christians learned that Africans, as lost tribes of Israel, were descendants of ancient Jews. But they also used this legacy to insert Africans into a universal history. Judaism, therefore, registered not only as a religion of the past but also as an African historical legacy. Christianity, as well, assumed a localized character. Generally defined by missionaries as a religion in opposition to indigenous traditions such as ancestral sacrifice, initiation into adulthood, and polygynous marriage, Christianity was engaged by Africans as an entry into a colonial modernity. As *ukukanya*, illumination, Christianity was the religion of literacy, industry, and market economy. Christianity, therefore, was not only a gospel of sin and salvation; it was also a religion of the colonial present. In the work of the historian and scholar of religion S. M. Molema, knowledge about Islam was cast in a specific African context. Against European representations of Islam as a militant religion, Molema found that Islam was a nonracial and egalitarian religion in contrast to the racist domination of Christian colonialism. In the hope of future liberation, Molema speculated that Islam might be the religion of the future for Africa.

Although knowledge about Judaism, Christianity, and Islam circulated through the British Empire, these South African renderings hint at local engagements with that circulation. In the empire of religion, knowledge about religion and religions was not merely consumed by the colonized but also produced and reproduced in its circulation through local situations. Turning from Semitic to Aryan in Max Müller's classification of religions, we recall how the colonial network linking South Africa and India resulted in the production of distinctive versions of Hinduism and Buddhism. Invoking the authority of Max Müller while serving as a lawyer in South Africa, Mohandas Gandhi defined Hinduism as *dharma*, a sense of duty like imperial duty, which was a religion shared by Aryans in the British Empire. Annie Besant, rejecting the authority of Max Müller when she was president of the Theosophical Society in India, defined Buddhism as a secret wisdom, shadowing the British Empire, which the Theosophist Patrick Bowen discovered among African secret brotherhoods in South Africa. If we were to reproduce these distinctive circulations as a survey of world religions, this South African history of Judaism, Christianity, Islam, Hinduism, and Buddhism would certainly seem strange and idiosyncratic, spinning out of control. But such a survey might call attention to the contingent character of the production, authentication, and circulation of knowledge about religion and religions in the empire of religion.

In the rise of the study of religion in the United States, knowledge about religion and religions also involved both imperial circulations and local engagements. For Morris Jastrow, ancient religions were imperial religions, in different shades, from the dark imperial religion of ancient Babylonia to the bright imperial religion of ancient Persia, with every shade in between. Certainly the darkness or light of empires, by this accounting, was measured by their persecution or toleration of the people of ancient Israel. Nevertheless, this ancient history provided a background for Jastrow to analyze the situation of Judaism, Christianity, and Islam in the contemporary Middle East. According to Jastrow, Judaism, as Orthodox, was understandable but "innocuous" religion, while Reformed Judaism was rational, modern religion, a religion among religions, in modern states. In its efforts to impose a Jewish state on the Middle East backed up by Western powers, however, political Zionism was dangerous. Christianity, which might have originated in the ancient motif of the dying and rising god, could also be rational and modern, but in the form of Christian Zionism, advocating a Jewish state in the Middle East "as a step leading not to the perpetuation but to the disappearance of the Jews," Christianity was dangerous.[98] Turning to Islam, Jastrow found this religion understandable as an adaptation of Judaism and Christianity, and he argued for the protection of Muslims in the Middle East from the imposition of any Jewish state. However, he also found Islam, displaying a "spirit of fanaticism," to be dangerous, but perhaps not as dangerous as pan-Germanism.

Throughout all of these renderings, knowledge about Judaism, Christianity, and Islam merged imperial circulations with specific, contingent situations, fraught with danger. In his analysis of a world at war, by turning to Zoroastrianism, which had been adopted by the bright Persian empire as its imperial religion, Jastrow amplified the danger as a cosmic struggle between good and evil, between civilization and the forces of nature. In this opposition, we might see traces of the great divide between the civilized and the primitive, since the primitive was associated with the savage, the wild, and the natural. However, by invoking the religion of Zarathustra, which had been classified by Max Müller as an Aryan religion, Jastrow was also strategically intervening in the Aryan ideology of racial supremacy emerging in Germany. Identifying German imperialism with the forces of nature, Jastrow employed the great divide between the civilized and the primitive in the study of religion to put Germans in the "savage slot" in the struggle for civilization. As we have seen in relation to South Africa, thinking about religion can be affected by a range of situated interests. In the United States, an academic study of religion emerged within a similar confluence of imperial forces, colonial interventions, local initiatives, and indigenous resources.

Imperial comparative religion merged knowledge and power, not in any simple social physics of cause and effect, as if the study of religion could cause imperial expansion, but in the ways in which knowledge about religion and religions circulated through the networks of empire. As we have seen, that knowledge could be used to support empire, but it also accompanied empire in its circulations through colonized peripheries, such as South Africa, in ways that simultaneously enabled and destabilized the production of knowledge about religion and religions in imperial comparative religion. Alternative knowledge, shaped by local factors, was also produced. In trying to understand the history of the study of religion, all of these forces and factors must be taken into consideration in discerning the ways in which knowledge about religion and religions was produced, authenticated, and circulated.

As we review the history of the study of religion, it is necessary but not sufficient to assert that the general idea of *religion* is a constructed category and that all kinds of ideas about specific *religions* have been invented. Although the empire of religion was certainly full of ideas, thinking was materially grounded. Therefore, we have to ask: Under what material conditions were these crucial terms in secular modernity produced, authenticated, and circulated? Although I have explored these material questions with particular attention to imperial exchanges with South Africa, many other stories can be told, stories about how knowledge was produced about religion and religions in many different places, all over the world, including within the United States.

In the end, I remain convinced that we cannot simply abandon the terms *religion* and *religions* because we are stuck with them as a result of a colonial, imperial, and now global legacy. What do we do with them? In tracking the history of the study of religion, I have used them as objects of analysis, focusing on their production, authentication, and circulation. In any critical history of the study of religion, they must be the objects of analysis. For the study of religion, however, they must be not objects but occasions for analysis, providing openings in a field of possibilities for exploring powerful classifications and orientations, cognitive capacities and constraints, and cultural repertoires of myth and fiction, ritual and magic, humanity and divinity. In reviewing the history of the study of religion, I have highlighted these enduring opportunities for analysis that inhere in such key terms for ongoing efforts of description, interpretation, explanation, and argumentation in the study of religion.

By acknowledging that the genealogy of the study of religion includes Friedrich Max Müller's classifications, E. B. Tylor's cognitive studies, Andrew Lang's cultural studies, and James Frazer's synthesis of available ethnographic data on ritual and magic, we are not necessarily subscribing to any of their theories, methods, or politics. How do we reject yet still retain these ancestors in the study of religion? We can depart from them, in the sense of leaving them behind, but we can also take them as significant points of departure for critical analysis in the study of religion.

However, if we are going to retain these imperial ancestors, we will need to bring them into the kind of history developed in this book, situating them in the imperial, colonial, and indigenous mediations in which knowledge about religion and religions has been generated. By locating these ancestors in such a material history, we can engage the challenge of combining critical reflection on our past, which sometimes seems to make knowing anything almost impossible, with creative possibilities for working through enduring categories in the study of religion to produce new knowledge.

Notes

PREFACE

1. Louis Henry Jordan, *Comparative Religion: Its Genesis and Growth* (Edinburgh: T & T Clark, 1905), 580.

2. J. F. van Oordt, *The Origin of the Bantu: A Preliminary Study* (Cape Town: Cape Times and Government Printers, 1907), 5.

3. David Chidester, *Savage Systems: Colonialism and Comparative Religion in Southern Africa* (Charlottesville: University Press of Virginia, 1996).

4. Eric J. Sharpe, *Comparative Religion: A History*, 2nd ed. (La Salle, IL: Open Court, 1986); J. Samuel Preus, *Explaining Religion: Criticism and Theory from Bodin to Freud* (New Haven, CT: Yale University Press, 1987); Walter H. Capps, *Religious Studies: The Making of a Discipline* (Minneapolis: Fortress Press, 1995).

5. Keith Irvine, foreword to *Life of a South African Tribe*, by Henri-Alexandre Junod, 2 vols. (New York: University Books, 1962), 1:viii, ix, cited by Jonathan Zittell Smith, "The Glory, Jest, and Riddle: James George Frazer and *The Golden Bough*" (PhD diss., Yale University, 1969), 139.

6. Jonathan Z. Smith, *"Adde Parvum Parvo Magnus Acervus Erit,"* in *Map Is Not Territory: Studies in the History of Religions*, by Smith (Chicago: University of Chicago Press, 1978), 240–64; Smith, "Classification," in *Guide to the Study of Religion*, ed. Willi Braun and Russell T. McCutcheon (London: Cassell, 2000), 35–56; Smith, "In Search of Place," in *To Take Place: Toward Theory in Ritual*, by Smith (Chicago: University of Chicago Press, 1987), 1–23; Smith, "Sacred Persistence: Toward a Redescription of Canon," in *Imagining Religion: From Babylon to Jonestown*, by Smith (Chicago: University of Chicago Press, 1982), 36–52; Smith, "The Unknown God: Myth in History," in Smith, *Imagining Religion*, 66–89; Smith, "The Bare Facts of Ritual," in Smith, *Imagining Religion*, 53–65.

CHAPTER ONE

The epigraph is from Eric J. Sharpe, "The Study of Religion in Historical Perspective," in *The Routledge Companion to the Study of Religion*, ed. John Hinnells (London: Routledge, 2005), 21.

1. F. Max Müller, *Introduction to the Science of Religion: Four Lectures Delivered at the Royal Institution with Two Essays on False Analogies, and the Philosophy of Mythology* (London: Longmans, Green, 1873), 68. On Friedrich Max Müller as founder of the study of religion, see Louis Henry Jordan, *Comparative Religion: Its Genesis and Growth* (Edinburgh: T & T Clark, 1905), 135–36;

Morris Jastrow Jr., *The Study of Religion* (London: Walter Scott, 1901), 44–45; Joachim Wach, *The Comparative Study of Religions*, ed. Joseph M. Kitagawa (New York: Columbia University Press, 1958), 3; Mircea Eliade, *The Sacred and the Profane: The Nature of Religion*, trans. Willard R. Trask (New York: Harcourt, Brace & World, 1959), 216; Jacques Waardenburg, *Classical Approaches to the Study of Religion: Aims, Methods, and Theories of Research*, 2 vols. (The Hague: Mouton, 1973–74), 1:13–14; Eric J. Sharpe, *Comparative Religion: A History*, 2nd ed. (LaSalle, IL: Open Court, 1986), 35. I have taken "Max Müller" as his surname because he did, his wife assumed that surname on their marriage, and he was entered as such ("Max Müller, Friedrich") in Arthur Anthony Macdonell, *Dictionary of National Biography Supplement*, 3 vols., ed. Sidney Lee (London: Elder Smith, 1901), 3:151–57.

2. Mountstuart Elphinstone, *The History of India*, 2 vols., 2nd ed. (London: John Murray, 1843), 2:286–87. See Paul Stevens and Rahul Sapra, "Akbar's Dream: Moghul Toleration and English/British Orientalism," *Modern Philology* 104, no. 3 (2007): 379–411.

3. Max Müller, *Introduction to the Science of Religion*, 23.

4. Ibid., 25.

5. Duncan Bell, *The Idea of Greater Britain: Empire and the Future of World Order, 1860–1900* (Princeton, NJ: Princeton University Press, 2007). The classic statements on Greater Britain are Charles Dilke, *Greater Britain: A Record of Travel in the English-Speaking Countries during 1866 and 1867* (London: Macmillan, 1868); J. R. Seeley, *The Expansion of England: Two Courses of Lectures* (London: Macmillan, 1883); and J. A. Froude, *Oceania, or England and Her Colonies* (London: Longmans, Green, 1886).

6. Edward W. Said, *Culture and Imperialism* (London: Chatto & Windus, 1993), 9.

7. Robert A. Stafford, *Scientist of Empire: Sir Roderick Murchison, Scientific Exploration, and Victorian Imperialism* (Cambridge: Cambridge University Press, 1989), 223. See James A. Secord, "King of Siluria: Roderick Murchison and the British Imperial Theme in Nineteenth-Century British Geology," *Victorian Studies* 25, no. 4 (1982): 413–42; Janet Browne, "A Science of Empire: British Biogeography before Darwin," *Revue de l'histoire des sciences* 45, no. 4 (1992): 453–75; Richard Drayton, *Nature's Government: Science, Imperial Britain, and the "Improvement" of the World* (New Haven, CT: Yale University Press, 2000).

8. Philip Dodd, "Englishness and the National Culture," in *Englishness: Politics and Culture 1880–1920*, ed. Robert Colls and Philip Dodd (London: Croom Helm, 1986), 2. For examples of the analysis of imperialism and human sciences, see Mark Bradley, ed., *Classics and Imperialism in the British Empire* (Oxford: Oxford University Press, 2010); Richard Hingley, *Roman Officers and English Gentlemen: The Imperial Origins of Roman Archaeology* (London: Routledge, 2000); Helen Tilley and Robert J. Gordon, eds., *Ordering Africa: Anthropology, European Imperialism, and the Politics of Knowledge* (Manchester: Manchester University Press, 2007).

9. Daniel Pick, *Faces of Degeneration: A European Disorder, c. 1848–c. 1918* (Cambridge: Cambridge University Press, 1989), 237.

10. Sharpe, "Study of Religion in Historical Perspective," 21.

11. David Fieldhouse, "Can Humpty-Dumpty Be Put Together Again? Imperial History in the 1980s," *Journal of Imperial and Commonwealth History* 12, no. 2 (1984): 9–23.

12. See Erwin H. Ackerknecht, "On the Comparative Method in Anthropology," in *Method and Perspective in Anthropology*, ed. Robert F. Spencer (Minneapolis: University of Minnesota Press, 1954), 117–25; Kenneth E. Bock, "The Comparative Method of Anthropology," *Comparative Studies in Society and History* 8, no. 3 (1966): 269–80; Alan Dundes, "The Anthropologist and the Comparative Method in Folklore," *Journal of Folklore Research* 23 (1986): 125–46; Fred Eggan, "Some Reflections on Comparative Method in Anthropology," in *Context and Meaning in Cultural Anthropology*, ed. Melford E. Spiro (New York: Free Press, 1965), 357–72; E. A. Hammel, "The Comparative Method in Anthropological Perspective," *Comparative Studies in Society and History* 22, no. 2 (1980): 145–55; Henry M. Hoenigswald, "On the History of the Comparative Method," *Anthropological Linguistics* 5, no. 1 (1963): 1–11.

13. Max Müller, *Introduction to the Science of Religion*, 25.

14. E. B. Tylor, *Primitive Culture*, 2 vols. (London: John Murray, 1871), 1:19.

15. For examples of imperial theorists—F. Max Müller, E. B. Tylor, J. F. McLennan, John Lubbock, Herbert Spencer, and James Frazer—cautioning that modern savages cannot be regarded as identical to primitive humans, see Valeer Neckebrouck, *Antropologie van de godsdienst: De andere zijde* (Louvain, Belgium: Leuven University Press, 2008), 117.

16. See Theodore Koditschek, *Liberalism, Imperialism, and the Historical Imagination: Nineteenth-Century Visions of Greater Britain* (Cambridge: Cambridge University Press, 2011).

17. Jonathan Zittell Smith, "The Glory, Jest, and Riddle: James George Frazer and *The Golden Bough*" (PhD diss., Yale University, 1969), 140-41.

18. James Frazer, *The Golden Bough: A Study in Comparative Religion*, 2 vols. (London: Macmillan, 1890), 1:218-19.

19. James Frazer, *The Golden Bough: A Study in Magic and Religion*, 12 vols., 3rd ed. (London: Macmillan, 1911-15), 4:36-37. See Nathaniel Isaacs, *Travels and Adventures in Eastern Africa*, 2 vols., ed. Louis Herman (1836; reprint, Cape Town: Van Riebeeck Society, 1936), 1:242.

20. F. Max Müller, *Contributions to the Science of Mythology*, 2 vols. (London: Longmans, Green, 1897), 1:183.

21. Hannah Arendt, *The Origins of Totalitarianism*, 2nd ed. (1951; New York: World, 1958), 151.

22. Bernard Porter, *The Absent-Minded Imperialists: Empire, Society, and Culture in Britain* (Oxford: Oxford University Press, 2004), 164.

23. Dorothy O. Helly and Helen Callaway, "Constructing South Africa in the British Press, 1890-92: The *Pall Mall Gazette*, the *Daily Graphic*, and *The Times*," in *Imperial Co-Histories: National Identities and the British and Colonial Press*, ed. Julie F. Codell (Madison, NJ: Fairleigh Dickinson University Press, 2003), 125.

24. William Kenneth, "The Church in Maritzburg: Being a Brief Report of the Work of the Church in the Diocese of Maritzburg during the year 1871," *Mission Life* 3 (1872): 421.

25. Thomas B. Jenkinson, *Amazulu: The Zulus, Their Past, History, Manners, Customs, and Language* (London: Allen, 1882), 55.

26. Hilary M. Carey, *God's Empire: Religion and Colonialism in the British World, c. 1801-1908* (Cambridge: Cambridge University Press, 2011), 27. See Hilary M. Carey, ed., *Empires of Religion* (Basingstoke: Palgrave Macmillan, 2008).

27. W. L. Distant, "On the Term 'Religion' as Used in Anthropology," *Journal of the Anthropological Institute* 6 (1877): 68. See Timothy Fitzgerald, *The Ideology of Religious Studies* (Oxford: Oxford University Press, 2000); Régis Debray, *Les communions humaines: Pour en finir avec "la religion"* (Paris: Fayard, 2005); Daniel Dubuisson, *The Western Construction of Religion: Myths, Knowledge, and Ideology*, trans. William Sayers (Baltimore: Johns Hopkins University Press, 2003).

28. C. P. Tiele, *Elements of the Science of Religion*, 2 vols. (Edinburgh: William Blackwood, 1897), 2:233, 1:4. See Arie L. Molendijk, "Tiele on Religion," *Numen* 46, no. 3 (1999): 237-68; Molendijk, "The Heritage of Cornelis Petrus Tiele (1830-1902)," *Nederlands Archief voor Kerkgeschiedenis* 80, no. 1 (2000): 78-114; Molendijk, "Religious Development: C. P. Tiele's Paradigm of Science of Religion," *Numen* 51, no. 3 (2004): 321-51; Molendijk, *The Emergence of the Science of Religion in the Netherlands* (Leiden: Brill, 2005).

29. Cornelius Donovan, "Abstract: On the Brain in the Study of Ethnology," *Journal of the Ethnological Society of London* 2, no. 4 (1870): 369; Donovan, *A Handbook of Phrenology* (London: Longmans, 1870).

30. Pascal Boyer, *Religion Explained: The Evolutionary Origins of Religious Thought* (New York: Basic Books, 2001); Harvey Whitehouse, *Modes of Religiosity: A Cognitive Theory of Religious Transmission* (Walnut Creek, CA: AltaMira Press, 2004). See Jeffrey Schloss and Michael Murray, eds., *The Believing Primate: Scientific, Philosophical, and Theological Reflections on the Origin of Religion* (Oxford: Oxford University Press, 2009).

31. Tylor, *Primitive Culture*, 2:410.

32. Daniel C. Dennett, *Breaking the Spell: Religion as a Natural Phenomenon* (New York: Viking, 2006), 327-28.

33. David N. Livingstone, "Evolution and Religion," in *Evolution: The First Four Billion Years*, ed. Michael Ruse and Joseph Travis (Cambridge, MA: Harvard University Press, 2009), 351.

34. Richard Dawkins, *The God Delusion* (London: Transworld, 2006), 13.

35. F. Max Müller, *Selected Essays on Language, Mythology, and Religion*, 2 vols. (London: Longmans, Green, 1881), 1:26.

36. Sharpe, *Comparative Religion*, 47-71.

37. Stephen Jay Gould, *Rock of Ages: Science and Religion in the Fullness of Life* (New York: Ballantine, 1999), 5.

38. Michael Ruse, *Darwinism and Its Discontents* (Cambridge: Cambridge University Press, 2006), 207.

39. W. J. T. Mitchell, *What Do Pictures Want? The Lives and Loves of Images* (Chicago: University of Chicago Press, 2005), 163. See Robert Alun Jones, *The Secret of the Totem: Religion and Society from McLennan to Freud* (New York: Columbia University Press, 2005).

40. Emile Durkheim, *The Elementary Forms of the Religious Life*, trans. Joseph Ward Swain (1912; New York: Free Press, 1965), 62.

41. James H. Leuba, *A Psychological Study of Religion: Its Origin, Function, and Future* (New York: Macmillan, 1912); Winston L. King, *Introduction to Religion* (New York: Harper and Row, 1954), 63; Jonathan Z. Smith, *Relating Religion: Essays in the Study of Religion* (Chicago: University of Chicago Press, 2004), 193.

42. Waardenburg, *Classical Approaches*; Sharpe, *Comparative Religion*; J. Samuel Preus, *Explaining Religion: Criticism and Theory from Bodin to Freud* (New Haven, CT: Yale University Press, 1987); Walter H. Capps, *Religious Studies: The Making of a Discipline* (Minneapolis: Fortress Press, 1995). See also Arie L. Molendijk and Peter Pels, eds., *Religion in the Making: The Emergence of the Sciences of Religion* (Leiden: Brill, 1998); Marjorie Wheeler-Barclay, *The Science of Religion in Britain, 1860-1915* (Charlottesville: University of Virginia Press, 2010).

43. Peter Harrison, *"Religion" and the Religions in the English Enlightenment* (Cambridge: Cambridge University Press, 1990); Guy G. Stroumsa, *A New Science: The Discovery of Religion in the Age of Reason* (Cambridge, MA: Harvard University Press, 2010); Brent Nongbri, *Before Religion: A History of a Modern Concept* (New Haven, CT: Yale University Press, 2013).

44. Hans G. Kippenberg, *Discovering Religious History in the Modern Age*, trans. Barbara Harshav (1997; Princeton, NJ: Princeton University Press, 2002).

45. Talal Asad, *Genealogies of Religion: Discipline and Reasons of Power in Christianity and Islam* (Baltimore: Johns Hopkins University Press, 1993); Asad, *Formations of the Secular: Christianity, Islam, Modernity* (Stanford, CA: Stanford University Press, 2003).

46. John P. Burris, *Exhibiting Religion: Colonialism and Spectacle at International Expositions, 1851-1893* (Charlottesville: University Press of Virginia, 2001).

47. Randall Styers, *Making Magic: Religion, Magic, and Science in the Modern World* (Oxford: Oxford University Press, 2004).

48. Tomoko Masuzawa, *The Invention of World Religions: Or, How European Universalism Was Preserved in the Language of Pluralism* (Chicago: University of Chicago Press, 2005).

49. P. J. Marshall, ed., *The British Discovery of Hinduism in the Eighteenth Century* (Cambridge: Cambridge University Press, 1970); Philip C. Almond, *The British Discovery of Buddhism* (Cambridge: Cambridge University Press, 1988). Recent works have uncovered the complex history and dedicated scholarship in Western discoveries of Asian religions. See Urs App, *The Birth of Orientalism* (Philadelphia: University of Pennsylvania Press, 2010); Suzanne L. Marchand, *German Orientalism in the Age of Empire: Religion, Race, and Scholarship* (Cambridge: Cambridge University Press, 2009).

50. Almond, *British Discovery of Buddhism*, 4.

51. Robert E. Frykenberg, "Constructions of Hinduism at the Nexus of History and Religion," *Journal of Interdisciplinary History* 23, no. 3 (1993): 523-50; Gauri Viswanathan, "Colonialism and the Construction of Hinduism," in *The Blackwell Companion to Hinduism*, ed. Gavin Flood (Malden, MA: Blackwell, 2003), 23-44; Esther Bloch, Marianne Keppens, and Rajaram Hedge, eds., *Rethinking Religion in India: The Colonial Construction of Hinduism* (London: Routledge, 2010).

52. Donald S. Lopez Jr., ed., *Curators of the Buddha: The Study of Buddhism under Colonialism* (Chicago: University of Chicago Press, 1995).

53. Richard King, *Orientalism and Religion: Post-Colonial Theory, India, and "the Mystic East"* (London: Routledge, 1999); Eric Reinders, *Borrowed Gods and Foreign Bodies: Christian Missionaries Imagine Chinese Religion* (Berkeley: University of California Press, 2004); T. H. Barrett, "Chinese Religion in English Guise: The History of an Illusion," *Modern Asian Studies* 39, no. 3 (2005): 509-33.

54. Donald S. Lopez Jr., introduction to Lopez, *Curators of the Buddha*, 12. See Hugh B. Urban, *Tantra: Sex, Secrecy, Politics, and Power in the Study of Religion* (Berkeley: University of California Press, 2003).

55. Brian K. Pennington, *Was Hinduism Invented? Britons, Indians, and the Colonial Construction of Religion* (Oxford: Oxford University Press, 2005); Phillip Wagoner, "Precolonial Intellectuals and the Production of Colonial Knowledge," *Comparative Studies in Society and History* 45, no. 4 (2003): 783-814.

56. Robert Ford Campany, "On the Very Idea of Religions (in the Modern West and in Early Medieval China)," *History of Religions* 42, no. 4 (2003): 287-319; Thomas David DuBois, ed., *Casting Faiths: Imperialism and the Transformation of Religion in East and Southeast Asia* (London: Palgrave Macmillan, 2009); Norman J. Girardot, *The Victorian Translation of China: James Legge's Oriental Pilgrimage* (Berkeley: University of California Press, 2002).

57. Rosalind Shaw, "The Invention of 'African Traditional Religion,'" *Religion* 20, no. 4 (1990): 339-53; Robin Derricourt, *Inventing Africa: History, Archaeology, and Ideas* (London: Pluto Press, 2011).

58. Paul S. Landau, *Popular Politics in the History of South Africa, 1400-1948* (Cambridge: Cambridge University Press, 2010), 235. See Landau, "Language," in *Missions and Empire*, ed. Norman Etherington (Oxford: Oxford University Press, 2005), 206-11. Major works in African studies that show how knowledge about religion was mediated through intercultural relations include Jean Comaroff and John L. Comaroff, *Of Revelation and Revolution*, vol. 1, *Christianity, Colonialism, and Consciousness in South Africa* (Chicago: University of Chicago Press, 1991); Johannes Fabian, *Out of Our Minds: Reason and Madness in the Exploration of Central Africa* (Berkeley: University of California Press, 2000); Birgit Meyer, *Translating the Devil: Religion and Modernity among the Ewe in Ghana* (Edinburgh: Edinburgh University Press, 1999); and J. D. Y. Peel, *Religious Encounter and the Making of the Yoruba* (Bloomington: Indiana University Press, 2000).

59. James L. Cox, *From Primitive to Indigenous: The Academic Study of Indigenous Religions* (Aldershot: Ashgate, 2007). See Afe Adogame, Ezra Chitando, and Bolaji Bateye, eds., *African Traditions in the Study of Religion in Africa: Emerging Trends, Indigenous Spirituality, and the Interface with other World Religions* (Burlington, VT: Ashgate, 2012); Ezra Chitando, "Sub-Saharan Africa," in *Religious Studies: A Global View*, ed. Gregory D. Alles (London: Routledge, 2007), 102-25; Frieder Ludwig and Afe Adogame, eds., *European Traditions in the Study of Religion in Africa* (Wiesbaden: Harrassowitz, 2004); T. O. Ranger, "African Traditional Religion," in *The World's Religions*, ed. Peter Clarke and Stewart Sutherland (London: Routledge, 2002), 106-14.

60. Stroumsa, *New Science*, 161.

61. Charles de Brosses, *Du culte des dieux fétiches, ou parallèle de l'ancienne religion de l'Egypte avec la religion actuelle de Nigritie* (Paris, 1760).

62. G. W. F. Hegel, *Lectures on the Philosophy of History*, trans. J. Sibree (London: Henry G. Bohn, 1856), 103.

63. Henry Rowley, *The Religion of the Africans* (London: W. Wells Gardner, 1877), 43.

64. "General Act of the Conference of Berlin (1885)," in *Colonial Rule in Africa: Readings from Primary Sources*, ed. Bruce Fetter (Madison: University of Wisconsin Press, 1979), 37.

65. Fred B. Fynney, *Zululand and the Zulus* (Maritzburg: Horne Brothers, 1880), 1. See S. J. R. Martin, "British Images of the Zulu, c. 1820-1879" (PhD diss., University of Cambridge, 1982).

66. J. A. Froude, *Lord Beaconsfield* (London: Sampson, Low, Marston, Searle & Rivington, 1890), 213.

67. Bernth Lindfors, "Charles Dickens and the Zulus," in *Africans on Stage: Studies in Ethnological Show Business*, ed. Bernth Lindfors (Bloomington: Indiana University Press, 1999), 62-80; Shane Peacock, "Africa Meets the Great Farini," in Lindfors, *Africans on Stage*, 81-106; Nichola Johnson, "Briton, Boer, and Black in Savage South Africa," in *Museums and the Appropriation of Culture*, ed. Susan Pearce (London: Athlone Press, 1994), 174-97.

68. Cited in Peacock, "Africa Meets the Great Farini," 86.

69. Veit Erlmann, "'Africa Civilised, Africa Uncivilised': Local Culture, World System, and South African Music," *Journal of Southern African Studies* 20, no. 2 (1994): 165-79; Erlmann, *Music, Modernity, and the Global Imagination: South Africa and the West* (Oxford: Oxford University Press, 1999).

70. J. G. Wood, *The Uncivilized Races; or, Natural History of Man, Being a Complete Account of the Manners and Customs, and the Physical, Social and Religious Condition and Characteristics of the Uncivilized Races of Men throughout the Entire World*, 2 vols. (London: George Routledge, 1868-70).

71. Henry Callaway, *The Religious System of the Amazulu*, ed. W. Wanger (Mariannhill, South Africa: Mission Press, 1913).

72. For a succinct summary, see John Wright, "Reflections on the Politics of Being 'Zulu,'" in *Zulu Identities: Being Zulu, Past and Present*, ed. Benedict Carton, John Laband, and Jabulani Sithole (Scottsville, South Africa: University of KwaZulu-Natal Press, 2008), 35-43.

73. Norman Etherington, "Christianity and African Society in Nineteenth-Century Natal," in *Natal and Zululand from Earliest Times to 1910: A New History*, ed. Andrew Duminy and Bill Guest (Pietermaritzburg: University of Natal Press, 1989), 275.

74. Patrick Harries, "Imagery, Symbolism, and Tradition in a South African Bantustan: Mangosuthu Buthelezi, Inkatha, and Zulu History," *History and Theory* 32, no. 4 (1993): 105-12.

75. Isaacs, *Travels and Adventures*, 2:248-49.

CHAPTER TWO

The epigraph is from A. C. Haddon, "Anthropology at the South African Meeting of the British Association for the Advancement of Science, 1905," *Science* 23, no. 587 (1906): 495.

1. J. Stark Browne, *Through South Africa with the British Association for the Advancement of Science* (London: James Speirs, 1906), 1. See Edna Bradlow, "The British Association's South African Meeting, 1905: 'The Flight to the Colonies' and Some Post Anglo-Boer War Problems," *South African Historical Journal* 46, no. 1 (2002): 42-62; Saul Dubow, "A Commonwealth of Science: The British Association in South Africa, 1905 and 1929," in *Science and Society in Southern Africa*, ed. Saul Dubow (Manchester: Manchester University Press, 2000), 66-99; O. J. R. Howarth, *The British Association for the Advancement of Science: A Retrospect, 1831-1921* (London: British Association, 1922), 127-30; Alan G. Morris, "The British Association Meeting of 1905 and the Rise of Physical Anthropology in South Africa." *South African Journal of Science* 98, nos. 7-8 (2002): 336-40.

2. Browne, *Through South Africa*, 13.

3. Ibid., 12. See Colin Holmes and A. H. Ion, "Bushido and the Samurai Image in British Public Opinion, 1894-1914," *Modern Asian Studies* 14, no. 2 (1980): 309-29; Inazo Nitobe, *Bushido, the Soul of Japan* (1899; New York: G. P. Putnam's, 1905).

4. Browne, *Through South Africa*, 12.

5. Ibid., 11–13.

6. Peter Harrison, *"Religion" and the Religions in the English Enlightenment* (Cambridge: Cambridge University Press, 1990), 39; David A. Pailin, *Attitudes to Other Religions: Comparative Religion in Seventeenth- and Eighteenth-Century Britain* (Manchester: Manchester University Press, 1984); Terry Thomas, "The Impact of Other Religions," in *Religion in Victorian Britain*, 4 vols., ed. Gerald Parsons (Manchester: Manchester University Press, 1995), 3:291–98.

7. Marian S. Benham, *Henry Callaway M.D., D.D., First Bishop of Kaffraria: His Life-History and Work: A Memoir* (London: Macmillan, 1896), 222. See Gwilym Beckerlegge, "Professor Friedrich Max Müller and the Missionary Cause," in *Religion in Victorian Britain*, vol. 5, *Culture and Empire*, ed. John Wolfe (Manchester: Manchester University Press, 1997), 177–220.

8. Henry Callaway, *A Fragment on Comparative Religion* (Natal: Callaway, 1874), 7.

9. Peter Kolb, *The Present State of the Cape of Good-Hope; or, A Particular Account of the Several Nations of the Hottentots: Their Religion, Government, Laws, Customs, Ceremonies, and Opinions: Their Art of War, Professions, Language, Genesis, etc.* Vol. 1, trans. Guido Medley (1719; London: W. Innys, 1731), 316.

10. Ernest Renan, "What Is a Nation?" in *Nation and Narration*, ed. Homi Bhabha (London: Routledge, 1990), 19.

11. Max Weber, "Politics as a Vocation," in *From Max Weber: Essays in Sociology*, ed. and trans. H. H. Gerth and C. Wright Mills (London: Routledge & Kegan Paul, 1948), 78.

12. See Rotem Kowner, "Becoming an Honorary Civilized Nation: Remaking Japan's Military Image during the Russo-Japanese War, 1904–1905," *Historian* 64, no. 1 (2001): 19–38.

13. Pernille Rudlin, *The History of Mitsubishi Corporation in London: 1915 to Present Day* (London: Routledge, 2000), 13.

14. Edouard Chavannes, "Collection of Chinese Bronze Antiques," *T'oung Pao*, 2nd ser., 12, no. 3 (1911): 435; Joseph Kitagawa, *On Understanding Japanese Religion* (Princeton, NJ: Princeton University Press, 1987), 304.

15. Takayoshi Matsuo, "The Japanese Protestants in Korea, Part One: The Missionary Activity of the Japan Congregational Church in Korea," trans. S. Takiguchi, *Modern Asian Studies* 13, no. 3 (1979): 415–16.

16. Jun'ichi Isomae, "The Discursive Position of Religious Studies in Japan: Masaharu Anesaki and the Origins of Religious Studies," *Method and Theory in the Study of Religion* 14, no. 1 (2002): 21–46; Michael Pye, "Modern Japan and the Science of Religions," *Method and Theory in the Study of Religion* 15, no. 1 (2003): 1–27. See Jason Ananda Josephson, *The Invention of Religion in Japan* (Chicago: University of Chicago Press, 2012).

17. Browne, *Through South Africa*, 11–13; David Randall-MacIver, "The Rhodesia Ruins: Their Probable Origin and Significance," *Geographical Journal* 27, no. 4 (1906): 325–36.

18. Felix von Luschan, "The Racial Affinities of the Hottentots," in *Addresses and Papers Read at the Joint Meeting of the British and South African Associations for the Advancement of Science Held in South Africa, 1905*, 4 vols. (Johannesburg: South African Association for the Advancement of Science, 1906), 3:111–18; republished as Felix von Luschan, *The Racial Affinities of the Hottentots* (London: Spottiswoode for the British and South African Associations, 1907).

19. Andrew Zimmermann, "Adventures in the Skin Trade: Physical Anthropology and the Colonial Encounter," in *Worldly Provincialism: German Anthropology in the Age of Empire*, ed. H. Glenn Penny and Matti Bunzl (Ann Arbor: University of Michigan Press, 2002), 163.

20. Ibid., 164.

21. Browne, *Through South Africa*, 237; see Felix von Luschan, "Bericht über eine Reise in Süd-Afrika [mit ein Diskussion über den Vortrag des Hrn v. Luschan]," *Zeitschrift für Ethnologie* 38, no. 6 (1906): 863–95, 904–25.

22. John M. Bridgman, *Revolt of the Hereros* (Berkeley: University of California Press, 1981); Tilman Dedering, "'A Certain Rigorous Treatment of All Parts of the Nation': The Annihilation of the Herero in German South West Africa, 1904," in *The Massacre in History*, ed. Mark Levine

and Penny Roberts (Oxford: Oxford University Press, 1999), 205-22; Horst Drechsler, *Let Us Die Fighting: The Struggle of the Herero and Nama against German Imperialism, 1884-1915*, trans. Bernd Zöllner (London: Zed Press, 1980).

23. Andrew Zimmermann, *Anthropology and Antihumanism in Imperial Germany* (Chicago: University of Chicago Press, 2001), 245.

24. Ibid., 168.

25. Simon J. Harrison, "Skulls and Scientific Collecting in the Victorian Military: Keeping the Enemy Dead in British Frontier Warfare," *Comparative Studies in Society and History* 50, no. 1 (2008): 285-303; Martin Legassick and Ciraj Rassool, *Skeletons in the Cupboard: South African Museums and the Trade in Human Remains, 1907-1917* (Cape Town: South African Museum and MacGregor Museum, 2000).

26. Erik Grimmer-Solem, "The Professors' Africa: Economists, the Elections of 1907, and the Legitimation of German Imperialism," *German History* 25, no. 3 (2007): 322; see Helmut Walser Smith, "The Talk of Genocide, the Rhetoric of Miscegenation: Notes on Debates in the German Reichstag concerning Southwest Africa, 1904-1914," in *The Imperialist Imagination: German Colonialism and Its Legacy*, ed. Sara Friedrichsmeyer, Sara Lennox, and Susanne Zantop (Ann Arbor: University of Michigan Press, 1998), 107-24.

27. Benjamin Madley, "From Africa to Auschwitz: How German South West Africa Incubated Ideas and Methods Adopted and Developed by the Nazis in Eastern Europe," *European History Quarterly* 35, no. 3 (2005): 429-64.

28. Bernard S. Cohn, *Colonialism and Its Forms of Knowledge* (Princeton, NJ: Princeton University Press, 1996), 4.

29. Catherine Hall, *Civilizing Subjects: Metropole and Colony in the English Imagination, 1830-1867* (Chicago: University of Chicago Press, 2002), 12.

30. Bernard Porter, *The Absent-Minded Imperialists: Empire, Society, and Culture in Britain* (Oxford: Oxford University Press, 2004).

31. Elizabeth Elbourne, "Indigenous Peoples and Imperial Networks in the Early Nineteenth Century: The Politics of Knowledge," in *Rediscovering the British World*, ed. Phillip Buckner and R. Douglas Francis (Alberta: University of Calgary Press, 2005), 59-86; Alan Lester, *Imperial Networks: Creating Identities in Nineteenth-Century South Africa and Britain* (London: Routledge, 2001).

32. Tony Ballantyne, *Orientalism and Race: Aryanism in the British Empire* (Basingstoke: Palgrave, 2002).

33. Ann Stoler and Carole McGranahan, "Reassessing Imperial Terrain," in *Imperial Formations*, ed. Ann Stoler, Carole McGranahan, and Peter Perdue (Santa Fe, NM: School for Advanced Research, 2007), 3-42.

34. Catherine Hall, "What Did a British World Mean to the British? Reflections on the Nineteenth Century," in Buckner and Francis, *Rediscovering the British World*, 36; see Catherine Hall and Sonya O. Rose, "Introduction: Being at Home with the Empire," in *At Home with the Empire: Metropolitan Culture and the Imperial World*, ed. Catherine Hall and Sonya O. Rose (Cambridge: Cambridge University Press, 2006), 1-31.

35. G. H. Darwin, "Address by the President of the British Association for the Advancement of Science," *Science* 22, no. 557 (1905): 225.

36. Browne, *Through South Africa*, 42.

37. David S. Evans, Terence J. Deeming, Betty Hall Evans, and Stephen Goldfarb, eds., *Herschel at the Cape: Diaries and Correspondence of Sir John Herschel, 1834-1836* (Cape Town: Balkema, 1969), 168.

38. Haddon, "Anthropology at the South African Meeting," 496.

39. Browne, *Through South Africa*, 47-50.

40. [Proceedings of the British Association], "Anthropology at the British Association South African Meeting, 1905," *Man* 5 (1905): 192.

41. E. Sidney Hartland, "Travel Notes in South Africa," *Folklore* 17, no. 4 (1906): 477.

42. Haddon, "Anthropology at the South African Meeting," 496.

43. Alice Werner, "Native Affairs in Natal," *Journal of the Royal African Society* 5, no. 17 (1905): 72. On indirect rule, see John Lambert, *Betrayed Trust: Africans and the State in Colonial Natal* (Pietermaritzburg: University of Natal Press, 1995); Mahmood Mamdani, *Citizen and Subject: Contemporary Africa and the Legacy of Late Colonialism* (Princeton, NJ: Princeton University Press, 1996); and Leroy Vail, introduction to *The Creation of Tribalism in Southern Africa*, ed. Leroy Vail (Berkeley: University of California Press, 1989), 1-19; but also see Michael R. Mahoney, "Racial Formation and Ethnogenesis from Below: The Zulu Case, 1879-1906," *International Journal of African Historical Studies* 36, no. 3 (2003): 559-83.

44. Jeff Guy, *The Maphumulo Uprising: War, Law, and Ritual in the Zulu Rebellion* (Scottsville, South Africa: University of KwaZulu-Natal Press, 2005), 5-6, 221.

45. James Stuart, *A History of the Zulu Rebellion 1906 and of Dinizulu's Arrest, Trial, and Expatriation* (London: Macmillan, 1913), 347n.

46. See Shula Marks, *Reluctant Rebellion: The 1906-8 Disturbances in Natal* (Oxford: Clarendon Press, 1970); Marks, "Class, Ideology and the Bambatha Rebellion," in *Banditry, Rebellion, and Social Protest in Africa*, ed. Donald Crummey (London: James Curry, 1986), 351-73; Sean Redding, "Governing the Zulu by Killing Them: Poll Tax and the Bambatha Rebellion in Natal and Zululand," in Redding, *Sorcery and Sovereignty: Taxation, Power, and Rebellion in South Africa, 1880-1963* (Athens: Ohio University Press, 2006), 89-123.

47. Browne, *Through South Africa*, 51.

48. [J. D. F. Gilchrist], "South African Meeting of the British Association," *Nature* 72, no. 1875 (1905): 561.

49. Veit Erlmann, "'Africa Civilised, Africa Uncivilised': Local Culture, World System, and South African Music," *Journal of Southern African Studies* 20, no. 2 (1994): 165-79; Erlmann, *Music, Modernity, and the Global Imagination: South Africa and the West* (Oxford: Oxford University Press, 1999).

50. Browne, *Through South Africa*, 51.

51. Ibid.

52. Bradlow, "British Association's South African Meeting," 58. On John Dube, see R. Hunt Davis, "John L. Dube, a South African Exponent of Booker T. Washington," *Journal of African Studies* 2, no. 4 (1976): 497-528; Heather Hughes, "Doubly Elite: Exploring the Life of John Langalibalele Dube," *Journal of Southern African Studies* 27, no. 3 (2001): 445-58; Hughes, *First President: The Life of John L. Dube, Founding President of the ANC* (Auckland Park, South Africa: Jacana, 2011); Shula Marks, "The Ambiguities of Dependence: John L. Dube of Natal," *Journal of Southern African Studies* 1, no. 2 (1975): 162-80.

53. "The Kaffirs of Natal," *Indian Opinion*, September 2, 1905; Mohandas K. Gandhi, *Collected Works of Mahatma Gandhi* (Delhi: Publications Division, Ministry of Information and Broadcasting Government of India, 1958-1994), 5:55. On Gandhi in South Africa, see Brian M. Du Toit, "The Mahatma Gandhi and South Africa," *Journal of Modern African Studies* 34, no. 4 (1996): 643-60; Maureen Swan, *Gandhi: The South African Experience* (Johannesburg: Ravan Press, 1985).

54. "The British Association: A Suggestion," *Indian Opinion*, August 26, 1905; Gandhi, *Collected Works*, 5:46-47.

55. A. C. Haddon, *Magic and Fetishism* (London: Archibald Constable, 1906); E. Sidney Hartland, *Primitive Paternity: The Myth of Supernatural Birth in Relation to the History of the Family*, 2 vols. (London: David Nutt, 1909-10); Hartland, *Ritual and Belief: Studies in the History of Religion* (New York: Charles Scribner's, 1914).

56. Anthropological Institute and Folklore Society, "A Plea for the Scientific Study of the Native Laws and Customs of South Africa: A Memorial Addressed by the Anthropological Institute and the Folklore Society to H.M. Secretary of State for the Colonies; and Subsequent Correspondence," *Man* 3 (1903): 73-74, 71.

57. Ibid., 71; Roderick Jones, "The Black Peril in South Africa," *Nineteenth Century* 55 (1904): 712. On the imperial trope of disappearing native populations, see Patrick Brantlinger, *Dark Vanishings: Discourse on the Extinction of Primitive Races, 1800–1930* (Ithaca, NY: Cornell University Press, 2003).

58. Hartland, "Travel Notes," 483.

59. George W. Stocking Jr., "Maclay, Kubary, Malinowski: Archetypes from the Dreamtime of Anthropology," in *Colonial Situations: Essays on the Contextualization of Ethnographic Knowledge*, ed. George W. Stocking Jr. (Madison: University of Wisconsin Press, 1993), 11.

60. Haddon, "Anthropology at the South African Meeting," 495.

61. Anthropological Institute and Folklore Society, "A Plea," 73, 72.

62. Werner, "Native Affairs," 79–80.

63. Michael R. Mahoney, "The Millennium Comes to Mapumulo: Popular Christianity in Rural Natal, 1866–1906," *Journal of Southern African Studies* 25, no. 3 (1999): 375–91.

64. A. C. Haddon, "South African Ethnology," in *Report of the Seventy-Fifth Annual Meeting of the British Association for the Advancement of Science, South Africa, 1905* (London: John Murray, 1906), 525; reprinted as "South African Ethnology (Presidential Address to Section H, British Association)," *Nature* 72 (1905): 471–79.

65. John Ferguson McLennan, "The Worship of Animals and Plants," *Fortnightly Review* 6 (1869): 407–27, 562–82; 7 (1870): 194–216; William Robertson Smith, *Lectures on the Religion of the Semites* (Edinburgh: Black, 1889). See Robert Alun Jones, *The Secret of the Totem: Religion and Society from McLennan to Freud* (New York: Columbia University Press, 2005).

66. F. Max Müller, *Contributions to the Science of Mythology*, 2 vols. (London: Longmans, Green, 1897), 1:201.

67. E. B. Tylor, "Remarks on Totemism, with Especial Reference to Some Modern Theories Respecting It," *Journal of the Anthropological Institute* 28 (1899): 138.

68. Ibid., 147.

69. Edmund Leach, "The Anthropology of Religion: British and French Schools," in *Nineteenth-Century Religious Thought in the West*, 3 vols., ed. Ninian Smart, John Clayton, Patrick Sherry, and Steven T. Katz (Cambridge: Cambridge University Press, 1985), 3:218.

70. W. J. T. Mitchell, *What Do Pictures Want? The Lives and Loves of Images* (Chicago: University of Chicago Press, 2005), 163.

71. James Urry, "Notes and Queries on Anthropology and the Development of Field Methods in British Anthropology, 1870–1920," *Proceedings of the Royal Anthropological Institute of Great Britain and Ireland for 1972* (London: Trübner, 1973), 45–57.

72. Folklore Society, "Notes and Queries on Totemism," *Folklore* 12, no. 4 (1901): 392.

73. Tylor, "Remarks on Totemism," 138.

74. W. Baldwin Spencer, *Spencer's Scientific Correspondence with Sir J. G. Frazer and Others*, ed. R. R. Marett and T. K. Penniman (London: Oxford University Press, 1932); W. Baldwin Spencer and Francis J. Gillen, *The Native Tribes of Central Australia*. London: Macmillan, 1899); Spencer and Gillen, "Some Remarks on Totemism as Applied to Australian Tribes," *Journal of the Anthropological Institute* 28 (1899): 275–80. See Sam D. Gill, *Storytracking: Texts, Stories, and Histories in Central Australia* (New York: Oxford University Press, 1998); Henrika Kuklick, "'Humanity in the Chrysalis Stage': Indigenous Australians in the Anthropological Imagination, 1899–1926," *British Journal for the History of Science* 39, no. 4 (2006): 535–68; Angus Nicholls, "Anglo-German Mythologics: The Australian Aborigines and Modern Theories of Myth in the Work of Baldwin Spencer and Carl Strehlow," *History of the Human Sciences* 20, no. 1 (2007): 83–114.

75. George McCall Theal, *Records of South-Eastern Africa*, vol. 7 (London: William Clowes, 1901), 404.

76. James G. Frazer, "South African Totemism," *Man* 1 (1901): 135–36.

77. Andrew Lang, N. W. Thomas, and G. W. Stow, "Bantu Totemism," *Folklore* 15, no. 2 (1904): 204.

78. N. W. Thomas, review of *The Native Races of South Africa: A History of the Intrusion of the Hottentots and Bantu into the Hunting Grounds of the Bushmen*, by G. W. Stow and G. M. Theal, *Folklore* 16, no. 3 (1905): 357.

79. E. Sidney Hartland, "The Totemism of the Bantu," in *Report of the Seventy-Fifth Annual Meeting of the British Association*, 527; [Proceedings of the British Association], "Anthropology," 190.

80. W. C. Willoughby, "Notes on the Totemism of the Becwana," in *Addresses and Papers Read at the Joint Meeting of the British and South African Associations*, 3:263-93. See Willoughby, *The Soul of the Bantu: A Sympathetic Study of the Magico-Religious Practices and Beliefs of the Bantu Tribes of Africa* (London: SCM Press; New York: Doubleday, 1928); Willoughby, *Nature Worship and Taboo: Further Studies in "The Soul of the Bantu"* (Hartford, CT: Hartford Seminary Press, 1932).

81. C. A. Wheelwright, "Native Circumcision Lodges in the Zoutpansberg District," *Journal of the Anthropological Institute* 35 (1905): 251-55; William Grant, "Magato and His Tribe," *Journal of the Anthropological Institute* 35 (1905): 266-70; A. E. Mabille, "The Basuto of Basutoland," *Journal of the Royal African Society* 5, nos. 19-20 (1906): 233-38, 351-76; J. W. Shepstone, "The Native Tribes of South Africa," in *Report of the Seventy-Fifth Annual Meeting of the British Association*, 532.

82. E. Gottschling, "The Bawenda: A Sketch of Their History and Customs," *Journal of the Anthropological Institute* 35 (1905): 365-86.

83. Henri-Alexandre Junod, "The Ba-Thonga of the Transvaal," in *Addresses and Papers Read at the Joint Meeting of the British and South African Associations*, 3:222-62.

84. Haddon, "Anthropology at the South African Meeting," 492.

85. William Crisp, "The Mental Capacity of the Bantu," in *Addresses and Papers Read at the Joint Meeting of the British and South African Associations*, 3:319-25; Luschan, "Racial Affinities of the Hottentots"; Louis Péringuey, "The Stone Age in South Africa," in *Report of the Seventy-Fifth Annual Meeting of the British Association*, 527-28; Péringuey, *The Stone Age in South Africa* (Cape Town: South African Museum, 1911); see Nick Shepherd, "State of the Discipline: Science, Culture, and Identity in South African Archaeology, 1870-2003," *Journal of Southern African Studies* 29, no. 4 (2003): 823-44; Pippa Skotnes, "'Civilised off the Face of the Earth': Museum Display and the Silencing of the /Xam," *Poetics Today* 22, no. 2 (2001): 299-321.

86. E. Sidney Hartland, "The Natives of South Africa: A Note on the Recent Bluebook (Cd. 904), with a Plea for Further Investigation," *Man* 2 (1902): 36.

87. Ibid.

88. Thomas Richards, *The Imperial Archive: Knowledge and the Fantasy of Empire* (London: Verso, 1993).

89. Susanne Zantop, *Colonial Fantasies: Conquest, Family, and Nation in Precolonial Germany, 1770-1870* (Durham, NC: Duke University Press, 1997).

90. Roger L. Janelli, "The Origins of Korean Folklore Scholarship," *Journal of American Folklore* 99, no. 391 (1986): 24-49; Andre Schmid, "Colonialism and the 'Korea Problem' in the Historiography of Modern Japan: A Review Article," *Journal of Asian Studies* 59, no. 4 (2000): 951-76.

91. Louis Henry Jordan, *Comparative Religion: Its Genesis and Growth* (Edinburgh: T & T Clark, 1905), 431; Thomas, "Impact of Other Religions," 294.

92. "From Constable's List," *Journal of Theological Studies* 13, no. 49 (1912): back matter.

93. Norman J. Girardot, "Max Müller's *Sacred Books* and the Nineteenth-Century Production of the Comparative Science of Religions," *History of Religions* 41, no. 3 (2002): 213-50.

94. F. Max Müller, "Preface to the Sacred Books of the East," in *The Upanishads*, vol. 1, ed. and trans. F. Max Müller (Oxford: Oxford University Press, 1879), xi.

95. Ibid., xiii.

96. Stephen Hay, "The Making of a Late-Victorian Hindu: M. K. Gandhi in London, 1888-1891," *Victorian Studies* 33, no. 1 (1989): 75-98; Jim Wilson, "Gandhi's God—A Substitute for the British Empire?" *Religion* 16, no. 4 (1986): 343-57.

97. Peter van der Veer, *Imperial Encounters: Religion and Modernity in India and Britain* (Princeton, NJ: Princeton University Press, 2001), 65.

98. Bal Gangadhar Tilak, *The Arctic Home of the Vedas* (Poona: Tilak Brothers, 1903); Dorothy M. Figueira, *Aryans, Jews, Brahmans: Theorizing Authority through Myths of Identity* (New York: State University of New York Press, 2002), 130-33.

99. Gandhi, *Collected Works*, 4:405-8.

100. "Hinduism," *Star* (Johannesburg), March 10, 1905; Gandhi, *Collected Works*, 4:368.

101. Gandhi, *Collected Works*, 3:241.

102. "Hinduism," *Star* (Johannesburg), March 10, 1905; Gandhi, *Collected Works*, 4:368.

103. "Hinduism," *Star* (Johannesburg), March 10, 1905; Gandhi, *Collected Works*, 4:368.

104. Gandhi, *Collected Works*, 3:9.

105. Ibid., 1:97-98; see Edwin Bryant and Laurie L. Patton, eds., *The Indo-Aryan Controversy: Evidence and Inference in Indian History* (London: Routledge, 2005).

106. "The Nelson Centenary: A Lesson," *Indian Opinion*, October 28, 1905; Gandhi, *Collected Works*, 5:111-12.

107. F. Max Müller, *India: What Can It Teach Us?* (London: Longmans, Green, 1883), 24.

108. Colonial Office Records, no. 179, vol. 189: Votes and Proceedings of Parliament, Natal, 1894; Gandhi, *Collected Works*, 1:96, 151.

109. Max Müller, *India*, 24.

110. J. Estlin Carpenter, "Congress of the History of Religions," *Folklore* 19, no. 2 (1908): 228-30; Ursula King, "A Question of Identity: Women Scholars and the Study of Religion," in *Religion and Gender*, ed. Ursula King (Oxford: Blackwell, 1995), 224.

111. R. R. Marett, *The Threshold of Religion*, 2nd ed. (1909; London: Metheun, 1914), 98.

112. W. H. T. Gairdner, *Echoes from Edinburgh, 1910: An Account and Interpretation of the World Missionary Conference* (New York: Fleming H. Revell, 1910), 149.

113. Ibid., 139, 141, 145.

114. J. Stanley Friesen, *Missionary Responses to Tribal Religions at Edinburgh, 1910* (Frankfurt am Main: Peter Lang, 1996), 32; World Missionary Conference, "Animistic Religions," in *The Missionary Message in Relation to Non-Christian Religions* (New York: Fleming H. Revell, 1910), 7.

115. Friesen, *Missionary Responses*, 36-42, 50-63.

116. W. E. B. Du Bois, "Editorial: The Races in Conference," *Crisis* 1 (December 1910): 17.

117. Felix von Luschan, "Anthropological View of Race," in *Papers on Inter-Racial Problems Communicated to the First Universal Races Congress Held at the University of London July 26-29, 1911*, ed. Gustav Spiller (London: P. S. King, 1911), 16, 22, 23.

118. Benoit Massin, "From Virchow to Fischer: Physical Anthropology and 'Modern Race Theories' in Wilhelmine Germany," in *Volksgeist as Method and Ethic: Essays on Boasian Ethnography and the German Anthropological Tradition*, ed. George W. Stocking Jr. (Madison: University of Wisconsin Press, 1996), 105.

119. Luschan, "Anthropological View of Race," 23, 24.

120. T. W. Rhys Davids, "Religion as a Consolidating and Separating Influence," in Spiller, *Papers on Inter-Racial Problems*, 62, 66.

121. Tongo Takebe and Teruaki Kobayashi, "Japan," in Spiller, *Papers on Inter-Racial Problems*, 134.

122. J. Tengo Jabavu, "The Native Races of South Africa," in Spiller, *Papers on Inter-Racial Problems*, 336-41.

CHAPTER THREE

The epigraph is from F. Max Müller, *Introduction to the Science of Religion: Four Lectures Delivered at the Royal Institution with Two Essays on False Analogies, and the Philosophy of Mythology* (London: Longmans, Green, 1873), 122-23.

1. F. Max Müller, *The Life and Letters of the Right Honourable Friedrich Max Müller*, ed. Georgina Adelaide Grenfell Max Müller, 2 vols. (London: Longmans, Green, 1902), 2:419.

2. F. Max Müller, *The Question of Right between England and the Transvaal: Letters by the Right Hon. F. Max Müller with rejoinders by Professor Theodore Mommsen* (London: Imperial South African Association, 1900), 5, 12.

3. Ibid., 6, 28.

4. Ibid., 1.

5. Ibid., 29.

6. Nirad C. Chaudhuri, *Scholar Extraordinary: The Life of Professor the Right Honourable Friedrich Max Müller, P. C.* (London: Chatto and Windus, 1974), 254.

7. Max Müller, *Question of Right*, 23.

8. Ibid., 11.

9. Max Müller, *Life and Letters*, 2:124-25, 157, 256-57.

10. Ibid., 2:191.

11. Eric J. Sharpe, *Comparative Religion: A History*, 2nd ed. (LaSalle, IL: Open Court, 1986), 35. See Ulrich Berner, "Africa and the Origin of the Science of Religion: Max Müller (1823-1900) and James George Frazer (1854-1941) on African Religions," in *European Traditions in the Study of Religion in Africa*, ed. Frieder Ludwig and Afe Adogame (Wiesbaden: Harrassowitz, 2004), 141-49; Norman J. Girardot, "Max Müller's *Sacred Books* and the Nineteenth-Century Production of the Comparative Science of Religions," *History of Religions* 41, no. 3 (2002): 213-50; Joseph M. Kitagawa and J. S. Strong, "Friedrich Max Müller and the Comparative Study of Religion," in *Nineteenth-Century Religious Thought in the West*, ed. Ninian Smart, John Clayton, Patrick Sherry, and Steven T. Katz, 3 vols. (Cambridge: Cambridge University Press, 1985), 3:179-205; Tomoko Masuzawa, "Our Master's Voice: F. Max Müller after a Hundred Years of Solitude," *Method and Theory in the Study of Religion* 15, no. 4 (2003): 305-28; Garry W. Trompf, "Friedrich Max Müller: Some Preliminary Chips from his German Workshop," *Journal of Religious History* 5, no. 3 (1969): 200-217; Lourens van den Bosch, "Friedrich Max Müller and His Contribution to the Science of Religion," in *Comparative Studies in the History of Religions*, ed. Erik Reenberg Sand and Jørgen Podemann Sørensen (Copenhagen: Museum Tusculanum Press, 1999), 11-39; Van den Bosch, *Friedrich Max Müller: A Life Devoted to the Humanities* (Leiden: Brill, 2002).

12. Max Müller, *Introduction to the Science of Religion*, 20.

13. F. Max Müller, *German Love: From the Papers of an Alien*, trans. Susanna Winkworth (London: Chapman and Hall, 1858), 118.

14. Ibid., 58.

15. Max Müller, *Introduction to the Science of Religion*, 12.

16. Ibid., 122-23.

17. Ibid., 106.

18. Ibid., 116.

19. F. Max Müller, *Natural Religion* (London: Longman, Green, 1889), 215.

20. F. Max Müller, *Anthropological Religion* (London: Longman, Green, 1892), 147.

21. F. Max Müller, *Lectures on the Science of Language*, 2nd ed. (London: Longmans, Green, 1862), 23, 49.

22. Max Müller, *Life and Letters*, 2:84.

23. Max Müller, *Natural Religion*, 505.

24. Max Müller, *Introduction to the Science of Religion*, 101.

25. Ieuan Ellis, *Seven Against Christ: A Study of "Essays and Reviews"* (Leiden: Brill, 1980), ix; Josef L. Altholz, *Anatomy of a Controversy: The Debate over "Essays and Reviews," 1860-1864* (Aldershot: Scolar Press, 1994), ix.

26. *Essays and Reviews* (London: John Parker, 1860), 338, 377.

27. Frederic Harrison, "Neo-Christianity," *Westminster Review*, n.s., 36 (October 1860): 295, 310.

28. Victor Shea and William Whitla, eds., *Essays and Reviews: The 1860 Text and Its Reading* (Charlottesville: University Press of Virginia, 2000), 27, 40.

29. John William Colenso, *The Pentateuch and Book of Joshua Critically Examined*, 7 vols. (London: Longman, Robert and Green, 1862-79), 1:vii.

30. Ibid., 1:150.

31. Jeff Guy, "Class, Imperialism, and Literary Criticism: William Ngidi, John Colenso, and Matthew Arnold," *Journal of Southern African Studies* 23, no. 2 (1997): 221.

32. Matthew Arnold, "The Bishop and the Philosopher (1863)," in *Archives of Empire*, vol. 2, *The Scramble for Africa*, ed. Barbara Harlow and Mia Carter (Durham, NC: Duke University Press, 2003), 331-34.

33. Ibid., 344.

34. John William Colenso, *Three Native Accounts of the Visit of the Bp. of Natal in September and October 1859 to Upande, King of the Zulus*, 3rd ed. (Pietermaritzburg: Magema, Mubi, 1901), 147; Guy, "Class, Imperialism, and Literary Criticism," 226.

35. Jeff Guy, *The View across the River: Harriette Colenso and the Zulu Struggle against Imperialism* (Cape Town: David Philip, 2001); Bridget Theron, "King Cetshwayo in Victorian England: A Cameo of Imperial Interaction," *South African Historical Journal* 56, no. 1 (2006): 60-87.

36. William Flavelle Monypenny and George Earle Buckle, *The Life of Benjamin Disraeli, Earl of Beaconsfield*, 4 vols. (London: John Murray, 1916), 3:100.

37. Max Müller, *Life and Letters*, 1:307, 372-73, 469.

38. F. Max Müller, *My Autobiography: A Fragment* (London: Longmans, Green, 1901), 294.

39. Max Müller, *Lectures on the Science of Language* (1862), 11.

40. F. Max Müller, *Lectures on the Science of Language*, second series (London: Longman, Green, Longman, Roberts, & Green, 1864), 580.

41. Ibid., 11-12.

42. W. H. I. Bleek, *Zulu Legends*, ed. J. A. Engelbrecht (1857; Pretoria: Van Schaik, 1952).

43. Robert J. Thornton, "The Elusive Unity of Sir George Grey's Library," *African Studies* 42, no. 1 (1983): 79-89.

44. W. H. I. Bleek, *A Comparative Grammar of South African Languages*, part 1 (London: Trübner, 1862); Bleek, *Reynard the Fox in South Africa; or, Hottentot Fables and Tales* (London: Trübner, 1864).

45. Neil Bennun, *The Broken String: The Last Words of an Extinct People* (London: Penguin, 2004); Pippa Skotnes, ed., *Claim to the Country: The Archive of Wilhelm Bleek and Lucy Lloyd* (Athens: Ohio University Press; Auckland Park, South Africa: Jacana Media, 2007).

46. W. H. I. Bleek and Lucy C. Lloyd, *Specimens of Bushman Folklore* (London: George Allen, 1911), 434-35; Andrew Bank, *Bushmen in a Victorian World: The Remarkable Story of the Bleek-Lloyd Collection of Bushman Folklore* (Cape Town: Double Storey, 2006), 103-27.

47. Max Müller, *Introduction to the Science of Religion*, 54-55.

48. Ibid., 56n1; see E. B. Tylor, "The Religion of Savages," *Fortnightly Review* 6 (1866): 80.

49. Max Müller, *Introduction to the Science of Religion*, 56.

50. Max Müller, *Natural Religion*, 341.

51. W. H. I. Bleek, *On the Origin of Language*, ed. Ernst Haeckel, trans. Thomas Davidson (New York: L. W. Schmidt, 1869), xv-xvi.

52. E. B. Tylor, *Primitive Culture*, 2 vols. (London: John Murray, 1871), 1:271.

53. Bleek, *Reynard the Fox*, xii; see Andrew Bank, "Evolution and Racial Theory: The Hidden Side of Wilhelm Bleek," *South African Historical Journal* 43, no. 1 (2000): 163-78.

54. Robert J. Thornton, "'This Dying Out Race': W. H. I. Bleek's Approach to the Languages of Southern Africa," *Social Dynamics* 9, no. 2 (1983): 1-10.

55. F. Max Müller, *Chips from a German Workshop*, vol. 4 (London: Longmans, 1875), 360-61; Max Müller, *Selected Essays on Language, Mythology, and Religion*, 2 vols. (London: Longmans, Green, 1881), 2:28.

56. Theophilus Hahn, *Tsuni-//Goam, the Supreme Being of the Khoi-Khoi* (London: Trübner, 1881), 1, 126; see F. Max Müller, "Mythology among the Hottentots," *Nineteenth Century* 11 (1882): 110-25.

57. Henry Callaway, *Nursery Tales, Traditions, and Histories of the Zulus*, 2 vols. (Springvale, South Africa: J. A. Blair; London: Trübner, 1866–68); Callaway, *The Religious System of the Amazulu* (1868–70; reprint, Cape Town: Struik, 1970); Callaway, "Native Zulu Clergy," *Mission Life* 3 (1872): 417–24; Callaway, "On Divination and Analogous Phenomena among the Natives of Natal," *Proceedings of the Anthropological Institute* 1 (1872): 163–83; Callaway, *A Fragment on Comparative Religion* (Natal: Callaway, 1874); Callaway, "South African Folk-Lore," *Cape Monthly Magazine* 16, no. 94 (February 1878): 109–10; Callaway, "On the Religious Sentiment amongst the Tribes of South Africa: Lecture Delivered at Kokstad," *Cape Monthly Magazine*, n.s., 2, no. 5 (1880): 87–102; Callaway, "A Fragment Illustrative of Religious Ideas among the Kafirs," *Folklore* 2, no. 4 (July 1880): 56–60.

58. Callaway to Bishop Gray, July 8, 1862, 9.10.c.6, manuscript collection, South African Library, Cape Town.

59. Marian S. Benham, *Henry Callaway M.D., D.D., First Bishop of Kaffraria: His Life-History and Work: A Memoir* (London: Macmillan, 1896), 215, 239, 341.

60. Max Müller, *Introduction to the Science of Religion*, 61.

61. Norman Etherington, *Preachers, Peasants, and Politics in Southeast Africa, 1835–1880: African Christian Communities in Natal, Pondoland, and Zululand* (London: Royal Historical Society, 1978), 68, 95, 102; Etherington, "Missionary Doctors and African Healers in Mid-Victorian South Africa," *South African Historical Journal* 19, no. 1 (1987): 80. See David Chidester, *Savage Systems: Colonialism and Comparative Religion in Southern Africa* (Charlottesville: University Press of Virginia, 1996), 152–72.

62. Callaway, *Religious System*, 22.

63. Ibid., 79–80.

64. Max Müller, *Natural Religion*, 516–17.

65. Max Müller, *Anthropological Religion*, 152.

66. F. Max Müller, *Contributions to the Science of Mythology*, 2 vols. (London: Longmans, Green, 1897): 1:203–5.

67. Les Switzer and Donna Switzer, *The Black Press in South Africa and Lesotho: A Descriptive Bibliographic Guide to African, Coloured, and Indian Newspapers, Newsletters, and Magazines, 1836–1976* (Boston: G. K. Hall, 1979), 249.

68. Max Müller, *Contributions to the Science of Mythology*, 1:204–5.

69. Ibid.

70. Society for Promoting Christian Knowledge, *May, the Little Bush Girl* (London: Society for Promoting Christian Knowledge, 1875), 29.

71. Wilhelm Schneider, *Die Religion der afrikanischen Naturvölker* (Münster: Aschendorff, 1891), 66.

72. Thomas B. Jenkinson, *Amazulu: The Zulus, Their Past, History, Manners, Customs, and Language* (London: W. H. Allen, 1882), 28.

73. Henry Rowley, *The Religion of the Africans* (London: W. Wells Gardner, 1877), 43.

74. Max Müller, *Life and Letters*, 2:191.

75. Max Müller, *Question of Right*, 5.

76. Antoinette Burton, "Making a Spectacle of Empire: Indian Travellers in Fin-de-Siècle London," *History Workshop Journal* 42 (1996): 127.

77. Lord Askwith, "Empire Exhibition: Seventy Years' Progress," *Daily Telegraph* (London), February 4, 1924, cited in Alexander C. T. Geppert, "True Copies: Time and Space Travels at British Imperial Exhibitions, 1880–1930," in *The Making of Modern Tourism: The Cultural History of the British Experience, 1600–2000*, ed. Hartmut Berghoff, Barbara Korte, Ralf Schneider, and Christopher Harvie (London: Palgrave, 2002), 233.

78. Max Müller, *Life and Letters*, 2:219, 223.

79. Steven Connor, "Myth and Meta-myth in Max Müller and Walter Pater," in *The Sun Is God: Painting, Literature, and Mythology in the Nineteenth Century*, ed. J. B. Bullen (Oxford: Clarendon Press, 1988), 221.

80. Alice Werner, "Native Affairs in Natal," *Journal of the Royal African Society* 5, no. 17 (1905): 72.

81. F. Max Müller, *Introduction to the Science of Religion*, new ed. (London: Longmans, Green, 1882), 68.

82. F. Max Müller, "Forgotten Bibles," *Nineteenth Century* 15 (1884): 1005.

83. Max Müller, *Natural Religion*, 203.

84. Max Müller, *Question of Right*, 11.

85. Frederick Temple, "Education of the World," in *Essays and Reviews*, 19.

86. Matthew Arnold, *Culture and Anarchy: An Essay in Political and Social Criticism* (London: Smith, Elder, 1869).

87. Peter H. Hoffenberg, *An Empire on Display: English, Indian, and Australian Exhibitions from the Crystal Palace to the Great War* (Berkeley: University of California Press, 2001).

88. Anthropological Institute, "Miscellaneous Business of the Meeting on June 1st, 1886," *Journal of the Anthropological Institute* 16 (1887): 175.

89. Max Müller, *Natural Religion*, 503-4.

90. J. G. Frazer, "Questions on the Manners, Customs, Religion, Superstition, etc. of Uncivilized or Semi-Civilized Peoples," *Journal of the Anthropological Institute* 18 (1888): 433.

91. Letter from William Ngidi, April 15, 1883, Killie Campbell Library, Colenso Collection, cited in Guy, "Class, Imperialism, and Literary Criticism," 241; G. W. Cox, *The Life of John William Colenso*, 2 vols. (London: Macmillan, 1888), 2:614.

92. Anthropological Institute, "Miscellaneous Business," 175.

93. Francis Galton, *The Art of Travel; or, Shifts and Contrivances Available in Wild Countries*, 4th ed. (1855; London: John Murray, 1867), 314-15.

94. E. Sidney Hartland, "On the Imperfection of Our Knowledge of the Black Races of the Transvaal and the Orange River Colony," *Journal of the Anthropological Institute* 30 (1900): 22-23, 24; A. C. Haddon, "A Plea for the Study of the Native Races in South Africa," *Nature* 63 (1900): 157-59. See Hartland, "Retiring Presidential Address," *Folklore* 12, no. 1 (1901): 15-40; Hartland, "Some Problems of Early Religion, in the Light of South African Folklore," *Man* 1 (1901): 27-28.

CHAPTER FOUR

The epigraph is from E. B. Tylor, *Primitive Culture*, 2 vols. (London: John Murray, 1871), 1:443.

1. C. Donovan, "Abstract: On the Brain in the Study of Ethnology," *Journal of the Ethnological Society of London* 2, no. 4 (1870): 369; see John van Wyhe, *Phrenology and the Origins of Victorian Scientific Naturalism* (Aldershot: Ashgate, 2004).

2. Anthropological Society, "Report of the Committee of Investigation," *Anthropological Review* 7 (1869): xvi-xvii; see George W. Stocking Jr., "What's in a Name? The Origins of the Royal Anthropological Institute (1837-71)," *Man*, n.s., 6, no. 3 (1971): 369-90.

3. Cornelius Donovan, *A Handbook of Phrenology* (London: Longmans, 1870), 34, 40, 93-94.

4. Johann Gaspar Spurzheim, *Phrenology, in Connexion with the Study of Physiognomy* (London: Treutel, Wurtz, and Richter, 1826), 154, 160, 71.

5. Donovan, *Handbook of Phrenology*, 134-35.

6. See, for example, Andrew Bank, "Of 'Native Skulls' and 'Noble Caucasians': Phrenology in Colonial South Africa," *Journal of Southern African Studies* 22, no. 3 (1996): 387-403.

7. On Tylor, see Joan Leopold, *Culture in Comparative and Evolutionary Perspective: E. B. Tylor and the Making of "Primitive Culture"* (Berlin: Dietrich Reimer, 1980); R. R. Marett, *Tylor* (London: Chapman & Hall, 1936); Laavanyan Ratnapalan, "E. B. Tylor and the Problem of Primitive Culture," *History and Anthropology* 19, no. 2 (2008): 131-42; Benson Saler, "E. B. Tylor and the Anthropology of Religion," in Saler, *Understanding Religion: Selected Essays* (Berlin: Walter de Gruyter, 2009), 51-57.

8. E. B. Tylor, *Anahuac; or, Mexico and the Mexicans, Ancient and Modern* (London: Longman, Green, Longman, and Roberts, 1861).

9. E. B. Tylor, "The Philosophy of Religion among the Lower Races of Mankind," *Journal of the Ethnological Society of London* 2, no. 4 (1870): 370.

10. George W. Stocking Jr., "Animism in Theory and Practice: E. B. Tylor's Unpublished 'Notes on Spiritualism,'" *Man*, n.s., 6, no. 1 (1971): 88-104.

11. Tylor, "Philosophy of Religion," 370.

12. Ibid.

13. Ibid., 379.

14. Ibid., 372.

15. Ibid., 373.

16. Ibid., 381.

17. Ibid.

18. John Lubbock, *The Origin of Civilization and the Primitive Condition of Man*, 5th ed. (1870; London: Longmans, Green, 1889), 287, citing Martin Karl Heinrich Lichtenstein, *Travels in Southern Africa in the Years 1803, 1804, 1805*, 2 vols., trans. Anne Plumptre (1811-12; Cape Town: Van Riebeeck Society, 1928), 1:313.

19. Eric J. Sharpe, *Comparative Religion: A History*, 2nd ed. (La Salle IL: Open Court, 1986), 47-71.

20. R. FitzRoy and C. R. Darwin, "A Letter, Containing Remarks on the Moral State of Tahiti, New Zealand, &c." *South African Christian Recorder* 2, no. 4 (September 1836): 221.

21. Charles R. Darwin, *The Autobiography of Charles Darwin, 1809-1882* (London: Collins, 1958), 85.

22. Charles R. Darwin, *The Descent of Man, and Selection in Relation to Sex*, 2 vols. (London: John Murray, 1871), 1:65.

23. F. W. Farrar, "On the Universality of Belief in God and in a Future State," *Anthropological Review* 2 (1864): ccxvii, citing George Brown, *Personal Adventures in South Africa* (London: Blackwood, 1855), 12.

24. Farrar, "On the Universality of Belief in God," ccxviii.

25. Darwin, *Descent of Man*, 1:65.

26. Charles R. Darwin, *The Descent of Man, and Selection in Relation to Sex*, 2nd ed., 2 vols. (London: John Murray, 1882), 1:93.

27. Darwin, *Descent of Man* (1871), 1:66n53, citing Lubbock, *Origin of Civilization*; John Ferguson McLennan, "The Worship of Animals and Plants," *Fortnightly Review* 7 (1869-70): 194-216; and Herbert Spencer, "The Origin of Animal Worship," *Fortnightly Review* 13 (May 1, 1870): 535-50.

28. Darwin, *Descent of Man* (1871), 1:66, citing E. B. Tylor, *Researches into the Early History of Mankind and the Development of Civilization* (London: John Murray, 1865), 6.

29. Darwin, *Descent of Man* (1871), 1:66.

30. Charles R. Darwin, *The Expression of Emotions in Man and Animals* (London: John Murray, 1872).

31. Francis Darwin, ed., *The Life and Letters of Charles Darwin*, 2 vols. (London: John Murray, 1887), 1:114; David Allan Feller, "Darwin, the Dog Lover," *Forbes*, February 5, 2009, www.forbes.com/2009/02/05/dogs-hunting-cambridge-university-opinions-darwin09_0205_david_allen_feller.html, accessed June 28, 2009.

32. Darwin, *Descent of Man* (1871), 1:58.

33. Ibid., 1:67.

34. Ibid., 1:67.

35. Herbert Spencer, *The Principles of Sociology*, vol. 1. (London: Williams and Norgate, 1871), 800.

36. George J. Romanes, "Fetichism in Animals," *Nature* 17, no. 426 (1877): 169; see Romanes, *Animal Intelligence* (London: Kegan Paul Trench, 1888).

37. Darwin, *Descent of Man* (1871), 1:68.

38. L. Owen Pike, "The Psychical Elements of Religion," *Anthropological Review* 8 (1870): lxiv.

39. Darwin, *Descent of Man* (1871), 1:68, citing Wilhelm Braubach, *Religion, Moral und Philosophie der Darwin'schen Artlehre und ihrer Natur und ihrem Charakter als kleine Parallele menschlich geistiger Entwicklung* (Leipzig: Neuwied, 1869), s.53.

40. Darwin, *Descent of Man* (1882), 1:96n78, citing W. Lauder Lindsay, "Physiology of Mind in the Lower Animals," *Journal of Mental Science* 17 (1871): 43.

41. Friedrich Schleiermacher, *The Christian Faith*, trans. H. R. Mackintosh (1830; London: T. T. Clark, 1999).

42. Spencer, *Principles of Sociology*, 800-801.

43. Romanes, "Fetichism in Animals," 169.

44. Darwin, *Descent of Man* (1871), 1:65.

45. See Matthew Day, "Godless Savages and Superstitious Dogs: Charles Darwin, Imperial Ethnography, and the Problem of Human Uniqueness," *Journal of the History of Ideas* 69, no. 1 (2008): 49-70.

46. F. Max Müller, *Natural Religion* (London: Longmans, Green, 1889), 69; see G. W. F. Hegel, *Werke*, 20 vols. (Frankfurt am Main: Suhrkamp, 1986), 11:58.

47. John H. King, *The Supernatural: Its Origin, Nature, and Evolution*, 2 vols. (London: Williams and Norgate, 1892), 1:87.

48. F. Max Müller, *Science of Thought* (London: Longmans, Green, 1887), 153; Max Müller, *The Life and Letters of the Right Honourable Friedrich Max Müller*, ed. Georgina Adelaide Grenfell Max Müller, 2 vols. (London: Longmans, Green, 1902), 2:468. See Elizabeth Knoll, "The Science of Language and the Evolution of Mind: Max Müller's Quarrel with Darwinism," *Journal of the History of Behavioral Sciences* 22, no. 1 (1986): 3-22; Gregory Schrempp, "The Re-education of Friedrich Max Müller: Intellectual Appropriation and Epistemological Antinomy in Mid-Victorian Evolutionary Thought," *Man*, n.s., 18, no. 1 (1983): 90-110; Lourens van den Bosch, "Language as the Barrier between Brute and Man: Friedrich Max Müller and the Darwinian Debate on Language," *Saeculum* 51, no. 1 (2000): 57-89.

49. "Review: Charles Darwin's *The Descent of Man*," *Athenaeum* 2262 (1871): 275.

50. Darwin to Asa Gray, May 22, 1860, in Darwin, *Life and Letters of Charles Darwin*, 2:312.

51. Thomas H. Huxley, "Science and 'Church Policy,'" *Reader* 4, no. 3 (December 1864): 821.

52. Leonard Huxley, ed., *Life and Letters of Thomas Henry Huxley*, 3 vols. (New York: D. Appleton, 1900), 1:237; see Bernard Lightman, "Victorian Sciences and Religions: Discordant Harmonies," *Osiris*, 2nd ser., 16 (2001): 343-66.

53. Tylor, "Philosophy of Religion," 372; Darwin, *Descent of Man* (1871), 1:66.

54. Lindsay, "Physiology of Mind," 30-82; Lindsay, "Mind in the Lower Animals," *Nature* 8, no. 187 (1873): 91-92; Lindsay, "The Pathology of Mind in the Lower Animals," *Journal of Mental Science* 23 (1877): 17-44; Lindsay, *Mind in the Lower Animals in Health and Disease*, 2 vols. (London: C. K. Paul, 1879).

55. W. Lauder Lindsay, "Mind in Plants," *Journal of Mental Science* 21 (1876): 532.

56. John Lubbock, "The President's Address," *Journal of the Proceedings of the Entomological Society of London* 5 (1866): lxiv.

57. James Hunt, "On the Negro's Place in Nature," *Journal of the Anthropological Society of London* 2 (1864): xv-lvi.

58. L. Owen Pike, "On the Alleged Influence of Race upon Religion," *Journal of the Anthropological Society of London* 7 (1869): cxxxv-cliii; see Ronald Rainger, "Race, Politics, and Science: The Anthropological Society of London in the 1860s," *Victorian Studies* 22, no. 1 (1978): 51-70.

59. Isaac Taylor, *The Origin of the Aryans: An Account of the Prehistoric Ethnology and Civilisation of Europe* (London: W. Scott, 1889), 247-49.

60. F. Max Müller, *Biographies of Words and the Home of the Aryas* (London: Longmans, Green, 1888), 120. See Stefan Arvidsson, "Aryan Mythology as Science and Ideology," *Journal of the American Academy of Religion* 67, no. 2 (1999): 327–54; Joan Leopold, "Friedrich Max Müller and the Question of Early Indo-Europeans (1847–1851)," *Etudes inter-ethniques* 7 (1984): 21–32; Maurice Olender, "The Danger of Ambiguity: Friedrich Max Müller," in *Languages of Paradise: Race, Religion and Philology in the Nineteenth Century*, by Olender, trans. Arthur Goldhammer (Cambridge, MA: Harvard University Press, 1992), 82–92.

61. Carl [*sic*] Vogt, *Lectures on Man: His Place in Creation, and in the History of the Earth*, ed. James Hunt (London: Longman, 1864), 82; J. McGrigor Allan, "On the Real Differences in the Minds of Men and Women," *Journal of the Anthropological Society of London* 7 (1869): cciv. See Evelleen Richards, "Darwin and the Descent of Woman," in *The Wider Domain of Evolutionary Thought*, ed. David Roger Oldroyd and Ian Langham (Dordrecht: Reidel, 1983), 57–111; Richards, "Huxley and Woman's Place in Science: The 'Woman Question' and the Control of Victorian Anthropology," in *History, Humanity, and Evolution*, ed. James R. Moore (Cambridge: Cambridge University Press, 1989), 253–84.

62. E. B. Tylor, "On Traces of the Early Mental Condition of Man," *Notes on the Proceedings at the Meetings of the Royal Institution of Great Britain* 5 (1867): 92.

63. Tylor, *Primitive Culture*, 1:31.

64. Ibid., 1:42.

65. E. B. Tylor, "On the Limits of Savage Religion," *Journal of the Anthropological Institute* 21 (1892): 300–301.

66. Charles Godfrey Leland, *Gypsy Sorcery and Fortune Telling* (London: T. Fisher Unwin, 1891), 13.

67. Karl Marx, *Capital*, vol. 1, *A Critique of Political Economy*, trans. Ben Fowkes (1867; London: Penguin, 1992), 372.

68. Ibid., 165.

69. "Fetishes," *All the Year Round* 11 (July 23, 1864): 569.

70. Ludwig Feuerbach, *The Essence of Christianity*, trans. George Eliot (New York: Harper Torchbooks, 1957), xxxix.

71. George Louis Leclerc, Comte de Buffon, *Natural History, General and Particular*, vol. 3, *The History of Man and Quadrupeds*, trans. W. Smellie (1749; London: Cadell and Davies, 1812), 530–31.

72. Adolf Bastian, *Beiträge zur vergleichenden Psychologie* (Berlin: Ferdinand Dümmler, 1868), 118–19, cited and translated by Patrick Wolfe, "Should the Subaltern Dream? 'Australian Aborigines' and the Problem of Ethnographic Ventriloquism," in *Cultures of Scholarship*, ed. S. C. Humphreys (Ann Arbor: University of Michigan Press, 1998), 66–67.

73. Spencer, *Principles of Sociology*, 150; James G. Frazer, *Totemism and Exogamy: A Treatise on Certain Early Forms of Superstition and Society*, 4 vols. (London: Macmillan, 1910), 1:212.

74. Tylor, *Primitive Culture*, 1:431.

75. Marian S. Benham, *Henry Callaway M.D., D.D., First Bishop of Kaffraria: His Life-History and Work: A Memoir* (London: Macmillan, 1896), 247.

76. Tylor, *Primitive Culture*, 1:380.

77. E. B. Tylor, "Fritsch's 'South African Races,'" *Nature* 9, no. 234 (1874): 481.

78. Tylor, *Primitive Culture*, 1:22–23.

79. Ibid., 1:430, citing Henry Callaway, *The Religious System of the Amazulu* (1868–70; reprint, Cape Town: Struik, 1970), 92, 126; Eugène Casalis, *The Basutos; or, Twenty-Three Years in South Africa* (London: James Nisbet, 1861), 245; Thomas Arbousset and François Daumas, *Narrative of an Exploratory Tour to the North-East of the Colony of the Cape of Good Hope*, trans. John Croumbie Brown (1842; Cape Town: A. S. Robertson, 1846), 12.

80. Callaway, *Religious System*, 228, 259–60, 316.

81. Tylor, *Primitive Culture*, 1:443.

82. Ibid., citing Callaway, *Religious System*, 228, 259-60, 316; and Callaway, "On Divination," 170.

83. Callaway, *Religious System*, 238-39.

84. Ibid., 238, 241.

85. Ibid., 237.

86. Tylor, *Primitive Culture*, 1:110, citing Callaway, *Religious System*, 241.

87. Andrew Lang, *The Making of Religion* (London: Longman, 1898), 114.

88. Callaway, *Religious System*, 238, 242.

89. Ibid., 246.

90. Ibid., 6.

91. Ibid., 142.

92. I have adapted the distinction between hermeneutics and energetics, with a different purpose, from Paul Ricoeur, who used the term *energetics*, to refer to dynamic energy flowing between the subconscious and consciousness. I use the term for dynamic energy flowing between dreaming and acting in the world. See Paul Ricoeur, *Freud and Philosophy: An Essay on Interpretation*, trans. Denis Savage (1965; New Haven, CT: Yale University Press, 1970).

93. Callaway, *Religious System*, 160-61.

94. Ibid., 146-47, 157.

95. Marguerite Poland, David Hammond-Tooke, and Leigh Voigt, *The Abundant Herds: A Celebration of the Nguni Cattle of the Zulu People* (Vlaeberg, South Africa: Fernwood Press, 2003).

96. Callaway, *Religious System*, 172.

97. Ibid., 190n50.

98. Ibid., 212.

99. Ibid., 206-7, 209.

100. Ibid., 185, 260.

101. Ibid., 187-88.

102. Ibid., 192.

103. Ibid., 260.

104. C. M. Doke and B. W. Vilakazi, *Zulu-English Dictionary*, 2nd ed. (Johannesburg: Witwatersrand University Press, 1958), 175.

105. David Chidester, *Religions of South Africa* (London: Routledge, 1992), 3-6.

106. Callaway, *Religious System*, 188-89.

107. Tylor, *Primitive Culture*, 2:387.

108. Ibid., 1:104.

109. Ibid., 1:98, 2:367; see Callaway, *Religious System*, 64, 222-25, 263.

110. Tylor, *Primitive Culture*, 1:104.

111. Callaway, "On Divination," 166-67.

112. Ibid., 184.

113. Callaway, *Religious System*, 249-50.

114. Tylor, "On the Limits of Savage Religion," 283, 298.

115. Tylor, *Primitive Culture*, 2:449, 451, 453.

116. Ibid., 1:453.

117. Alfred Russel Wallace, "Physical Science and Philosophy," *Academy* 3 (February 15, 1872): 71.

118. Lang, *Making of Religion*, 70.

119. Emile Durkheim, *The Elementary Forms of the Religious Life*, trans. Joseph Ward Swain (1912; New York: Free Press, 1965), 86.

120. Tomoko Masuzawa, "Troubles with Materiality: The Ghost of Fetishism in the Nineteenth Century," *Comparative Studies in Society and History* 42, no. 2 (2000): 242-67.

121. Marx, *Capital*, 163.

CHAPTER FIVE

The epigraph is from H. Rider Haggard, *She* (London: Longmans, Green, 1887), 157.

1. Arthur Conan Doyle, *The Complete Sherlock Holmes* (London: Penguin, 2009), 127. For an analysis of Sherlock Holmes the Orientalist, see Pinaki Roy, *The Manichean Investigators: A Postcolonial and Cultural Rereading of the Sherlock Holmes and Byomkesh Bakshi Stories* (New Delhi: Sarup, 2008), 124-39.

2. Doyle, *Complete Sherlock Holmes*, 485, 52-88.

3. Ibid., 887.

4. Andrew Lang, "The Novels of Sir Arthur Conan Doyle," *Quarterly Review* 200 (July 1904): 178; cited in William S. Baring-Gould, *The Annotated Sherlock Holmes*, 2 vols. (New York: Clarkson N. Potter, 1967), 1:655.

5. Andrew Lang, "The Supernatural in Fiction," in *Adventures among Books*, by Lang (London: Longman, 1905), 279. See Lang, "Realism and Romance," *Contemporary Review* 52 (1887): 683-93.

6. H. Rider Haggard, "About Fiction," *Contemporary Review* 51 (1887): 172.

7. Robert Michalski, "Towards a Popular Culture: Andrew Lang's Anthropological and Literary Criticism," *Journal of American Culture* 18, no. 3 (1995): 16. See Robert Crawford, "Pater's *Renaissance*, Andrew Lang, and Anthropological Romanticism," *English Literary History* 53, no. 4 (1986): 849-79.

8. Andrew Lang, *Essays in Little* (New York: Scribner, 1901), 200; Martin Green, *Dreams of Adventure, Deeds of Empire* (New York: Basic Books, 1979), 233.

9. H. Rider Haggard, *King Solomon's Mines* (1885; London: Macdonald, 1965), 19.

10. Brian Street, *The Savage in Literature* (London: Routledge, 1975), 74.

11. Eric J. Sharpe, *Comparative Religion*, 2nd ed. (LaSalle, IL: Open Court, 1986), 58-65; Walter H. Capps, *Religious Studies: The Making of a Discipline* (Minneapolis: Fortress Press, 1995), 83-84; Marjorie Wheeler-Barclay, *The Science of Religion in Britain, 1860-1915* (Charlottesville: University of Virginia Press, 2010), 104-39. See Antonius Petrus Leonardus de Cocq, *Andrew Lang, a Nineteenth-Century Anthropologist* (Tilburg, Netherlands: Zwijsen, 1968); Andrew Duff-Cooper, "Andrew Lang: Aspects of His Work in Relation to Current Social Anthropology," *Folklore* 97, no. 2 (1986): 186-205; Roger Lancelyn Green, *Andrew Lang: A Critical Biography* (Leicester: Edmund Ward, 1946); Green, *Andrew Lang* (London: Bodley Head, 1962); Eleanor de Selms Langstaff, *Andrew Lang* (Boston: Twayne, 1978); George W. Stocking Jr., *After Tylor: British Social Anthropology, 1888-1951* (Madison: University of Wisconsin Press, 1995), 50-63.

12. *Times* (London), July 22, 1912, 11, cited in Duff-Cooper, "Andrew Lang," 187.

13. R. R. Marett, *A Jerseyman at Oxford* (Oxford: Oxford University Press, 1941), 169.

14. Salomon Reinach, *Orpheus: A General History of Religions*, trans. Florence Simmonds (New York: G. P. Putnam, 1909), 3.

15. Salomon Reinach, "Andrew Lang," *Quarterly Review* 218 (April 1913): 218.

16. H. Rider Haggard, *The Days of My Life*, 2 vols. (London: Longmans, Green, 1926), 1:229-31.

17. John Buchan, *Andrew Lang and the Border* (London: Oxford University Press, 1933), 1.

18. Fred B. Fynney, *Zululand and the Zulus* (Maritzburg: Horne Brothers, 1880).

19. Haggard, *Days of My Life*, 1:235.

20. Laurence Kitzan, *Victorian Writers and the Image of Empire: The Rose-Colored Vision* (Westport, CT: Greenwood Press, 2001), 47. On H. Rider Haggard, see Peter Berresford Ellis, *H. Rider Haggard: A Voice from the Infinite* (London: Routledge & Kegan Paul, 1978); Wendy R. Katz, *Rider Haggard and the Fiction of Empire: Critical Study of British Imperial Fiction* (Cambridge: Cambridge University Press, 1987); Tom Pocock, *Rider Haggard and the Lost Empire* (London: Weidenfeld & Nicolson, 1993). *King Solomon's Mines*, in particular, has been analyzed as a key text in British imperialism and gendered, sexual, environmental, and colonial domination. Laura Chrisman, "Gendering Imperial Culture," in *Cultural Readings of Imperialism: Edward Said and*

the Gravity of History, ed. Keith Ansell-Pearson, Benita Parry, and Judith Squires (New York: St. Martin's, 1997), 290–303; Gail Ching-Liang Low, *White Skin/Black Masks: Representation and Colonialism* (London: Routledge, 1996); Anne McClintock, *Imperial Leather: Race, Gender, and Sexuality in the Colonial Contest* (London: Routledge, 1995).

21. Alfred Milner, *The Nation and the Empire* (London: Constable, 1913), xxxii; Alan Sandison, "John Buchan: The Church of Empire," in *The Wheel of Empire,* by Sandison (New York: St. Martin's Press, 1967), 25–45.

22. John Buchan, *The African Colony: Studies in the Reconstruction* (Edinburgh: Blackwood, 1903), 397, 390. See Saul Dubow, "Colonial Nationalism, the Milner Kindergarten, and the Rise of 'South Africanism,' 1902–1910," *History Workshop Journal* 43 (1997): 53–85; Dubow, "Imagining the 'New' South Africa in the Era of Reconstruction," in *The Impact of the South African War,* ed. David Omissi and Andrew Thompson (Basingstoke: Palgrave, 2002), 76–95.

23. Janet Adam Smith, *John Buchan: A Biography* (London: Hart-Davis, 1965); Andrew Lownie, *John Buchan: Presbyterian Cavalier* (London: Constable, 1995); Paul Rich, " 'Milnerism and a Ripping Yarn': Transvaal Land Settlement and John Buchan's Novel *Prester John,* 1901–1910," in *Town and Countryside in the Transvaal: Capitalist Penetration and Popular Response,* ed. Belinda Bozzoli (Johannesburg: Ravan Press, 1983), 412–33; Peter Henshaw, "John Buchan from the 'Borders' to the 'Berg': Nature, Empire, and White South African Identity, 1901–1910," *African Studies* 62, no. 1 (2003): 3–32.

24. Andrew Lang, "King Solomon's Mines," *Saturday Review* 60 (October 10, 1885): 485–86.

25. Douglas Blackburn and N. W. Thomas, "Animal Superstitions among the Zulus, Basutos, Griquas, and Magatese, and the Kafirs of Natal," *Man* 4 (1904): 181.

26. Andrew Lang, "Edward Burnett Tylor," in *Anthropological Essays Presented to Edward Burnett Tylor in Honour of His 75th Birthday, Oct. 2 1907,* ed. W. H. R. Rivers, R. R. Marett, and Northcote W. Thomas (Oxford: Clarendon Press, 1907): 1.

27. John Buchan, *Greenmantle* (1916; Oxford: Oxford University Press, 1993), 24.

28. Andrew Lang, *Magic and Religion* (London: Longmans, Green, 1901), 240.

29. Andrew Lang, "At the Sign of the Ship," *Longman's Magazine* 28 (October 1896): 632.

30. Andrew Lang, *Myth, Ritual, and Religion,* 2 vols. (1899; London: Longmans, Green, 1906), 2:358–59.

31. R. H. Codrington, *The Melanesians: Studies in Their Anthropology and Folk-Lore* (Oxford: Clarendon Press, 1891), 123, 357.

32. Cited in Stocking, *After Tylor,* 43–44.

33. R. H. Codrington, "Letter to Max Müller" (July 7, 1877), cited in *Lectures on the Origin and Growth of Religion,* by F. Max Müller (London: Longmans, Green, 1878), 55; see Codrington, *Melanesians,* 118.

34. Andrew Lang, *The Making of Religion* (London: Longmans, Green, 1898), 226; Henry Callaway, *The Religious System of the Amazulu* (1868–70; reprint, Cape Town: Struik, 1970).

35. Andrew Lang, *Cock Lane and Common-Sense* (London: Longmans, Green, 1894), x.

36. Haggard, *She,* 125.

37. H. Rider Haggard, *Allan Quatermain* (London: Longmans, 1887), 157.

38. Lilias Rider Haggard, *The Cloak That I Left: A Biography of the Author Henry Rider Haggard K.B.E.* (London: Hodder and Stoughton, 1951), 53.

39. Ibid.

40. Duncan Bell, "The Idea of a Patriot Queen? The Monarchy, the Constitution, and the Iconographic Order of Greater Britain, 1860–1900," *Journal of Imperial and Commonwealth History* 34, no. 1 (2006): 3–22.

41. Haggard, *She,* 4, 170.

42. Andrew Lang, *Custom and Myth* (London: Longmans, Green, 1884), 233.

43. John Buchan, *Prestor John* (Boston: Houghton Mifflin, 1910), 73. Prester John, of course,

alludes to the medieval legend of a powerful Christian king in Africa. See David Chidester, *Christianity: A Global History* (San Francisco: HarperCollins, 2000), 337, 343. On Ethiopianism, see David Chidester, *Religions of South Africa* (London: Routledge, 1992), 114-22.

44. Buchan, *African Colony*, 397.

45. Andrew Lang, *XXII Ballades in Blue China* (London: Kegan Paul, 1880), 40, cited in Stocking, *After Tylor*, 56; George W. Stocking Jr., *Delimiting Anthropology: Occasional Inquiries and Reflections* (Madison: University of Wisconsin Press, 2002), 145.

46. James Anson Farrer, *Primitive Manners and Customs* (London: Chatto & Windus, 1879), xii; see Farrer, *Zululand and the Zulus* (London: Kirby and Endean, 1879).

47. F. Max Müller, *Introduction to the Science of Religion: Four Lectures Delivered at the Royal Institution with Two Essays on False Analogies, and the Philosophy of Mythology* (London: Longmans, Green, 1873).

48. E. B. Tylor, *Primitive Culture*, 2 vols. (London: John Murray, 1871).

49. Jeremy Stolow, "Religion and/as Media," *Theory, Culture, and Society* 22, no. 4 (2005): 136.

50. Andrew Lang, "Mythology and Fairy Tales," *Fortnightly Review* 13 (1873): 622; Richard M. Dorson, ed., *Peasant Customs and Savage Myths: Selections from the British Folklorists*, 2 vols. (Chicago: University of Chicago Press, 1968), 1:197.

51. Lang, *Custom and Myth*, 125.

52. Lang, "Mythology and Fairy Tales," 625; Dorson, *Peasant Customs and Savage Myths*, 1:200.

53. Lang, *Myth, Ritual, and Religion*, 1:110, citing Callaway, *Religious System*, 384-85.

54. Lang, "Mythology and Fairy Tales," 630; Dorson, *Peasant Customs and Savage Myths*, 1:206.

55. Lang, *Making of Religion*, 226-27; see Lang, "South African Religion," in Lang, *Magic and Religion*, 224-40.

56. J. M. Orpen, "A Glimpse into the Mythology of the Maluti Bushmen," *Cape Monthly Magazine*, n.s., 9 (1874): 1-10; W. H. I. Bleek, "Remarks on Orpen's 'Mythology of the Maluti Bushmen,'" *Cape Monthly Magazine*, n.s., 9 (1874): 10-13.

57. Lang, *Making of Religion*, 210.

58. Ibid., 229.

59. Ibid., 228.

60. H. Rider Haggard, *Nada the Lily* (1892; London: Macdonald, 1963), xii.

61. Ibid.

62. Ibid., 98.

63. Ibid., 187-88.

64. Buchan, *Prester John*, 96.

65. Ibid., 120.

66. Andrew Lang, "Protest of a Psycho-Folklorist," *Folklore* 6, no. 3 (1895): 236-48.

67. Edward Clodd, "In Memorium: Andrew Lang (1844-1912)," *Folklore* 23, no. 3 (1912): 361.

68. Alfred Russel Wallace, *Miracles and Modern Spiritualism*, rev. ed. (1874; London: George Redway, 1896; reprint, New York: Arno, 1975); see Peter Pels, "Spiritual Facts and Super-visions: The 'Conversion' of Alfred Russel Wallace," *Etnofoor* 8, no. 2 (1995): 69-91.

69. George W. Stocking Jr., "Animism in Theory and Practice: E. B. Tylor's Unpublished 'Notes on Spiritualism,'" *Man* 6, no. 1 (1971): 88-104. On Victorian spiritualism, see Roger Luckhurst, "Knowledge, Belief, and the Supernatural at the Imperial Margin," in *The Victorian Supernatural*, ed. Nicola Bown, Carolyn Burdett, and Pamela Thurschwell (Cambridge: Cambridge University Press, 2004): 197-216; Janet Oppenheim, *The Other World: Spiritualism and Psychical Research in England, 1850-1914* (Cambridge: Cambridge University Press, 1985).

70. Lang, *Making of Religion*, 72, citing Callaway, *Religious System*, 232.

71. David Leslie, *Among the Zulus and Amatongas* (Edinburgh: Edmonston, 1875), 55.

72. Lang, *Cock Lane*, 78; H. Rider Haggard, *Allan's Wife* (London: Spencer Blackett, 1889), 94.

73. Andrew Lang, *The Origins of Religion* (London: Watts, 1908), 94.

74. Haggard, *Nada the Lily*, 22.

75. H. Rider Haggard, *She and Allan* (London: Longmans, Green, 1921), 233.

76. H. Rider Haggard, *The Wizard* (Bristol: J. W. Arrowsmith, 1896), 236; H. Rider Haggard, *Lysbeth: A Tale of the Dutch* (London: Longmans, Green, 1901), 289.

77. Buchan, *Prester John*, 72. See Roger Luckhurst, *The Invention of Telepathy* (Oxford: Oxford University Press, 2002).

78. Buchan, *Prester John*, 105. See Pamela Thurschwell, *Literature, Technology, and Magical Thinking, 1880–1920* (Cambridge: Cambridge University Press, 2001).

79. Buchan, *Prester John*, 263.

80. Haggard, *King Solomon's Mines*, 87.

81. Tylor, *Primitive Culture*, 1:5.

82. Lang, *Origins of Religion*, 95.

83. C. de B. Webb and J. B. Wright, eds., *The James Stuart Archive of Recorded Oral Evidence Relating to the History of the Zulu and Neighbouring Peoples*, vol. 3 (Durban: University of Natal Press, 1976), 171.

84. Lang, *Myth, Ritual, and Religion*, 1:172–73.

85. Ibid., 1:111.

86. Ibid., 1:109–10.

87. Ibid., 1:113.

88. Ibid., 1:110.

89. H. Rider Haggard, *Cetywayo and His White Neighbours* (London: Trübner, 1882), 22.

90. Ibid., 23.

91. Theophilus Shepstone, "Questions Proposed by His Excellency the Lieutenant-Governor and Answers by the Secretary for Native Affairs, October 16, 1863," in *British Documents on Foreign Affairs, Natal and Zululand, 1856–1879*, ed. David Throup (Bethesda, MD: University Publications of America, 1995), 35.

92. *Government Commission on Native Law and Custom* (1881; Cape Town: Government Printer, 1883), 68.

93. Theophilus Shepstone, "Letter to the Editor," *Natal Mercury*, January 19, 1892, cited in *Healing Traditions: African Medicine, Cultural Exchange, and Competition in South Africa, 1820–1948*, by Karen E. Flint (Athens: Ohio University Press, 2008), 107.

94. Haggard, *Cetywayo*, 19.

95. Ibid.

96. John William Colenso, *Ten Weeks in Natal: A Journal of a First Tour of Visitation among the Colonists and Zulu Kafirs of Natal* (London: Macmillan, 1855), 116–17.

97. H. Rider Haggard, "A Zulu War Dance," *Gentleman's Magazine* 243 (July 1877): 101.

98. Ibid., 104–6. See Jeff Guy, *The Maphumulo Uprising: War, Law, and Ritual in the Zulu Rebellion* (Scottsville, South Africa: University of KwaZulu-Natal Press, 2005).

99. Cited in Carolyn Hamilton, *Terrific Majesty: The Powers of Shaka Zulu and the Limits of Historical Invention* (Cambridge, MA: Harvard University Press; Cape Town: David Philip, 1998), 73.

100. Terence Ranger, "The Invention of Tradition in Colonial Africa," in *The Invention of Tradition*, ed. Eric Hobsbawm and Terence Ranger (Cambridge: Cambridge University Press, 1983), 212.

101. H. Rider Haggard, "The Tale of Isandhlwana and Rorkes Drift," in *The True Story Book*, ed. Andrew Lang, 2nd ed. (London: Longmans, Green, 1893), 132–52.

102. Neil Parsons, "'No Longer Rare Birds in London': Zulu, Ndebele, Gaza, and Swazi Envoys to England, 1882–1894," in *Black Victorians/Black Victoriana*, ed. Gretchen Holbrook Gerzina (New Brunswick, NJ: Rutgers University Press, 2003), 117.

103. H. Bartle Frere, "On Systems of Land Tenure among Aboriginal Tribes in South Africa," *Journal of the Anthropological Institute* 12 (1883): 262, 263, 265.

104. Ibid., 271–72.

105. Ibid., 275.

106. E. B. Tylor, "The Philosophy of Religion among the Lower Races of Mankind," *Journal of the Ethnological Society of London* 2, no. 4 (1870): 381.

107. Haggard, *Allan Quatermain*, 154.

108. Haggard, *King Solomon's Mines*, 183.

109. Buchan, *Prester John*, 100.

110. Ibid., 141.

111. Ibid., 202.

112. Patrick Brantlinger, *Rule of Darkness: British Literature and Imperialism, 1830–1914* (Ithaca, NY: Cornell University Press, 1988), 229.

113. H. Rider Haggard, *Child of Storm* (London: Cassell, 1913), vi.

114. Andrew Lang, *Books and Bookmen* (London: Longmans, Green, 1886), 51.

115. Andrew Lang, introduction to *Poetical Works of Sir Walter Scott*, ed. Andrew Lang, 2 vols. (London: Adam and Charles Black, 1895), 1:xx.

116. Andrew Lang, *In the Wrong Paradise, and Other Stories* (London: K. Paul, Trench, 1886), iii.

117. Haggard, *Allan Quatermain*, 13.

118. Haggard, *Cetywayo*, liii.

119. Ibid.

120. Haggard, *Child of Storm*, 89–90. See H. Rider Haggard, "The Zulus: The Finest Savage Race in the World," *Pall Mall Magazine* 41, no. 182 (1908): 764–70.

121. Haggard, *Allan Quatermain*, 4–6.

122. Lang, *In the Wrong Paradise*, iii.

123. R. R. Marett, "Andrew Lang: Folklorist and Critic," *Folklore* 23, no. 3 (1912): 365.

124. Lang, *In the Wrong Paradise*, iii–iv.

125. Marett, "Andrew Lang," 364.

126. Lang, *In the Wrong Paradise*, 283, 285.

127. Ibid., 284–85.

128. Ibid., 180. See Julie Sparks, "At the Intersection of Victorian Science and Fiction: Andrew Lang's 'Romance of the First Radical,'" *English Literature in Transition, 1880–1920* 42, no. 2 (1999): 125–42.

129. Lang, *In the Wrong Paradise*, 185–186. Here Lang is satirizing theories of the origin of language in imitation (the "bow-wow" theory) or interjections (the "pooh-pooh" theory) as they had been designated by F. Max Müller, *Lectures on the Science of Language* (London: Longmans, Green, 1861), 344–56; *Lectures on the Science of Language*, second series (London: Longman, Green, Longman, Roberts, & Green, 1864), 88–92.

130. Talal Asad, *Formations of the Secular: Christianity, Islam, Modernity* (Stanford, CA: Stanford University Press, 2003), 14–15.

131. [Andrew Lang], *He* (London: Longmans, Green, 1887), frontispiece.

132. Lang, *Essays in Little*, 200.

133. Max Weber, "Science as a Vocation," in *From Max Weber: Essays in Sociology*, ed. and trans., H. H. Gerth and C. Wright Mills (London: Routledge & Kegan Paul, 1948), 139.

134. Andrew Lang, "General Essay on the Works of Charles Dickens," in *Reprinted Pieces*, by Charles Dickens (London: Chapman & Hall, 1899), xv–xvi; Stewart Guthrie, *Faces in the Clouds: A New Theory of Religion* (Oxford: Oxford University Press, 1993), 58.

135. Andrew Lang, introduction to *The Personal History of David Copperfield*, by Charles Dickens, 2 vols. (London: Chapman & Hall, 1897), 1:2–3.

136. Laura Chrisman, "The Imperial Unconscious? Representations of Imperial Discourse," *Critical Quarterly* 32, no. 3 (1990): 38–58; Chrisman, *Rereading the Imperial Romance: British Imperialism and South African Resistance in Haggard, Schreiner, and Plaatje* (Oxford: Clarendon Press, 2000).

137. Carolyn Burdett, "Romance, Reincarnation, and Rider Haggard," in Bown, Burdett, and Thurschwell, *Victorian Supernatural*, 217-31.

138. Michael Saler, "'Clap If You Believe In Sherlock Holmes': Mass Culture and the Re-enchantment of Modernity, c. 1890-c. 1940," *Historical Journal* 46, no. 3 (2003): 604.

139. Haggard, *She*, 4, 157.

CHAPTER SIX

The epigraph is from R. R. Marett and T. K. Penniman, eds. *Spencer's Scientific Correspondence with Sir J. G. Frazer and Others* (Oxford: Clarendon, 1932), 41, cited in Robert Ackerman, *J. G. Frazer, His Life and His Work* (Cambridge: Cambridge University Press, 1987), 157.

1. Henri-Alexandre Junod, *The Life of a South African Tribe*, 2 vols., 2nd ed. (London: Macmillan, 1927), 1:492.

2. Ibid.

3. Ibid., 1:492-95. See Lorenzo Macagno, "Missionaries and the Ethnographic Imagination: Reflections on the Legacy of Henri-Alexandre Junod (1863-1934)," *Social Sciences and Missions* 22, no. 1 (2009): 55-88.

4. Marc Epprecht, "'Unnatural Vice' in South Africa: The 1907 Commission of Enquiry," *International Journal of African Historical Studies* 34, no. 1 (2001): 121-40; Ross G. Forman, "Randy on the Rand: Portuguese African Labor and the Discourse on 'Unnatural Vice' in the Transvaal in the Early Twentieth Century," *Journal of the History of Sexuality* 11, no. 4 (2002): 570-609.

5. Patrick Harries, "The Anthropologist as Historian and Liberal: H-A Junod and the Thonga," *Journal of South African Studies* 8, no. 1 (1981): 37. See James Bryce, *Impressions of South Africa* (London: Macmillan, 1897); Bryce, *The Relations of the Advanced and Backward Races of Mankind* (Oxford: Clarendon Press, 1902).

6. Junod, *Life of a South African Tribe*, 2nd ed., 1:1.

7. James G. Frazer, "Questions on the Manners, Customs, Religion, Superstition, etc. of Uncivilized or Semi-Civilized Peoples," *Journal of the Anthropological Institute* 18 (1889): 431-40; Junod, *Life of a South African Tribe*, 2nd ed., 1:6.

8. Henri-Alexandre Junod, *Les Ba-Ronga: Etude ethnographique sur les indigénes de la baie de Delgoa* (Neuchâtel, Switzerland: Attinger, 1898); James Frazer, *The Golden Bough: A Study in Magic and Religion*, 12 vols., 3rd ed. (London: Macmillan, 1911-15), 1:152, 153, 268, 286; 2: 205.

9. Ibid., 1:268.

10. Marcel Mauss and Henri Hubert, *Sacrifice: Its Nature and Function*, trans. W. D. Halls (1898; Chicago: University of Chicago Press, 1964); Marcel Mauss and Henri Hubert, *A General Theory of Magic*, trans. Robert Brain (1902-3; London: Routledge, Kegan Paul, 1975); Emile Durkheim, *The Elementary Forms of the Religious Life*, trans. Joseph Ward Swain (1912; New York: Free Press, 1965).

11. Junod, *Life of a South African Tribe*, 2nd ed., 1:3.

12. Henri-Alexandre Junod, "The Ba-Thonga of the Transvaal," *South African Journal of Science* 3 (1905): 255.

13. Junod, *Life of a South African Tribe*, 2nd ed., 1:4-5.

14. Ibid., 1:444.

15. Edmund Leach, "Golden Bough or Gilded Twig?" *Daedalus* 90, no. 2 (1961): 381.

16. R. R. Marett, *The Threshold of Religion*, 2nd ed. (London: Methuen, 1914), 176.

17. Junod, *Life of a South African Tribe*, 2nd ed., 2:451, 368, 369-70.

18. Ibid., 2:451.

19. Ibid., 2:370.

20. William Robertson Smith, *Lectures on the Religion of the Semites*, first series, 1st ed. (Edinburgh: Black, 1889). On William Robertson Smith, see T. O. Beidelman, *W. Robertson Smith*

and the Sociological Study of Religion (Chicago: University of Chicago Press, 1974); John Sutherland Black and George Chrystal, *The Life of William Robertson Smith* (London: Adam and Charles Black, 1912); William Johnstone, ed., *William Robertson Smith: Essays in Reassessment* (Sheffield: Sheffield Academic Press, 1995); Robert Alun Jones, "Robertson Smith and James Frazer on Religion: Two Traditions in British Social Anthropology," in *Functionalism Historicized: Essays on British Social Anthropology*, ed. George W. Stocking Jr. (Madison: University of Wisconsin Press, 1984), 31–58; Bernhard Maier, *William Robertson Smith: His Life, His Work, and His Times* (Tübingen, Mohr Siebeck, 2009); Robert A. Segal, "William Robertson Smith: Sociologist or Theologian?" *Religion* 38, no. 1 (2008): 9–24; Margit Warburg, "William Robertson Smith and the Study of Religion," *Religion* 19, no. 1 (1989): 41–61; Marjorie Wheeler-Barclay, "Victorian Evangelicalism and the Sociology of Religion: The Career of William Robertson Smith," *Journal of the History of Ideas* 54, no. 1 (1993): 59–78.

21. William Robertson Smith, *Religion of the Semites*, 2nd ed. (1894; London: Adam and Charles Black, 1914), 234; E. B. Tylor, *Primitive Culture*, 2 vols. (London: John Murray, 1871): 2:346.

22. Peter Kolb, *Caput Bonae Spei Hodiernum* (Nürnberg: Peter Conrad Monath, 1719), 1:205; Robertson Smith, *Religion of the Semites*, 234n2.

23. Robertson Smith, *Religion of the Semites*, 297–300.

24. A. H. Sayce, "Review: William Robertson Smith, *Religion of the Semites*," *Academy* 36 (November 30, 1889): 357–58.

25. James G. Frazer, "William Robertson Smith," in *Sir Roger de Coverley and Other Literary Pieces*, by Frazer (London: Macmillan, 1894), 207.

26. On Frazer, see Robert Ackerman, "Frazer on Myth and Ritual," *Journal of the History of Ideas* 36, no. 1 (1975): 115–34; Ackerman, *J. G. Frazer*; Ackerman, *The Myth and Ritual School: J. G. Frazer and the Cambridge Ritualists* (New York: Garland, 1991); Ackerman, ed., *Selected Letters of Sir J. G. Frazer* (Oxford: Oxford University Press, 2005); Robert Fraser, *The Making of the Golden Bough: The Origins and Growth of an Argument* (New York: St. Martin's Press, 1990); Jonathan Z. Smith, "When the Bough Breaks," in *Map Is Not Territory: Studies in the History of Religions*, by Smith (Leiden: Brill, 1978), 208–39.

27. Ackerman, *J. G. Frazer*, 153–57, 244–45, 269–70; for his notebooks on Africa, see James G. Frazer, *Anthologia Anthropologica: The Native Races of Africa and Madagascar* (London: Lund Humphries, 1938).

28. Ackerman, *J. G. Frazer*, 157.

29. James G. Frazer, *The Golden Bough: A Study in Magic and Religion*, abridged ed. (London: Macmillan, 1922), 49.

30. Robertson Smith, *Religion of the Semites*, 440.

31. James G. Frazer, "The Prytaneum, the Temple of Vesta, the Vestals, Perpetual Fires (1885)," in *Garnered Sheaves: Essays, Addresses, and Reviews*, by Frazer (London: Macmillan, 1931), 64.

32. Ibid., 64–65, citing Charles John Andersson, *Lake Ngami; or, Explorations and Discoveries during Four Years' Wanderings in the Wilds of South Western Africa* (London: Hurst and Blackett, 1856), 223.

33. Andersson, *Lake Ngami*, iv, 201.

34. Marion Wallace, "'Making Tradition': Healing, History, and Ethnic Identity among Otjiherero-Speakers in Namibia, c. 1850–1950," *Journal of Southern African Studies* 29, no. 2 (2003): 370; see Brigitte Lau, "Conflict and Power in Nineteenth-Century Namibia," *Journal of African History* 27, no. 1 (1986): 29–39.

35. Wallace, "Making Tradition," 362.

36. Frazer, "Prytaneum," 66–67.

37. R. R. Marett, *Psychology and Folklore* (London: Methuen, 1920), 173–74.

38. James G. Frazer, *Totemism and Exogamy: A Treatise on Certain Early Forms of Superstition and Society*, 4 vols. (London: Macmillan, 1910), 2:388; see James G. Frazer, "South African Totemism," *Man* 1 (1901): 135–36.

39. Frazer, *Golden Bough*, 3rd ed., 1:350, 2:224; see James G. Frazer, "Savage Childhood: The Infant Kaffir," *Daily Mail* (London), Books supplement, November 24, 1906; Dudley Kidd, *The Essential Kafir* (London: Macmillan, 1904); Kidd, *Savage Childhood* (London: Macmillan, 1906).

40. Frazer, *Totemism and Exogamy*, 2:386; James G. Frazer, *The Fear of the Dead in Primitive Religion* (London: Macmillan, 1933), 51.

41. Harries, "Anthropologist as Historian and Liberal," 45-50; see Patrick Harries, *Butterflies and Barbarians: Swiss Missionaries and Systems of Knowledge in South-East Africa* (London: James Currey; Athens: Ohio University Press, 2007).

42. Henri-Alexandre Junod, "The Native Language and Native Education," *Journal of the African Society* 5, no. 17 (1905): 6, 9.

43. Edmund Leach, "The Anthropology of Religion: British and French Schools," in *Nineteenth-Century Religious Thought in the West*, 3 vols., ed. Ninian Smart, John Clayton, Patrick Sherry, and Steven T. Katz (Cambridge: Cambridge University Press, 1985), 3:218-19.

44. Junod, *Life of a South African Tribe*, 2nd ed., 1:7.

45. Junod, "Ba-Thonga of the Transvaal," 222-62.

46. Junod, *Life of a South African Tribe*, 2nd ed., 1:6, 125, 447-48.

47. Arnold van Gennep, *The Rites of Passage*, trans. Monika B. Vizedom and Gabrielle L. Caffee (1909; Chicago: University of Chicago Press, 1960).

48. Junod, *Life of a South African Tribe*, 2nd ed., 1:74, 167-68, 327-28, 483.

49. Ibid., 2:395.

50. Henri-Alexandre Junod, *The Life of a South African Tribe*, 2 vols., 1st ed. (London: Macmillan, 1912-13), 2:362.

51. Junod, *Life of a South African Tribe*, 2nd ed., 2:388.

52. Junod, *Life of a South African Tribe*, 1st ed., 2:412; 2nd ed., 2:451.

53. Junod, *Life of a South African Tribe*, 1st ed., 2:361.

54. Junod, *Life of a South African Tribe*, 2nd ed., 2:387.

55. Junod, *Life of a South African Tribe*, 1st ed., 2:388-89; 2nd ed., 2:427-28.

56. Junod, *Life of a South African Tribe*, 2nd ed., 2:427.

57. Junod, *Life of a South African Tribe*, 1st ed., 2:412; 2nd ed., 2:451.

58. Junod, *Life of a South African Tribe*, 1st ed., 2:412.

59. Junod, *Life of a South African Tribe*, 2nd ed., 2:454.

60. Junod, *Life of a South African Tribe*, 1st ed., 2:382; 2nd ed., 2:419.

61. James G. Frazer, *The Golden Bough: A Study in Comparative Religion*, 2 vols. (London: Macmillan, 1890); Frazer, *The Golden Bough: A Study in Magic and Religion*, 2nd ed., 3 vols. (London: Macmillan, 1900).

62. Junod, *Life of a South African Tribe*, 1st ed., 2:382; 2nd ed., 2:418.

63. Junod, *Life of a South African Tribe*, 2nd ed., 2:419-20n1.

64. Junod, *Life of a South African Tribe*, 1st ed., 2:358.

65. Junod, *Life of a South African Tribe*, 1st ed., 2:373; 2nd ed., 2:405.

66. Junod, *Life of a South African Tribe*, 1st ed., 2:356; 2nd ed., 2:381-82.

67. Junod, "Ba-Thonga of the Transvaal," 246-47.

68. Malyn Newitt, *A History of Mozambique* (London: Hurst, 1995), 492-93; Sheila T. van der Horst, *Native Labour in South Africa* (Oxford: Oxford University Press, 1942), 216-17.

69. Junod, *Life of a South African Tribe*, 2nd ed., 2:311.

70. Junod, *Life of a South African Tribe*, 1st ed., 2:365-66; 2nd ed., 2:393-94.

71. Junod, *Life of a South African Tribe*, 1st ed., 2:366; 2nd ed., 2:394. On migrant labor and rites of passage, see P. A. McAllister, "Work, Homestead, and the Shades: The Ritual Interpretation of Labour Migration among the Gcaleka," in *Black Villagers in an Industrial Society*, ed. Philip Mayer (Cape Town: Oxford University Press, 1980), 205-53; McAllister, *Xhosa Beer Drinking Rituals: Power, Practice, and Performance in the South African Rural Periphery* (Durham, NC: Carolina Academic Press, 2006).

72. Junod, *Life of a South African Tribe*, 2nd ed., 1:494-95.

73. Frazer, *Golden Bough*, 3rd ed., 10:vi.

74. Zackie Achmat, "'Apostles of Civilized Vice': 'Immoral Practices' and 'Unnatural Vice' in South African Prisons and Compounds, 1890-1920," *Social Dynamics* 19, no. 2 (1993): 92-110; Patrick Harries, "Symbols and Sexuality: Culture and Identity on the Early Witwatersrand Gold Mines," *Gender and History* 2, no. 3 (1990): 318-36; Harries, *Work, Culture, and Identity: Migrant Labourers in Mozambique and South Africa, c. 1860-1910* (London: James Currey, 1994), 200-208; T. Dunbar Moodie, with Vivienne Ndatshe and British Sibuyi, "Migrancy and Male Sexuality on the South African Gold Mines," *Journal of Southern African Studies* 14, no. 2 (1998): 228-56; Moodie, with Vivienne Ndatshe, *Going for Gold: Men, Mines, and Migration* (Johannesburg: Witwatersrand University Press; Berkeley: University of California Press, 1994); Isak Niehaus, "Renegotiating Masculinity in the South African Lowveld: Narratives of Male-Male Sex in Labour Compounds and in Prisons," *African Studies* 61, no. 1 (2002): 77-97.

75. William Gemmill, introduction to Henri-Philippe Junod, *Bantu Heritage* (Johannesburg: Hortors, for the Transvaal Chamber of Mines, 1938), i.

76. William R. Bascom, review of *Bantu Heritage*, by H. P. Junod, *American Anthropologist* 43, no. 1 (1941): 107.

77. Junod, *Bantu Heritage*, 92; see Wilmot G. James, "From Segregation to Apartheid: Miners and Peasants in the Making of a Racial Order, South Africa, 1930-1952" (PhD diss., University of Wisconsin-Madison, 1982), 144; Alan H. Jeeves, *Migrant Labour in South Africa's Mining Economy: The Struggle for the Gold Mines' Labour Supply, 1890-1920* (Kingston, Ontario: McGill-Queens University Press, 1985), 115.

78. Jonny Steinberg, *The Number: One Man's Search for Identity in the Cape Underworld and Prison Gangs* (Johannesburg: Jonathan Ball, 2004), 47.

79. Charles van Onselen, *The Small Matter of a Horse: The Life of "Nongoloza" Mathebula, 1867-1948* (Johannesburg: Ravan, 1984); Van Onselen, *New Babylon, New Nineveh: Everyday Life on the Witwatersrand, 1886-1914* (Johannesburg: Jonathan Ball, 2001), 368-97.

80. Steinberg, *Number*, 18.

81. Ibid., 54-55.

82. Frazer, *Golden Bough*, abridged ed., 60.

83. Frazer, *Fear of the Dead in Primitive Religion*, 51, citing Junod, *Life of a South African Tribe*, 2nd ed., 2:372.

84. Frazer, *Golden Bough*, abridged ed., 61.

85. Ibid., 62-78, citing Junod, *Ba-Ronga*, 66-67.

86. Frazer, *Golden Bough*, abridged ed., 46.

87. Junod, "Ba-Thonga of the Transvaal," 255.

88. Frazer, *Golden Bough*, abridged ed., 91.

89. Michael Taussig, *The Magic of the State* (London: Routledge, 1997).

90. Junod, *Life of a South African Tribe*, 1st ed., 1:2.

91. Ibid.

92. Ibid., 1:2-3.

93. Ibid., 1:3.

94. James G. Frazer, "The Scope and Method of Mental Anthropology (1920)," in Frazer, *Garnered Sheaves*, 244.

95. Frazer, "Scope and Method of Mental Anthropology," 246.

96. Harries, *Butterflies and Barbarians*, 232.

97. Emile Durkheim, review of *Les Ba-Ronga*, by Junod, *L'Année sociologique* 3 (1898-99): 370-72; Marcel Mauss, review of *Les Ba-Ronga*, by Junod, *L'Année sociologique* 3 (1898-99): 220-22, reprinted in *Oeuvres 3: Cohésion sociale et divisions de la sociologie*, by Mauss (Paris: Minuit, 1969), 126-28; Harries, *Butterflies and Barbarians*, 211.

98. See Ivan Strenski, *Contesting Sacrifice: Religion, Nationalism, and Social Thought in France*

(Chicago: University of Chicago Press, 2002); Strenski, *Theology and the First Theory of Sacrifice* (Leiden: Brill, 2003).

99. Randall Styers, *Making Magic: Religion, Magic, and Science in the Modern World* (Oxford: Oxford University Press, 2004), 87-90.

100. Durkheim, *Elementary Forms of the Religious Life*, 62, 60.

101. Nicole Belmont, *Arnold van Gennep: The Creator of French Ethnography*, trans. Derek Coltman (Chicago: University of Chicago Press, 1979); Rosemary Lévy Zumwalt, *The Enigma of Arnold van Gennep (1873-1957): Master of French Folklore and Hermit of Bourg-la-Reine* (Helsinki: Academia Scientiarum Fennica, 1988).

102. Arnold van Gennep, *Tabou et totémisme à Madagascar: Etude descriptive et théorique* (Paris: Leroux, 1904).

103. Arnold van Gennep, *Mythes et légendes d'Australie: Etudes d'ethnographie et de sociologie* (Paris: Guilmoto, 1906).

104. Arnold van Gennep, *Les rites de passage* (Paris: Emile Noury, 1909); Marcel Mauss, review of *Les rites de passage*, by van Gennep, *Année sociologique* 11 (1910): 200-202; Wouter W. Belier, "Arnold van Gennep and the Rise of French Sociology of Religion," *Numen* 41, no. 2 (1994): 141-62.

105. Harries, *Butterflies and Barbarians*, 214.

106. Victor Turner, *The Ritual Process: Structure and Anti-Structure* (London: Routledge & Kegan Paul, 1969).

107. W. D. Hammond-Tooke, *Imperfect Interpreters: South Africa's Anthropologists, 1920-1990* (Johannesburg: Witwatersrand University Press, 1997); Adam Kuper, *South Africa and the Anthropologist* (London: Routledge, 1987); Kuper, "South African Anthropology: An Inside Job," in *Among the Anthropologists: History and Context in Anthropology*, by Kuper (London: Athlone Press, 1999), 145-71.

108. Marcel Mauss, "A propos de la guerre du Transvaal," *Mouvement Socialiste*, February 15, 1902, 293; see Mauss, "La guerre du Transvaal," *Mouvement Socialiste*, June 1, 1900, 644-45.

109. Marcel Fournier, *Marcel Mauss: A Biography*, trans. Jane Marie Todd (Princeton, NJ: Princeton University Press, 2005), 146.

110. Cited in Gary Wilder, *The French Imperial Nation-State: Negritude and Colonial Humanism between the Two World Wars* (Chicago: University of Chicago Press, 2005), 64. See Emmanuelle Sibeud, "The Elusive Bureau of Colonial Ethnography in France, 1907-1925," in *Ordering Africa: Anthropology, European Imperialism, and the Politics of Knowledge*, ed. Helen Tilley and Robert J. Gordon (Manchester: Manchester University Press, 2007), 49-66.

111. Lucien Lévy-Bruhl, *How Natives Think*, trans. Lilian A. Clare (1910; Princeton, NJ: Princeton University Press, 1985), 44. See Lévy-Bruhl, *Primitive Mentality*, trans. Lilian A. Clare (1922; London: Allen & Unwin, 1923); Lévy-Bruhl, *The "Soul" of the Primitive*, trans. Lilian A. Clare (1927; New York: Macmillan, 1928); Lévy-Bruhl, *The Notebooks on Primitive Mentality*, trans. Peter Rivière (1949; Oxford: Blackwell, 1975).

112. Roger Caillois, *Man and the Sacred*, trans. Meyer Barash (1939; Urbana: University of Illinois Press, 2001), 139.

113. Ibid., 151.

CHAPTER SEVEN

The epigraph is from Leo Frobenius, *Histoire de la civilisation africaine*, trans. H. Back and D. Ermont (Paris: Gallimard, 1936), 79, cited in *The World and Africa: An Inquiry into the Part Which Africa Has Played in World History*, by W. E. B. Du Bois (New York: Viking Press, 1947), 79.

1. W. E. B. Du Bois, *The Souls of Black Folk: Essays and Sketches*, 2nd ed. (Chicago: A. C. McClurg, 1903), 196.

2. Ibid., 192.

3. W. E. B. Du Bois, *The Negro* (New York: Henry Holt, 1915), 242.

4. Du Bois, *Souls of Black Folk*, 198.

5. Du Bois, *The Negro*, 9.

6. Du Bois, *Souls of Black Folk*, 198.

7. Cynthia D. Schrager, "Both Sides of the Veil: Race, Science, and Mysticism in W. E. B. Du Bois," *American Quarterly* 48, no. 4 (1996), 584-85. See William James, *The Varieties of Religious Experience* (1902; New York: Macmillan, 1961), 114-59.

8. W. E. B. Du Bois, *Black Folk: Then and Now* (New York: Henry Holt, 1939), vi. See Julia E. Liss, "Diasporic Identities: The Science and Politics of Race in the Work of Franz Boas and W. E. B. Du Bois, 1894-1919," *Cultural Anthropology* 13, no. 2 (1998): 127-66.

9. Franz Boas, "Instability of Human Types," in *Papers on Inter-Racial Problems Communicated to the First Universal Races Congress Held at the University of London July 26-29, 1911*, ed. Gustav Spiller (London: P. S. King, 1911), 99-103; W. E. B. Du Bois, "The Negro Race in the United States of America," ibid., 348-64.

10. J. Tengo Jabavu, "The Native Races of South Africa," in Spiller, *Papers on Inter-Racial Problems*, 337.

11. Francis Paul Prucha, ed., *Documents of United States Indian Policy*, 3rd ed. (Lincoln: University of Nebraska Press, 2000), 158-60. See Tisa Wenger, *We Have a Religion: The 1920s Pueblo Indian Dance Controversy and American Religious Freedom* (Chapel Hill: University of North Carolina Press, 2009).

12. William T. Hagan, "Reformers' Images of the American Indians: The Late Nineteenth Century," in *"They Made Us Many Promises": The American Indian Experience, 1524 to the Present*, ed. Philip Weeks (Wheeling, IL: Harlan Davidson, 2002), 152.

13. David Murray, *Matter, Magic, and Spirit: Representing Indian and African American Belief* (Philadelphia: University of Pennsylvania Press, 2007), 212.

14. Charles A. Eastman, "The North American Indian," in Spiller, *Papers on Inter-Racial Problems*, 370. See Eastman, *Indian Boyhood* (New York: McClure, Phillips, 1902); Eastman, *The Soul of an Indian* (New York: Houghton Mifflin, 1911); and Lucy Maddox, *Citizen Indians: Native American Intellectuals, Race, and Reform* (Ithaca, NY: Cornell University Press, 2005).

15. Melville J. Herskovits, *The Myth of the Negro Past* (New York: Harper & Brothers, 1941); E. Franklin Frazier, *The Negro Church in America* (New York: Schocken, 1963). See Albert J. Raboteau, *Slave Religion: The "Invisible Institution" in the Antebellum South* (New York: Oxford University Press, 1978), 48-87.

16. Du Bois, *The Negro*, 124.

17. Eric J. Sharpe, *Comparative Religion: A History*, 2nd ed. (La Salle, IL: Open Court, 1986), 47-71; Edmund Leach, "The Anthropology of Religion: British and French Schools," in *Nineteenth-Century Religious Thought in the West*, 3 vols., ed. Ninian Smart, John Clayton, Patrick Sherry, and Steven T. Katz (Cambridge: Cambridge University Press, 1985), 3:215-62.

18. Johannes Fabian, *Time and the Other: How Anthropology Makes Its Object* (New York: Columbia University Press, 1983).

19. James Bryce, *Impressions of South Africa* (London: Macmillan, 1897), 90.

20. Robert Hamill Nassau, *Fetichism in West Africa: Forty Years' Observation of Native Customs and Superstitions* (New York: Scribner, 1904). See also Stephen Septimus Farrow, *Faith, Fancies, and Fetich; or, Yoruba Paganism: Being Some Account of the Religious Beliefs of the West African Negroes, Particularly of the Yoruba Tribes of Southern Nigeria* (London: Society for Promoting Christian Knowledge, 1926).

21. Du Bois, *The Negro*, 124. On missionary theories of African religious degeneration, see David Chidester, *Savage Systems: Colonialism and Comparative Religion in Southern Africa* (Charlottesville: University Press of Virginia, 1996), 89-92.

22. Du Bois, *The Negro*, 125.

23. William Pietz, "Fetish," in *Critical Terms for Art History*, ed. Robert S. Nelson and Richard Shiff (Chicago: University of Chicago Press, 1996), 201. See Peter Melville Logan, *Victorian Fetishism: Intellectuals and Primitives* (Albany: State University of New York Press, 2009).

24. Mary H. Kingsley, *West African Studies*, 2nd ed. (1899; London: Macmillan, 1901), 107.

25. Nassau, *Fetichism in West Africa*, 36.

26. Chidester, *Savage Systems*, 39, 41, 47, 52, 88, 75, 78, 94, 96, 103, 120, 180-81, 190.

27. Richard Burton, *Lake Regions of Central Africa*, 2 vols. (London: Longman, Green, Longman, and Roberts, 1860), 2:341-57; James Augustus Grant, *A Walk across Africa; or, Domestic Scenes from my Nile Journal* (Edinburgh: W. Blackwood, 1864), 145; René Caillié, *Travels through Central Africa to Timbuctoo*, 2 vols. (London: Colburn and Bentley, 1830), 1:303.

28. Bryce, *Impressions of South Africa*, 89.

29. Du Bois, *The Negro*, 150. For his overview of Muslim and Christian missions, see 128-30.

30. Ibid., 188-89; Nassau, *Fetichism in West Africa*, 274.

31. Du Bois, *Souls of Black Folk*, 196; Du Bois, *The Negro Church* (Atlanta: Atlanta University Press, 1903), 5-6; Du Bois, *Economic Co-operation among Negro Americans* (Atlanta: Atlanta University Press, 1907), 24; *The Negro*, 188-89.

32. William R. Bascom, *The Yoruba of Southwestern Nigeria* (New York: Holt, Rinehart & Winston, 1969); Bascom, *Shango in the New World* (Austin: African and Afro-American Research Institute, University of Texas, 1972).

33. Maurice Olender, *The Languages of Paradise: Race, Religion, and Philology in the Nineteenth Century*, trans. Arthur Goldhammer (Cambridge, MA: Harvard University Press, 1992).

34. Du Bois, *Black Folk*, 107-8.

35. Rudolf Otto, *The Idea of the Holy: An Inquiry into the Non-Rational Factor in the Idea of the Divine and Its Relation to the Rational*, 2nd ed., trans. John Harvey (1917; Oxford: Oxford University Press, 1950).

36. Rudolf Otto, "Vom Wege," *Die Christliche Welt* 25 (1911): 709, cited in Gregory D. Alles, "Rudolf Otto, Cultural Colonialism, and the 'Discovery' of the Holy," in *Religion and the Secular: Historical and Colonial Formations*, ed. Timothy Fitzgerald (London: Equinox, 2007), 196-97.

37. Rudolf Otto, "Deutsche Kulturaufgaben im Ausland," *Der Ostasiatische Lloyd* 26, no. 23 (1912): 483-85; see Gregory D. Alles, ed., *Rudolf Otto: Autobiographical and Social Essays* (Berlin: Mouton de Gruyter, 1996), 104-14.

38. Friedrich Schleiermacher, *On Religion: Speeches to Its Cultured Despisers*, trans. Richard Crouter (1799; Cambridge: Cambridge University Press, 1996), 114. See David Chidester, *Christianity: A Global History* (San Francisco: HarperCollins, 2000), 493-94.

39. Otto, "Vom Wege," 709, cited in Alles, "Rudolf Otto, Cultural Colonialism," 197.

40. Du Bois, *Black Folk*, 198.

41. Du Bois, *The Negro*, 189; *Black Folk*, 198.

42. Du Bois, *World and Africa*, 43.

43. Ibid., 79; Frobenius, *Histoire de la civilisation africaine*, 79. The 1936 edition is a translation of Frobenius, *Kulturgeschichte Afrikas: Prolegomena zu einer historischen Gestaltlehre* (Zurich: Phaidon, 1933).

44. Du Bois, *World and Africa*, x-xi.

45. Emil Torday, *Camp and Tramp in African Wilds: A Record of Adventures, Impressions, and Experiences during Many Years Spent among the Savage Tribes round Lake Tanganyika and Central Africa, with a Description of Native Life, Character, and Customs* (London: Seeley, Service, 1913), 76; Johannes Fabian, *Anthropology with an Attitude: Critical Essays* (Stanford, CA: Stanford University Press, 2001), 124.

46. Cited in Fabian, *Anthropology with an Attitude*, 154.

47. Wilhelm Schmidt, *The Origin and Growth of Religion: Facts and Theories*, trans. H. J. Rose

(London: Methuen, 1935); Joseph Campbell, *The Masks of God: Primitive Mythology* (1959; New York: Viking Press, 1969).

48. Leo Frobenius, *Leo Frobenius: An Anthology*, ed. Eike Haberland, trans. Patricia Crampton (Wiesbaden: Franz Steiner, 1973), 20.

49. Du Bois, *World and Africa*, 79; Frobenius, *Histoire de la civilisation africaine*, 79.

50. William Pietz, "The Problem of the Fetish, I, II, and IIIa," *Res: Anthropology and Aesthetics* 9 (Spring 1985): 5-17; 13 (Spring 1987): 23-45; 16 (Autumn 1988): 105-23.

51. William Smith, *A New Voyage to Guinea* (London: Nourse, 1744), 26.

52. Malgorzata Irek, "From Berlin to Harlem: Felix von Luschan, Alain Locke, and the New Negro," in *The Black Columbiad: Defining Moments in African American Literature and Culture*, ed. Werner Sollors and Maria Diedrich (Cambridge, MA: Harvard University Press, 1994), 174-84.

53. Robert Hertz, "R.-H. Nassau, Fetichism in West Africa," *Année Sociologique* 9 (1904-5): 193.

54. Marcel Mauss, *Oeuvres 2: Représentations collectives et diversité des civilisations* (Paris: Minuit, 1969), 244-45; cited in *Blank Darkness: Africanist Discourse in French*, by Christopher L. Miller (Chicago: University of Chicago Press, 1985), 49; and William Pietz, "Fetishism and Materialism: The Limits of Theory in Marx," in *Fetishism as Cultural Discourse*, ed. Emily Apter and William Pietz (Ithaca, NY: Cornell University Press, 1993), 133.

55. Du Bois, *World and Africa*, 158; Frobenius, *Histoire de la civilisation africaine*, 56.

56. As Robin D. G. Kelley has observed, Césaire, Senghor, and others in the Négritude movement drew inspiration from Frobenius. Kelley, "A Poetics of Anticolonialism," *Monthly Review* 51, no. 6 (1999), http://monthlyreview.org/author/robindgkelley, accessed June 30, 2011. See Suzanne Césaire, "Leo Frobenius and the Problem of Civilization," in *Refusal of the Shadow: Surrealism and the Caribbean*, ed. Michael Richardson, trans. Richardson and Krzysztof Fijalkowski (London: Verso, 1996), 82-87; Léopold Sédar Senghor, "The Lessons of Leo Frobenius," in Frobenius, *Leo Frobenius*, vii.

57. Léopold Senghor, *Liberté 3: Négritude et civilisation de l'universal* (Paris: Editions du Seuil, 1977), 13.

58. Senghor, "Lessons of Leo Frobenius," vii-viii; Senghor, *Liberté 3*, 399-400.

59. Sandra Adell, *Double Consciousness/Double Bind: Theoretical Issues in Twentieth-Century Black Literature* (Urbana: University of Illinois Press, 1994), 31-34.

60. Léopold Senghor, "The Revolution of 1889 and Leo Frobenius," in *Africa and the West: The Legacies of Empire*, ed. Isaac James Mowoe and Richard Bjornson, trans. Richard Bjornson (Westport, CT: Greenwood Press, 1986), 86-87.

61. Senghor, "Lessons of Leo Frobenius," xi.

62. Du Bois, *World and Africa*, 149.

63. John Lubbock, *The Origin of Civilization and the Primitive Condition of Man*, 5th ed. (1870; London: Longmans, Green, 1889), 205-10.

64. Edward Clodd, *Myths and Dreams* (London: Chatto and Windus, 1885), 13.

65. Alfred C. Haddon, *Magic and Fetishism* (London: Archibald Constable, 1906), 84-85. For similar renderings, see Frank Byron Jevons, *An Introduction to the History of Religion*, 8th ed. (1896; London: Methuen, 1921), 28.

66. Placide Tempels, *Bantu Philosophy*, trans. Colin King (1945; Paris: Présence Africaine, 1959), 25.

67. Pietz, "Problem of the Fetish I," 7.

68. Karl Marx, *Capital*, 2 vols., trans. Samuel Moore and Edward Aveling (1867; London: Lawrence and Wishart, 1974), 1:81.

69. On Christian translation, see Lamin Sanneh, "Missionary Translation in African Perspective: Religious and Theological Themes," in *Translating the Message: The Missionary Impact on Culture*, 2nd ed., by Sanneh (1989; Maryknoll, NY: Orbis, 2008), 191-228; Andrew Walls, "The

Translation Principle in Christian History," in *The Missionary Movement in Christian History*, by Walls (Maryknoll, NY: Orbis, 1996), 26-42.

70. Henk J. van Rinsum, "'Knowing the African': Edwin W. Smith and the Invention of African Traditional Religion," in *Uniquely African? African Christian Identity from Cultural and Historical Perspectives*, ed. James L. Cox and Gerrie ter Haar (Trenton, NJ: Africa World Press. 2003), 39-66.

71. Edwin W. Smith, ed., *African Ideas of God: A Symposium* (London: Edinburgh House Press, 1950); John S. Mbiti, *Concepts of God in Africa* (London: SPCK, 1970); Malcolm J. McVeigh, *God in Africa: Concepts of God in African Traditional Religion and Christianity* (Cape Cod, MA: Claude Stark, 1974).

72. Robin Horton, "African Conversion," *Africa* 41, no. 2 (1971): 85-108. See Terence Ranger, "The Local and the Global in South African Religious History," in *Conversion to Christianity: Historical and Anthropological Perspectives on a Great Transformation*, ed. Robert W. Hefner (Berkeley: University of California Press, 1993), 65-98.

73. See Rosalind Shaw, "The Invention of 'African Traditional Religion,'" *Religion* 20, no. 4 (1990): 339-53.

74. Bascom, *Shango in the New World*; Leonard E. Barrett, *Soul Force: African Heritage in Afro-American Religion* (Garden City, NY: Anchor Press, 1974); George Eaton Simpson, *The Shango Cult in Trinidad* (Rio Piedras: Institute of Caribbean Studies, University of Puerto Rico, 1965); Margarite Fernández Olmos and Lizabeth Paravisini-Gebert, eds., *Sacred Possessions: Vodou, Santeria, Obeah, and the Caribbean* (New Brunswick, NJ: Rutgers University Press, 1997).

75. Frantz Fanon, *The Wretched of the Earth*, trans. Constance Farrington (1961; London: Penguin, 1967), 43.

76. Du Bois, *Souls of Black Folk*, 198.

77. Achille Mbembe, "African Modes of Self-Writing," *Public Culture* 14, no. 1 (2002): 239.

CHAPTER EIGHT

The epigraph is from S. M. Molema, *The Bantu Past and Present: An Ethnographical and Historical Study of the Native Races of South Africa* (Edinburgh: W. Green, 1920), 176.

1. C. de B. Webb and J. B. Wright, eds., *The James Stuart Archive*, vol. 1 (Pietermaritzburg: University of Natal Press, 1976), 217.

2. Ibid., 246.

3. Ibid., 217.

4. Ibid., 232.

5. Ibid., 246, 232, 246-47.

6. Ibid., 238.

7. Ibid., 247.

8. Ibid., xiv. On James Stuart and his archive, see John Wright, "Making the James Stuart Archive," *History in Africa* 23 (1996): 333-50; Wright, "Ndukwana kaMbengwana as an Interlocutor in the History of the Zulu Kingdom, 1897-1903," *History in Africa* 38 (2011): 343-68; Carolyn Hamilton, *Terrific Majesty: The Powers of Shaka Zulu and the Limits of Historical Invention* (Cambridge, MA: Harvard University Press; Cape Town: David Philip, 1998), 130-67; Hamilton, "Backstory, Biography, and the Life of the James Stuart Archive," *History in Africa* 38 (2011): 319-41; Benedict Carton, "Fount of Deep Culture: Legacies of the 'James Stuart Archive' in South African Historiography," *History in Africa* 30 (2003): 87-106.

9. Webb and Wright, *James Stuart Archive*, vol. 1, 93.

10. E. Sidney Hartland, "Retiring Presidential Address," *Folklore* 12, no. 1 (1901): 15-40; Hartland, "Travel Notes in South Africa," *Folklore* 17, no. 4 (1906): 472-87; Hartland, "Bantu and South Africa," in *Encyclopedia of Religion and Ethics*, 13 vols., ed. James Hastings (Edinburgh: Clark, 1908-26), 2:350-67.

11. E. B. Tylor, *Primitive Culture*, 2 vols. (London: John Murray, 1871), 1:384.

12. Peter Kolb, *The Present State of the Cape of Good-Hope*, trans. Guido Medley (1719; London: W. Innys, 1731); Charles John Andersson, *Lake Ngami; or, Explorations and Discoveries during Four Years' Wanderings in the Wilds of South Western Africa* (London: Hurst and Blackett, 1856), 201; Dudley Kidd, *The Essential Kafir* (London: Macmillan, 1904), 65.

13. Mary H. Kingsley, "The Fetish View of the Human Soul," *Folklore* 8, no. 2 (1897): 139-40.

14. Edwin Sidney Hartland, *Ritual and Belief: Studies in the History of Religion* (New York: Charles Scribner's, 1914), 24.

15. Ibid., 23.

16. Mary H. Kingsley, "West Africa, from an Ethnologist's Point of View," *Transactions of the Liverpool Geographical Society* 6 (1897): 65.

17. Mary H. Kingsley, *West African Studies*, 2nd ed. (1899; London: Macmillan, 1901), 431. See Bernard Porter, *Critics of Empire: British Radicals and the Imperial Challenge* (1968; London: I. B. Taurus, 2008), 241.

18. Hartland, "Retiring Presidential Address," 16; Katherine Frank, *A Voyager Out: The Life of Mary Kingsley* (London: I. B. Taurus, 2004), 297. See Dea Birkett, *Mary Kingsley: Imperial Adventures* (London: Macmillan, 1992).

19. F. Max Müller, "Preface to the Sacred Books of the East," in *The Upanishads*, vol. 1, ed. and trans. Max Müller (Oxford: Oxford University Press, 1879), xiii.

20. F. Max Müller, *Contributions to the Science of Mythology*, 2 vols. (London: Longmans, Green, 1897): 1:204-5.

21. uNemo, "Zig Zag Notes for Zulu Scholars I," *Inkanyiso yase Natal*, March 22, 1895.

22. uNemo, "Zig Zag Notes for Zulu Scholars IV," *Inkanyiso yase Natal*, April 12, 1895.

23. uNemo, "Zig Zag Notes for Zulu Scholars V," *Inkanyiso yase Natal*, May 10, May 24, 1895.

24. uNemo, "Zig Zag Notes for Zulu Scholars V," *Inkanyiso yase Natal*, May 10, 1895.

25. uNemo, "Zig Zag Notes for Zulu Scholars I," *Inkanyiso yase Natal*, April 5, 1895.

26. uNemo, *Isigama, ukuti nje, inncwadi yamazwi esingisi ecasiselwe ngokwabantu* (Pinetown, Natal: Mariannhill Mission Press, n.d. [1890s]). Bryant was confirmed as the author of this text by C. M. Doke, *Bantu: Modern Grammatical, Phonetical, and Lexicographical Studies since 1860* (London: P. Lund, Humphries, 1945), 75. See Axel-Ivar Berglund, *Zulu Thought-Patterns and Symbolism* (1976; Bloomington: Indiana University Press, 1989), 25-26.

27. Alfred T. Bryant, *A Zulu-English Dictionary* (Durban: P. Davis, 1905), 7.

28. Ibid., 758.

29. See David Chidester, "The Unknown God," in *Savage Systems: Colonialism and Comparative Religion in Southern Africa*, by Chidester (Charlottesville: University Press of Virginia, 1996), 116-72; William H. Worger, "Parsing God: Conversations about the Meaning of Words and Metaphors in Nineteenth-Century Southern Africa," *Journal of African History* 42, no. 3 (2001): 417-47; and Jennifer Weir, "Whose Unkulunkulu?" *Africa* 75, no. 2 (2005): 203-19.

30. Bryant, *Zulu-English Dictionary*, 104.

31. Ibid., 105.

32. A. T. Bryant, *Olden Times in Zululand and Natal* (London: Longmans, Green, 1929). See John Wright, "A. T. Bryant and 'The Wars of Shaka,'" *History in Africa* 18 (1991): 409-25.

33. A. T. Bryant, *The Zulu People as They Were before the White Man Came* (Pietermaritzburg: Shuter & Shooter, 1949), 56, 69.

34. Shula Marks, "South Africa—'The Myth of the Empty Land,'" *History Today* 30, no. 1 (1980): 7-12.

35. Norman Etherington, "Barbarians Ancient and Modern," *American Historical Review* 116, no. 1 (2011): 43. See Edwin Bryant and Laurie L. Patton, eds., *The Indo-Aryan Controversy: Evidence and Inference in Indian History* (London: Routledge, 2005).

36. Bryant, *Zulu People*, 450-52.

37. A. T. Bryant, "The Zulu Cult of the Dead," *Man* 17 (1917): 140-45.

38. A. T. Bryant, "Mental Development of the South African Native," *Eugenic Review* 9 (1917): 44–45.

39. Tylor, *Primitive Culture*, 1:443.

40. Sigmund Freud, *Totem and Taboo*, in *The Standard Edition of the Complete Psychological Works of Sigmund Freud*, ed. and trans. James Strachey and Anna Freud, 24 vols. (London: Hogarth, 1953–74), 13:87.

41. Ibid., 13:1.

42. T. O. Beidelman, *W. Robertson Smith and the Sociological Study of Religion* (Chicago: University of Chicago Press, 1974), 50. See Celia Brickman, "Primitivity, Race, and Religion in Psychoanalysis," *Journal of Religion* 82, no. 1 (2002): 53–74.

43. Blake Burleson, *Jung in Africa* (New York: Continuum, 2005).

44. Wulf Sachs, *Psycho-Analysis: Its Meaning and Practical Applications* (London: Cassell, 1934).

45. Ellen Hellmann, "Native Life in a Johannesburg Slum Yard," *Africa* 8, no. 1 (1935): 34–62.

46. Wulf Sachs, *Black Hamlet: The Mind of an African Negro Revealed by Psychoanalysis* (London: Geoffrey Bles, 1937), 12, 13. See Saul Dubow, "Wulf Sachs's Black Hamlet: A Case of 'Psychic Vivisection'?" *African Affairs* 92, no. 369 (1993): 519–56; Jonathan Crewe, "*Black Hamlet*: Psychoanalysis on Trial in South Africa," *Poetics Today* 22, no. 2 (2001): 413–33.

47. Sachs, *Black Hamlet: The Mind of an African Negro*, 19.

48. Ibid., 22.

49. Ibid., 23.

50. Ibid., 27.

51. Ibid., 49.

52. Wulf Sachs, *Black Anger* (Boston: Little, Brown, 1947), 36.

53. Sachs, *Black Hamlet: The Mind of an African Negro*, 280.

54. Ibid., 174.

55. Ibid., 286.

56. Sachs, *Black Anger*, 52.

57. H. I. E. Dhlomo, "African Attitudes to the European," *Democrat*, December 1, 1945, cited in Saul Dubow, "Introduction: Part One," in *Black Hamlet*, by Wulf Sachs (Johannesburg: Witwatersrand University Press, 1996), 30, 37.

58. Sachs, *Black Hamlet: The Mind of an African Negro*, 31.

59. Henri A. Junod, *Zidji: Etude de Moeurs Sud-Africaines* (Saint-Blaise, Switzerland: Foyer Solidariste, 1911). See Bronwyn Strydom, "Belonging to Fiction? A Reconsideration of H. A. Junod in the Light of His Novel *Zidji*," *African Historical Review* 40, no. 1 (2008): 101–20.

60. George McCall Theal, *History and Ethnography of Africa South of the Zambesi*, 3 vols. (London: Allen & Unwin, 1907–10), 1:84, 86.

61. Magema M. Fuze, *The Black People and Whence They Came: A Zulu View*, ed. A. T. Cope, trans. H. C. Lugg (Pietermaritzburg: University of Natal Press, 1979), iv, 9. On Fuze, see Hlonipha Mokoena, *Magema Fuze: The Making of a Kholwa Intellectual* (Scottsville, South Africa: University of KwaZulu-Natal Press, 2011). On the Zulu and lost tribes, see Tudor Parfitt, *The Lost Tribes of Israel: The History of a Myth* (London: Weidenfeld & Nicolson, 2002), 217–21.

62. Petros Lamula, *UZulukaMalandela: A Most Practical and Concise Compendium of African History* (Durban: Star Printing Works, 1924); Paul la Hausse de Lalouvière, *Restless Identities: Signatures of Nationalism, Zulu Ethnicity, and History in the Lives of Petros Lamula (c. 1881-1948) and Lymon Maling (1889-c. 1936)* (Pietermaritzburg: University of Natal Press, 2000), 102.

63. John Henderson Soga, *The Ama-Xosa: Life and Customs* (London: Kegan Paul, Trench, Trübner, 1931), 145. See Soga, *The South-Eastern Bantu* (Johannesburg: Witwatersrand University Press, 1930).

64. John Dube, *Jeqe the Bodyservant of King Tshaka*, trans. J. Boxwell (Lovedale, South Africa: Lovedale Press, 1951). See Isabel Hofmeyr, *The Portable Bunyan: A Transnational History of the Pilgrim's Progress* (Princeton, NJ: Princeton University Press, 2004), 151–72.

65. Thomas Mofolo, *The Traveller of the East*, trans. Harry Ashton (London: Society for Promoting Christian Knowledge, 1934).

66. Thomas Mofolo, *Chaka, an Historical Romance*, trans. F. H. Dutton (Oxford: Oxford University Press, 1931).

67. Thomas Mofolo, *Traveller to the East*, ed. Stephen Gray, trans. Harry Ashton (London: Penguin, 2007), 88; Mofolo, *Chaka, a New Translation*, trans. Daniel P. Kunene (London: Heinemann, 1981), 47.

68. Daniel P. Kunene, *Thomas Mofolo and the Emergence of Written Sesotho Prose* (Johannesburg: Ravan Press, 1989), 143.

69. Ibid., 147.

70. Ibid., 149.

71. Ibid., 174. See Bernth Lindfors, "The Ambiguity of Evil in Thomas Mofolo's *Chaka*," in *Comparative Approaches to African Literatures*, ed. Bernth Lindfors (Amsterdam: Rodopi, 1994), 39–44.

72. Eugène Casalis, *The Basutos; or, Twenty-Three Years in South Africa* (London: James Nisbit, 1861); D. F. Ellenberger, with J. C. MacGregor, *History of the Basuto: Ancient and Modern* (London: Caxton, 1912).

73. C. G. Seligman, "Dreams and Dream Interpretation," in *Religion and Art in Ashanti*, ed. R. S. Rattray (Oxford: Clarendon Press, 1927), 197–204; Seligman, "The Unconscious in Relation to Anthropology," *British Journal of Psychology* 18, no. 4 (1928): 373–87.

74. Wilfrid Dyson Hambly, review of *Chaka: An Historical Romance*, *American Anthropologist*, n.s., 34, no. 2 (1932): 350.

75. Jane Starfield, "A Dance with the Empire: Modiri Molema's Glasgow Years, 1914–1921," *Journal of Southern African Studies* 27, no. 3 (2001): 479–503.

76. Molema, *Bantu Past and Present*, 27.

77. Ibid., 32.

78. Ibid., 164; Henry Drummond, *Tropical Africa* (London: Hodder & Stoughton, 1888), 60.

79. Molema, *Bantu Past and Present*, 172.

80. Tylor, *Primitive Culture*, 1:383.

81. Marie Jean Guyau [*sic*], *The Non-religion of the Future: A Sociological Study* (London: William Heinemann, 1897), 2.

82. James H. Leuba, *A Psychological Study of Religion: Its Origin, Function, and Future* (New York: Macmillan, 1912), 41.

83. In response to Winston L. King's assertion that Leuba's catalog proved that defining religion was a "hopeless task," Jonathan Z. Smith proposed, "The moral of Leuba is not that religion cannot be defined, but that it can be defined, with greater or lesser success, more than fifty ways." Winston L. King, *Introduction to Religion* (New York: Harper and Row, 1954), 63; Jonathan Z. Smith, *Relating Religion: Essays in the Study of Religion* (Chicago: University of Chicago Press, 2004), 193.

84. James Frazer, *The Golden Bough: A Study in Magic and Religion*, 2nd ed., 3 vols. (London: Macmillan, 1900), 1:63.

85. William James, *The Varieties of Religious Experience* (1902; London: Collier Macmillan, 1961), 59.

86. Molema, *Bantu Past and Present*, 176.

87. Ibid., 199–200; Edward Gibbon, *The History of the Decline and Fall of the Roman Empire*, 8 vols. (Oxford: Talboys and Wheeler, 1827), 1:272, 275.

88. For the phrase "savage slot," see Michel-Rolph Trouillot, "Anthropology and the Savage

Slot: The Poetics and Politics of Otherness," in *Global Transformations: Anthropology and the Modern World*, by Trouillot (London: Palgrave Macmillan, 2003), 7-28.

89. Molema, *Bantu Past and Present*, 334-35; W. E. B. Du Bois, *Souls of Black Folk: Essays and Sketches*, 2nd ed. (Chicago: A. C. McClurg, 1903), 262.

90. Molema, *Bantu Past and Present*, 176.

91. Henry Callaway, *Religious Sentiment amongst the Tribes of South Africa* (Kokstad, South Africa: Callaway, 1874), 4.

92. Adam Kuper, "South African Anthropology: An Inside Job," *Paideuma* 45 (1999): 85.

93. Max Gluckman, "The Realm of the Supernatural among the South-Eastern Bantu," 2 vols. (DPhil thesis, Oxford University, 1936). See Gluckman, "Zulu Women in Hoecultural Ritual," *Bantu Studies* 9 (1935): 255-71; Gluckman, "Social Aspects of First Fruits Ceremonies among the South-Eastern Bantu," *Africa* 11, no. 1 (1938): 25-41.

94. Jean Comaroff and John L. Comaroff, "On the Founding Fathers, Fieldwork, and Functionalism: A Conversation with Isaac Schapera," *American Ethnologist* 15, no. 3 (1988): 555.

95. Isaac Schapera, "The Present State and Future Development of Ethnographical Research in South Africa," *Bantu Studies* 8 (1934): 258.

96. See Chidester, *Savage Systems*, 252-53. On Eiselen and apartheid, see Cynthia Kros, *The Seeds of Separate Development: Origins of Bantu Education* (Pretoria: Unisa Press, 2010).

97. On the opposition between English and Afrikaner anthropology, see John S. Sharp, "The Roots and Development of Volkekunde in South Africa," *Journal of Southern African Studies* 8, no. 1 (1981): 16-36; and Robert Gordon, "Apartheid's Anthropologists: The Genealogy of Afrikaner Anthropology," *American Ethnologist* 15, no. 3 (1988): 535-53. But see also Sharp, "Serving the *Volk*? Afrikaner Anthropology Revisited," in *Culture Wars: Context, Models, and Anthropologists' Accounts*, ed. Deborah James, Evie Plaice, and Christina Toren (London: Berghahn, 2010), 32-44.

98. W. M. Eiselen and Isaac Schapera, "Religious Beliefs and Practices," in *The Bantu-Speaking Tribes of South Africa: An Ethnographical Survey*, ed. Isaac Schapera (London: George Routledge, 1937), 247-70. Eiselen and Schapera noted (247n1) that they derived their general theory of Bantu religion, as ancestor worship, from the local expert W. C. Willoughby, in *The Soul of the Bantu: A Sympathetic Study of the Magico-Religious Practices and Beliefs of the Bantu Tribes of Africa* (London: SCM Press; New York: Doubleday, 1928). For the religious beliefs and practices of various "tribal" groupings, they relied upon Monica Hunter, *Reaction to Conquest: Effects of Contact with Europeans on the Pondo of South Africa* (London: Oxford University Press, 1936); Henri-Alexandre Junod, *The Life of a South African Tribe*, 2 vols., 2nd ed. (London: Macmillan, 1927); Eileen Jensen Krige, *The Social System of the Zulus* (London: Longmans Green, 1936); Soga, *Ama-Xosa*; and Hugh A. Stayt, *The Bavenda* (London: Oxford University Press, 1931).

99. John B. Vickery, *Literary Impact of "The Golden Bough"* (Princeton, NJ: Princeton University Press, 1973).

100. H. I. E. Dhlomo, "Drama and the African," *South African Outlook* 66 (October 1, 1936); reprinted in *English in Africa* 4, no. 2 (1977): 3. See Tim Couzens, *The New African: A Study of the Life and Work of H. I. E. Dhlomo* (Johannesburg: Ravan Press, 1985); Nick Visser and Tim Couzens, eds., *H. I. E Dhlomo: Collected Works* (Johannesburg: Ravan Press, 1985).

101. Jane Ellen Harrison, *Ancient Art and Ritual* (London: Williams & Norgate, 1913), 253. On Harrison, see Mary Beard, *The Invention of Jane Harrison* (Cambridge, MA: Harvard University Press, 2000); Annabel Robinson, *The Life and Work of Jane Ellen Harrison* (Oxford: Oxford University Press, 2002); Marjorie Wheeler-Barclay, "Jane Ellen Harrison: The Redefinition of Religion," in *The Science of Religion in Britain, 1860-1915*, by Wheeler-Barclay (Charlottesville: University of Virginia Press, 2010), 215-42.

102. H. I. E. Dhlomo, "Nature and Variety of Tribal Drama," *Bantu Studies* 13 (1939); reprinted in *English in Africa* 4, no. 2 (1977): 34; Harrison, *Ancient Art and Ritual*, 18.

103. Dhlomo, "Nature and Variety of Tribal Drama," 34.

104. Dhlomo, "Drama and the African," 3.

105. Harrison, *Ancient Art and Ritual*, 43–44.

106. Ibid., 44.

107. Dhlomo, "Nature and Variety of Tribal Drama," 35.

108. Ibid., 27.

109. Ibid., 35.

110. Harrison, *Ancient Art and Ritual*, 50; James Frazer, *The Golden Bough: A Study in Magic and Religion*, 12 vols., 3rd ed. (London: Macmillan, 1911–15), 5:5.

111. Dhlomo, "Nature and Variety of Tribal Drama," 33, 35.

112. H. I. E. Dhlomo, "African Drama and Research," *Native Teachers' Journal* 18 (April 1939); reprinted in *English in Africa* 4, no. 2 (1977): 20.

113. Dhlomo, "Drama and the African," 7.

114. Ibid., 5.

115. Dhlomo, "Nature and Variety of Tribal Drama," 34.

116. Ibid., 30.

117. Dhlomo, "African Drama and Research," 21–22.

118. Ibid., 19.

119. Ibid., 19; Dhlomo cites Vico with no reference, but probably from J. B. Bury, *The Idea of Progress: An Inquiry into Its Origin and Growth* (London: Macmillan, 1920), 269.

120. John Buchan, *Greenmantle* (1916; Oxford: Oxford University Press, 1993), 24.

121. Du Bois, *Souls of Black Folk*, 262.

122. Dudley Kidd, *Kafir Socialism and the Dawn of Individualism* (London: Adam & Charles Black, 1908), 217–18.

123. Molema, *Bantu Past and Present*, 337; B. L. Putnam Weale, *The Conflict of Colour: The Threatened Upheaval throughout the World* (London: Macmillan, 1910), 236.

124. Molema, *Bantu Past and Present*, 341; G. W. Leitner, "Muhammadanism," in *Religious Systems of the World: National, Christian, and Philosophic*, ed. William Sheowring and Conrad W. Thies (London: Swan Sonnenschein, 1890), 253.

125. Dhlomo, "Nature and Variety of Tribal Drama," 35.

126. H. I. E. Dhlomo, "Why Study Tribal Dramatic Forms?" *Transvaal Native Education Quarterly*, March 1939; reprinted in *English in Africa* 4, no. 2 (1977): 24.

127. Thomas R. Trautmann, *Aryans and British India* (Berkeley: University of California Press, 1997), 211. See Stefan Arvidsson, *Aryan Idols: Indo-European Mythology as Ideology and Science* (Chicago: University of Chicago Press, 2006), 46.

CHAPTER NINE

The epigraph is from Annie Besant, "Theosophy and Imperialism: A Lecture Delivered in 1902," in *Essays and Addresses*, vol. 4, *India*, by Besant (London: Theosophical Publishing Society, 1913), 197.

1. Timothy H. Parsons, *Race, Resistance, and the Boy Scout Movement in British Colonial Africa* (Athens: Ohio University Press, 2004), 51–52; John Springhall, *Youth, Empire, and Society: British Youth Movements, 1883–1942* (London: Croom Helm, 1977), 57.

2. Robert Baden-Powell, *Scouting for Boys: A Handbook for Instruction in Good Citizenship*, ed. Elleke Boehmer (1908; Oxford: Oxford University Press, 2004), 40.

3. Robert Baden-Powell, *Lessons from the 'Varsity of Life* (London: C. Arthur Pearson, 1933), 76. See Jeff Guy, "Imperial Appropriations: Baden-Powell, the Wood Badge, and the Zulu *Iziqu*," in *Zulu Identities: Being Zulu, Past and Present*, ed. Benedict Carton, John Laband, and Jabulani Sithole (Scottsville, South Africa: University of KwaZulu-Natal Press, 2008), 193–213.

4. Jeff Guy, *The Maphumulo Uprising: War, Law, and Ritual in the Zulu Rebellion* (Scottsville, South Africa: University of KwaZulu-Natal Press, 2005), 5-6, 221.

5. Charles Lindholm, *Culture and Authenticity* (Oxford: Blackwell, 2008).

6. "Dr. Besant Receives 'The Silver Wolf,'" *Theosophist* 54, no. 3 (December 1932): 295-99.

7. Ashis Nandy and Shiv Visvanathan, "Modern Medicine and Its Non-Modern Critics: A Study of Discourse," in *Dominating Knowledge: Development, Culture, and Resistance*, ed. Frédérique Appfel Marglin and Stephen A. Marglin (Oxford: Oxford University Press, 1990), 162.

8. Besant, "Theosophy and Imperialism," 197.

9. Ibid., 176.

10. Annie Besant, *Britain's Place in the Great Plan: Four Lectures Delivered in London, June and July 1921* (London: Theosophical Publishing House, 1921), 53. See Gauri Viswanathan, *Outside the Fold: Conversion, Modernity, and Belief* (Princeton, NJ: Princeton University Press, 1998), 177-207.

11. Annie Besant, *The Ancient Wisdom: An Outline of Theosophical Teachings* (Adyar, Madras: Theosophical Publishing House, 1897), 2-3.

12. Ibid., 231.

13. Ibid., 310.

14. E. Denison Ross, introduction to *Religions of the Empire: A Conference on Some Living Religions within the Empire*, ed. William Loftus Hare (London: Camelot Press; New York: Macmillan, 1925), 3.

15. Richard Hughes Seager, ed., *The Dawn of Religious Pluralism: Voices from the World's Parliament of Religions, 1893* (La Salle, IL: Open Court, 1993); Seager, *The World's Parliament of Religions: The East/West Encounter, Chicago, 1893* (Bloomington: Indiana University Press, 1995); Eric J. Ziolkowski, ed., *A Museum of Faiths: Histories and Legacies of the 1893 World's Parliament of Religions* (Atlanta: Scholars Press, 1993).

16. Mustafa Khan, "The Spirit of Islam," in Hare, *Religions of the Empire*, 86.

17. William Loftus Hare, "A Sketch of Modern Religious Congresses," in Hare, *Religions of the Empire*, 8-14.

18. Khan, "Spirit of Islam," 86; G. P. Malalasekera, "Influence of Buddhism on Education in Ceylon," in Hare, *Religions of the Empire*, 175.

19. N. C. Sen, "Brâhma Samâj," 284; The Bahâ'i Assembly, "The Bahâ'i Cause," 304, both in Hare, *Religions of the Empire*.

20. Tyssul Davis, "Summing Up," in Hare, *Religions of the Empire*, 516.

21. Pandit Shyam Shankar, "Orthodox Hinduism or Sanâtana Dharma," 32; Rai Bahadur Jagmander Lal Jaini, "Jainism," 230, both in Hare, *Religions of the Empire*.

22. Francis Younghusband, *South Africa of Today* (London: Macmillan, 1898). See Patrick French, *Younghusband: The Last Great Imperial Adventurer* (London: HarperCollins, 1995); George Seaver, *Francis Younghusband: Explorer and Mystic* (London: John Murray, 1952).

23. Francis Younghusband, *The Heart of Nature; or, the Quest for Natural Beauty* (London: John Murray, 1921), 168.

24. Ibid., 149.

25. Francis Younghusband, "Opening Address," in Hare, *Religions of the Empire*, 15, 25, 17.

26. Francis Younghusband, "Man and Nature," in Hare, *Religions of the Empire*, 410.

27. Victor Branford, "Primitive Occupations: Their Ideals and Temptations," 424; J. Arthur Thomson, "The Naturalist's Approach to Religion," 417, both in Hare, *Religions of the Empire*.

28. The Venerable Archdeacon Williams, "Some Account of the Maori Beliefs," 332-46; Richard St. Barbe Baker, "Beliefs of Some East African Tribes," 347-55; L. W. G. Malcolm, "Some Aspects of the Religion of the West African Negro," 368-400, all in Hare, *Religions of the Empire*.

29. Alice Werner, "An Introductory Note on Primitive Religion," in Hare, *Religions of the Empire*, 330.

30. Mweli T. D. Skota, ed., *The African Yearly Register: Being an Illustrated National Biographical Dictionary (Who's Who) of the Black Folks in Africa* (Johannesburg: R. L. Esson, 1930), 334. A sighting of Albert Thoka at the conference was reported by a participant, who noted, "Several dusky Africans flitted in and out including Mr. Albert Thoka." William Loftus Hare, "A Parliament of Living Religions," *Open Court* 38, no. 12 (1924): 713.

31. Albert Thoka, "The Bantu Religious Ideas," in Hare, *Religions of the Empire*, 358.

32. Ibid., 356-59, 357. J. P. Dameron, *Spiritism: The Origin of All Religions* (San Francisco: Dameron, 1885), 65: "'Therefore,' says Agassiz, 'to understand God we must study His works in nature, and the more we learn of it the more we will know of Him.'"

33. Younghusband, "Man and Nature," 405, 404.

34. Thoka, "Bantu Religious Ideas," 360, 364, 366, 367.

35. J. Tengo Jabavu, "The Native Races of South Africa," in *Papers on Inter-Racial Problems Communicated to the First Universal Races Congress Held at the University of London July 26-29, 1911*, ed. Gustav Spiller (London: P. S. King, 1911), 337.

36. Marcus Braybrooke, "Francis Younghusband: Founder of the World Congress of Faiths," *Journal of Ecumenical Studies* 41, nos. 3-4 (2004): 456-62.

37. Francis Younghusband, ed., *A Venture of Faith: Being a Description of the World Congress of Faiths Held in London, 1936* (London: Michael Joseph, 1936; New York: Dutton, 1937); James B. Pratt, review of *A Venture of Faith, Journal of Religion* 18, no. 1 (1938): 126.

38. C. J. Bleeker, "Epilegomena," in *Historia Religionem II: Religions of the Present*, ed. C. J. Bleeker and Geo Widengren (Leiden: Brill, 1971), 649.

39. Peter van der Veer, *Imperial Encounters: Religion and Modernity in India and Britain* (Princeton, NJ: Princeton University Press, 2001), 65; Wouter J. Hanegraaff, *New Age Religion and Western Culture: Esotericism in the Mirror of Secular Thought* (Leiden: Brill, 1996), 443. On Theosophy, see Bruce F. Campbell, *Ancient Wisdom Revived: A History of the Theosophical Movement* (Berkeley: University of California Press, 1980); Joy Dixon, *Divine Feminine: Theosophy and Feminism in England* (Baltimore: Johns Hopkins University Press, 2001); Peter Washington, *Madame Blavatsky's Baboon: Theosophy and the Emergence of the Western Guru* (London: Martin Secker & Warburg, 1993).

40. H. P. Blavatsky, *The Secret Doctrine: The Synthesis of Science, Religion, and Philosophy* (London: Theosophical Publishing Company, 1888), 1:xxiii, xli; F. Max Müller, *Introduction to the Science of Religion: Four Lectures Delivered at the Royal Institution with Two Essays on False Analogies, and the Philosophy of Mythology* (London: Longmans, Green, 1873), 23, 257. See J. Jeffrey Franklin, *The Lotus and the Lion: Buddhism and the British Empire* (Ithaca, NY: Cornell University Press, 2008), 74-77.

41. "Professor Max Müller," *Supplement to the Theosophist* (January 1889): xxxv-xxxvi.

42. F. Max Müller, "Esoteric Buddhism," *Nineteenth Century* 33 (1893): 775. Max Müller's exchange with A. P. Sinnett was reprinted in Max Müller, *Last Essays, Second Series: Essays on the Science of Religion* (London: Longmans, Green, 1901), 79-170. See Donald S. Lopez Jr., "The Science of Buddhism," in *Buddhism and Science: A Guide for the Perplexed*, by Lopez (Chicago: University of Chicago Press, 2008), 153-96; Alex Owen, *The Place of Enchantment: British Occultism and the Culture of the Modern* (Chicago: University of Chicago Press, 2004), 30-34; Peter Pels, "Occult Truths: Race, Conjecture, and Theosophy in Victorian Anthropology," in *Excluded Ancestors, Inventible Traditions: Essays toward a More Inclusive History of Anthropology*, ed. Richard Handler (Madison: University of Wisconsin Press, 2000), 11-41.

43. F. Max Müller, *Theosophy or Psychological Religion* (London: Longmans, Green, 1893), xvi.

44. Edward Clodd, "Presidential Address," *Folklore* 7, no. 1 (1896): 39.

45. "On the Watch-Tower," *Lucifer: A Theosophical Magazine* 12, no. 69 (May 15, 1893): 182-83.

46. Mark Bevir, "Theosophy and the Origins of the Indian National Congress," *International*

Journal of Hindu Studies 7, nos. 1-3 (2003): 99-115. See W. Travis Hanes III, "On the Origins of the Indian National Congress: A Case Study of Cross-Cultural Synthesis," *Journal of World History* 4, no. 1 (1993): 69-98.

47. Patrick Bowen, "The Ancient Wisdom in Africa," *Theosophist* 48, no. 11 (August 1927): 549-50.

48. Ibid., 553, 555.

49. Ibid., 555.

50. P. G. Bowen, *The Occult Way* (London: Theosophical Publishing House, 1933), 31-32.

51. Bowen, "Ancient Wisdom in Africa," 557.

52. P. G. B. Bowen, "Africa's White Race," *Theosophical Path* 42, no. 2 (October 1932): 183.

53. Bowen, "Ancient Wisdom in Africa," 557-58.

54. H. T. Edge, "H. P. Blavatsky on the Mission of Theosophy," *Theosophical Path* 6, no. 3 (March 1914): 147; Annie Besant, "The Sphinx of Theosophy," *Lucifer: A Theosophical Magazine* 6 (August 1890): 453. See H. P. Blavatsky, *Key to Theosophy* (London: Theosophical Publishing Company, 1889), 175; Annie Besant, *The Seven Principles of Man* (London: Theosophical Publishing Society, 1904).

55. P. G. Bowen, "The New Age," *Theosophical Path* 43, no. 2 (1933): 178.

56. Bowen, "Ancient Wisdom in Africa," 559.

57. Annie Besant, *The Riddle of Life and How Theosophy Answers It* (London: Theosophical Publishing Society, 1911), 35.

58. Bowen, "Africa's White Race, 179.

59. Robert Bowen, "The 'Secret Doctrine' and Its Study," in *An Invitation to the Secret Doctrine*, ed. Grace F. Knoche (Pasadena: Theosophical University Press, 1988), 1-6.

60. P. G. Bowen, "*Amazwi Wo Mamdala*: The Sayings of the Ancient One," *Theosophical Path* 42, no. 2 (October 1932): 185-90; Bowen, *The Sayings of the Ancient One* (London: Rider, n.d. [1935]).

61. Bhagavan Das, *The Essential Unity of All Religions*, 2nd ed. (1932; Benares: Kashi, 1939), 193-97.

62. Eleanor Stakesby-Lewis, "The Mystery Tradition of Africa," *Theosophist* 72, nos. 5-6 (1951): 322-27, 420-25.

63. Patrick Bowen, "The Ancient Wisdom in Africa," *Studies in Comparative Religion* 3, no. 2 (1969): 96-102. Bowen's African theosophy has been cited as factual by Joseph Head and S. L. Cranston, *Reincarnation: The Phoenix Fire Mystery* (New York: Julian Press, 1977), 191; Robert Kastenbaum, *Is There Life after Death? The Latest Evidence Analysed* (London: Prion, 1997), 190; and Mathole Motshekga, founder of the Kara Heritage Institute in South Africa. See David Chidester, *Wild Religion: Tracking the Sacred in South Africa* (Berkeley: University of California Press, 2012), 152-75.

64. Steven Wasserstrom, *Religion after Religion: Gershom Scholem, Mircea Eliade, and Henry Corbin at Eranos* (Princeton, NJ: Princeton University Press, 1999); Thomas Hakl, *Eranos: An Alternative Intellectual History of the Twentieth Century*, trans. Christopher McIntosh (Montreal: McGill-Queens University Press, 2012).

65. W. Richard Comstock, "Religion, Literature, and Religious Studies: A Sketch of Their Modal Connections," *Notre Dame English Journal* 14, no. 1 (1981): 15. See Immanuel Kant, *Critique of Pure Reason*, trans. Paul Guyer and Allen W. Wood (Cambridge: Cambridge University Press, 1998), 321.

66. Bruce Lincoln, *Theorizing Myth: Narrative, Ideology, and Scholarship* (Chicago: University of Chicago Press, 1999), 50-51, 211. See Howard Gaskill, ed., *The Reception of Ossian in Europe* (London: Thoemmes Continuum, 2004).

67. Henry Callaway, *The Religious System of the Amazulu* (1868-70; reprint, Cape Town: Struik, 1970), 94.

68. John William Colenso, *Ten Weeks in Natal: A Journal of a First Tour of Visitation among the Colonists and Zulu Kafirs of Natal* (Cambridge: Macmillan, 1855), 57-59. See William H. Worger,

"Parsing God: Conversations about the Meaning of Words and Metaphors in Nineteenth-Century Southern Africa," *Journal of African History* 42, no. 3 (2001): 435-36.

69. Henry Callaway, *Religious Sentiment amongst the Tribes of South Africa* (Kokstad, South Africa: Callaway, 1874), 12.

70. Max Müller, *Introduction to the Science of Religion*, 185.

71. E. B. Tylor, *Primitive Culture*, 2 vols. (London: John Murray, 1871), 1:88-89.

72. Ibid., 1:399-400.

73. Andrew Lang, *The Making of Religion* (London: Longmans, Green, 1898), 178.

74. Andrew Lang, *Custom and Myth* (London: Longmans, Green, 1884), 237.

75. Andrew Lang, *Myth, Ritual, and Religion*, 2 vols. (London: Longmans, Green, 1901), 1:109-10.

76. James Frazer, *The Golden Bough: A Study in Magic and Religion*, 12 vols., 3rd ed. (London: Macmillan, 1911-15), 6:184-85; Callaway, *Religious System*, 145.

77. Frazer, *Golden Bough*, 3rd ed., 6:200.

78. Russell T. McCutcheon, ed., *The Insider/Outsider Problem in the Study of Religion: A Reader* (London: Cassell, 1999).

79. Jeppe Sinding Jensen, "Revisiting the Insider-Outsider Debate: Dismantling a Pseudo-Problem in the Study of Religion," *Method and Theory in the Study of Religion* 23, no. 1 (2011): 31.

80. Paul Christopher Johnson, *Secrets, Gossip, and Gods: The Transformation of Brazilian Candomblé* (Oxford: Oxford University Press, 2002), 9.

81. Gauri Viswanathan, "The Ordinary Business of Occultism," *Critical Inquiry* 27, no. 1 (2000): 1-20.

82. E. B. Tylor, "On the Limits of Savage Religion," *Journal of the Anthropological Institute* 21 (1892): 283, 298.

83. James G. Frazer, "The Scope and Method of Mental Anthropology (1920)," in *Garnered Sheaves: Essays, Addresses, and Reviews*, by Frazer (London: Macmillan, 1931), 246.

84. Lang, *Myth, Ritual, and Religion*, 2:358-59.

85. Frazer, "Scope and Method of Mental Anthropology," 244.

86. Phil Macnaghten and John Urry, *Contested Natures* (London: Sage, 1998), 104-29.

87. Carlo Ginzburg, *Threads and Traces: True False Fictive*, trans. Anne C. Tedeschi and John Tedeschi (Berkeley: University of California Press, 2012), 21.

CHAPTER TEN

The epigraph is from Morris Jastrow Jr., *Aspects of Religious Belief and Practice in Babylonia and Assyria* (New York: G. P. Putnam's, 1911), 4-5.

1. Martin Luther King Jr., "The Origin of Religion in the Race," in *The Papers of Martin Luther King, Jr.*, vol. 1, *Called to Serve, January 1929-June 1951*, ed. Clayborne Carson, Ralph E. Luker, and Penny A. Russell (Berkeley: University of California Press, 1992), 392-406. The essay relies upon D. Miall Edwards, *The Philosophy of Religion* (London: Hodder & Stoughton, 1924).

2. Susan K. Harris, *God's Arbiters: Americans and the Philippines, 1898-1902* (Oxford: Oxford University Press, 2011), 129-53.

3. Ruth Oldenziel, "Islands: The United States as a Networked Empire," in *Entangled Geographies: Empire and Technopolitics in the Global Cold War*, ed. Gabrielle Hecht (Cambridge, MA: MIT Press, 2011), 13-42. See Howard Zinn, Mike Konopacki, and Paul Buhle, *A People's History of the American Empire* (New York: Henry Holt, Metropolitan Books, 2008).

4. Frederick D. Maurice, *The Religions of the World and Their Relations to Christianity* (London: John W. Parker, 1847), 255. See David Chidester, *Savage Systems: Colonialism and Comparative Religion in Southern Africa* (Charlottesville: University Press of Virginia, 1996), 131-32.

5. Huston Smith, *The Religions of Man* (New York: Harper and Row, 1958), 8. See Russell T. McCutcheon, *Manufacturing Religion: The Discourse of Sui Generis Religion and the Politics of Nostalgia* (New York: Oxford University Press, 1997), 180-81.

6. Ken Stice, "Religious Factors in Special Operations" (1997), www-cgsc.army.mil/chap /COURSES/W-REL/STICE/sf-relig.doc, accessed January 20, 2002.

7. Eric Patterson, *Politics in a Religious World: Building a Religiously Literate U.S. Foreign Policy* (New York: Continuum, 2011), 11. See Stephen Prothero, *Religious Literacy: What Every American Needs to Know—And Doesn't* (San Francisco: HarperCollins, 2007).

8. Thomas A. Tweed, "An American Pioneer in the Study of Religion: Hannah Adams (1755- 1831) and her *Dictionary of All Religions,*" *Journal of the American Academy of Religion* 60, no. 3 (1992): 437-64.

9. James Freeman Clarke, *Ten Great Religions: An Essay in Comparative Theology* (Boston: James R. Osgood, 1871); Samuel Johnson, *Oriental Religions and Their Relation to Universal Religion,* 3 vols. (Boston: Houghton Mifflin, 1872, 1877, 1885); Morris Jastrow Jr., *The Study of Religion* (London: Walter Scott, 1901).

10. Joseph M. Kitagawa, "The History of Religions in America," in *The History of Religions: Essays in Methodology,* ed. Mircea Eliade and Joseph M. Kitagawa (Chicago: University of Chicago Press, 1959), 1-30.

11. T. W. Rhys Davids, *Buddhism: Its History and Literature* (New York: G. P. Putnam's, 1896). See Carl T. Jackson, *The Oriental Religions and American Thought: Nineteenth-Century Explorations* (Westport, CT: Greenwood Press, 1981); Thomas A. Tweed, *The American Encounter with Buddhism, 1844-1912: Victorian Culture and the Limits of Dissent* (1992; Chapel Hill: University of North Carolina Press, 2000).

12. James Turner, *Religion Enters the Academy: The Origins of the Scholarly Study of Religion in America* (Athens: University of Georgia Press, 2011), 56. See D. G. Hart, *The University Gets Religion: Religious Studies in American Higher Education* (Baltimore: Johns Hopkins University Press, 1999); Murray G. Murphey, "On the Scientific Study of Religion in the United States, 1870-1980," in *Religion and Twentieth-Century American Intellectual Life,* ed. Michael J. Lacey (New York: Cambridge University Press, 1989), 136-71.

13. A. C. Haddon, "Anthropology at the South African Meeting of the British Association for the Advancement of Science, 1905," *Science* 23, no. 587 (1906): 495; Michel-Rolph Trouillot, "Anthropology and the Savage Slot: The Poetics and Politics of Otherness," in *Global Transformations: Anthropology and the Modern World,* by Trouillot (London: Palgrave Macmillan, 2003), 7-28.

14. Lee D. Baker, *Anthropology and the Racial Politics of Culture* (Durham, NC: Duke University Press, 2010), 69.

15. Morris Jastrow Jr., *The Religion of Babylonia and Assyria* (Boston: Ginn, 1898). See Harold S. Wechsler, "Pulpit or Professoriate: The Case of Morris Jastrow, Jr.," *American Jewish History* 74, no. 4 (1985): 338-55; Kathryn Lofton, "Liberal Sympathies: Morris Jastrow and the Science of Religion," in *American Religious Liberalism,* ed. Leigh E. Schmidt and Sally M. Promey (Bloomington: Indiana University Press, 2012), 251-69.

16. Morris Jastrow Jr., "The Historical Study of Religions in Universities and Colleges," *Journal of the American Oriental Society* 20 (1899): 318. See Jastrow, "Recent Movements in the Historical Study of Religions in America," *Biblical World,* n.s., 1, no.1 (1893): 24-32.

17. Jastrow, *Study of Religion,* 51; Crawford Howell Toy, *Introduction to the History of Religions* (Boston: Ginn, 1913).

18. George Foot Moore, *History of Religions,* 2 vols. (New York: Charles Scribner's, 1913, 1919), 1:v.

19. C. P. Tiele, "Religions," *Encyclopaedia Britannica,* 9th ed. (Edinburgh: Adam & Charles Black, 1884), 20:359.

20. Jastrow, *Study of Religion,* 117.

21. Ibid., 100, 106.

22. Ibid., 333.

23. Ibid., 335.

24. Ibid., 336.

25. Daniel G. Brinton, *Myths of the New World: A Treatise on the Symbolism and Mythology of the Red Race of America* (New York: Leypoldt & Holt, 1868), i.

26. Daniel G. Brinton, *The Religious Sentiment, Its Source and Aim: A Contribution to the Science and Philosophy of Religion* (New York: Henry Holt, 1876); Brinton, *Races and Peoples: Lectures on the Science of Ethnography* (New York: N.D.C. Hodges, 1890), 48.

27. Daniel G. Brinton, "The Peoples of the Philippines," *American Anthropologist* 11, no. 10 (1898): 293; "Professor Blumentritt's Studies of the Philippines," *American Anthropologist*, n.s., 1, no. 1 (1899): 122. See Lee D. Baker, "Daniel G. Brinton's Success on the Road to Obscurity, 1890–99," *Cultural Anthropology* 15, no. 3 (2000): 394–423.

28. Daniel G. Brinton, *Religions of Primitive Peoples* (New York: G. P. Putnam's Sons, 1897), 6.

29. Ibid., 24.

30. Ibid., 56, 66–67, 72, 93, 168–69.

31. E. B. Tylor, *Primitive Culture*, 2 vols. (London: John Murray, 1871), 1:326, 1:390–91, 2:6, 17.

32. Ibid., 2:290–96.

33. Ibid., 2:302–3.

34. E. B. Tylor, *Anahuac; or, Mexico and the Mexicans, Ancient and Modern* (London: Longman, Green, Longman, and Roberts, 1861), 206, 212.

35. James Mooney, "Sacred Formulas of the Cherokees," in *Seventh Annual Report of the Bureau of Ethnology, 1885–86*, ed. John W. Powell (Washington, DC: Government Printing Office, 1891), 318.

36. Lewis H. Morgan, *Ancient Society; or, Researches in the Lines of Human Progress from Savagery, through Barbarism to Civilization* (New York: Henry Holt, 1877), vii.

37. Ibid., 115–16.

38. John W. Powell, *Report on the Methods of Surveying the Public Domain* (Washington, DC: Government Printing Office, 1878), 15.

39. See Tisa Wenger, "Indian Dances and the Politics of Religious Freedom, 1870–1930," *Journal of the American Academy of Religion* 79, no. 4 (2011): 850–78; Wenger, *We Have a Religion: The 1920s Pueblo Indian Dance Controversy and American Religious Freedom* (Chapel Hill: University of North Carolina Press, 2009).

40. John W. Powell, "From Savagery to Barbarism, Annual Address of the President, Delivered February 3, 1885," *Transactions of the Anthropological Society of Washington* 3 (1885): 173.

41. John W. Powell, "From Barbarism to Civilization," *American Anthropologist* 1, no. 2 (1888): 109.

42. James Mooney, "The Ghost Dance Religion and the Sioux Outbreak of 1890," in *Fourteenth Annual Report of the Bureau of American Ethnology, 1892–1893*, ed. John W. Powell (Washington, DC: Government Printing Office, 1896), 783. See Gregory E. Smoak, *Ghost Dances and Identity: Prophetic Religion and American Indian Ethnogenesis in the Nineteenth Century* (Berkeley: University of California Press, 2006).

43. Mooney, "Ghost Dance Religion," 928.

44. John W. Powell, *On Primitive Institutions* (Philadelphia: Dando, 1896), 17–20.

45. Robert H. Lowie, *Primitive Religion* (1924; London: George Routledge, 1936), 51.

46. Ibid., 251; see 251–58.

47. William Wells Newell, "The Importance and Utility of the Collection of Negro Folklore," in *Strange Ways and Sweet Dreams: Afro-American Folklore from the Hampton Institute*, ed. Donald J. Waters (1894; Boston: G. K. Hall, 1983), 186.

48. Ibid., 189.

49. Curtis J. Evans, "The Social Sciences and the Professional Discipline of Black Religion," in *The Burden of Black Religion*, by Evans (Oxford: Oxford University Press, 2008), 105–40.

50. Joseph Alexander Tillinghast, *The Negro in Africa and America* (1902; New York: Negro Universities Press, 1968), v, 205.

51. Frederick Morgan Davenport, *Primitive Traits in Religious Revivals: A Study in Mental and Social Evolution* (New York: Macmillan, 1905), 45-59; see Davenport, "The Religion of the American Negro," *Contemporary Review* 88 (September 1905): 369-75.

52. Davenport, *Primitive Traits*, ix, 15.

53. Ibid., 45.

54. Ibid., 47.

55. Ibid., 50.

56. Ibid., 57-58.

57. Ann Taves, *Fits, Trances, and Visions: Experiencing Religion and Explaining Experience from Wesley to James* (Princeton, NJ: Princeton University Press, 1999), 294.

58. George Barton Cutten, *The Psychological Phenomena of Christianity* (1908; New York: Charles Scribner's, 1909), 170-71.

59. Newbell Niles Puckett, *Folk Beliefs of the Southern Negro* (Chapel Hill: University of North Carolina Press, 1926), vii.

60. Ibid., 576-82.

61. Cited in Robert Hemenway, introduction to *Mules and Men*, by Zora Neale Hurston (Bloomington: Indiana University Press, 1978), xix-xx.

62. Paul Radin, *Primitive Man as Philosopher* (New York: D. Appleton, 1927), 380; see 379-84.

63. George Foot Moore, *Literature of the Old Testament* (New York: Henry Holt, 1913); Moore, *Judaism in the First Centuries of the Christian Era*, 3 vols. (Cambridge, MA: Harvard University Press, 1927-30).

64. George Stephen Goodspeed, *A History of the Babylonians and Assyrians* (New York: Charles Scribner's, 1902); Goodspeed, *A History of the Ancient World* (New York: Charles Scribner's, 1904).

65. Zachary Lockman, *Contending Visions of the Middle East: The History and Politics of Orientalism*, 2nd ed. (Cambridge: Cambridge University Press, 2010), 97. See Bruce Kuklick, *Puritans in Babylon: The Ancient Near East and American Intellectual Life, 1880-1930* (Princeton, NJ: Princeton University Press, 1996).

66. James Henry Breasted, *Ancient Times: A History of the Early World* (Boston: Ginn, 1916). See Jeffrey Abt, *American Egyptologist: The Life of James Henry Breasted and the Creation of His Oriental Institute* (Chicago: University of Chicago Press, 2011).

67. James Henry Breasted, "The Place of the Near Orient in the Career of Man and the Task of the American Orientalist," *Journal of the American Oriental Society* 39 (1919): 168.

68. James Henry Breasted, *The Conquest of Civilization* (New York: Harper & Brothers, 1926), 112.

69. Jastrow, *Aspects of Religious Belief and Practice*, 4-5.

70. Gil Anidjar, *Semites: Race, Religion, Literature* (Stanford, CA: Stanford University Press, 2008), 28. See Maurice Olender, *Race and Erudition* (Cambridge, MA: Harvard University Press, 2009).

71. Jastrow, *Aspects of Religious Belief and Practice*, 63.

72. Ibid., 291, 350.

73. Andrew Lang, *Magic and Religion* (London: Longmans, Green, 1901), 76-204.

74. Jastrow, *Aspects of Religious Belief and Practice*, 414.

75. Morris Jastrow Jr., *Hebrew and Babylonian Traditions: The Haskell Lectures Delivered at Oberlin College in 1913, and Since Revised and Enlarged* (New York: Charles Scribner's, 1914), 62.

76. Morris Jastrow Jr., *The War and the Bagdad Railway: The Story of Asia Minor and Its Relation to the Present Conflict* (Philadelphia: J. B. Lippincott, 1917), 134.

77. Morris Jastrow Jr., *The Eastern Question and Its Solution* (Philadelphia: J. B. Lippincott, 1920), 155; Jastrow, *War and the Bagdad Railway*, 146.

78. Jastrow, *Eastern Question*, 132.

79. Ibid., 135.

80. Morris Jastrow Jr., *Zionism and the Future of Palestine: The Fallacies and Dangers of Political Zionism* (New York: Macmillan, 1919).

81. Ibid., 11.

82. Jastrow, *Eastern Question*, 135.

83. Morris Jastrow Jr., *The War and the Coming Peace: The Moral Issue* (Philadelphia: J. B. Lippincott, 1918), 8.

84. Ibid., 46, 48-49.

85. Ibid., 49.

86. Ibid., 50.

87. Ibid., 63-64.

88. Ibid., 74.

89. Walter Benjamin, "Theses on the Philosophy of History," in *Illuminations*, by Benjamin, trans. Harry Zohn (New York: Schocken, 1968), 256.

90. Jastrow, *War and the Coming Peace*, 65.

91. Jastrow, *War and the Bagdad Railway*, 25.

92. Jastrow, *Study of Religion*, 336.

93. Clifford Geertz, "Religion as a Cultural System," in *Anthropological Approaches to the Study of Religion*, ed. Michael Banton (London: Tavistock, 1966), 1.

94. Clifford Geertz, "Shifting Aims, Moving Targets: On the Anthropology of Religion," *Journal of the Royal Anthropological Institute*, n.s., 11, no. 1 (2005): 13.

95. Talal Asad, ed. *Anthropology and the Colonial Encounter* (London: Ithaca Press, 1973); Asad, "Anthropological Conceptions of Religion: Reflections on Geertz," *Man* 18, no. 2 (1983): 237-59. See Talal Asad, *Genealogies of Religion: Discipline and Reasons of Power in Christianity and Islam* (Baltimore: Johns Hopkins University Press, 1993); Asad, *Formations of the Secular: Christianity, Islam, Modernity* (Stanford, CA: Stanford University Press, 2003).

96. William Dwight Whitney, *Max Müller and the Science of Language: A Criticism* (New York: D. Appleton, 1892).

97. Breasted, *Conquest of Civilization*, 112.

98. Jastrow, *Zionism*, 16.

Index